THE BOMBING OF AUSCHWITZ

Should the Allies Have Attempted It?

The

BOMBING

of

AUSCHWITZ

———

SHOULD THE ALLIES HAVE ATTEMPTED IT?

———

Edited by

MICHAEL J. NEUFELD *and* MICHAEL BERENBAUM

UNIVERSITY PRESS OF KANSAS

PUBLISHED IN ASSOCIATION WITH THE
UNITED STATES HOLOCAUST MEMORIAL MUSEUM

To Karen, with love, MJN

To Yehoshua ben Harav Moonish Gershon ben Yehoshua
To Joshua Boaz Berenbaum, who is a blessed addition to our family—
and so much more! MB

The original hardcover edition of this book was published by St. Martin's Press, 175 Fifth Avenue, New York, NY 10010. This edition, with an updating preface, is published by arrangement with the volume editors and with the United States Holocaust Memorial Museum, 100 Raoul Wallenberg Place, SW, Washington, DC 20024-2126.

Published by the University Press of Kansas (Lawrence, Kansas 66049), which was organized by the Kansas Board of Regents and is operated and funded by Emporia State University, Fort Hays State University, Kansas State University, Pittsburg State University, the University of Kansas, and Wichita State University

Library of Congress Cataloging-in-Publication Data

The bombing of Auschwitz : should the allies have attempted it? /
edited by Michael J. Neufeld and Michael Berenbaum.
   p.   cm.
Originally published: New York : St. Martin's Press, 2000.
Original ed. was based on a symposium held April 30, 1993, at the Smithsonian Institution, sponsored jointly by the National Air and Space Museum and the United States Holocaust Memorial Museum.
"Published in association with the United States Holocaust Memorial Museum."
Includes bibliographical references and index.
ISBN 0-7006-1280-7 (pbk. : alk. paper)
1. Auschwitz (Concentration camp)—Congresses. 2. World War, 1939 1945—Aerial operations—Congresses. 3. Holocaust, Jewish (1939 1945)—Poland—Congresses. I. Neufeld, Michael J., 1951
II. Berenbaum, Michael, 1945
D.805.G3B5848 2003
940.53′1853858—dc21

2003047928

British Library Cataloguing-in-Publication Data is available.

Printed in the United States of America

10 9 8 7 6 5 4 3 2 1

The paper used in this publication meets the minimum requirements of the American National Standard for Permanence of Paper for Printed Library Materials Z39.48-1984.

CONTENTS

PREFACE TO THE PAPERBACK EDITION   ix

PREFACE   x

ACKNOWLEDGMENTS   xvi

INTRODUCTION TO THE CONTROVERSY *by Michael J. Neufeld*   1

I. ALLIED KNOWLEDGE *and* CAPABILITIES   11

1. THE ALLIES AND THE HOLOCAUST
   by Gerhard L. Weinberg   15
2. AUSCHWITZ PARTIALLY DECODED
   by Richard Breitman   27
3. ALLIED AIR POWER: OBJECTIVES AND CAPABILITIES
   by Tami Davis Biddle   35
4. THE AERIAL PHOTOS OF THE AUSCHWITZ-BIRKENAU
   EXTERMINATION COMPLEX
   by Dino A. Brugioni   52

II. BOMBING AUSCHWITZ: FOR *and* AGAINST   59

5. THE CONTEMPORARY CASE FOR THE FEASIBILITY
   OF BOMBING AUSCHWITZ
   by Martin Gilbert   65
6. THE ALLIES AND AUSCHWITZ: A PARTICIPANT'S VIEW
   by Gerhart M. Riegner   76
7. THE BOMBING OF AUSCHWITZ RE-EXAMINED
   by James H. Kitchens III   80
8. THE BOMBING OF AUSCHWITZ REVISITED:
   A CRITICAL ANALYSIS
   by Richard H. Levy   101
9. COULD THE ALLIES HAVE BOMBED
   AUSCHWITZ-BIRKENAU?
   by Stuart G. Erdheim   127
10. BOMBING AUSCHWITZ: U.S. FIFTEENTH
    AIR FORCE AND THE MILITARY ASPECTS
    OF A POSSIBLE ATTACK
    by Rondall R. Rice   157

III. NEW PERSPECTIVES *on the* CONTROVERSY — 181

11. AUSCHWITZ
    by Walter Laqueur — 186
12. BOMBING AUSCHWITZ AND THE POLITICS OF THE
    JEWISH QUESTION DURING WORLD WAR II
    by Henry L. Feingold — 193
13. MONDAY-MORNING QUARTERBACKING AND THE
    BOMBING OF AUSCHWITZ
    by Williamson Murray — 204
14. THE BOMBING OF AUSCHWITZ: COMMENTS ON A
    HISTORICAL SPECULATION
    by Richard G. Davis — 214
15. THE FAILURE TO RESCUE AND CONTEMPORARY
    AMERICAN JEWISH HISTORIOGRAPHY OF THE
    HOLOCAUST: JUDGING FROM A DISTANCE
    by Deborah E. Lipstadt — 227

IV. DOCUMENTS — 237

1. PRELIMINARIES
    1.1 I. G. Farben Auschwitz Aiming Point Report, 21 January 1944 — 240
    1.2 Vrba-Wetzler and Rosin-Mordowicz Reports, April and June 1944
         (excerpts) — 242

2. THE FIRST APPEALS TO THE AMERICANS
    2.1 Memorandum, Roswell McClelland to Col. Alfred de Jonge,
         25 May 1944 — 249
    2.2 "Report on a Discussion between Y. Gruenbaum and Mr.
         Pinkerton . . . June 2, 1944." — 250
    2.3 Meeting of the Executive of the Jewish Agency, Jerusalem, 11 June
         1944 (excerpt) — 252
    2.4 Jacob Rosenheim to Henry Morgenthau, 18 June 1944 — 254
    2.5 Maj. Gen. Thomas R. Handy, Memorandum for the Record,
         23 June 1944 — 254
    2.6 John W. Pehle, War Refugee Board, Memorandum of 24 June
         1944 — 256
    2.7 Leland Harrison to Cordell Hull, Secretary of State, 24 June 1944 — 256
    2.8 Memorandum, J.W. Pehle to John McCloy, Assistant Secretary of
         War, 29 June 1944 — 257
    2.9 War Refugee Board Memorandum, Benjamin Akzin to L. S.
         Lesser, 29 June 1944 — 258
    2.10 A. Leon Kubowitzki, World Jewish Congress, to J. W. Pehle, 1
         July 1944 — 259

2.11 Memorandum, Col. Harrison A. Gerhardt, to John J. McCloy,
     3 July 1944   260
2.12 J. J. McCloy, War Department, to J.W. Pehle, War Refugee
     Board, 4 July 1944   260

3. THE APPEAL TO THE BRITISH
3.1 British Intercept of Cable from Richard Lichtheim to Jewish
    Agency, 26 June 1944   261
3.2 Yisrael Gruenbaum, Jerusalem, to Chaim Barlas, Istanbul, 30 June
    1944   262
3.3 Foreign Secretary Anthony Eden to Winston Churchill, 3 July 1944   262
3.4 Aide-Memoire by Chaim Weizmann and Moshe Shertok, 6 July
    1944   263
3.5 Telegram, Moshe Shertok to David Ben-Gurion and Nahum
    Goldmann, 6 July 1944   264
3.6 Memorandum, Anthony Eden to Winston Churchill, 6 July 1944   266
3.7 Winston Churchill to Anthony Eden, 7 July 1944   266
3.8 Anthony Eden to Sir Archibald Sinclair, Secretary of State for Air,
    7 July 1944   267
3.9 Sir Archibald Sinclair to Anthony Eden, 15 July 1944   267
3.10 Sinclair's Assistant Private Secretary to Vice-Chief of Air Staff,
     26 July 1944   269
3.11 Deputy Chief of Air Staff Bottomley to Acting Chief of Air Staff,
     2 August 1944   269
3.12 G. W. P. Grant, Air Ministry, to V. F. W. Cavendish-Bentinck,
     Foreign Office, 13 August 1944   269
3.13 Richard Law, Foreign Office, to Sir Archibald Sinclair, 1 September
     1944   270
3.14 Deputy Chief of Air Staff Bottomley to Lt. Gen. Carl Spaatz,
     6 September 1944   270

4. THE LATER APPEALS TO THE AMERICANS
4.1 J. J. Smertenko to President Franklin D. Roosevelt, 24 July 1944   271
4.2 A. Leon Kubowitzki, World Jewish Congress, to John J. McCloy,
    9 August 1944   273
4.3 John J. McCloy to A. Leon Kubowitzki, 14 August 1944   274
4.4 I. L. Kenen, "Report of Meeting with John W. Pehle . . . ,"
    16 August 1944 (excerpt)   274
4.5 War Refugee Board Memorandum, B. Akzin to J. W. Pehle,
    2 September 1944   275
4.6 John W. Pehle to John J. McCloy, 3 October 1944   277
4.7 Memorandum, Col. Harrison A. Gerhardt, to John J. McCloy,
    5 October 1944   277
4.8 John W. Pehle to John J. McCloy, 8 November 1944   278

4.9   Memorandum by H. H. F., War Department General Staff,
        14 November 1944   279
4.10 John J. McCloy to John W. Pehle, 18 November 1944   279

NOTES   281
SELECT BIBLIOGRAPHY   327
ABOUT THE EDITORS   331
ABOUT THE CONTRIBUTORS   333
COPYRIGHT ACKNOWLEDGMENTS   337
INDEX   339

PREFACE TO THE PAPERBACK EDITION

Michael J. Neufeld
Michael Berenbaum

Since the original publication of this collection in fall 2000, there have been two especially noteworthy additions to the bombing of Auschwitz debate that readers and researchers may wish to consult.

Joseph Robert White has published the first detailed examination of the response of the SS to possible and actual air raids on the Auschwitz-Birkenau-Monowitz complex. White's article appears in "Target Auschwitz: Historical and Hypothetical Responses to Allied Attack," *Holocaust and Genocide Studies* 16:1 (Spring 2002), 54–76. (See also Paul B. Miller's critique and White's response in the Spring 2003 issue.) On the basis of original records of the Auschwitz camp, White argues that the SS could have found alternate means to continue gassing Jews, and thus the actual impact of any hypothetical raid on the Birkenau gas-chamber/crematoria buildings would likely not have reduced the SS's ability to carry out mass murder. In line with Gerhard Weinberg's contribution to this volume, White believes that an Allied attack on Auschwitz-Birkenau might well have had symbolic and political importance, but there was little chance for it to be actually effective.

Michael Beschloss, in his new book *The Conquerors: Roosevelt, Truman and the Destruction of Hitler's Germany, 1941–1945* (New York: Simon and Schuster, 2002), pp. 65–67, reveals evidence that Assistant Secretary of War John J. McCloy may have consulted Roosevelt on the question of bombing the Birkenau crematoria, contrary to public statements McCloy made throughout his life. In a private conversation in 1986 with Henry Morgenthau III, preserved on a tape kept in the latter's papers in Cambridge, Massachusetts, McCloy asserted that he had talked to Roosevelt in 1944 and that the President had rejected the idea out of hand as ineffective. FDR allegedly said: "They'll only move it [the death factory] down the road a little way." If this evidence is accepted, it would indicate that an American raid on Auschwitz-Birkenau was not merely unlikely in the historical circumstances of 1944, but actually almost impossible. Any appeal or military proposal to the President would have been rejected. This evidence of course does not undermine any ex post facto arguments for the moral and political desirability of bombing Auschwitz-Birkenau, such as those made by several contributors to this book, whether supported with arguments for the effectiveness of possible raids, or not.

PREFACE

Michael Berenbaum

THE OPENING OF a new museum on the National Mall is not an everyday occurrence; it happens once a decade or so, and the cultural institutions of Washington, D.C., are usually most gracious in acknowledging their new neighbors. Thus, when the United States Holocaust Memorial Museum opened its doors to the public in April 1993, the component parts of the Smithsonian Institution sponsored exhibitions, lectures, and symposia to mark the occasion. The welcome extended to the new museum by these distinguished senior institutions was especially gratifying, for the museum's place among the memorials, monuments, museums, and institutions on the National Mall was not then secure.

Planners of the United States Holocaust Memorial Museum were often asked, "What is a memorial museum to the Holocaust—an essentially European event—doing among the landmarks of the American capital, celebrating American culture and the achievements of the United States?" The Holocaust Memorial Museum was denied permission to demolish a building, known as Annex II, that would have permitted an unimpeded view of the museum from the Mall, in no small measure because the National Capital Planning Commission did not want it to have such prominence on the Mall. Preopening surveys had indicated significant resistance to the presence of the Holocaust Memorial Museum *on* the Mall, but little opposition when it was described as *in proximity to* the Mall. In the *Report to the President,* the charter document given to President Jimmy Carter recommending the creation of a memorial museum, the President's Commission on the Holocaust suggested an answer: "If the present branches of the Smithsonian represent the accomplishments of civilization, the Holocaust illuminates an alternative dimension of human experience. . . . The fact that this process of destruction was committed by one of the most cultured and technologically advanced societies adds a sober dimension to the progress of humanity celebrated by the Smithsonian. . . . The memorial/museum would allow the presentation of a more complete picture of civilization, a greater vision of its promises and dangers."

Given the enormous success of the Holocaust Museum, measured in part by the lines of visitors that surround the building most mornings and the length of time that Americans devote to a Holocaust Museum visit, the question of the museum's place on the Mall seems long settled. Yet, in April 1993, the warm welcome was critical to its acceptance. Among the institutions that convened a conference in honor of the museum's opening was the National Air and Space Museum. In actuality, there were probably only two topics appropriate to that institution and to the Holocaust Museum—the role of German scientists in the development of the American rocket program and the question of the bombing of Auschwitz. The former would have been more disquieting to the constituency of the Air and Space Museum, and the latter topic had become emblematic of the Allied wartime record during the Holocaust.

"Why wasn't Auschwitz bombed?" is one of the most basic questions that students of the Holocaust ask. It ranks alongside "Why didn't the Jews resist?" as a simple and often innocent question that gives voice to the astonishment at the magnitude of the crime, and the ineffective response of the victims and the bystanders. Yet, the more one studies the question of resistance, the more one feels competent to respond to the issue or to reshape it in such a way that an answer becomes possible. The question, "Why wasn't Auschwitz bombed?" gnaws, not just at the student, but at the scholar as well.

The question, "Why wasn't Auschwitz bombed?" has been posed by American presidents and to American presidents. It is linked to the earliest days of the U.S. Holocaust Memorial Museum. In their first meeting, Jimmy Carter handed Elie Wiesel, the Jewish concentration-camp survivor and author who was chairman of the President's Commission on the Holocaust, a copy of the soon-to-be-released photographs of Birkenau developed by Dino A. Brugioni and Robert G. Poirier (see chapter 4).

Wiesel had been in Buna-Monowitz when the bombs were dropped on the camp. He had written: "Then we began to hear the airplanes. Almost at once the barracks began to shake. 'They're bombing Buna,' someone shouted. I thought of my father but I was glad all the same. To see the whole works go up in fire—what revenge! . . . We were not afraid. And yet, if a bomb had fallen on the blocks, it alone would have claimed hundreds of lives on the spot. We were no longer afraid of death; at any rate, not of that death. Every bomb filled us with joy and gave us new confidence in life."

Two months after meeting the president, in his address at the first National Days of Remembrance Ceremony at the Capitol Rotunda on 24 April 1979, Wiesel responded to his gift: "The evidence is before us: The world knew and kept silent. The documents that you, Mr. President, handed to the Chairman of your Commission on the Holocaust, testify to that effect. . . . Still when Hungarian Jews began arriving there [at Auschwitz] feeding the flames with ten or twelve thousand persons a day, nothing was done to stop or delay the process. Not one bomb was dropped on the railway tracks to the death camps." Wiesel was to repeat this accusation to Presidents Ronald Reagan and Bill Clinton.

The conference in honor of the opening of the Holocaust Museum was organized by Michael Neufeld, the National Air and Space Museum's curator for World War II history, and his colleagues. They made the important decision to have all sides represented at the conference—those who believe that Auschwitz *could* have been bombed and *should* have been bombed, and those who believe that it *could not* have been bombed or, knowing what was then known, *should not* have been bombed.

The debate was intense, as it should have been, and in the ensuing years, the debate only intensified. Attacks on the Allied wartime record with regard to the Holocaust were more prevalent, and the attackers more persuasive than the defenders. Then several new voices emerged in defense of the Roosevelt administration's policy toward the Final Solution, the one large black mark on FDR's record. Richard H. Levy, a retired nuclear engineer, tackled the issue fiercely. I invited him to make a presentation at what was then called the United States Holocaust Research Institute (which has now devolved into the Center for Advanced Holocaust Studies). His conclusions, toned down from their original fervor but not changed in substance, were then published in the journal *Holocaust and Genocide Studies*. They invited a rejoinder from Stuart G. Erdheim and from David S. Wyman. Erdheim's is reprinted here (see Chapter 9); Wyman did not wish to have his work republished.

Among the documents that Levy brought forth were the minutes of a meeting of the Jewish Agency in which the issue of bombing Auschwitz was discussed. Since one may presume that the Jewish Agency in Jerusalem was neither anti-Semitic nor indifferent to the plight of the Jews of Europe, its discussion of the bombing issue would seemingly not involve questions of motivations, but merely the issue of what was known about Auschwitz, the nature of the camp, the fate of its prisoners, the feasibility of bombing, and the danger that it would pose to Jewish inmates. The decision not to recommend bombing is, therefore, seemingly dispositive. It meant that even those individuals deeply concerned about Jewish fate, knowing what they knew then, did not recommend bombing. Israeli historians Shabtai Teveth and Dina Porat believe that this decision was reversed, but thus far no conclusive documentation has been discovered. David Wyman and Stuart Erdheim share the view that the Jewish Agency Executive changed its mind. On the other hand, some non-Zionist Israeli journalists, such as Tom Segev, see in the Executive's documented decision not to endorse bombing an indictment of the Zionists.

The Bombing of Auschwitz endeavors to present all sides of the debate. Major commentators who have written on the Holocaust, on American and Allied policy toward the Jews, and on military history, and representing diverse points of view, are included. Original documents are presented so that readers can gain a keener sense of the climate of the debate and see for themselves some of the raw material from which scholars have drawn their opinions.

The contributors are divided over the answers to several basic questions: what was known about the Holocaust? When was it known? By whom? In what context? Most contributors are mindful of Walter Laqueur's important distinction between knowledge and information. What, in retrospect, may be interpreted as knowledge may have at the time seemed like disparate bits of information that, in retrospect, take on far greater significance than they had at the time. If information reached one part of an organization, it did not necessarily reach other parts; and it may have been understood in such a way that the question itself was never raised. If the president or another American leader had a meeting with Jewish leaders or Polish couriers, what other issues were of concern to him that day? What were his expectations in advance of the meeting? What was of interest to him during the meeting?

Most people who ask, "Why wasn't Auschwitz bombed?" presume that if the full scope of what was happening at Auschwitz had been known, something would have been done. So the failure to act must have been related to an inability to perceive what was happening, to put all the disparate pieces of data together to understand the whole, and to thus gain the will, the urgent determination, to act. Perhaps historians and the general public cushion themselves from the more frightening conclusion that the events taking place at Auschwitz were known and that something was possible, but it wasn't worth the effort or the risk. In an age of CNN and the atrocities of Bosnia, Rwanda, and Kosovo future historians will be unable to avoid confronting such unpleasant—but not necessarily untruthful—realities.

Just to take the most recent example, major political, military, and moral leaders opposed American efforts in Kosovo. Pessimistic as to the efficacy of military action, they were willing to agree to the status quo ante, horrible as it was. And while bombing Yugoslavia provoked, in John J. McCloy's words of 1944, "even more vindictive action," it seems to have been effective. Military experts will properly argue that the precision bombing of today cannot be compared to the crude bombing of 1944, and that the United States was totally mobilized for its efforts to defeat Nazi Germany in battle, but the issue of bombing is joined, at least for the public.

What could have been done about Auschwitz—and when—is also subject to debate. Was bombing feasible? When? From what airfields would the bombers have taken off, and where would they have landed? What airplanes would have been used? What escorts would have been required, and at what cost of personnel and matériel?

Did the plight of the Jews matter? To whom and how deeply? Were American Jews effective or ineffective in advancing the cause of their brethren abroad? Did they comprehend their plight? Were they compromised by their fears of anti-Semitism, or by the fears they shared with American political leaders that the world war would be perceived as a Jewish war?

Was there a will to come to their assistance? If there was a will, might there not have been a way?

Beneath the historical evaluation, moral judgments emerge because of the magnitude of the crime of Auschwitz and the futility of the direct response. In his book, *We Are Our Brothers' Keepers,* Haskel Lookstein wrote: "The Final Solution may have been unstoppable by American Jewry, but it should have been unbearable for them. And it wasn't. This is important, not alone for our understanding of the past, but for our sense of responsibility in the future." Lookstein's conclusions as to responsibility to the future are perhaps even more compelling now when the failure to act during the Holocaust was invoked time and again as justification for American bombing in Kosovo by American leaders. The Holocaust analogy, inaccurate as it may be, was used to justify the use of American military forces for essentially humanitarian purposes seemingly un-related to direct national interests. As of this writing, bombing alone—massive and sustained bombing, coupled with support for guerrillas on the ground—seems to have succeeded in defeating the Serbians, which will only heighten the temptation for a technological response to ethnic cleansing and other prelimi-nary acts of genocide in the future. While the same concerted action was not possible in 1944, one could say of American officials, "The Final Solution may have been unstoppable by the American government—except as a result of complete military victory over the Germans—but it should have been unbear-able for them. And it wasn't." Might not the same verdict be reached regarding other Allied governments, the Vatican, and others?

Lookstein is a rabbi, but heed Walter Laqueur who writes in chapter 11: "Next to nothing was done. The fatalists may still claim that nothing could have been done. All we know is that it wasn't even tried." The "fatalists" seem rather confident that, had Auschwitz been bombed, it would have had no impact. It might have inconvenienced the Germans for a while and imposed greater hard-ships on those Jews who survived the assault. Such may have also been the reasoning of those fatalists who suggested dire consequences for American in-tervention in Bosnia; yet only after the bombing there was American diplomacy able to have at least some impact on the course of the genocide. The same seemingly holds true in Kosovo.

Others argue that the powerlessness of the Jews and their precariousness were reasons why nothing was done. In chapter 12, Henry L. Feingold speaks of the Jews as outside the "universe of obligation" that informs the Western world. If Feingold is correct, then our responsibility toward the future is to broaden the universe of obligation. Anti-Semitism, Richard G. Davis argues, is not a sufficient explanation of why nothing was done; it does not explain in-action in other mass exterminations of the twentieth century (see chapter 14). The powerlessness of the victims invites their victimization. Armenians, Cam-bodians, Rwandans, and Yugoslavs just did not have a constituency in the West. We must, therefore, increase the power of the voices that speak on behalf of the victims—those that plead their cause, that call attention to their plight. To the Jewish community, statehood and empowerment are required in order to avoid victimization. These obligations to the future lead to interpretations of the past.

And what of those who say, "America did all that it could do. We tried our best; we did our utmost within the constraints of our power. The Final Solution was unstoppable." Even if they are correct in their understanding of the past, they impoverish our collective future. The final moral judgment must be: *it should have been unbearable.*

ACKNOWLEDGMENTS

I

THE BOMBING OF Auschwitz had its origins in the 30 April 1993 symposium at the Smithsonian Institution jointly sponsored by the National Air and Space Museum (NASM), a division of the Smithsonian, and the United States Holocaust Memorial Museum (USHMM). I would like to thank those who contributed their efforts to make the symposium possible. The idea for the meeting, which was suggested by the U.S. Holocaust Memorial Council before the museum itself was finished, came to fruition because of the support of the former director of the National Air and Space Museum, Martin Harwit, and the work of his special assistant, Steven Soter, now at the Hayden Planetarium, American Museum of Natural History. Dr. Soter also suggested the name of the symposium, which is the title of this book. Tom Crouch of NASM, then chairman of the aeronautics department, aided in planning the symposium, and Helen Mc-Mahon and Pamela Blalock provided valuable professional expertise in organizing the meeting. Sara Bloomfield and Brewster Chamberlin of the Holocaust Council and Museum contributed both advance support for and participation in the symposium.

During the long, arduous course toward publication, Michael Berenbaum provided me with invaluable advice, not only through his suggestions about reshaping and expanding *The Bombing of Auschwitz* to make it more useful to scholars and general readers, but also through his crucial support inside USHMM for the book's publication. I also benefited from the hard work and wise counsel of Benton Arnovitz, USHMM director of academic publications, who solved the many difficult organizational and contractual problems that arose during the book's creation. After NASM withdrew from the project in 1996, Alan Ullberg of the Smithsonian office of the general counsel provided helpful support in making the legal transition to exclusive Holocaust Museum support, as did USHMM legal counsel Stuart Bender, who also reviewed the complex book contract negotiations.

At a late stage of the project, I was also greatly aided by a number of USHMM staffers; my thanks to Paul Thomas for his help with legal and copyright matters, Mary Ann Leonard for library and interlibrary loan support, and Aleisa Fishman (assisted by interns Erin Mishkin and Lindsay Harris) for invaluable aid in manuscript assembly and editing.

Throughout the long gestation of this book, I also received, as always, the unstinting love, support, and advice of my wife, Karen Levenback.

Michael J. Neufeld

II

Words of gratitude are in order. Michael Neufeld was responsible for much of the organizing of the original conference. He was responsible for collecting the manuscripts, soliciting new contributions, communicating with the authors, negotiating with them, and editing their work. His was the unenviable task of pressing and pressuring, and of seeing that all work came in on time and met his exacting standards. He did it all with charm, competence, and grace. My contributions were offering occasional advice and reviewing manuscripts. In my work as director of the United States Holocaust Research Institute, I did have a hand in the publication of Richard Levy's work and later the rejoinder of Stuart Erdheim. And I did have a hand in pushing *The Bombing of Auschwitz* toward publication and creating its present form. But please permit me to acknowledge with gratitude the disproportionate and ever-wise contribution of Michael Neufeld to this work.

When we undertook the publication of this book, both Michael Neufeld and I were working for federal institutions that received a large measure of their budget from Congress. I was successful in persuading my colleagues at the United States Holocaust Memorial Museum that a balanced book on a controversial topic was appropriate even for a publicly supported museum. However, Michael Neufeld's superiors at the National Air and Space Museum were more reluctant to participate, given the controversies that had beset their institution over a proposed exhibition.

It is hoped by all scholars that the Holocaust Memorial Museum, despite its recent controversies, and other federally supported museums will not shy away from publishing serious, accurate, and competent scholarship by persons of diverse and often conflicting opinions so that an informed readership can come to its own judgment. We need not endorse each view or each opinion to believe that it is worthy of publication and to remain committed to the importance of the issue.

With the publication of *The Bombing of Auschwitz,* I discharge my final obligations to the museum and its former research institute. I wish to acknowledge the work of my former colleague Aleisa Fishman, a young and talented historian who works in the academic publication branch. Her efforts were undertaken with skill and persistence. Paul Thomas, the museum's copyright coordinator, was very helpful with permissions. The library staff of the museum must be thanked for its efforts. In particular, I want to mention Teresa Amiel Polin, who works with the photo archives, whom I neglected to thank in a previous publication for her knowledge and wisdom.

Above all, thanks are due to Benton Arnovitz, the museum's director of academic publications, who has compiled for the museum a rather distinguished series of Holocaust publications. Dr. Walter Reich, former director of the museum, must be recognized for having the courage to permit the publication of this book. Two colleagues at the Survivors of the Shoah Visual History Foundation must be thanked: Susan Bernath, my dutiful assistant, and Joshua Harris, who assisted in scanning documents.

I am mindful of a chapter in life coming to a final close. But ends can also be wonderful beginnings.

Michael Berenbaum

INTRODUCTION TO THE CONTROVERSY

Michael J. Neufeld

FOR MORE THAN three decades after the end of World War II, the question of why the Allies did not bomb the Auschwitz-Birkenau death camp, or the rail lines leading to it, was a footnote to history. A few survivors and a few scholars raised the question—but almost no one paid any attention to it. That changed in May 1978, with the publication of David S. Wyman's "Why Auschwitz Was Never Bombed" in the journal *Commentary*.[1] Wyman's thesis—that the gas chamber/crematoria complexes at Auschwitz, and perhaps the rail lines as well, could have and should have been attacked by Allied bombers in the summer and fall of 1944—provoked not only a rush of letters to *Commentary*, most of them favorable, but also a very similar article in *Commonweal*, and some supportive commentary in the op-ed sections of the newspapers.[2]

The popularity of Wyman's thesis, and the American media's largely positive reaction to it, was reinforced in 1979 when two leading CIA photo-interpreters, Dino A. Brugioni and Robert Poirier, released a report on Allied reconnaissance photographs of the Auschwitz complex, taken as part of the bombing campaign against the I. G Farben factories at Auschwitz III-Monowitz, not five miles from the gas chambers.[3] Using modern equipment much superior to that available to their counterparts in World War II, Brugioni and Poirier were able to magnify photos unwittingly made of Auschwitz II–Birkenau, showing rail cars on the new Birkenau siding and even Jewish arrivals being marched to their death. Another picture they discovered was especially resonant: taken from an American B-24 on 13 September 1944, it showed just-released bombs intended for I. G. Farben framed against the crematoria (because of the forward momentum of the aircraft, bombs had to be released before the target). Here, it seemed, was visual proof of Wyman's thesis.

In the years that followed, opposition was confined mostly to letters to the editors from World War II aviators who questioned both the technical feasibility of bombing and Wyman's damning critique of the Roosevelt administration for its inaction. One of the first was Milt Groban, a Fifteenth Air Force radar navigator-bombardier who participated in the first Monowitz raid of 20 August 1944.[4] He not only questioned the accuracy of American "precision bombing," but also the efficacy of railroad bombing, and he asked whether the administration's claim that it could not divert forces away from critical military campaigns of that summer, such as the invasion of France, was not legitimate after all. He even raised a question that has been examined precious little since: whether the Nazis would not have found other ways to kill Jews if the gas chambers had been destroyed, such as by mass shooting. Well over a million Jews, out of a total of the five to six million who perished in the Holocaust, had been murdered that way between 1941 and 1943.[5]

The publication of Bernard Wasserstein's *Britain and the Jews of Europe* in 1979, but especially the appearance of Martin Gilbert's *Auschwitz and the Allies* in 1981, added another dimension to the public debate: awareness of the parallel failure of the British to take any action.[6] In late June and early July 1944, representatives of the Jewish Agency for Palestine appealed to Winston Churchill's government to bomb Auschwitz and the rail lines carrying hundreds of thousands of Hungarian Jews to their death—the unprecedentedly rapid implementation of the Final Solution in Hungary being the proximate cause of the appeals to both the United States and the United Kingdom. Despite Churchill's 7 July injunction to his foreign minister, Anthony Eden, to "get anything out of the Air Force you can and invoke me if necessary," once again nothing was done. Gilbert's book was less focused on making a case for bombing than was Wyman's subsequent, but at least equally influential, *The Abandonment of the Jews: America and the Holocaust 1941–1945* (1984); however, it did broaden the discussion beyond the United States and its failure to bomb. However, because of the greater difficulty of making a case for the Royal Air Force attacking Auschwitz, and because of indigenous American factors, the debate about whether the camp or the rail lines could have been bombed has been primarily American since the beginning.[7]

Explaining why Wyman's arguments have struck a chord on this side of the Atlantic, and why there was no significant debate before 1978, would require a more substantive treatment than we have space for here. Clearly, one answer was simply the effective way Wyman marshaled his research and arguments. He was able to show that Fifteenth Air Force bombers based in Italy had attacked I. G. Farben–Monowitz four times between August and December 1944 because of its synthetic-oil plant, yet the appeals to Washington to bomb the camp were dismissed by Assistant Secretary of War John J. McCloy with excuses that seem, with hindsight, disingenuous.[8] Wyman also outlined a number of alternate scenarios for attacking Birkenau or perhaps the rail lines (he has acknowledged the marginal efficacy of the latter) with medium bombers or fighter-bombers, which would in theory have been more accurate than the heavy bombers used against Monowitz and other oil targets in the region. And when he published *The Abandonment of the Jews*, Wyman was able to place the failure to bomb in the larger context of what appears now to many to be the shocking indifference of the Allies to the Holocaust. Wyman's book also did much to spread further the influence of the bombing thesis.

[2]

The deeper cultural reasons why Wyman's arguments were well received by the American public, and especially by the Jewish community, must include the gradual decline of anti-Semitism and the rise of pro-Israeli sentiment in American society after 1945, and the not unrelated rise of interest in the Holocaust. It is difficult to imagine now to what extent the Holocaust, the Shoah, or the Final Solution—whatever one wishes to call it—was peripheral to the public memory of World War II before the 1960s. The Holocaust, a term that came into widespread use only during the sixties, was equally little studied in academia. Two oft-cited seminal events took place in 1961: the trial of Adolf Eichmann in Israel and the publication of Raul Hilberg's *The Destruction of the European Jews*. But that book was not immediately accepted by a scholarly community unwilling to discuss the topic. According to Deborah E. Lipstadt, it was only at the time of the 1967 Arab-Israeli War that the murder of the European Jews began to find a wider echo in the American Jewish community, as well as outside it (see chapter 15). The following year, Arthur D. Morse's pioneering *While Six Million Died* (with the U.S. subtitle *A Chronicle of American Apathy*) raised for the first time a forceful critique of the failure of the Roosevelt administration, and of the United States generally, to respond to the reports of the murder of the Jews. Henry L. Feingold's more scholarly *The Politics of Rescue* followed in 1970.[9] Thus, when Wyman published his article in 1978, Americans were much more attuned to the history of the Holocaust and to the issue of the responsibility of bystanders than they had been a decade or two before. Symptomatic of that climate, 1978 was also the year of the melodramatic but much watched television miniseries, *Holocaust*.

One other factor that must have contributed to the instant popularity of the Wyman thesis: the appeal of air power as a technocratic, relatively bloodless (for Americans anyway) "quick fix." From the Air Corps Tactical School's infatuation with "precision bombing" between World Wars I and II, to the "precision-guided weapons" of the Gulf War and beyond, American culture has been in love with the idea that aircraft could drop bombs that would fix some military or political problem without undue losses on its part—indeed in the Kosovo war this scenario actually appears to have come true.[10] The idea that the Allies could have bombed Auschwitz and thus done something about the Holocaust inevitably had and has appeal in this context, especially because Auschwitz had become the symbol of the Holocaust by the 1970s. (In fact, roughly eighty percent of the Jews were murdered elsewhere and by means other than Zyklon B gas.) Moreover, the simplicity and symbolism of an air attack on Auschwitz was—and is—much easier for most people to grasp than are the complexities of immigration and refugee policy (save perhaps for an emblematic story like the voyage of the SS *St. Louis*). Yet David Wyman and his critics would probably agree that far more could have been saved if the door had been opened wide to Jewish refugees in the 1930s. On the other hand, the prospects for rescue after World War II started, and the failure of the Western powers to do much about it, have been bitterly disputed in the scholarly community, but that debate has had less impact on the public than has the specific question of bombing Auschwitz.[11]

With the exception of an attack on Wyman's *Abandonment of the Jews* by the eminent historian of the Shoah, Lucy Dawidowicz—whose real focus was the anti-Roosevelt, pro-rescue tone of Wyman's book—little was done to oppose the bombing-of-Auschwitz thesis in the scholarly community until the 1990s.[12] In part, this was due to the traditional, and not unjustified, reluctance of professional historians to become enmeshed in debates about counterfactual, "what if" history. Another factor was the marginality of military and aviation history to the mainstream of the community, a marginality that has only been partially remedied in recent years. The first attempts to write scholarly articles critiquing Wyman were thus left to Richard Foregger, a physician and World War II army field surgeon. Foregger's first article appeared in mid-1987 in a semipopular journal associated with the U.S. Air Force, *Aerospace Historian*. It focused on technical issues such as the doubtful accuracy of heavy bombers, the inadequate intelligence on the camp available to American forces, the strength of the German defenses (a factor Wyman tended to dismiss), and the likely ineffectiveness of bombing rail lines at ranges of hundreds of miles. Subsequently, Foregger published other articles focused on specific technical issues.[13]

Foregger's work made little impression on the Holocaust-history community or the wider public, and it did not go unchallenged even in the pages of *Aerospace Historian*.[14] The prevailing opinion among aviation and military historians, however, was largely dismissive of the thesis that Auschwitz could have been or should have been bombed. Historians in that world who I talked to in the early and mid-1990s viewed it as "Monday-morning quarterbacking" and ex post facto history. They considered Wyman and his followers to be naive about the history and realities of World War II air power. When James H. Kitchens III, a historian and archivist then working for the Air Force, published (without official support) the first full-scale scholarly attempt to refute Wyman in 1994 (see chapter 7), he noted that "the Holocaust studies community and that of air power history [had] passed like ships in the night"—that is, there had been almost no communication.

Kitchens's article, which concentrated mostly on technical issues such as intelligence, aircraft ranges and accuracies, and German defenses, did help alter that situation, in part because it provoked David Wyman to respond. Subsequently, heated exchanges broke out in the pages of the *Journal of Military History*, where Kitchens's article appeared, and in *Holocaust and Genocide Studies*, which printed another antibombing article by retired nuclear engineer Richard H. Levy, and a defense of the Wyman thesis by filmmaker and theologian Stuart G. Erdheim (see chapters 8 and 9). Independently, an Air Force officer, Rondall R. Rice, added a critique of Kitchens and Foregger (see chapter 10). Thus, in the last several years, the two sides have been talking to each other, although to a large extent it remains "a dialogue of the deaf," as Henry L. Feingold puts it (see chapter 12). To the pro-bombing side, the evidence that Wyman marshaled of Allied capabilities is so convincing, and the moral issues of bombing are so compelling, as to make the opposition's competence and viewpoint inherently suspect. To the antibombing side, the Wyman thesis is based on unrealistic expectations of bombing accuracy and on a historical second-guessing of Allied wartime leaders. The focus on the technical issues of aircraft capabilities and deployments of Allied and German forces and, in the case of Levy, on questions of whether Jewish leaders even supported the bombing, have left some historians, not to mention members of the public, a bit lost. It is rather difficult to sort out what is true and what is excessively influenced by hindsight. Nonetheless, this debate has helped clarify the technical issues of bombing and has raised interesting new insights into broader questions of the overall Allied attitudes to the fate of the Jews, as *The Bombing of Auschwitz* hopes to demonstrate.

A GUIDE FOR THE PERPLEXED

The origin of this collection goes back to a joint symposium held by the U.S. Holocaust Memorial Museum and the Smithsonian Institution's National Air and Space Museum on 30 April 1993, only days after the Holocaust Museum's highly successful opening. Because much has transpired in the controversies of the last several years, the original speeches of that conference have been re-written as essays, or have been entirely replaced by updated contributions. We have also added recently published material, including the latest contributions to the controversy in part II ("Bombing Auschwitz: For and Against") and an essay on "The Allies and the Holocaust" by noted World War II historian Gerhard L. Weinberg in part I ("Allied Knowledge and Capabilities"). Moreover, there are five entirely new commentaries by prominent historians Walter Laqueur, Henry L. Feingold, Williamson Murray, Richard G. Davis, and Deborah E. Lipstadt in part III ("New Perspectives on the Controversy"). In addition, we have included a selection of the most important original documents of 1944 in part IV, giving readers the opportunity to assess some of the evidence for themselves. Because these documents are largely framed by the appeals to bomb and their rejection, they do not give a picture of the larger framework in which the Allied leadership operated in the midst of a total war with many, apparently much more urgent priorities. But they do give one a more immediate view of what actually happened inside the British and American bureaucracies. Because the issues involved are quite complex, I would like to mention a few things that the reader should keep in mind while perusing this collection.

The Timing of Bombing and Its Relationship to the Hungarian Holocaust

One fact that all participants in the debate agree on is that the window for Allied air forces to do anything that might have retarded the murder of the Jews was small and came very late in the game: about six months in the summer and fall of 1944. At that point, the Nazis' "Final Solution of the Jewish Question" had been an ongoing enterprise for three years and (depending on one's estimates for the total death toll) had already killed around five million people. The Operation Reinhard death camps exclusively devoted to gassing by carbon monoxide—Treblinka, Sobibor, and Belzec—had been out of operation for nearly a year or more, and Lublin-Majdanek was overrun by Soviet troops in July 1944. Chelmno was mostly inactive. The camps in the East, including Auschwitz, were simply beyond the range of Allied air forces until spring 1944, when southern Italian bases around Foggia were put into full operation and the U.S. Fifteenth Air Force was given sufficient long-range fighter escorts. The first reconnaissance photographs of the I. G. Farben-Auschwitz facilities were taken 26 February and 4 April. However the first raids against synthetic-oil targets in the Upper Silesian coal basin around Auschwitz did not take place until July and August because the Fifteenth was heavily occupied with attacks on the Rumanian oil complex of Ploesti and on tactical and strategic targets in greater Germany, Italy, and southern France—attacks that helped pave the way for the invasions of France in June and August. When the window of opportunity opened depends on whether one believes that only the Fifteenth's heavy bombers come into consideration, or whether one accepts Wyman's various scenarios for special operations by smaller aircraft. The window definitely closed in November, when Reichsführer-SS Heinrich Himmler ordered the end of the gassing operations and the destruction of the Auschwitz crematoria to cover up the evidence, a fact not known in the West immediately.

The origin of the appeals to bomb Auschwitz-Birkenau, or the rail lines that led to it, was entirely unrelated to the specific readiness of Allied air forces. Rather, it emanated in May and June 1944 from the Slovakian Jewish underground, which was witnessing the horrifyingly rapid mass deportation and murder of the Hungarian Jews that had begun in earnest in mid-May. By various routes, these appeals reached Jewish and rescue groups in the West, along with summaries of reports by Slovakian Jewish escapees from Auschwitz that described the gassing process in detail, notably the Vrba-Wetzler report, selections from which are included in part IV. The appeals were tied specifically to stopping the deportations and focused initially on cutting the rail lines from Hungary to Upper Silesia. Thus, when the Hungarian government under Admiral Miklós Horthy ordered an end to the deportations on 7 July out of fear of Allied bombing and retaliation, it induced confusion in Western governments and undercut what little willingness there was to take the appeals seriously. However, reports continued to circulate about the resumption of deportations from Hungary, which indeed was a serious and threatening possibility. Meanwhile, the SS fed its death chambers with new deportees from Poland, Greece, the Netherlands, and elsewhere, a reality not well understood in the West. Also inducing confusion was the bizarre offer from Eichmann in April 1944, conveyed by the Budapest Jewish representative Joel Brand, to sell a million Jews for trucks.[15] There was no possibility that the Allies would have dealt with the Nazis, but this offer became mixed up with other rescue discussions, notably the bombing appeals from the Palestinian Jews to London.

The Feasibility of Bombing

As David Wyman was able to show at the outset, it is impossible to claim that Auschwitz-Birkenau could not have been bombed. In fact, the Fifteenth Air Force did drop bombs on it *by accident* on 13 September 1944, when SS barracks were hit by bombs falling short of their intended industrial targets. The question rather becomes one of the likelihood of hitting the four main gas chamber/crematoria complexes along the west side of Birkenau, and the likelihood that bombs would have fallen in profusion on the rows and rows of adjacent prisoner barracks. Accuracy is thus the central issue, but related to it are questions of what aircraft besides heavy bombers could have been deployed at the considerable range of about a thousand kilometers (620 miles) from southern Italian bases, if one wanted to look for forces that might have been more accurate than the heavies. Range is a tricky statistic, because it depends on the mix of fuel, armament, and bombs carried on specific types of aircraft. While the Allies might have hypothetically mounted special missions with Royal Air Force (RAF) Mosquitoes or with U.S. Army Air Forces (USAAF) P-38s or B-25 medium bombers, these scenarios are, in my opinion, hypothetical and problematic. Normally, only USAAF B-17 and B-24 heavy bombers (with escorts) operated over Auschwitz, beginning in July 1944. Accuracy by heavy bombers depended heavily on clear weather and weak defenses, and on average only something like two or three percent of such bombs fell directly on target in World War II; the crematoria presented small targets at that. Wyman has carefully laid out various scenarios, but it is fair to say that he takes an optimistic view of the possibilities. Regarding the intelligence data needed to mount a special mission, it is now clear that the Allies had a great deal of information about Auschwitz in various places in the complex bureaucratic structure of the combined British-American war effort. However, it is not entirely clear how straightforward it would have been to assemble it.

How many lives would have been saved by a raid on Birkenau? The usual upper limit is given by Wyman's estimate of 150,000, if the Fifteenth had knocked out the gas chambers permanently on 7 July, the day of the first raid on an oil complex in the region. Yet Wyman (and more recently his defender, Stuart G. Erdheim) has broached the possibility of saving considerably more lives if the Allies had made a decision much earlier to try to stop the Hungarian Holocaust. On the other hand, Wyman's harshest critics do not believe that a single life would have been saved, and they conclude that many would have been taken by indiscriminate bombing of the prisoner barracks. Between the two extremes, a little-discussed third position is offered by Gerhard L. Weinberg in "The Allies and the Holocaust." Weinberg accepts the argument that bombing would likely have saved no one, as the SS would have easily found other means to keep up the murder rate, but an air raid would have been a symbol of the Allies' will to do something to protest the genocide. (See chapter 1.)

As for railway bombing, it was entirely natural that the Slovakian underground wanted the Allies to cut the lines on which the death trains from Hungary were moving. However, this task would have been extremely difficult at the ranges involved. Tactical air power was not available in profusion, and the odds of heavy bombers cutting rail lines and knocking out bridges were very poor. Attacking a town with marshaling yards en route might have offered a slightly better chance. But rail lines and some bridges could have been repaired easily by German crews, and deportation trains diverted to other routes, as the Nazis did not care what happened to the individuals inside. Readers may make up their own minds, but I believe that *at best* the pace of deportation might have been slowed slightly if the Allies had attacked while the Hungarian trains were still moving; however, this was nearly impossible as the appeals did not even reach the top leadership in the West until about the time the Horthy government ordered a halt. Otherwise, one must again construct an alternate, more palatable reality in which the Allied governments had the will to oppose the Holocaust with military force much earlier, leading to a special attack in the spring.

Two issues relating to the third major Allied power, the Soviet Union, are worth mentioning. Some commentators have noted that, after the smashing success of the Soviet summer offensive that began on 22 June, Red Air Force tactical units were much closer to the gas chambers than were American bombers based in Italy. Given the disinterest of Stalin and the Communist leadership in the Holocaust, no one has taken the idea very seriously (see Henry L. Feingold, chapter 12). Alternately, the USAAF could have carried out a so-called shuttle raid against Auschwitz, in which U.S. heavy bombers used Soviet Ukrainian bases as staging points toward more distant targets. But the shuttle raids were greatly hampered by East-West tension, and the Lower Silesian region was already within range of Italian bases; it is thus unclear to me why this scenario merits any consideration.

Hindsight and the Problems of Counterfactual History

The various hypothetical scenarios offered for an attack on Auschwitz bring forth the central problem of the whole debate: how far can one go in constructing counterfactual, "what if" histories, and what are the limits to judging the morality of actors in the past? It is well to keep in mind Holocaust historian Michael Marrus's commentary on the literature criticizing the West for inaction:

> In assessing this work, we should note that many of these analyses center explicitly on what did *not* happen—an awkward approach for the historian. Information on the Holocaust was not digested, Jews were not

admitted, Jewish communities failed to unite, Allied governments spurned rescue suggestions, and access to Auschwitz was not bombed. It is, essentially, a negative report—the history of inaction, indifference, and insensitivity. It should be obvious there is a pitfall here: in any such assessment, there is great danger that the historian will apply to subjects the standards, value systems, and vantage point of the present, rather than those of the period being discussed. We believe that people should have acted otherwise, and we set out to show why they did not. Occasionally the thrust of such work is an extended lament that the people being written about did not live up to our standards. This temptation is the historians' form of hubris: to yield fully to it is to denounce the characters we describe for not being like ourselves.[16]

That chasm between then and now is well illustrated by the debate about the nonbombing of Auschwitz-Birkenau—indeed, the illumination of this chasm may be the most useful contribution of the debate. Judged from a post-1960s or post-1978 perspective, the relative apathy with which the genocide against the Jews was regarded in World War II—despite a number of strongly worded Allied statements—and the disinterest in taking any concrete military action, seem astonishing, even appalling. The Holocaust simply was not an important issue on the public or military agenda of World War II, in part because it was not perceived in the vivid way it is now—nameless millions were dying, although many refused to even believe that.[17] For the supreme Allied leadership in the West (not to mention the East), there were many more urgent priorities, such as doing everything militarily possible to win the war as soon as possible; rescuing refugees, Jewish or otherwise, just got in the way. Additionally, the anti-Semitism of Allied populations also tied the hands of Roosevelt, Churchill, and Stalin—or they let it tie their hands. They did not want to give Nazi propaganda minister Josef Goebbels more ammunition for his claims that the Allies were fighting for, and were secretly controlled by, the Jews. Anti-Semitism, in fact, does not appear to have been a direct factor in any of the rejections of appeals for bombing Auschwitz or the rail lines, but it formed an important context for the Holocaust's lack of centrality to the war effort—which brings home again the chasm in attitudes between then and now.

Another chasm was that which existed between the Western leadership and the concentration-camp prisoners. Under the circumstances of the war, it was extraordinarily difficult for the air force commanders or civilian bureaucrats to comprehend what it was like to be a prisoner in Auschwitz. By and large, the vivid images we can now conjure just were not there. Thus, Allied leaders found it difficult to comprehend that an inmate in the camp would prefer to be killed in an air raid if it meant something was being done to destroy the death machine—although in reality prisoners looked up at the bombers in the summer of 1944 and asked why. A few imaginative individuals, like Benjamin Akzin at the War Refugee Board in

Washington, did use the information at hand to comprehend the prisoners' horrifying situation, but they were exceptions. Without explicit and sustained pressure from Roosevelt or Churchill, I believe it is difficult to imagine that the air forces would have been moved to act. And that again requires the construction of an alternate, more palatable reality than the one that actually happened.

All of this points out the dangers of looking with hindsight on 1944 and expecting the actors and ordinary citizens of that time to look at the genocide in the same terms we do. On the other hand, academic historians too often dismiss "counterfactual" history as a pointless exercise in wishful thinking; it is one reason why amateur historians have taken a prominent part in the bombing-of-Auschwitz debate. In reality, as Walter Laqueur argues in chapter 11, almost any historian who constructs an interpretation of the past gives some thought to the alternative endings that might have been, either because it helps to explain why events almost inevitably had to turn out the way they did, or the opposite: it illuminates the very chanciness of the outcome. With the decline of influence of deterministic theories of historical change, such as Marxism and modernization theory, interest has risen in the contingencies and accidents of history.[18] Moreover, some debates about the past, like whether Auschwitz should have been bombed, or Hiroshima and Nagasaki not bombed, also seem so compelling to the public or to scholars on moral and political grounds, that they will be debated whether we like it or not. It is thus incumbent on professional historians to try to ground such hypothetical histories in the best research possible, while constraining undue speculation within the bounds of what the realities and mentality of that time were, as opposed to our own.

In conclusion, I think it is fair to say that Auschwitz II-Birkenau could definitely have been bombed by the same U.S. heavy bomber forces that were bombing I. G. Farben-Monowitz. Whether that would have been effective or not, you, the reader, must decide. Railroad bombing, on the other hand, seems likely to have been a failure under any circumstances. How much validity one imparts to the alternate scenarios for bombing Auschwitz, and for the decision-making about doing so, depends in part on what one believes is permissible in constructing counterfactual histories. But even if one were to doubt the validity of any speculations not tightly constrained by what actually happened, the debate over whether the Allies should have bombed Auschwitz has helped us to understand the chasm between 1944 and the present; has helped to illuminate the nature of Allied reactions to the Holocaust; has shed new light on the operations of Allied air forces and intelligence agencies; and has shined a spotlight on ourselves and why we are moved by this question.

Part I

ALLIED

KNOWLEDGE

and

CAPABILITIES

———

CENTRAL ISSUES IN deciding whether the Allies should have attempted to bomb the Auschwitz-Birkenau crematoria complex, or the rail lines leading to it, are (1) how much the Western Allies knew and (2) what the capability of their air forces was. Research during the past twenty years, including the recent declassification of secret signals intelligence sources, has shown that much more was known about Auschwitz than was believed at the time of the publication of David Wyman's 1978 article advocating bombing, or Martin Gilbert's 1981 book *Auschwitz and the Allies.* These revelations have only intensified the questions that Wyman and others have raised about whether the Allies shared complicity with the Nazis by doing little or nothing about the Holocaust. Brugioni and Poirier's 1979 discovery of the 1944 aerial reconnaissance photos of the Auschwitz complex also has fueled questions about how easy it would have been for Allied air planners to assemble the necessary intelligence for a special mission, if one had been ordered.

The first chapter, "The Allies and the Holocaust," by eminent World War II historian Gerhard L. Weinberg, provides a valuable overview of American and British attitudes toward the persecution and ultimate genocidal murder of the European Jews, and the domestic, international, and military constraints under which the Allies acted. Weinberg feels strongly that some of the literature on this question has gone too far in making the Allies complicit, when all responsibility must be laid at the door of the actual murderers. He also discusses some of the intelligence knowledge of the Holocaust, available in the West through ULTRA decrypts of German ENIGMA ciphers, which points toward the contribution of Richard Breitman in chapter 2. In his assessment of the likelihood of a successful raid on Birkenau, Weinberg is skeptical about the ability of the Allies to actually halt the killing, whatever the results of a raid. He points out the hardened commitment to mass murder of the Jews on the part of the agencies of National Socialist Germany, particularly the SS, and the personal motivations SS men had to keep the process going. Nonetheless, he raises the question of whether a symbolic raid on Auschwitz would not have signaled the Allies' commitment to actively oppose the genocide—assuming such a commitment had existed.

Adapted from a chapter in his important book, *Official Secrets* (1998), Richard Breitman's "Auschwitz Partially Decoded" examines in more detail what ULTRA information the Allies had, as well as what information came to the West from the Polish underground sources. Martin Gilbert's view that little concrete information was known about the camp or the gassing facilities until the late spring of 1944, and the arrival of summaries of the Vrba-Wetzler report, has greatly influenced the Auschwitz bombing debate. Breitman is able to show conclusively, however, that the Allies knew about Auschwitz as early as 1943. The question remains as to whether—in the tremendous, twenty-four-hour-a-day operation that was ULTRA—the decoded police ciphers were not buried in the mass of more urgent military information needed to fight a gigantic and desperate war. Moreover, the distribution of ULTRA intelligence was extremely tightly held to protect the secret.

In chapter 3, Tami Davis Biddle's "Allied Air Power: Objectives and Capabilities" steps back to survey what became the Combined Bomber Offensive in 1943, and what that tells us about the capabilities and preoccupations of the RAF and USAAF. She notes the slow and ineffectual beginning of the RAF bomber offensive and the ultimate switch to indiscriminate night area bombing of German cities as the only effective means to hit back at Nazi Germany. As a result, RAF Bomber Command had no capability to attack Auschwitz, even though appeals were launched as early as 1941, before gassing operations began. Later, as capabilities improved markedly, Bomber Command's aircraft were still inappropriate for the mission, except possibly special attack squadrons of Mosquitoes. In any case, Bomber Command's commander, Air Marshal Sir Arthur (Bomber) Harris, was stubbornly committed to the area bombing strategy. The USAAF strategic bomber forces were weak before 1943, and faced severe problems with the chosen strategy of daylight "precision" attacks on German targets. Only in 1944, with more forces, adequate escort fighters, and new bases in the Mediterranean, did the capability to attack targets in eastern Europe appear. Even then, U.S. Strategic Air Forces (USSTAF) were preoccupied with very important tasks in preparing the way for D-Day and wearing down German military and industrial capabilities in a bloody war of attrition. In view of USSTAF commander Gen. Carl A. (Tooey) Spaatz's focus on the oil campaign in the summer of 1944, and the ongoing attacks on the Western European transportation infrastructure, Biddle shows that all requests to bomb Auschwitz and the rail lines seemed like diversions to Allied military leaders.

Finally, in chapter 4, retired CIA photo-interpreter and intelligence specialist Dino A. Brugioni looks at the photographs of the Auschwitz complex he originally unveiled in 1979, and discusses why the photo-interpreters of 1944 entirely missed their significance. First, they were preoccupied with higher-priority projects linked to the critical military events of 1944, notably the invasion of Western Europe. And second, they were limited by their lack of understanding of the nature of the death camps and of the genocide; by superficial training; and by photo-enlarging equipment that was greatly inferior to that available to Brugioni and Poirier in 1978–79. Thus, he concludes, it is not surprising that the interpreters paid no attention to the photographs of Birkenau taken by accident on runs over I. G. Farben–Monowitz. It is Brugioni's professional opinion, however, that the photo-interpreters in Italy or England "would have quickly located the gas chambers and crematoria" if they had been provided with the detailed description of the camp made by escaped prisoners Rudolf Vrba and Alfred Wetzler.

Michael J. Neufeld

1

THE ALLIES AND THE HOLOCAUST

Gerhard L. Weinberg

In the years before the systematic killing of Jews began, the persecution of Jews by the German government was widely reported in the media of the time, as well as followed and described in reports home by the diplomatic representatives of foreign powers stationed in Germany. It is, however, important to recall that at the time practically no one inside or outside Germany anticipated that these measures were steps on the road to mass murder. The actions of the German government were generally understood, perhaps we should now say misunderstood, both by the victims and the bystanders, as a return to the kinds of persecutions and restrictions imposed on Jews in prior centuries, not as steps on the road toward a new policy.

Since these events in Germany coincided in time with the great world depression, it was particularly difficult for Jews to emigrate from Germany—and subsequently German-annexed Austria—to other countries. At a time of massive unemployment and enormous difficulties in financing government relief measures, all countries were reluctant to receive refugees who had been deprived of most of their assets by their former country and would be competing for the already scarce jobs in any new home. The uproars over immigration at a time of economic difficulties which we have witnessed in Europe and the United States in the most recent past should remind us that a time when unemployment was from three to five times as high as it has been in many countries recently was not an auspicious moment for the acceptance of large numbers of refugees.

On the contrary, most states adopted measures to restrict immigration; one of the few steps President Herbert Hoover took to cope with the Depression in the United States was to have regulations issued to make the issuance of visas within the quotas allowed by the existing American immigration legislation dependent on a showing that the individual allowed into the country would not become a public charge. It was this procedural restriction which would greatly hamper filling the available quota during the early years of the Nazi regime.

After his reelection in 1936, President Roosevelt felt sufficiently secure politically to insist on a more lenient interpretation of the rules, thereby allowing a substantially greater number of visas to be issued. As a result, the United States accepted about twice as many Jewish refugees as the rest of the world put together: about 200,000 out of 300,000.[1] It must be recalled, however, that at the time the overwhelming majority of Americans opposed the admission of refugees, and that Roosevelt acted in the face of strong and politically damaging criticism for what was generally considered a pro-Jewish attitude by him personally and by his administration.

Great Britain followed a restrictive immigration policy of its own, and the relaxation after the pogrom of November 1938 would have the effect of saving many lives but was at the time intended for, and restricted to, those who had prospects of leaving Great Britain for the United States or another country after what was expected to be a short time. In the 1930s, of course, Britain was also the mandatory power for Palestine. It had partitioned Palestine in the early 1920s into two mandates and had prohibited Jewish immigration into the larger of the two, called Trans-Jordan from a typically colonialist perspective because it was the other side of the river from London.

As is generally known, the British government abandoned its original intention of further partitioning the smaller of the two, now called Palestine, into three parts: a small Jewish unit, a much larger Arab one and an international zone; instead the British government issued a general limitation on Jewish immigration which was to end entirely in the near future unless the Arabs approved—as they were not expected to. What is not so generally known, or when known is not considered in connection with the infamous 1939 White Paper, is that this step was taken as a part of a general reorientation of British policy which was to prove of decisive positive significance for the survival of many Jews.

A most important factor in the decision to close Palestine to Jewish immigration was the belief in London that the troops which had to be stationed there to contain the Arab uprising—at the time the largest deployment of British active duty troops anywhere—were needed in England against the contingency of war with Germany. As the British government turned in the winter of 1938–39 from the policy of appeasement to one of resistance to German aggression, the military imperatives of the new policy included not only the first-ever introduction of conscription in peacetime but also the need to transfer troops from Palestine to the home islands so that a new British Expeditionary Force for deployment on the continent against Germany could begin to be formed. Furthermore, any new war with Germany was expected to require the large-scale recruitment and employment of troops from India, troops which were expected to be heavily Muslim in religion. In this context, the shift from appeasing Germany to very likely fighting Germany entailed a reverse shift toward the Arabs from fighting their uprising to appeasing their demands for a cessation of Jewish immigration into Palestine.

I do not want to suggest that there were no other motives, and I certainly am not denying the generally anti-Jewish and pro-Arab attitudes of most of those then in the British Foreign and Colonial Offices who had anything to do with the Middle East, but it does seem to me that this interrelated double-reversal of British policy illuminates a point about most policies of the major powers in the years before and during World War II: the whole issue of the fate of the Jews was entirely marginal to the considerations which drove policy choices.[2] Today, with the Holocaust seen quite properly as one of the defining events of the 20th century, we are inclined to examine the developments of the period 1933–45 in a perspective which places that event at the center. To understand the decisions made by leaders and governments at the time, however, we must recognize that for them entirely different issues were dominant. To them, the fate of the Jews was a very marginal consideration—if it entered into their thinking at all—and both enormously negative as well as enormously positive effects on the fate of the Jews resulted from choices which were made completely or almost completely without any regard to those effects.

This point should be kept in mind when we examine one of the most fascinating aspects of the beginnings of the systematic killing of Jews which is still shrouded in secrecy and about which we have only the vaguest and most tantalizing hints. Whatever the differences in interpretation by scholars as to what they tell us about the decision-making process in Germany with regard to the "Final Solution," the periodic reports of the *Einsatzgruppen*, the killing squads which accompanied the German military in the invasion of the Soviet Union, constitute one of the most important sources we have on the early stages of the actual process of mass murder. These reports are too well known to need detailed discussion here. What is not sufficiently taken into account by the existing literature is that the British decoding experts at Bletchley Park had broken the German police code in which similar reports, or summaries of them, together with other regular reports on SS camps were sent to Berlin.

Let me quote from a book on the subject by Peter Calvacoressi, one who worked at Bletchley. He asserts in *Top Secret Ultra*: "There is a peculiarly horrible example of the links between cyphers of different grades. The basic problem in cryptography is to get randomness ... At one point the German cryptographers responsible for finding entirely random settings for an Enigma cypher thought that they had hit on a bright solution. Every day the concentration camps rendered returns giving the numbers of prisoners who had been delivered to the camp that day, the number who had died or been killed, and the number of surviving inmates at the end of the day. These were truly random figures. They were reported in a medium-grade cypher and the recipients passed them on to their Enigma colleagues who used them in determining the settings of a particular Enigma cypher. B[letchley] P[ark] was reading that medium-grade cypher and it realized too that these daily concentration camp returns were being used in Enigma. So these sad, grisly statistics of human suffering and indignity played a part which the piteous victims never dreamed of."[3]

There is more evidence. An Appendix in Volume 2 of F. H. Hinsley's *British Intelligence in the Second World War* makes it clear that the British were reading German police ciphers with a high degree of regularity.[4] The messages to which Calvacoressi alludes seem to be the daily returns from the spring of 1942 to February 1943 from Dachau, Buchenwald, Auschwitz and seven other camps to which Hinsley refers.[5] Furthermore, the messages read at the time included what originally certainly sounded like *Einsatzgruppen* reports or preliminary summaries of them. Hinsley writes: "Between 18 July and 30 August 1941 police decrypts on at least seven occasions gave details of mass shootings, in the central sector, of victims described variously as 'Jews,' 'Jewish plunderers,' 'Jewish bolshevists' or 'Russian soldiers' in numbers varying from less than a hundred to several thousand."[6]

The reason that we have had to rely on deductions from these and a few similar comments in the secondary literature is that the original decrypts remained closed to research until April 1996, and others, if they survive at all, are intended to be closed to access in perpetuity. The decision to keep these records closed is, of course, not Hinsley's, but his description of the issue deserves quotation. After explaining that in the published volumes of his official history of British intelligence precise references are provided for documents already open or likely to be made available, even if after a lengthy interval, he continues: "But it would have served no useful purpose to give precise references to the domestic files of the intelligence-collecting bodies, which are unlikely ever to be opened in the Public Record Office. We have been permitted—indeed encouraged—to make use of these files in our text and we have done so on a generous scale, but in their case our text must be accepted as being the only evidence of their contents that can be made public. This course may demand from our readers more trust than historians have the right to expect, but we believe they will agree that it is preferable to the alternative, which was to have incorporated no evidence for which we could not quote sources."[7]

No sources were cited for the police reports, including quotations from them; at the time of publication, all these documents fell into the category of permanent withholding. In April 1996 the National Security Agency—presumably with the agreement of the government in London—released through the National Archives a huge collection of materials pertaining to deciphering operations by the Allies and the Axis, before, during, and after World War II. Included among these records is a set of British decrypts of German *Ordnungspolizei* (order police, regular uniformed police) reports of mass killings in the newly occupied Soviet territories from July to September 1941. These appear to be some of the documents cited by Hinsley; the set was turned over to United

States authorities at an as yet unknown later date. They demonstrate that not only the notorious *Einsatzgruppen* but also the regular German police units were engaged in the mass slaughter of Jews from the earliest days of the German campaign in the East. What can be learned from future releases of Allied decrypts—such as the concentration camp returns cited by Hinsley and Calvacoressi—remains to be seen. Here is an issue on which scholars in the United Kingdom and the United States might try to work; the need to maintain secrecy about intercepted German World War II concentration camp reports is difficult to understand.

This reference to records of World War II which are still kept secret in Washington and London calls for reference to another group of records also still closed which may turn out to be of interest for research on the Holocaust: the "Floradora" material. These are the decodes of German diplomatic World War II traffic. The point which is too often overlooked is that such intercepts not only shed light on the knowledge of the British and American governments at the time, in this case among other topics about the German program of systematically killing Jews, but that in addition in some cases the intercepts are likely to be the only surviving texts of documents of which the German originals are missing from the German archives because of destruction during the war. The United States Holocaust Memorial Museum has made a major effort to locate and microfilm material in the archives of the former Soviet Union pertaining to the Holocaust; perhaps it could try to get at some of the documents which are in British and American archives but are still kept closed as effectively as the Soviet archives once were.

The point of all this is that the governments of the Western Allies knew considerably more detail about the Holocaust somewhat earlier than previously recognized by scholars. This comment is not meant to detract from the fine books dealing with this subject, Walter Laqueur's *The Terrible Secret*[8] and Richard Breitman and Walter Laqueur's *Breaking the Silence,*[9] but to suggest some new avenues for future exploration at a time when the argument that certain records cannot be made accessible to scholars is becoming less and less plausible. Furthermore, there are likely to be all sorts of other important hitherto unknown materials on the Holocaust in these records.

It should always be remembered that during World War II Allied intercepting and decoding capabilities steadily improved—just as the proportion of German records which survives equally steadily decreases each year of the war. For the later portion of the war, therefore, the Allied intercepts are increasingly likely to be the only surviving record. What makes this even more important for scholars of the Holocaust is that one significant side-effect of the strategic bombing offensive was that the disruption of German transportation and communications systems in the last year of the war obliged the Germans to resort to wireless systems for messages which in earlier times were entrusted for security reasons to cables, the mail, and messengers and thereby protected against interception and decoding. If and when the remaining Allied intercepts and decodes are opened up, we may expect to learn a great deal more about the later stages of the Holocaust.

To return to the events of 1941 and their relationship to the Allies, we need to consider more carefully than has been the case hitherto the German plans for and Allied measures against German projects in the Middle East and North Africa. In the fall of 1941 German planning, which had originally anticipated a drive into the Middle East in the winter of 1941–42 as a follow-up to the defeat of the Soviet Union, shifted the time-table into 1942. There was, however, one aspect of this project which, at least in Hitler's thinking, had not changed. In late July he had assured the Croatian Minister of Defense that all Jews would disappear from Europe and predicted that Hungary would be the last country to give up its Jewish inhabitants. In November he made it clear that the project of killing Jews was by no means confined to Europe. As he explained to the Grand Mufti of Jerusalem, the Jews not only of Europe but everywhere else were to be killed; his expression refers to Jews living outside Europe, those living among *"aussereuropäischen Völker."*[10] Since the Mufti was presumably more interested in the Middle East than, say Australia or Latin America, Hitler spelled out for him that Germany intended the destruction, *"Vernichtung"* is the word recorded by the interpreter, of Jews living in the Arab world.[11]

What this latter term meant at the time was the Jewish community in Palestine and the then still substantial Jewish communities in Syria, Iraq, Iran, the Arabian peninsula, Egypt, and French Northwest Africa. And the Germans were indeed expecting to take over these areas, among other reasons so that their Jewish inhabitants could be killed, as was already being done in the newly occupied portions of the USSR. As I have just pointed out, German drives from Libya through Egypt into Palestine, across Turkey into Syria and Iraq, and across the Caucasus into the Middle East from the North were already being planned. Because a number of relevant documents on this have been published for years, I would mention only Hitler's draft Directive No. 32 of 11 June 1941 as a prominent example.[12] Two aspects of this issue have not received the attention they deserve.

In the first place, German interests were not limited to the Middle East and the northeast African route into it. As Norman Goda has clearly demonstrated, Hitler anticipated German control over important portions of Northwest Africa, primarily as a basis for his anticipated war against the United States.[13] The Jewish community of Morocco was thus at risk as was that of Palestine. Secondly, the Allied forces which defended Egypt against German advances and those which subsequently landed in Northwest Africa were primarily responsible for the survival of the Jewish population in the Middle East. Certainly no Jewish state in Palestine, however configured, would have emerged had all of the Jews in the then British mandate been killed during World War II.

There were several preconditions for this success of the Western Allies. One was the decision of President Roosevelt in April of 1941 to open the Red Sea to American shipping and thereby assist in the defense of Egypt once the British had conquered Italian East Africa. A second such precondition was Roosevelt's decision of June 1942 to turn over to the British the tanks of this country's first armored division so that Rommel's rush into the Middle East could be halted and reversed after the surrender of Tobruk. Though essential to the survival of the Jewish community of Palestine, these decisions were clearly taken without reference to that consideration. The other major precondition was, however, very much connected with the question of the Holocaust, but ironically in a reverse fashion.

The British forces which defended the southern approach to Palestine through Egypt were made up to a very substantial extent of troops from India, two-thirds of them Moslem.[14] It is, of course, obvious that these men did not volunteer for the Indian Army in order to defend Jews; but that is, among other things, what they were in fact doing in the North African campaign. Although this cause of British concern over Moslem opinion about Jewish immigration into Palestine is rarely mentioned in the literature, it was obvious enough to those in charge of the British war effort. The British 8th Army is always referred to as "British"; that a majority of its soldiers did not come from the United Kingdom is generally forgotten by both writers and readers of history. But it was not forgotten by either their commanders (one of whom came out of the Indian Army himself) or by the authorities in London.

The point that again needs to be emphasized is that the decision of the London government in the summer of 1940 to try very hard to defend the British position in the Middle East, even if that meant leaving her Far Eastern, South Asian, and Southeast Asian positions open to attack by Japan, like most of the other choices made by Britain and the United States which had such a profound effect on the course of the Holocaust, was made without reference to it. This may make it a little less surprising that the triumph of that British policy, and the association of the United States with it, in the last months of 1942 and the first months of 1943 would have a double effect on Germany's hopes of killing the world's Jews, one restricting those hopes and one facilitating a portion of their realization.

The way in which the Allied victory restricted Germany's program should be obvious but is rarely mentioned. The turning of the tide in the war, obvious in the Mediterranean theater in the winter 1942–43 (I shall turn to the Eastern Front in a moment) meant that Nazi expectations of victory and the slaughter of all the world's Jews had been thwarted. In effect, the Allies had saved about two-thirds of the globe's Jews from the fate the Germans intended for them. On the other hand, the collapse of the Fascist regime in Italy, which was both an expected and an obvious by-product of the Allied victory in North Africa, would open up to the Germans the opportunity to kill many Jews in Italy and in Italian-controlled portions of Europe who had hitherto been protected by the unwillingness of the Italian diplomatic and military leadership to cooperate with the German murder program.[15] As is well known, the Germans utilized what they saw as the opportunity opened up by the Italian surrender to try to include the Jews of Italy, the Italian islands in the Aegean, and the Italian occupation zones in France, Yugoslavia, and Greece into their killing program, and many thousands of Jews lost their lives as a result. Although this aspect of the Mediterranean campaign has received the attention it quite properly deserves, one ought not to overlook the fact that literally millions of Jews were saved by the same success of the Allies.

If the choices and decisions of Britain and the United States mentioned up to this point were, on the whole, taken without regard to their positive or negative implications for the Jews whom the Germans intended to kill or were actually in the process of killing, there was one further element in the situation which tended to reinforce the existing inclination to disregard the Holocaust even as it was under way. German propaganda throughout the war years took the line that the Jews had caused the war and either controlled the countries aligned against Germany or influenced those who did exercise power. This concept had been included in the phraseology of Hitler's original public declaration on 30 January 1939, of his expectation that in any new war the Jews would be killed. This propaganda line was a central one in the subsequent years, and for a very good reason: it was correctly believed in Berlin that it was an effective one. Although the anti-Semitic sentiments of large portions of the British and American public certainly did not extend to any wish for the Jews to be killed, on the other hand any hint that their government was taking major steps to assist the Jews at their time of greatest danger was certain to evoke the strongest opposition.

At a time when there was in practice very little that could be done to assist Germany's Jewish victims by the Western Powers, who were losing the war on land until the end of 1942, losing the war at sea until the fall of 1943, and who were unable to assure victory in the war in the air until February–March 1944, the leadership in both London and Washington wanted nothing to happen on the home fronts that might discourage their peoples. Victory over the Axis was the first priority, a subject to which I shall return. In the meantime, anything that might be seen as giving substance to the German propaganda line that the Allies were fighting not for the survival of their own peoples in life and in freedom but for the interests of the Jews was pushed aside.

The Soviet Union had made it a matter of national policy to disregard the anti-Semitic policies and actions of the German government. Obsessed with the fatuous notion that fascism was the tool of monopoly capitalism, there was neither understanding of nor reaction to the persecution of Jews by the Nazis at the time—and, one might add, after the war until the collapse of the Soviet system a few years ago. It can, in fact, be argued that the official Communist Party line sedulously spread throughout the Soviet Union, combined with the

Nazi-Soviet Pact of 1939, contributed to the early successes of the German killing program during 1941 in that it led many citizens of the Soviet Union to expect that the Germans would behave in any occupied portions of the country rather the way they had in the preceding war when huge Russian territories had also been under temporary German occupation. By the time people discovered that this was a serious mistake, many Jews who might have made a greater effort to escape the Germans were already dead.

But just as the Soviet policy which had this effect as a terrible by-product was adopted for reasons having nothing to do with the Holocaust, so the major contribution which the Red Army made toward the containment of the German killing program was also unaffected by any consideration for the prospective Jewish victims. Keeping the German army away from a substantial proportion of the Jews living in the USSR as well as contributing to the defeat of Germany's attempt to control the globe obviously made for the saving of Jewish lives inside and outside the country. This point has already been made in connection with the Western Allies; it certainly must be mentioned once more in this context. And in this context, furthermore, belongs the successful defense by the Red Army of the Caucasus in the late summer of 1942 when it looked for a moment that the German army might be able to break from the north into the Middle East with its large Jewish communities. The Soviets were mainly concerned about defending their country, and the Western Allies were terrified, to put it mildly, that the Axis might gain control of the oil resources of that region; the survival of the Jews of Palestine, Syria, Iran, and Iraq was, however, as surely due to the Soviets holding the Germans in the Caucasus as to the British holding in the Western Desert of Egypt.

During the course of 1944, as the tide of the war either had turned or was turning in favor of the Allies, two issues related to the Holocaust came increasingly to the fore then, and both have received considerable attention since 1945—or rather, since serious discussion of the Holocaust began in the 1960s. These were the possibilities of rescue and interference; that is, the prospects for rescuing Jews threatened by the killing program and/or of interfering with the mechanics of that program by such steps as the bombing of killing centers or the railway routes to them. These issues will be discussed separately, but only with reference to the Western Allies since the Soviet Union had no interest in either of them a priori.

There were some minimal possibilities of rescuing Jews, but they were minimal indeed. The most recent examination of the subject by Shlomo Aronson and Richard Breitman shows that whatever the details of the various rescue schemes, there were very tight limits on what could be done.[16] These limits were largely the result of German insistence on the sorts of trades and concessions which were impossible—and which they knew to be impossible—for the Allies to accept. A tiny number was saved in a variety of projects in which Jewish organizations, the War Refugee Board, and various neutral agencies and persons like Raoul Wallenberg played significant roles, and it is entirely possible that more might have been done. The major obstacle, however, was on the German side, a point which is too often overlooked.

The fixation on rescue attempts and their very limited success has tended to divert attention from the enormous efforts made by the Germans—including practically every agency of the German government—to maximize the killing and minimize any rescues.[17] This is not to ignore the resistance of the British to most rescue attempts which involved getting the rescued into Palestine and of the Americans to most rescue attempts likely to bring Jewish refugees to the United States.[18] It is in this context that the title of Monty Penkower's book, *The Jews Were Expendable,* seems entirely appropriate.[19] Before too long we may expect to see books with the titles *The Baha'i Were Expendable* and *The Bosnian Moslems Were Expendable.* But those titles should not divert all attention from those primarily responsible for the killing: the killers.

This is a major consideration too often omitted from examinations of the other issue now frequently discussed, namely the possibilities of interfering with the killing process, primarily by bombing. This question really comes up only from the summer of 1944 on when the Western Allies had finally defeated the German air force, had succeeded in establishing a firm bridgehead in Normandy, and had taken the airfields in central Italy from which airplanes could reach almost any portion of Europe still controlled by the Germans. Let me put forward the theory that what could have been done, and in my opinion should have been done, is essentially what the United States recently did with the dropping of air supplies to some isolated portions of Bosnia: the clear and public indication of a policy preference opposed to the established policy of one side even if there is little or no prospect of providing substantial practical assistance.

An excellent example of this from World War II is the supplies which the Allies attempted to drop by air to the Polish resistance forces which had risen against the Germans in Warsaw. These efforts no doubt showed where the British and Americans stood, and they also certainly helped the morale of those active in the uprising; but the practical effect was nearly nil. Perhaps the effort made enabled the Poles to prolong their resistance for a few days longer than would otherwise have been possible, but the outcome could not be in doubt.

One further point should be made in this connection. When the Western Allies sent planes to Warsaw, this was done over the strong objections of the commanders in the affected theaters of war. They always had other targets and priorities; this is particularly obvious from the records of the Allied command in Italy. In wartime there are invariably competing demands for all military resources, and the diversion of such resources in the fall of 1944 to the futile effort to assist the Polish uprising in Warsaw was ordered from the top.[20]

The aspect of the debate over the possible bombing of Auschwitz or the railways leading to it which has been too readily overlooked is that of the

German side. By 1944 the murderers were both hardened and exper
were, it should be noted, proud of their activities and what they
their great accomplishment. The notorious Stroop report on the de
the Warsaw Ghetto should be reread from this perspective: it show
boasted of what they were doing.[21] They were completely committ
careers as professional killers, and not only because of their ideological stance.
By 1944 it was obvious to all of them that this was their road to advancement
and to medals. It is not a coincidence that promotions and decorations invariably occupy such a central place in military and pseudo-military hierarchies;
these are the visible signs of success.

Furthermore, those involved in the program to kill all Jews the Germans
could reach knew very well, most especially by the summer of 1944, that this
was not only their route to higher rank and higher decorations but their best
chance of exemption from conscription if they were still in civilian positions
and from far more dangerous duty at the front if they were in uniform. It may
be a nasty way to put it, but these were, after all, nasty people. For them, killing
Jews, most of whom had no weapons, was vastly preferable to serving at the
front where those with whom one had to deal had plenty of weapons, especially
in this stage of the war.

Those active in the killing program had by this time an enormous vested
interest in its continuation and in their own participation in it. Already in the
preceding year, 1943, there are signs that the vast number of Jews killed in 1941
and 1942 had led those inside the apparatus of murder to search Europe for
new categories of victims, whether these were Jews still protected in some way
by Germany's satellites and allies or new categories for the death factories: Sinti
and Roma, those of mixed ancestry, the so-called *Mischlinge*, or other categories.[22]

The idea that men who were dedicated to the killing program, and who saw
their own careers and even their own lives tied to its continuation, were likely
to be halted in their tracks by a few line-cuts on the railways or the blowing
up of a gas-chamber is preposterous. The notion that people who had by the
summer of 1944 encompassed by one means or another the deaths of well over
four million and quite probably over five million Jews lacked the persistence,
ingenuity, and means to kill the majority of Hungary's seven hundred thousand
Jews defies all reason. It would have required greater exertions and more ingenuity on their part—and would perhaps have produced an additional medal
and an additional promotion for those who in the face of great obstacles had
carried out their Führer's design.

On the other hand, such an action by the Western Allies would have made
something of an important assertion of policy, would have encouraged desperate
victims in their last days and hours, might have inspired a few additional persons to provide aid and comfort to the persecuted, and might even have enabled
a tiny number to escape the fate planned for them by the Germans. As it is,

absence of such essentially symbolic action leaves a blot on the record of ..e Allies and, possibly more effectively than any other development of those horrendous years, gives the lie to the endless stories about the alleged power of the Jews in the world: in the hour of supreme agony, all the Jewish organizations on earth could not get one country to send one plane to drop one bomb.

In connection with the last stage of the war and of the Holocaust, one additional significant aspect of the policy of Britain and the United States needs review. Time and again during the war both governments responded to those who urged more drastic steps to assist the victims of the German killing program with the argument that the most important thing was to win the war as quickly as possible. Victory would end the killing, and anything that might delay victory would only hurt, not help, those whom the Germans had marked out as victims. It is frequently claimed that this was not only a silly answer, but that there was something mendacious about it because most of Europe's Jews were killed before victory was in fact attained. This issue ought in future research to be given a far more careful scrutiny.

Given the determination of the Germans to fight on to the bitter end, and given their equally fierce determination to slaughter Jews into the last moments of the Third Reich, there were, as is well known, thousands of deaths every day into the final days of the war; and many of the surviving camp inmates had been so weakened by hunger and disease that thousands more died even after liberation. In this connection, it might be worthwhile to consider how many more Jews would have survived had the war ended even a week or ten days earlier—and conversely, how many more would have died had the war lasted an additional week or ten days. Whatever numbers one might put forward in such speculations, one thing is or ought to be reasonably clear: the number would be greater than the total number of Jews saved by the various rescue efforts of 1943–45.

Every single life counts, and every individual saved counts. There cannot be the slightest doubt that more efforts could have been made by an earlier establishment of the War Refugee Board and by an number of other steps and actions. The general picture in terms of overall statistics would not, in my judgment, have been very different; but the record of the Allies would have been brighter, and each person saved could have lived out a decent life. The exertions of the Allies in World War II saved not only themselves but also the majority of the world's Jews. But the shadow of doubt that enough was not done will always remain, even if there were really not many things that could have been done. Any examination of the failure to do more must, however, carefully avoid a most dangerous shift in the apportioning of responsibility. It is the killers, whether in an office, a murder squad, or a killing center, who bear the central responsibility for their deeds. Any general distribution of blame, the "we are all guilty" syndrome, only serves to exculpate the truly guilty. And those were not to be found among the Allies.

2

AUSCHWITZ PARTIALLY DECODED

Richard Breitman

WHEN DID THE West first learn about mass extermination of Jews at Auschwitz-Birkenau? Western governments clearly had special sources of information not available to the public at that time. Walter Laqueur once suggested that British intelligence must have learned about Auschwitz quite early during the Holocaust from its decodes of various types of German radio messages, but the documentary evidence to validate his conclusion was not then available, and some of it may have been destroyed.[1] In contrast, Martin Gilbert has argued that, despite the existence of some Polish intelligence reports mentioning Nazi activities at Auschwitz, the real significance of Auschwitz-Birkenau remained obscured to the West until mid-1944, when escapees from the camps managed to get very detailed accounts of their experiences and of camp operations to the outside world.[2] Few other scholars have ventured into this particular controversy about Auschwitz, although it is now clear that during the war Western governments received plenty of information about the Nazi "Final Solution" of the Jewish question.[3]

One aspect of this subject—Polish treatment of information about Auschwitz and about the Holocaust—has been explored in detail. In August 1943 the Polish government-in-exile in London promoted the notion of a British bombing mission directed at Auschwitz designed to achieve a mass liberation of prisoners,[4] but this suggestion is not clear evidence of how much the British government knew. In a study of the Polish government David Engel argued that the Poles highlighted atrocities against Polish prisoners at Auschwitz and played down reports about killings of Jews there. In short, the Polish government was partly responsible for the West's lack of knowledge. Engel's interpretation, although between Laqueur's and Gilbert's, is closer to the latter.[5]

Questions raised about the secrecy of Nazi operations at Auschwitz are relevant to the debate about bombing the gas chambers and crematoria at Birkenau. No one in the West could think about or plan to bomb Auschwitz until there was clear and convincing evidence of why it was needed and some consideration of whether it was logistically feasible. Despite continuing government resistance to declassification of World War II intelligence records, some recent openings of selected British intelligence documents now make it possible to look in greater detail at contemporary intelligence records about Auschwitz.

From its headquarters at Oranienburg, outside Berlin, the SS Economic-Administrative Main Office (WVHA)—which oversaw the array of extermination camps, concentration camps, factory camps, labor camps, other types of camps, and SS economic enterprises—liked to use radio communication. The WVHA, like most branches of the SS, used the sophisticated Enigma coding machine. Although British codebreakers managed to decipher a good number of Enigma codes used by the German military, they were less successful with the SS. But the British were able to break at least one Enigma key used by the WVHA beginning in December 1940 and read the SS communications, with many ups and downs, until late in the war.[6] In the process, they picked up some glimpses of activities related to the Holocaust and some specific items about Auschwitz-Birkenau.

SS officials sent top-secret information only by courier, not by radio. But one WVHA radio instruction was itself a revealing indicator of the nature of activities at the camps. On 11 June 1942, one or more of the concentration camp commanders[7] who had received previous instructions about radio secrecy learned that reports of executions carried out were no longer to be considered top secret (*Geheime Reichssache*), but only secret. It meant that the camp commanders could report executions by radio to the WVHA, and it implied that there was something considerably more sensitive than simple shootings of prisoners.[8] The British decodes of WVHA messages also picked up traces, often partly garbled, of meetings between Adolf Eichmann, in charge of removing and transporting Jews, and various concentration- and extermination-camp officials.[9]

Substantial information about Auschwitz was made available in signals communications in part because it was a collection of camps with different purposes, some less secret than others. Auschwitz had started out as a concentration camp mostly for various categories of Poles; it began a dramatic expansion in 1941. Auschwitz II (Birkenau) became the center of mass extermination in 1942, and an I. G. Farben synthetic rubber (Buna) factory at Monowitz, Auschwitz III, absorbed many of those prisoners capable of hard labor.[10]

Auschwitz, particularly Auschwitz III, needed laborers, and that kind of information could go out by radio. The Reich Security Main Office (RSHA) stated that unexplained internal political reasons made it impossible to ship some thousand German Jews capable of labor to Auschwitz on 3 and 4 June 1942,[11] but the Nazi puppet-state of Slovakia cooperated to fill the gap. New transports of Jews from Slovakia to Auschwitz began on 16 June; the purpose was deployment for labor.[12] Trainloads of Slovak Jews from March 1942 on were among the first who underwent "selection" at Auschwitz—the able-bodied spared temporarily for hard labor: the children, elderly, and weak sent to the gas chambers. The transports of 16–20 June, however, consisted of adults apparently needed and used as laborers—for the time being.[13] In November 1942 the British learned that 396 prisoners were involved in construction at the Buna camp, and 1,568 worked in the Buna factory itself.[14]

Information about Birkenau and the factory-style process of mass murder was more difficult to locate in British decodes of German radio messages, but it was there. In a partially garbled decode in June 1942, *SS-Brigadeführer* Dr. Hans Kammler, the head of construction for the WVHA and the builder of camps and camp installations, alluded to a chimney for the crematorium.[15] At that time additional gas chambers and crematoria were under construction at Birkenau.[16]

The British also picked up reports of a number of meetings among WVHA chief Oswald Pohl, Kammler, and Rudolf Höss, commandant of Auschwitz.[17] These meetings apparently were connected with high-level dissatisfaction with the pace of resolving the Jewish question, complications caused by transportation bottlenecks in hindering shipments of Jews, and construction of new extermination facilities.[18] Himmler himself went to Auschwitz for a two-day inspection on 17–18 July 1942 and observed the gassing of one selection of Jews. He then authorized a major expansion and gave commandant Höss a promotion. Following that visit, he went straight to Lublin and observed operations at at least one of Globocnik's extermination camps, Sobibor.[19] Neither trip, however, showed up in the decodes—as far as we know. Based on the documents released to this point, it would have been very difficult for British analysts to make a connection in mid-1942 between transports of Jews to Auschwitz and the new killing installations there from the decodes alone, and there is no sign that British intelligence did so. More suggestive was a later (November 1942) message that Auschwitz urgently needed six hundred gas masks to equip its new guards, but that, too, was only one little piece of a picture.[20]

Still, there were other, more indirect ways for British intelligence to get at the reality. Himmler and his subordinates had a liking for good records and for statistics. In early 1943 the WVHA passed along to the various camps an order from Himmler to compile the prisoner population each year since 1933 by category: political prisoners, criminals, Jews, Poles, Spanish communists, and Russians. Himmler wanted to know how many each camp had released each year, and how many had died.[21] If the returns were sent by radio (which is most unlikely), reports of them have not survived or have not been declassified. During 1942, however, a number of camps, Auschwitz among them, reported by radio almost daily, the number of additions and subtractions to the camp prisoner population. Following instructions, they also broke down their total number of prisoners by the major categories—Germans, Jews, Poles, and Russians. With one big exception (explained below), British intelligence could and did, with some delay, track the changing population and mortality at Auschwitz.[22]

In January–March 1942 the number of Jews was in the hundreds. Beginning in April, it moved into the thousands, which reflected the arrival of deportees from Slovakia, and by late July it exceeded 10,000. The peak number was just over 12,000 in August; then the official Jewish population began to decline. In August 1942, 6,829 men and 1,525 women died in the camp. From 1 September on, "natural" deaths were no longer to be sent by radio—only in writing.[23]

These statistics covered only the number of prisoners registered at the Auschwitz camps. The death total included those shot or beaten to death as well as those who died of disease or starvation. They *omitted* all Jews (and the smaller number of Gypsies) selected for the gas chambers immediately upon arrival. This omission—was it too a cloaking device?—might have imposed a critical handicap in interpreting Auschwitz's role, but other forms of intelligence could and should have compensated for it.

From early in the war British intelligence read German railway decodes, and from February 1941 on, a Railway Research Service within the Ministry of Economic Warfare analyzed German rail transportation, too.[24] (If they still exist, these decodes are apparently still classified.) Some WVHA messages also referred to shipments of categories of Jews to Auschwitz. A mid-July 1942 message explained that a particular transport from France was not filled with Jews; the implication was that the others were. An October 1942 message referred in passing to transports of Jews from Polish, Czech, and Dutch territory.[25] The railway decodes must have contained even more detailed information, so British intelligence analysts must have known about the scale of deportations. They also knew from the data that the Auschwitz camp population was not taking in Jews in numbers comparable to what the transports must have brought, and that Jews were not departing. Had Auschwitz become one of the largest cities of Europe? There was only one logical conclusion about the fate of Jews transported there. But specific British intelligence conclusions about Auschwitz-Birkenau either have not survived or remain classified.[26]

The British also received through the intelligence organization of the Polish government-in-exile a series of reports from Polish agents and couriers about activities at Auschwitz and other extermination camps. (For present purposes, what mattered most were Polish reports actually passed to the British and the Americans, not the larger body of information that reached the Polish government in London.) Information from human sources, especially escaped prisoners, took much longer to reach London and contained hearsay as well as eyewitness testimony. Nonetheless, the Polish underground reports were an important complement to, and confirmation of, British signals intelligence.

A Polish agent based in London, Tadeusz Chciuk-Celt, parachuted into Poland twice. His first visit came at the end of December 1941, and he remained through mid-June 1942. He went from Poland to Budapest and sent a report to London in the fall of 1942 about mass executions and the expansion of Auschwitz's capacity to absorb victims. Chciuk-Celt's original reports were lost or remain classified, but he wrote up some of his experiences for publication in 1945 and afterwards.[27] His account also is consistent with the pattern formed by those contemporary documents not still classified.

On 15 November 1942 the Polish underground reported that tens of thousands, mostly Jews and Soviet POWs, had arrived at Auschwitz "for the sole purpose of their immediate extermination in gas chambers." This information reached the Polish government in London by 27 November.[28] The Directorate of Civilian Resistance in Poland reported on 23 March 1943 that a new crematorium was disposing of about 3,000 persons per day in Auschwitz-Birkenau, of which most were Jews.[29] This report was very close to what postwar reconstruction would establish as the actual situation at that time. Crematorium IV had begun to operate on March 22—one day earlier—and Crematorium V started up about two weeks later. Together they had the capacity to deal with 3,000 bodies per day.

The report of the new crematorium, sent by Stefan Korbonski in underground Poland to London, appeared in April 1943 in a Polish bulletin called *Poland Fights*. Through the middle of 1942, according to this publication, there had been 63,340 prisoners registered at Auschwitz-Birkenau. Another 22,000 persons had arrived at the camp, but were simply liquidated without being registered. Among the unregistered were 4000 Poles, 10,000 Jews, and 8500 Soviet POWs. Also included was another estimate that 57,000 people had died at Auschwitz-Birkenau of illness, exhaustion, or execution.[30]

On 18 April 1943, the day before the Warsaw ghetto uprising began, a Polish underground courier[31] who had made his way to London drafted a long report about his stay in Poland and Europe from roughly November 1941 until October 1942.[32] He made some errors in his report, and there were some overly optimistic comments about the prevailing relationship between Poles and Jews in Poland, but he also had detailed information about Auschwitz:

I lived in Oswiecim [Auschwitz] for a number of weeks. I know the conditions well, because I investigated them. . . . I had the most detailed information of what is going on there from people [Polish prisoners] who were freed. When I left Oswiecim at the end of September [1942], the number of registered prisoners was over 95,000. . . . Among the latter [unregistered were] 20,000 Russian prisoners of war who were brought there in the summer of 1940 [1941] as well as masses of Jews brought there from other countries. The POWs died from starvation. Jews were exterminated en masse.

On the basis of information I collected and on the spot, I can ascertain that the Germans applied the following killing methods. a) gas chambers: the victims were undressed and put into those chambers where they suffocated; b) electric chambers: Those chambers had metal walls. The victims were brought in and then high-tension electric current was introduced; c) the so-called Hammerluft system. This is a hammer of the air [presumably some sort of air pressure killing]. d) shooting, often killing every tenth person.

The first three methods were said to be the most common. Obviously, there were false elements (the electric chambers and Hammerluft system) and deductions in this account, gathered from a variety of sources. Nonetheless, the courier left little doubt that large numbers of Jews were being gassed at Birkenau:

> Gestapo men stood in a position which enabled them to watch in gas masks the death of the masses of victims. The Germans loaded the corpses and took them outside Auschwitz by means of huge shovels. They made holes where they buried the dead, and then they covered the holes with lime. Burning of victims by means of electric ovens was seldom applied [in this period]. This is because in such ovens only about 250 people could be burned within twenty-four hours.[33]

This Polish courier met in London with Dr. Ignacy Schwarzbart, a member of the Polish National Council and a representative of the World Jewish Congress. On 27 April Schwarzbart sent a report of this meeting and about this document to the Representation of Polish Jews in the United States within the World Jewish Congress. He asked his recipients to keep the information strictly confidential. But the American government had this information, too, because its Censorship Office inspected all transatlantic mail, summarized relevant and useful information, then sent it on its way.[34] The British must have had this information from Polish intelligence or even through a direct debriefing of the courier. The information remained unpublished at the courier's request, but the Western governments had it. In arguing that the killing operations at Birkenau remained secret, Martin Gilbert commented on this document: "There is no evidence, however, that its revelations made any impression or that it was quoted or mentioned again."[35] But do we have access to all Western intelligence records about this report?

On 18 May Polish military intelligence in London prepared another report on conditions in Poland that was sent by diplomatic pouch to Washington; a copy in Polish was given to the Joint Chiefs of Staff in June. Again there was updating of information regarding Auschwitz-Birkenau, this time from new underground sources. The total number of people killed at Auschwitz-Birkenau through December 1942 was now said to be 640,000, including 65,000 Poles, 26,000 Soviet POWs, and 520,000 Jews.[36]

In May 1943 the Polish Embassy in London gave the British Foreign Office another first-hand (largely accurate) account of the killing process at Treblinka, which the author thought was the center for the extermination of Europe's Jews.

[32]

Nonetheless, the report mentioned other such killing centers, and Auschwitz (Oswiecim) was listed.[37]

The flow of information about Auschwitz continued. A December 1943 Polish military intelligence report from a Polish woman, codenamed Wanda, reached London at the end of January 1944. Wanda had apparently also written about Auschwitz-Birkenau earlier and was believed to be completely reliable. Her report was given to the U.S. liaison to the Allied governments-in-exile and to the American military attaché in London, with the request to give it as wide publicity as possible. Copies were sent to OSS London and eventually to Washington. Wanda claimed that, through September 1942, 468,000 non-registered Jews had been gassed at Auschwitz-Birkenau. Then during the next eight months, 60,000 Jews had arrived from Greece, 50,000 from Slovakia and Bohemia-Moravia, 60,000 from Holland, Belgium, and France, as well as 11,000 others; 98 percent of the recent arrivals were gassed. So Wanda's grand total as of early June 1943 was 645,000 Jews gassed.

She, too, described the processes of selection and killing:

Each convoy arriving at Auschwitz is unloaded. Men are separated from women and then packed haphazard in a mass. Children and women are put into cars and lorries and taken to the gas chamber in Brzezinka. There they are suffocated with the most horrible suffering lasting ten to fifteen minutes, the corpses being thrown out through an aperture and cremated. Before entering the gas chambers, the condemned must be bathed. At present, three large crematoria have been erected in Birkenau-Brzezinka for 10,000 people daily which are ceaselessly cremating bodies and which the neighboring population call "the eternal fire."

Wanda also mentioned that the overwhelming majority of Gypsies from Greece and southern France were gassed immediately.[38]

Martin Gilbert argued that the West lacked information about the gas chambers and crematoria disposing of huge numbers of Jews at Auschwitz until four prisoners escaped in April–May 1944 and their accounts filtered out to the West in June.

From the first week of May 1942 until the third week of June 1944 the gas chambers at Auschwitz-Birkenau had kept their secret both as the principal mass murder site of the Jews of Europe and also as the destination of so many hundreds of deportation trains from France, Holland, Belgium, Italy, Greece, and elsewhere.[39]

But as we have seen, such information was available. British intelligence analysts may have had some difficulty for a time in untangling the various functions of the Auschwitz camps, but historians cannot see how they tried to do so, given that relevant British documents are still classified or have been destroyed.

It is certainly true that the very detailed report about Auschwitz and Birkenau compiled by two escapees, Rudolf Vrba and Alfred Wetzler, gave Western governments in mid-1944 many new details and brought fundamentally new information to the public in Britain and the United States. It may also have swayed some officials who had managed to discount all earlier sources of information, but we do not know. Still, for British intelligence officials who had had access to the decodes or to Polish intelligence, the Vrba-Wetzler report was not the first to reveal that huge numbers of Jews were being killed at Auschwitz-Birkenau or that poison gas was an essential part of the process. British intelligence knew enough about Auschwitz-Birkenau to preclude one argument: that lack of information was a part of the reason why Auschwitz was never bombed.

3

ALLIED AIR POWER: OBJECTIVES AND CAPABILITIES

Tami Davis Biddle

TODAY, THE QUESTION of whether the Allies could and should have bombed Auschwitz is addressed through the lens of postwar images and ways of understanding. Those who take it up do so in the framework of a modern *mentalité*, embracing the sensitivities, the language, and the metaphors of the late twentieth century. This is inevitable because historians always bring their own era to bear on their interpretation of the past. We view evidence though modern filters and lenses; we base our judgments on contemporary standards and assumptions. In many respects, this feature of history writing is helpful as it enables us to attempt to use the past for the betterment of the future.

But while we must recognize and even embrace the influence of the present on history writing, we also must make our best efforts to comprehend historical events in the context of their own time. Failure to do so puts us in the position of basing our analyses and our judgments on artificial premises unrelated to the realities of the past. The purpose of this essay is to help ground the discussion of the bombing of Auschwitz-Birkenau in a foundation that recognizes the objectives, capabilities, and priorities of the World War II Allied air forces: the Royal Air Force (RAF) and the United States Army Air Forces (USAAF). This chapter will not address specific scenarios in detail, as these are undertaken by other contributors to this volume. Rather, it will offer an overview designed to inform readers generally about the Allied air forces during World War II, highlighting both the constraints and pressures under which they operated. After providing a general review of the air force record in the early years of the war, the chapter will focus on the hectic summer of 1944, when information arriving from Auschwitz escapees prompted Jewish representatives to implore Allied leaders to attack the camp or the rail lines leading to it.

On 4 January 1941, a brief report on the camp at Oswiecim (Auschwitz), along with a request to bomb the camp, was sent directly to Air Marshal Sir Richard

Peirse, head of the RAF's Bomber Command. At that time, Auschwitz, while a concentration camp, had not yet acquired the machinery of mass extermination that would turn it into Europe's most infamous site of mass killing. The report, forwarded by Count Stephan Zamoyski on behalf of the commander-in-chief of the Polish army, had been sent from Poland to the Rubens Hotel in London, the temporary home of the General Headquarters (G.H.Q.) of the Polish army. It alleged that Oswiecim was one of the "worst orgainized [sic] and most inhuman concentration camps" with conditions that are "incredible." After describing generally the location of the camp, the report stated: "The prisoners implore the Polish Government to have the camp bombed. The destruction of the electrified barbed wire, the ensuing panic and darkness prevailing, [mean that] the chances of escape would be great."[1]

Peirse forwarded the report to Sir Charles Portal, chief of the air staff. He attached a covering letter that stated: "I cannot here assess the political value of such an expedition, but if you judge it to be a desirable diversion then this is to let you know that from the point of view of distance I could undertake it with a small Wellington force under suitable moonlight conditions."[2] In his response four days later, Portal argued that "an attack on the Polish concentration camp at Oswiecim is an undesirable diversion for our bomber force and unlikely to achieve its purpose. The weight of bombs that could be carried to a target at this distance with the limited force available, would be very unlikely to cause enough damage to enable prisoners to escape." Portal told Peirse to communicate that position to the Poles.[3]

On 15 January, Peirse wrote directly to Gen. W. Sikorski at the Polish G.H.Q. and told him that an attack on the camp at Oswiecim "is not a practical proposition." He said that, first, British bomber forces were fully committed to the attack on Germany's industrial resources—an attack that he speculated "[was] likely to precipitate a crisis in Germany's war economy this year." He added that this required Bomber Command to use every opportunity to strike vital targets, pointing out that "the weather conditions which would enable us to attack targets in Poland are just those which allow us to engage our major targets in Germany." Second, he argued that an attack on Oswiecim was unlikely to achieve the hoped-for result: namely, the escape of prisoners made possible by the destruction of the camp's barbed-wire fences and nearby ammunition dumps. Peirse continued: "Air bombardment of this nature would need to be extremely accurate if serious casualties were not to be caused among the prisoners themselves. Such accuracy cannot be guaranteed." He closed by telling Sikorski: "I am so sorry to have to give you this answer, but I know you will appreciate the reasons and the fact that only by rigid concentration of our bomber forces on the main objectives are we likely to be effective against our common enemy."[4]

This exchange is notable for a number of reasons. First, it represents a very early request to bomb Auschwitz. Second, it is striking that Sir Richard Peirse revealed a basic willingness to consider the mission, and that he regretted having to give a negative response. And third, it is noteworthy that the language Sir Charles Portal used in responding negatively to Peirse was remarkably similar to that which would be used when requests to bomb Auschwitz were put forward again in the summer of 1944.

While certainly we must admire Peirse's spirit, his comments reveal a misplaced optimism about the strategic bombing campaign in the early years of its operation, and a failure to fully confront the many weaknesses of Bomber Command at that time. (Indeed, the latter would help to bring an end to his command of the force by the end of the year.) His speculation—in his reply to Sikorski—that British bombing might provoke a crisis in Germany in 1941 was wildly optimistic. In the early years of the war, Bomber Command was a small, technically unsophisticated force that coped poorly with German defenses and, more often than not, failed to find and hit targets successfully. Already by May 1940, the attrition its crews had suffered at the hands of German fighters had forced British bombers to operate at night. But night flying naturally complicated efforts at finding targets, and never totally solved the problem of high attrition rates. During August 1942, for instance, losses in Bomber Command's No. 4 Group were a staggering ten percent; at such a rate, only a small handful of total crew members could be expected to survive the full complement of required missions. Many of the worst losses were partly a result of inherent faults and failures in the airplanes used early in the war.[5]

The full weight of Bomber Command's weakness was brought home to Peirse and the Air Ministry in the summer of 1941. At that time, the results of Britain's first full-scale bomb-damage assessment (based on extensive photo-reconnaissance) would reveal that of total bomber sorties flown, only about one in five bombers was getting within five miles of its designated target.[6] Initially, Peirse was so staggered by these results (known as the "Butt Report" after the civil servant who compiled and evaluated the statistics) that he doubted they could be true. And Prime Minister Winston Churchill, who had been harboring doubts for some time about the effectiveness of Bomber Command, told Portal: "It is an awful thought that perhaps three-quarters of our bombs go astray."[7]

The results ultimately forced the British into the unavoidable conclusion that if they were to continue the bomber offensive at all, they would have to aim for the only targets large enough to find: cities. In mid-February 1942, this was set forth in a new directive stating that henceforth, Bomber Command's aim points would be the built-up residential areas of cities, and the principal object would be to undermine "the morale of the enemy population and in particular of the industrial workers." Sir Arthur Harris, who became the new head of Bomber Command just a week later, committed himself fully to the directive. Harris believed firmly that sustained, extensive attacks on German industrial cities would undermine the Reich's war-making capability to the point of un-sustainability, bringing the quickest possible end to the war.[8] In order to im-prove their ability to operate at night, the British developed radar bombing aids that increased in sophistication throughout the war.

In light of the fact that well under half of Bomber Command's planes were getting into the general vicinity of their targets, it is hard to imagine how a 1941 raid on such a distant and small target as Auschwitz would have had much chance of success, especially since the raid envisioned—one designed to enable the prisoners to escape—would have had to be exceptionally precise. Portal's reservations were realistic: he was correct to claim that the bombload that a two-engine Wellington bomber could have carried to such a remote target would have been too small to insure that—in the unlikely event the crew could have found the camp—the facilities could have been damaged enough to have allowed prisoners to escape.

His argument that an attack on the concentration camp "is an undesirable diversion for our bomber force" may sound bureaucratic and perhaps even callous to the modern ear, but it must be remembered that RAF leaders believed the central purpose of Bomber Command was to wage an offensive against the German war machine—an offensive designed to erode the sources of Hitler's power. The sooner and more efficiently that could be done, the sooner a remedy could be given to all those suffering under the boot of the Third Reich. As a place, Auschwitz at that time bore none of the significance it holds today. Portal would not have felt a particular sense of urgency about it. Certainly, terrible things were happening there, but that was true for much of Europe in 1941. Also, Bomber Command's limited assets were stretched thin, meaning that there were always direct trade-offs involved in targeting decisions: attacking one target meant foregoing another, and planners had to make constant efforts to assess the most promising use of scarce resources.

Peirse tried to explain this resource trade-off in his final reply to Sikorski. Though in hindsight we may think him foolish for assuming that his airplanes might soon precipitate a crisis in the German war economy, it is unfair to assume that he spoke the words disingenuously. Optimism that progress was being made and that a breakthrough was just around the corner was one of the most enduring (if, in hindsight, curious) qualities of the British bomber offen-sive.

Neither Peirse nor Portal was in a position to assess a raid on Auschwitz on political grounds, as they had no authority in political matters. By 1942, how-ever, Allied politicians became increasingly involved in the issue of German concentration camps and extermination programs. In December, further infor-mation on atrocities taking place in occupied Europe prompted the Allies and associated governments-in-exile to make a formal declaration in condemnation of the Nazi policy of "cold-blooded extermination."[9] In the same month, Chur-chill responded to pressure from the Polish ambassador by raising with his War

Cabinet the possibility of air reprisals against the Germans for their mass executions in Poland. But Portal was emphatically opposed to reprisal raids as a matter of principle; he believed that they would not deter German behavior, and might instead invite retaliation against British crews shot down over Germany. Another issue entered into his thinking as well: he told the prime minister that Hitler "has so often stressed that this is a war by the Jews to exterminate Germany that . . . a raid, avowedly conducted on account of the Jews, would be an asset to enemy propaganda."[10]

But if Portal was unwilling to entertain the idea of raids designated specifically as reprisals for German atrocities, and if he believed that, due to Bomber Command's operational limitations, a raid on the camp itself could not be considered, then the Allies were left with few means to directly affect German behavior toward the Jews of Europe. The truth was that in 1941, after the Nazis had formalized the Final Solution as policy, the Allies were weak militarily. As a result, they were unable to do much to directly impede the accelerating march of the Nazi horrors in Europe—horrors that seemed almost incomprehensible even in light of the available accounts.[11]

In 1942, the United States was only just beginning to muster its offensive capabilities. Most of the year was spent building airplanes, training pilots, and erecting the infrastructure (airfields, supply areas, etc.) necessary to wage an air campaign. While the war in Europe had made it politically possible for President Franklin Roosevelt to authorize notable increases in American defense expenditures prior to 1941, full-scale mobilization began only after the bombing of Pearl Harbor. Only in July 1941 had Roosevelt asked the secretaries of war and the navy to prepare an estimate of overall production requirements needed to defeat the potential enemies of the United States. This led to the first comprehensive plan detailing the requirements and targeting objectives for an air campaign in Europe—a plan that called for the production of over 60,000 aircraft. The usual problems of overnight production increases made themselves felt, and planes "in production" were not necessarily combat-ready. Early combat types underwent almost constant modification based on initial operational experience.[12] USAAF bombers began venturing over the coast of France only in August 1942; not until the following February would they begin to make bombing runs over Germany proper. Most of the early raids were small-scale and cautious. Through this period, death camps at Chelmno, Sobibor, Treblinka, Belzec, Majdanek, and Auschwitz would be the scenes of unspeakable and unprecedented catastrophe for the Jews of Europe.

The British, struggling to build up their own aerial force and greatly frustrated by the slow progress of the American effort, sought to persuade the Americans to join them in the nighttime area offensive against German cities. Churchill took a leading role in this, going directly to Roosevelt and his aide Harry Hopkins. But the Americans remained committed to a different course: the use of daylight, high-altitude, self-defending bomber raids (without fighter escort) against selected targets. Their approach rested on the assumption that concentrated attacks on a few key—or "bottleneck"—industries in the German economy were the most efficient way to slow and ultimately halt the Nazi war machine. The British, unable to persuade their stubborn allies that daylight operations deep into Germany would be too costly, ultimately had to stand back and allow them to make their own mistakes.[13]

At the Casablanca conference of January 1943, the Americans and the British agreed to a program of round-the-clock bombing designed to dislocate and destroy the German war economy, and to bring about a collapse of the morale of the German people. The directive emerging from the conference accommodated both the American and British approaches and was, in essence, an agreement to disagree. Specific targeting guidance was worked out in the succeeding months. Based heavily on the work of the newly formed American intelligence group, the Committee of Operations Analysts (COA), the resulting "Pointblank" directive prioritized attacks on the German aircraft industry and its supporting industries (viewing such a step as essential to all subsequent operations).[14]

It was expected that Americans would bomb industrial targets by day, and the British would complement the effort by attacking the surrounding area by night.[15] Though all plans for the Combined Bomber Offensive (CBO) went through the Allied Combined Chiefs of Staff (CCS), coordination between the British and the Americans was not subject to rigid rules. British and American field commanders retained a good deal of control over the day-to-day operation of their forces. Not infrequently, however, targeting demands representing emergencies or overriding strategic priorities were imposed on field commanders by national or Allied high command. Germany's naval war against Britain's supply lifeline, for instance, kept a significant number of Allied bombers committed to attacking submarine pens, even though the pens proved to be largely impervious to Allied bombs. These missions, though dutifully carried out, were sometimes resented by air force commanders who felt that they prevented a concentration of effort on the central task of strategic bombardment, thereby slowing progress toward Germany's final defeat. Sir Arthur Harris, who believed that the quickest and surest way to victory was to smash German industrial cities, lashed out repeatedly against the "diversionists" who kept Bomber Command from devoting sustained attention to its main focus.[16]

Most of the time, however, political authorities did not interject themselves into targeting decisions for strategic air forces. Such decisions were complex, dependent on contingent factors (like weather), and subject to special types of technical knowledge and expertise. Not even Churchill, who routinely involved himself in all manner of military details, was a major force in targeting decisions. Though he showed a tendency to want to micromanage Bomber Command early on, the overwhelming demands on his time prevented him from indulging this predeliction except on occasion. Roosevelt's policy was noninterventionist.[17]

American bombers suffered at the hands of Luftwaffe pilots, and by late 1943, American air leaders finally were persuaded that unescorted daylight raids deep into enemy territory were too costly to be continued. Sealing this decision were two raids on ball-bearing production facilities at Schweinfurt, Germany, flown in August and October 1943. In the second raid, 198 of the 291 bombers sent out either did not return at all, or came back damaged.[18] Facing the collapse of their entire strategic bombing campaign, the Americans were forced to take radical action. But they chose to change tactics rather than targets. Relying on an expanded production base back home, they built long-range escort fighters in great numbers, and brought them into the European theater as quickly as possible. These fighters, equipped with auxiliary fuel tanks, were able to escort bombers to Germany and defend them over German airspace.

Not only had the RAF failed to provoke a collapse in Germany, but it was also struggling mightily—and increasingly unsuccessfully—against German defenses, especially night fighters. American planners realized that failure to defeat the German air force would jeopardize a cross-channel invasion: clearly, an all-out effort against the Luftwaffe was required as quickly as possible. By flying to targets that the Germans felt obliged to defend, American bombers drew German fighters into the skies, whereupon American fighters were free to engage them in deadly dogfights. This hard-fought aerial battle of attrition, carried on through the winter and spring of 1943–44, eventually broke the back of the Luftwaffe by putting an unbearable strain on its supply of aircraft, fuel, and pilots.[19]

This campaign diverged quite a lot from the prewar expectations of air planners, but in the end it served its purpose. Naturally, its success benefited the British as well: the toll it took—on German fighter pilots in particular— made it more difficult for the Germans to defend adequately against night bombing.[20] It helped clear the way for D-Day, and it opened the door to a more extensive bombing campaign, waged by the joint forces of Bomber Command, the U.S. Eighth Air Force (based in the United Kingdom since 1942), and the newly formed Fifteenth Air Force, based in Italy. The Fifteenth, formed in November 1943 over the objections of the British who thought it would further dilute the strength of the Eighth, became part of the U.S. Strategic Air Forces (USSTAF), under the overall command of Gen. Carl A. Spaatz.[21]

Throughout the war in Europe, the Americans maintained their focus, in theory at least, on selective bombing of particular industries, while the British concentrated on their general area offensive against German cities. This distinction, however, ought not to lead to a conclusion—drawn too often both at the time and after the war by the American press (and encouraged by the USAAF)—that the Americans were capable of "pinpoint" targeting, or "pickle-barrel" bombing. The frequently used but inappropriate phrase "precision bombing" helped create misleading impressions and memories of American

World War II bombing. These impressions have, inevitably, affected the discussion of whether Auschwitz could have or should have been bombed.

Concerns about possible public reaction to World War II strategic bombing prompted USAAF officials to be very careful about how the American bombing campaign in Europe was characterized. Sensitivities about civilian deaths and possible violations of the law of war had cropped up throughout the interwar years whenever long-range bombing was discussed, and at the outset of war in 1939, President Roosevelt had called upon the belligerent powers to confine their aerial attacks to legitimate military targets. After the United States entered the war, American airmen did not wish to associate themselves with British "city bombing" for fear that this would raise uncomfortable questions and possibly compromise their all-important bid for service independence after the war.[22] In addition, American airmen genuinely believed in the theory of selective targeting, and had faith in tools such as the B-17 bomber (designed originally to strike ships at sea) and the Norden bombsight. The emphasis placed on these tools, and the attention they received by the press, helped to convey the impression that American bombing was indeed "precise."

In fact, there was no such thing as "precision" bombing during World War II. To the extent that the term is relevant at all, it is in respect to the work of a handful of specially trained British units rather than that of the USAAF. American bombers flew to their targets in formation, and attacked in combat "boxes" of (usually) eighteen to twenty-one aircraft. The lead aircraft in each box controlled the direction and path to the target. Early in the war, the bombardier in each plane was responsible for delivering his bombs on the target. This was changed, however, in the early months of 1943, when individual sighting was abandoned and replaced by a procedure in which all aircraft dropped their bombs on a signal from the leader of the combat box. Because each box covered a sizable stretch of real estate below, the result was, inevitably, pattern bombing. Under combat conditions, when bombers had to contend with fighters, antiaircraft fire, and smoke, it became very difficult indeed to bomb in tight patterns.[23]

Because the USAAF was a daylight force dependent on good visibility for best effectiveness, it struggled in poor weather. As the war progressed, continuous cloud cover over Europe forced the Americans to rely in daylight on radar aids similar to those the British used at night. Hopes that the establishment of the Fifteenth Air Force would provide a way around north European weather problems foundered on long stretches of cloud over Italy in the fall and winter of 1943–44. And the Fifteenth suffered too from inevitable start-up problems and shortages, especially of photo-reconnaissance equipment.[24] If the Americans were going to maintain an acceptable tempo of operations in their bombing campaign, they would have to fly even in bad conditions. Thus, by the autumn of 1943, the Americans found themselves relying on radar bombing aids, and adding a considerable proportion of incendiary bombs to the ordnance mix carried by their bombers. But while this provided a higher operational tempo, it meant decreased accuracy.[25]

Throughout the war, the USAAF maintained its identity as a visual bombing force; thus, it did not equip and train as extensively with radar aids as the RAF did. As a result, American crews never became as skilled as their British counterparts when bombing on instruments. Therefore, in periods of bad weather, the overall accuracy of American crews was no better than—and was frequently worse than—that of Bomber Command. In blind (nonvisual) bombing undertaken between October and December 1943, for instance, the USAAF achieved accuracy rates no better than those documented by the RAF's Butt Report in 1941.[26]

Even after gaining experience, American bomber crews found that accurate bombing could be highly elusive. In one 1943 raid against Stuttgart, not a single one of the 338 B-17s sent out reached its primary target.[27] And months later, during a raid flown on 29 April 1944, only one of the eleven combat wings sent to bomb the railway facilities in the Friedrichstrasse section of Berlin was able to get its bombs within five miles of the aim point.[28] Even if bombs were released over the target, they did not necessarily fall where they should or cause the damage intended. The U.S. Strategic Bombing Survey (USSBS), an extensive investigation of American World War II bombing, revealed this difficulty. During 57 American raids against three German synthetic-oil plants, only 12.9 percent of the bombs dropped fell within the plant perimeter (no less than 87.1 percent fell over the surrounding countryside). Of these, only 2.2 percent actually hit damageable buildings and equipment.[29]

Though the RAF was continuously trying to improve its accuracy by developing and using special instruments, aids, and techniques, in 1943 it remained essentially an area bombing force that used city centers as aim points. In the winter of 1943–44, Bomber Command concentrated on intensive bombing of Berlin—a prolonged campaign in which Sir Arthur Harris invested unwarranted hopes and expectations. While the RAF occasionally carried out special missions demanding much higher accuracy than could be obtained by standard heavy bomber raids, these required careful planning, entailed extreme risks, and frequently exacted heavy losses.[30] Missions flown on behalf of the Special Operations Executive (SOE) were looked on with some skepticism by Portal and with outright hostility by Harris, who felt they diverted crucial resources away from Bomber Command.[31]

Just as the Allied air forces were gaining an upper hand over the Luftwaffe and beginning to pay attention to other potentially lucrative targets like the German oil supply, they were called upon to help in the direct preparation for the Allied invasion of France (Operation Overlord). Though air commanders accepted this "diversion" as inevitable, they sought to carry it out on their own terms by linking it to their own targeting priorities. But this effort was unsuccessful: the Supreme Allied Commander, Gen. Dwight Eisenhower, and his deputy, Air Marshal Sir Arthur Tedder, had other ideas. In March 1944, Eisenhower, and Tedder—who would direct Allied air forces from mid-April to mid-September—had concluded that strategic bombers would provide the most immediate help to Overlord by bombing the transportation and communications networks (mainly railroads) serving the Normandy region. This would prevent the Germans from resupplying and reinforcing the battle areas around the Allied beachhead.[32]

Allied bomber crews tried to bomb as accurately as they could when operating in France, and USAAF bombers used visual sighting as often as possible. Still, about a hundred French civilians died in each one of the visually sighted attacks waged on French railyards in the preinvasion period.[33] The bombing effort dedicated to Overlord was vast because it aimed to destroy a significant portion of the rail net supplying the Normandy region, and because the Germans naturally sought to repair the damage as quickly as possible. The effort against transportation targets, continued in Germany later in the war, brought dramatic results.[34] But it demanded a sustained commitment of resources to insure that the Allies stayed ahead of German repairs.

Allied strategic bombers were kept exceedingly busy throughout the spring and summer. In addition to paving the way for the Normandy landing and then helping to support the ground forces afterward, Allied bombers both assisted the ground war on the Italian front and helped prepare for an additional Allied landing in southern France. Seeking to use overwhelming air power to quicken the breakout from the Normandy beachhead, Allied leaders called on heavy bombers to provide close support to troops in the field. Though such operations could be very effective, they did not always live up to expectations. In addition, they entailed serious risks due to the challenges of controlling a large and inherently inaccurate force. The heavy bomber missions flown in support of Lt. Gen. Omar Bradley's Operation Cobra in late July 1944, for instance, were a mixed blessing. Though they aided the Allied advance, they killed over one hundred American troops and wounded hundreds more.[35]

The inability of Allied supply lines to keep pace with the advance of ground troops caused the diversion of an entire bomber combat wing (approximately two hundred B-24 bombers) to the ferrying of supplies to forward troops. The preparation for and execution of Operation Market Garden (August–September 1944), an airborne assault on the Arnhem region, also placed serious demands on Allied strategic bombers: under dangerous and ultimately costly conditions, they shuttled supplies forward for the paratroops, and engaged in close support operations.[36]

Heavy bombers were called on as well to perform other pressing tasks, including the attack on V-1 and V-2 launch sites and factories (Operation Crossbow). General Spaatz lamented the high priority placed on the Crossbow raids because the hardened launch sites were nearly impervious to even the biggest bombs. Nonetheless, because of the incessant V-1 attacks on England (over three hundred V-1s were launched on 15–16 June) and the threat posed by the more dangerous V-2s, there seemed no choice but to prioritize Crossbow raids. Indeed, in July and August 1944, the Allied air forces sent 16,566 sorties against V-weapon targets, one quarter of their total tonnage for those months.[37]

Spaatz was more interested in another use of heavy bombers that was quickly gaining momentum: the attack on the German oil supply. Indeed, General Spaatz had become so convinced that this was the German "Achilles' heel" that he had tried to persuade Eisenhower to make oil attacks the centerpiece of the pre-Overlord bombardment, thereby combining preinvasion preparations with the main American air campaign against the German war machine.[38] Though he failed in his effort, he nonetheless continued to lobby hard for leeway to attack oil targets.

The Fifteenth had begun its campaign against oil when it attacked Ploesti, Rumania, on 5 April 1944, causing enough damage to encourage planners to authorize further attacks. Eisenhower, who was fundamentally sympathetic to Spaatz's interest in oil, gave the USSTAF commander some room in the spring to test out the efficacy of such attacks. In May, the Fifteenth went back to Ploesti repeatedly, and the Eighth attacked synthetic oil at a number of sites including Zwickau, Merseburg-Leuna, and Politz.[39] In a memo to Deputy Supreme Commander Sir Arthur Tedder in late June, Eisenhower drew up a bombing directive which, though it ranked Crossbow first, added that "when we have favorable conditions over Germany and when the entire Strategic Air Force cannot be used against Crossbow, we should attack—a. Aircraft industry; b. Oil; c. Ball bearings; d. Vehicular production."[40]

Spaatz's intuition about oil was supported by Ultra intelligence indicating that the Germans were facing critical fuel shortages, and were deeply concerned about their situation. Information to this effect arrived steadily over the months. On 9 July, Ultra deciphered a message from Luftwaffe chief Reichsmarschall Hermann Goering: "The deep inroads made into the supply of aircraft fuel demand the most stringent reduction in flying. Drastic economy is absolutely essential."[41] Indeed, the Germans were so concerned about their oil situation that they transferred large numbers of antiaircraft guns from their cities to the synthetic-oil plants.[42] Spaatz was determined to dedicate every single bomber he had to the attack on the German oil supply. He believed that every clear day suitable for visual bombing (and not given over to Eisenhower's other priorities) had to be dedicated to oil—to the effort to stop the Germans, literally, in their tracks.[43]

By late summer, Spaatz felt even more pressure to strike at German oil while he could, because British intelligence informed him that the Germans were instituting an extensive program to repair the facilities as quickly as possible. Spaatz believed he was in an all-out race: his bombers were pitted against both the German labor force and the prospect of worsening weather in the fall.[44] With each passing week, the Axis oil situation was further compromised as

Soviet armies advanced westward and laid claim to the resources of Eastern Europe. A September memorandum from the British chiefs of staff supported Spaatz's priorities, claiming: "It has become abundantly clear over the past few months that the enemy is faced with an increasingly critical situation in regard to his oil supplies. To exploit his difficulties fully it is essential that the attack of his oil resources be pressed home at maximum intensity and on the widest scale possible."[45]

In July 1944, the Eighth had been able to send missions into Germany twelve times: four missions were aimed at oil targets, while the others focused on aircraft production facilities, ball-bearing plants, and the experimental rocket facility at Peenemünde. Due to cloud cover, over half those missions ultimately had to employ radar bombing. The Fifteenth Air Force flew fifteen strategic missions in July, thirteen of them against oil facilities. These raids were particularly costly due to the toll taken by German antiaircraft guns. In August and early September, the Eighth and Fifteenth Air Forces continued to divide their resources between supporting the ground campaign, attacking V-weapons sites, and attacking strategic targets—mainly oil. The Eighth flew seven missions against German oil, and the Fifteenth flew thirteen missions against German and Balkan oil.[46]

On a handful of occasions over the summer, the USAAF used "shuttle" bases in the Soviet Union as layover points for raids deep into central Europe. American air commanders placed hope in the program as a means of reaching important targets—particularly oil—in Central and Eastern Europe, which were difficult or impossible to reach otherwise.[47] But the shuttle program—which began in June—was star-crossed from the start: throughout its brief life, it was fraught with severe problems and difficulties. In the end, it hardly justified the hopes placed in it or the time and resources devoted to it. The Soviets heavily scrutinized all the targets the Americans proposed to attack on such missions, and made using the bases very problematical and complex, both bureaucratically and logistically.[48]

Due to the demands on the strategic bomber forces for ground support, and to the continuing problems with the Russians and the shuttle bases, very few shuttle missions were flown in July and August. On 15 August, however, Gen. Eisenhower received a message from Washington urging him to undertake a supply-dropping mission to help the besieged Poles in Warsaw. (The Russians had called upon the Warsaw Poles to rise against the Germans, and then stood aside as they were crushed in the effort.) Permission was sought from the Soviets to use the shuttle bases, but the Soviets refused to cooperate. Denouncing the Poles as reckless, and claiming that they had risen prematurely, the Soviets would not authorize the use of their bases for Allied supply drops, despite vigorous diplomatic efforts and a direct appeal from Roosevelt and Churchill. Indeed, they even declined to allow the Allies to overfly Soviet-occupied Hungary on the long journey to help the Poles.[49] After a pause of two weeks, the

Americans renewed the appeal, and the Soviets finally and reluctantly gave their approval (on 11 September) for the use of shuttle bases. The very last shuttle operation was flown on 18 September, when 107 B-17s dropped over twelve hundred containers of supplies into Warsaw—the vast majority of which, it was discovered later, reached the Germans, not the Poles.[50]

At the outset of the Warsaw crisis in August, Prime Minister Churchill—whose attention to the issue had a profound influence on Allied action—had prevailed upon the RAF commander in the Mediterranean, Sir John Slessor, to use his Italy-based force (specifically No. 205 Group) to fly supplies to the Poles. Slessor believed that the idea had little chance of success, and objected to it strenuously. Nonetheless, he responded to Churchill's wishes by going ahead anyway (in early August), ultimately relying heavily on Polish volunteer forces to fly the dangerous and costly missions. The Allied supply drops were put together hurriedly, and due to the difficulty of the mission and the distance involved, they were not successful in getting much help to the desperate Poles. In his autobiography, Slessor explained: "Air supply to Poland was always the most difficult and dangerous of our special operations from the Mediterranean. The dropping zones were anything between seven and nine hundred miles from base, mostly over enemy-held country, and there was little or nothing in the way of meteorological information or radio aids in the area."[51]

In late September, Churchill kept the pressure on for the Americans to attempt a second supply drop into Warsaw. Roosevelt ordered the second mission to go ahead, but he did so against the advice of the War Department and the Air Staff, which had concluded that such missions were "costly and hopeless."[52] As it was, the Soviets again denied the Americans landing rights, and the mission was not flown before the crisis ended, on Soviet terms, in October.

Meanwhile, Spaatz continued to argue that the main Allied air effort be directed against oil, and he hoped that Bomber Command might join vigorously in the effort. By mid-1944, Bomber Command had become a highly capable force, able to deliver vast quantities of bombs with ever-increasing accuracy against industrial targets. When Bomber Command went after oil targets, the results were unfailingly dramatic. However, weather, and Harris's determined belief that cities were the only target that really mattered, kept Bomber Command's effort against oil down to 14 percent of total bombs dropped during the last three months of 1944. (By contrast, cities received 53 percent of bombs dropped by the force.) If this disappointed Spaatz, it also caused friction between Harris and the British chiefs of staff, who were convinced that oil showed the most promise as a means to victory.[53]

Very poor weather for visual bombing also had a negative impact on Spaatz's own oil campaign during the last quarter of 1944. Increasingly vigorous German ground defenses further hindered American progress, and overall bombing accuracy fell off a dramatic 40 percent.[54] Although American bomber raids had choked off production of aviation fuel in mid-September, poor weather in

October allowed the Germans to rebound. This trend continued through November and December, helping to facilitate a German counteroffensive at the end of the year. The Allies, who at one point during the summer had been optimistic about a possible victory over Germany in 1944, now had to look ahead to another year of war.

It was during this intensely busy summer of 1944—when Allied leaders were in constant, urgent turmoil over how to best use their military assets—that new requests to bomb Auschwitz or the rail lines to it began to make their way to Allied government agencies. The requests were spurred by the arrival of more detailed information than had ever before been available about the atrocities occurring at the death camp in southwest Poland. Informed by accounts of Auschwitz provided by escapees, and moved by the knowledge that deportations to the death camp were ongoing, Jewish representatives from a number of different organizations implored Allied governments to consider bombing the railway lines leading to the camp, and the camp itself.[55] In the United States, the War Department acted as the principal agent in the American decision, although some Air Force officers—including Gen. Spaatz—ultimately were made aware of the discussions about the camp. In Britain, the prime minister, the foreign secretary, the secretary of state for air, and members of the Foreign Office all took part, at one time or another, in the debate over Auschwitz.

On 18 June, Jacob Rosenheim of the New York office of Agudas Israel World Organization addressed letters to American government officials asking them to consider paralyzing the rail traffic from Hungary to Poland in an effort to halt ongoing Jewish deportations. In late June 1944, John Pehle, the executive director of the War Refugee Board (WRB), raised the bombing issue with John McCloy, the assistant secretary of war. Pehle's approach was guarded; he had doubts about whether to press the issue. McCloy's job, in what was perhaps the single most powerful federal bureaucracy at the time, enabled him to set agendas and influence the use of resources. Though a civilian, he advocated for the interests and needs of the military.[56] Shortly after Pehle's approach, McCloy and the War Department ruled against the request on the grounds that it was "impracticable" and "could be executed only by diversion of considerable air support essential to the success of our forces now engaged in decisive operations."[57] This answer was consistent with the overall policy of the War Department articulated in an internal memorandum that read: "We must constantly bear in mind that the most effective relief which can be given victims of enemy persecution is to insure the speedy defeat of the Axis."[58]

In early July, after hearing a report on Auschwitz from Foreign Minister Anthony Eden, Prime Minister Churchill chose to use his power to set some action in motion. He charged Eden to confer with the RAF to see what could be done. The secretary of state for air, Sir Archibald Sinclair, responded to Eden's inquiry on 15 July, by explaining that bombing the railways was not feasible because only an enormous concentration of bombers had been able to interrupt communications, and "the distance of Silesia from our bases entirely rules out anything of the kind." He argued further that Auschwitz-Birkenau was too far to be considered as a realistic target for a night operation by Bomber Command, which had its assets concentrated in England. But he suggested that the Americans might be persuaded to consider it—adding though that it would be a "costly and hazardous" operation. He revealed himself to be pessimistic, as well, about the possibility of a breaching operation designed to get weapons into the hands of prisoners.[59]

On 2 August, the matter was discussed with Gen. Spaatz, who was reported to have been "most sympathetic," although the historical record provides little further detail. The process of acquiring photographic intelligence of the camp, essential for planning a raid of any type, was then set in motion in Britain. The Air Ministry needed the cooperation of the Foreign Office in this, but Foreign Office personnel dragged their heels. In early September, they called off the process, citing the "very great technical difficulties" involved in the operation.[60]

While calls for bombing the rail lines continued to arrive in Washington, so too did appeals for direct attacks on the Auschwitz-Birkenau complex. But Pehle's contact with McCloy on the issue gave him little encouragement that action might be forthcoming. In September and October, the matter surfaced again in the United States, and at one point garnered attention from the operations division of the War Department. From there it moved into the Air Force operational plans division where Gen. Spaatz's deputy for operations, Gen. Frederick Anderson, considered it and recommended against action.[61]

In November, after the full text of the Auschwitz escapees' report became available in Washington, the issue of bombing the camps was taken to the War Department one more time. The further level of detail and explanation available in the full text galvanized a newly motivated John Pehle into action. He released the escapees' report to the press, and wrote a memo to John McCloy in which he stated: "Until now . . . I have been hesitant to urge the destruction of these camps by direct, military action. But I am convinced that the point has now been reached where such action is justifiable if it is deemed feasible by competent military authorities."[62] But once more, the War Department declined to take action, explaining the decision in language that was somewhat more detailed, but in essence not very different from that used in response to earlier requests. The memo, signed by the War Department's Maj. Gen. J. E. Hull, argued that "at the present critical stage of the war in Europe, our strategic air forces are engaged in the destruction of industrial target systems so vital to our effort that we cannot afford diversion. . . . The positive solution to this problem is the earliest possible victory over Germany, to which end we should exert our entire means." He concluded: "The proposal is of very doubtful feasibility and is unacceptable from a military standpoint at this time in that it would be a diversion from our strategic bombing effort and the results would not justify the high losses likely to result from such a mission."[63] In late November, as the Soviet army continued its advance westward, the Nazis ordered the killing machinery at Auschwitz destroyed. The camp was captured by the Red Army on 27 January 1945.

Requests to bomb Auschwitz or the railways leading to it were repeatedly declined by Anglo-American authorities. Over time, the language they used in their explanations of nonaction remained strikingly constant. Historians interested in this issue are obliged to do all they can to evaluate this official response and understand the possible meanings behind it.

The history of both the interwar period and World War II is full of examples of a deaf ear being turned to the Jews. Wrenching evidence of insensitivity and prejudice can be found in the documents, and they are jarring, painful, and infuriating to the historian who reads them. Few scholars who examine the many heartfelt pleas for Allied help regarding Auschwitz can fail to be moved by them. And they are all the more powerful because of the conscientious and thoughtful way in which they were put forward.

We know, of course, that there were individuals in both the State Department and the Foreign Office who were unwilling to prioritize Jewish concerns. And we may surely lament the initially guarded efforts of John Pehle—whose job it was to bring attention to those concerns—to make his case to those agencies with some authority over military resources. John McCloy, who had both the influence and the opportunity to press the case, at no point felt compelled to campaign on behalf of those making requests for action.[64] Though Churchill did at least begin an initiative, both he and Roosevelt were— unfortunately—preoccupied with other things. Nonetheless, it would oversimplify a complex problem and do an injustice to the history of events if we were to argue that Auschwitz was not bombed simply because Allied policymakers were callous or morally obtuse.

Those in positions of authority perceived serious difficulties inherent in any proposal to bomb either the railways or the camp. Requests to bomb the railways were seen through the lens of the pre-Overlord transportation campaign, which had required a vast and sustained dedication of Allied resources. And requests to bomb the camp itself were unavoidably affected by the very real and legitimate concerns (felt acutely by military planners even if not fully evident to others) about the limitations and inaccuracy of Allied bombers. Finally, as the foregoing discussion has stressed, the Allies were facing constant and profoundly difficult decisions about how to allocate their overtaxed resources most effectively in the summer of 1944. They were seeking to finish off the war as quickly as possible, and they believed—at least before the Germans renewed their ground offensive late in the year—that victory was within their grasp. This sense of urgency caused them to feel that every single use of their assets was crucial to speeding an imminent German defeat. The constant and debilitating difficulties surrounding the shuttle flights meant that an attack on Auschwitz through that means would not have readily suggested itself. And the disappointing experience of the Warsaw uprising might have further disinclined military officials against another operation that, at the time, might have sounded similar.

It is certainly true that raids on oil targets were often flown within easy reach of Auschwitz in 1944. In fact, the synthetic-oil and rubber plant at Monowitz, just a few miles from the Auschwitz main camp, was first designated a target for U.S. bombers on 18 July 1944, and was bombed for the first time on 20 August.[65] But this fact (better understood in hindsight than at the time) does not imply that simply diverting bombers to the camp would have been an obvious or easily undertaken choice in 1944. Both time and careful effort would have been needed to transform the idea into a reality. It would have been necessary, first of all, to make Auschwitz an emergency priority target (following a debate that would win the support of the highest political and military authorities). It would also have been necessary to make Auschwitz the subject of a dedicated, extensive photo-reconnaissance evaluation to guide the operational planning for the raid. And operational planners would have had to accept the likelihood of mission failure, large numbers of collateral casualties among the prisoners, or both. Similarly, making the camp the object of a special RAF raid would have required sustained efforts to reprioritize those resources dedicated to ongoing special missions—such as dropping weapons to resistance fighters in France—and special training by crews tasked with the operation.

In 1944, military planners were consumed by a plethora of immediate warfighting demands and problems. They were unlikely—without further information and outside pressure—to have taken a special initiative that would have shifted resources away from operations that they were charged, organizationally, to prioritize, and that, they genuinely believed would be "decisive" in Germany's defeat. Overcoming the momentum of the war effort would have required great and sustained efforts by someone—or some agency—with broad influence and authority.

The decision taken for nonaction in the summer and fall of 1944 was made in the swirling vortex of competing wartime priorities, partial information, and confusion. It was taken at a time when Auschwitz was a distant and still poorly understood place that did not seem to have the same overriding claim on Allied resources as the Normandy invasion, the battle of France, the Nazis' V-weapon launch sites, or the ongoing, costly ground battles in Italy. That it did not was due in part to the inattention and insensitivities of those husbanding and directing Allied resources. But it was due, as well, to the limitations of those resources and the overwhelming and profoundly diverse demands of a voracious and omnivorous war.

4

THE AERIAL PHOTOS
OF THE AUSCHWITZ-BIRKENAU
EXTERMINATION COMPLEX

Dino A. Brugioni

My INTEREST IN Nazi concentration and death camps was piqued by the television program *Holocaust* in 1978. I was a member of a bomber crew during World War II and knew about the discovery of Nazi atrocities during and after the war. I also knew that aerial reconnaissance was an important intelligence tool and played a significant role during that war. My interest in reconnaissance continued when I was hired by the Central Intelligence Agency in 1948 and I later became one of the founding fathers of the National Photographic Interpretation Center. I have always been a strong advocate of the application of aerial photography to historical research and analysis.

After viewing the TV program, I consulted maps of the Auschwitz area and noted that the Auschwitz camps were in perfect alignment with the I. G. Farben synthetic fuel and rubber plant only 8 kilometers away. I reasoned that on any reconnaissance and bombing of the Farben plant, the aircraft would also be flying over the Birkenau extermination complex. Having flown as an aerial photographer on some missions during World War II, I was also aware that the cameras were turned on coming on to an assigned target and the film run out over and after the target. I wondered if, by chance, activity at the extermination complex would have been seen on these runs. Working with my colleague, Robert Poirier, and on our own time at the National Photographic Interpretation Center, we ordered film taken during reconnaissance and bombing missions of the Farben plant. Much to our surprise, we did indeed see considerable activity relating to the Holocaust at both Auschwitz I (the original main camp) and Auschwitz II (Birkenau) that had been completely overlooked since 1944 and early 1945.

We used 1978 technology on the World War II film, including modern light tables and microstereoscopes. World War II photo interpreters used four-power stereoscopes and paper prints. We had enlarged some of the photos thirty-five times and could see people being marched to their death and being processed for slave labor, as well as the movement of large groups of inmates to the many small factories near the complex.

We displayed our findings at a press conference held at the National Archives and published our analysis in an unclassified CIA monograph that was available to the public.[1] When the study and photos were released the most frequently asked questions were and still are: Why was Auschwitz not bombed? Why did the World War II photo interpreters not identify the horrifying activities perpetrated at this complex, or was it not possible for them to do so? How could something so hideous have been overlooked? Why did the photo interpreters fail to note the unusually large size and unique configuration of Birkenau and know that it was not a conventional "prison camp"? Why were the large number of boxcars on the Birkenau sidings never questioned, considering the obvious lack of industrial installations within the camp? Most importantly, why did the photo interpreters not spot the four separately secured extermination areas, each of which contained unique facilities—an undressing room, a gas chamber and a crematorium?

I searched the records and reports produced by the concerned reconnaissance and organizational units and have concluded that five major factors influenced these shortcomings.

TASKING

Tasking is a military intelligence term meaning requirement imposed, on a photo interpreter, for instance, to procure specific information needed to formulate intelligence about a specific enemy target or targets. During World War II, photo interpreters operated under an elaborate tasking and priority system to produce intelligence from aerial photography. Searching for or doing detailed analysis on concentration camps was not a specific assigned task. Photographs were searched to find indications of enemy build-ups or military movements. This was called first-phase exploitation. Of prime concern were concentrations or movements of troops that posed threats to Allied operations, either current or planned. In addition, the photographs were scanned for evidence of reprisal weapons (V-1 cruise missile and V-2 ballistic missile sites), flak and searchlights, coastal defenses, material dumps and depots, camps and barracks, field works and defense lines, construction work or demolition activity, and road, rail, port and inland waterway transport activity. As D-Day approached, coastal shipping, beach obstacles, mine fields and strongpoints were added to the watch list.

Photo interpreters were also tasked to perform detailed analysis on a variety of significant tactical and strategic targets. Concentration and extermination camps were not considered significant targets. A target folder was created for each significant target and was described at the time as being the interpreter's "most important aid." The target folder contained the target requirement, a night target map, a small-scale illustration of the target, a large-scale illustration of the target with annotations and a target information sheet giving all known and pertinent details with regard to the target.

The target chart for the Auschwitz (Oswiecim) area was centered on the I. G. Farben "Buna" synthetic fuel and rubber plant and did not include either the Auschwitz I or Birkenau camps. The specific detailed interpretation tasking was to report on the progress of the construction of the plant. Later an added requirement was to report on the extent and effect of Allied bombing. A review of all photo interpretation reports created on the Farben plant reveals the interpreters' principal concern was the bomb damage and production stoppages at the plant. There is not a single reference to either the Auschwitz I or Birkenau camps, which were covered on the same photographic runs. The Monowitz (Monowice) camp (Auschwitz III), next to the plant, was correctly identified as a concentration camp.

PRIORITY PROJECTS

The principal units performing interpretation of photographs taken over Germany or German-occupied territories were the Allied Central Interpretation Unit at the Royal Air Force station Medmenham in England and the Mediterranean Allied Photo Reconnaissance Wing in Italy. These organizations worked on a twenty-four-hour-a-day basis and in 1943–44 were heavily involved in the planning of the Normandy and Southern France invasions. Support to the Normandy landings alone required an estimated half-million photo interpretation man-hours. The stepped-up Allied bombing offensive of German strategic industries in 1944, which included synthetic fuel plants, also involved extensive photographic analysis and assessment. Other high-priority projects included searching for and destruction of V-1 and V-2 sites, jet aircraft plants, and submarine production facilities. Photo interpreters were also employed in the planning and execution of special bombing missions over critical targets. The volumes of material being received for photo interpretation must also be considered. The daily intake for the Allied Central Interpretation Unit averaged 25,000 negatives and 60,000 prints. By V-E Day, over five million prints were in storage. More than 40,000 reports had been prepared from these prints.

TRAINING

Interpreter trainees were normally sent to a four- to six-week course that explained the identification of military equipment: airplanes, tanks, artillery, ships and the like. Senior photo interpreters, organized in sections, worked on more specific subjects such as bomb damage assessment, rail and road transportation, ports and shipping, military installations, inland waterway transportation, aircraft plants and airfields, radar and electronics, V-1 and V-2 installations, enemy defenses, armor and artillery, and petroleum refineries. No photo interpreters were assigned to do detailed interpretations of concentration or extermination camps. As nearly as I can determine, no tasking was ever imposed to conduct aerial reconnaissance of such camps. Photography that was acquired of these camps was a by-product of the reconnaissance of nearby strategic installations. Photo interpreters were not directed to locate or interpret such camps, and they did not try to determine which camps were unique or different, that is, which contained gas chambers or crematoria.

Photo interpreters were provided with hundreds of so-called photographic keys to aid them in the identification of newly photographed targets. These keys were manuals, each containing photographs and details of previously identified targets. Annotation and text provided guidance on the unique characteristics (called "signatures" or "indicators") of targets that could be used to identify a newly photographed target. No such keys were prepared about any of the types of installations and camps involved in what is now known as the Holocaust. For that matter, no photo interpreters experienced in identifying such installations were available to compile such keys.

There was a key prepared on a typical labor or construction camp. The existence of such a camp was often an indication or "signature" of a nearby underground installation or construction of massive defensive fortifications along French coasts in preparation for the invasion.

No detailed photo intelligence study was ever done on any of the major concentration and extermination camps; in truth, no distinctions were ever made among the various types of camps. A variety of descriptive terms were used indiscriminately, although some of the camps were much larger and more complex than others. The following terms were used to describe these camps: slave labor camps, labor camps, construction camps, forced labor camps, prisons, concentration camps and internment camps. The most frequent and descriptive term used, however, was "hutted camps." The term, of British derivation, was originally used to describe a series of prefabricated buildings similar in appearance to British Nissen huts or the later American Quonset huts, and was carried over into the interpretation field. The term "extermination camp" was never used in any of this reporting.

In searching the aerial photography, the photo interpreters would have little difficulty spotting the hundreds of concentration camps in Germany and German-occupied lands. These were usually set in forested areas or valleys, apart from towns or cities. The camps were surrounded with barbed wire and watch towers. The barracks building did not conform to known forms of architecture. They were, for the most part, of wooden construction, mostly of one story and several standard sizes. Most were prefabricated or of the "tar paper" variety. Frequently, the administrative buildings and guards' quarters were in a separate enclosure, often near the main gate of the camp.

The main effort in World War II, with respect to the camps, was to locate those which contained Allied prisoners of war. In this effort, the photo interpreters were provided pertinent data and locations of specific camps. In addition to the barracks and security features, other indicators were provided which interpreters could use in making identification. In most cases there were no associated industrial plants near POW camps. Most POW camps had an exercise area. The barracks were usually arranged on both sides of a central street and a cleared area separated the barracks from the enclosure wall. The extensive open area between the barracks and the enclosure wall was intended to prevent escapes.

PRECEDENCE

Photo interpreters depend heavily on precedence or existing knowledge about a subject or installation. I did not find a single reference in which interpreters were told to look for gas chambers or crematoria that were killing thousands each day. There was simply no historical or intelligence precedence for genocide on such a scale. Most World War II photo interpreters I have spoken to found this concept unbelievable, unimaginable and completely incongruous. It was not until Allied troops captured such camps that photos taken at ground level were made available.

It must be quickly added that during World War II information from human sources and communication intelligence was not available to most interpreters. Photo interpreters, for the most part, worked in a vacuum while interpreting and reported only what they saw on the photography. My research also confirms that the information provided about Auschwitz provided by two escapees, Rudolf Vrba and Alfred Wetzler, was never made available to those interpreting the Farben plant photos. It is my professional opinion that had such information been provided to the interpreters they would have quickly located the gas chambers and crematoria.

PHOTO INTERPRETATION EQUIPMENT

By modern standards, the photo interpretation equipment used in World War II can only be described as primitive. Photo interpreters used stereoscopes with lenses capable of a magnification four times the original imagery (about like that of a magnifying glass). In addition, tube magnifiers with a magnification of seven were also used in scanning the aerial photos. Photo interpreters performed the interpretation from contact paper prints rather than with film duplicates, as is done at the present time. We know today that the negatives from which the Auschwitz contact prints were made in World War II could have been enlarged up to thirty-five times.

Concomitant with the tragic failure of photo interpreters to identify the extermination complex was the equally tragic failure of major Allied air commands to be aware that aerial photography of the complex existed. There had been appeals from a number of sources to bomb the complex, the rail yards, the rail bridges and rail lines over major rivers leading to Auschwitz. Those appeals we now know reached the highest levels including Prime Minister Winston Churchill and the immediate subordinates of President Franklin D. Roosevelt. When concern was given to a plan for possible bombing of the complex, officials of the Air Ministry, the Royal Air Force and US Strategic Air Forces bemoaned the lack of coverage of the plant and the distance to Auschwitz. In fact, photos had been taken by the Fifteenth Air Force and were available at the Allied Central Interpretation Unit at Medmenham, fifty miles outside London. The photos were also at the Mediterranean Allied Photo Reconnaissance Wing in Italy, which was commanded by Col. Elliott Roosevelt, the President's son. By the time the Soviet Army reached Auschwitz on January 27, 1945, the Allies had photographed the Birkenau extermination complex at least thirty times.

Part II

BOMBING AUSCHWITZ: FOR

and

AGAINST

FROM THE BEGINNING of the modern debate over the feasibility of bombing Auschwitz-Birkenau or the rail lines leading to it, David S. Wyman's contribution has defined the terms of the controversy. The editors of this book wanted to include his work, and sought to reprint a recent version of his seminal 1978 article as further refined in his highly praised book, *The Abandonment of the Jews*.[1] Professor Wyman declined republication of the article in the current volume—a decision we regret. In order to set the debate that follows in context, a brief summary of his most salient points is useful.

According to Wyman, the confluence of "three circumstances" in the spring and early summer of 1944 made the bombing of Auschwitz-Birkenau, or the rail lines leading to it, "critically important and militarily possible." First, the Hungarian Holocaust got underway with the Nazis concentrating the Hungarian Jews for deportation beginning in May. Second, Rudolf Vrba and Alfred Wetzler escaped from Birkenau in April and gave to the Slovakian Jewish underground a detailed report, a summary of which filtered out to the West by June. Finally, in May 1944 U.S. Fifteenth Air Force "reached full strength" in Italy and began attacking industrial facilities in eastern and central Europe.[2]

From late May onward, the ongoing catastrophe in Hungary, reinforced by the vivid description of the horrors of Auschwitz given by Vrba and Wetzler, sparked a series of appeals from Jewish sources to the American and British governments to bomb the rail lines or the crematoria. In Washington these appeals were rejected with little or no study by the War Department, based, Wyman asserts, on a secret policy to refuse all appeals to divert U.S. military forces to rescue refugees or civilians persecuted by the Axis powers. This policy had been adopted in February in response to President Franklin Roosevelt's establishment of the War Refugee Board, which a number of historians have interpreted as a belated concession to those who were asking for some response to the Nazi persecution of the European Jews. Wyman also discusses the bureaucratic resistance in the British government to bombing Auschwitz, despite direct support for the idea from Prime Minister Winston Churchill. In the late summer and fall of 1944, pressure for an attack again mounted in Washington, and in November even John Pehle, Director of the War Refugee Board, reluctantly joined the advocates after receiving the full text of the Vrba-Wetzler report. Again, however, the War Department—guided in this matter by Assistant Secretary of War John J. McCloy—rejected all appeals with what Wyman sees as disingenuous arguments about the unfeasibility of such a mission.

In contrast to the statements of the American and British military bureaucracies, Wyman believes that the Allied air forces could have disabled the Nazi murder machine without much trouble. He offers four basic scenarios: 1) a diversion of some U.S. B-17 and B-24 heavy bombers of Fifteenth Air Force from a raid on the Auschwitz IG Farben plant, which was attacked four times between August and December 1944; 2) a lower-altitude and presumably more accurate bombing raid by B-25 medium bombers from Fifteenth Air Force; 3) a dive-bombing raid by two-engine P-38 fighters, such as was carried out on the Rumanian Ploesti oil complex on 10 June 1944; and 4) a precision raid by Royal Air Force De Havilland Mosquitos from the special units that carried out attacks on Gestapo facilities in Western Europe. Such a diversion of forces for political ends was actually carried out in the case of the airlift to the Warsaw Uprising in August/September 1944, so the excuses that were offered at the time are unconvincing, Wyman asserts. Moreover, the Germans did not have the manpower to begin mass shootings again, so the net result is that tens to hundreds of thousands of Jewish deportees could have been saved from the gas chambers, if the Allies had only had the political will to do something.

Wyman's conclusions are seconded in two revised speeches from the 30 April 1993 NASM-USHMM symposium. Martin Gilbert's contribution, "The Contemporary Case for the Feasibility of Bombing Auschwitz" (chapter 5), is derived from his influential 1981 book, *Auschwitz and the Allies*. Like Wyman, Gilbert presents a parallel narrative of the failure of the appeals to bomb Auschwitz in both Britain and the United States, with detailed attention being paid to the British situation. Gilbert quotes from an interview with the famous RAF Bomber Command hero of the "Dambusters" squadron, Group Captain Leonard Cheshire, V. C., in which he stated that his forces could have carried out a special attack. Gilbert also responds to an early version of James H. Kitchens III's critique of the bombing thesis, as given in the symposium.

Chapter 6, "The Allies and Auschwitz: A Participant's View," is the contribution of one of the original actors in the 1944 appeals, Gerhart Riegner, a German-Jewish refugee lawyer who was a key leader in the World Jewish Congress in Geneva. Those present at the symposium were very fortunate to hear the personal testimony of Dr. Riegner, who played a historic role in informing the West about the Holocaust. He still feels betrayed by the lack of any Allied response to the appeals from Slovakia and Hungary that he passed on to London and Washington; he believes that he was lied to, and that the Allied leadership therefore shared some complicity in the Holocaust.

Following in the footsteps of the pioneering work of Richard Foregger, airpower historian James H. Kitchens III presents the other side: the first full scholarly case against the Wyman thesis. His essay, "The Bombing of Auschwitz Re-examined" (1994), is reproduced here in chapter 7. (Dr. Kitchens did not wish to modify his original article, nor respond further to David Wyman, believing that such debate is not likely to be productive.) After presenting an overview of the historiography of the controversy up to 1992, Kitchens then concentrates primarily on the technical limitations that, he claims, would have made a successful raid on Birkenau and the rail lines highly unlikely. He believes that a heavy bomber raid might well have missed the crematoria altogether, while killing many prisoners; that railroad bombing was guaranteed to be in-effective; that intelligence knowledge adequate to organize a special mission against Birkenau was not on hand; and that the specialized and medium-range aircraft would either not have had the range to reach the complex or would not have been well suited to such a difficult mission. Moreover, he asserts that, just as Wyman and other advocates overrate the likelihood of a successful raid, they underrate the strength of German defenses. Kitchens adds that such a raid on the camp would also have been illegal under the rules of war and the Hague Conventions. This latter argument has found no support even among his fellow skeptics, given the horrors of Birkenau and the indiscriminate attacks on German and Japanese cities by Allied air forces during the war, propaganda about "precision bombing" and "industrial targets" notwithstanding.

In chapter 8, Richard H. Levy provides a second attack on the Wyman thesis in "The Bombing of Auschwitz Revisited: A Critical Analysis," which was first published in 1996. Levy reprises many of the technical arguments given by Kitchens, sometimes with new and interesting details, and he reemphasizes the argument that alternate methods of killing could be found. Levy also introduces two new elements to the debate. First, he claims that Jewish groups were far from united behind the proposals to bomb Auschwitz and the rail lines from Hungary. In particular, he emphasizes the vote of the Jewish Agency Executive (JAE) in Palestine on 11 June 1944 not to support bombing, and the opposition of A. Leon Kubowitzki, head of the rescue department of the World Jewish Congress in New York, to attacking the camp with aircraft, given the probability of killing prisoners. Second, he emphasizes "command considerations," assert-ing that an order to bomb could only have come from Roosevelt or Churchill, given the chain of command and the political character of such a raid.

Stuart G. Erdheim's 1997 essay, "Could the Allies Have Bombed Auschwitz-Birkenau?," reprinted here as chapter 9, is the first full-length response to the critiques of the Wyman thesis by James Kitchens and Richard Levy.[3] Through a detailed examination of various technical issues, including bombing accuracy, intelligence, German defenses, and aircraft ranges, Erdheim attempts to show that the Allies could quite certainly have put together a special mission with heavy bombers, medium bombers, or fighter-bombers—just as Wyman origi-nally proposed—and could have destroyed the gas chambers and crematoria as early as spring 1944. Erdheim contributes much new and interesting information about the state of German defenses and about the success of other special mis-sions that have been cited by Wyman and others as models for an Auschwitz raid.

Quite independently of Erdheim, and without knowledge of his work or that of Richard Levy, Rondall R. Rice, an Air Force officer and historian, published a second detailed defense of the Wyman thesis in 1999. It leaves aside the hy-pothetical scenarios for Royal Air Force raids and focuses on the likely instru-ment of any Allied attack on Auschwitz-Birkenau (assuming that the requisite political will had existed in Washington): the U.S. heavy bombers of Fifteenth Air Force. His "Bombing Auschwitz: U.S. Fifteenth Air Force and the Military Aspects of a Possible Attack," which appears in this volume as chapter 10, comes to many of the same conclusions as does Erdheim regarding the ability of American forces to overcome the defenses and mount a successful riad on the Birkenau crematoria. The unique contribution of Rice's article comes, however, in his detailed knowledge of Air Force procedures for calculating bombing accuracy, and from his detailed examination of Fifteenth Air Force procedures and operations. Rice makes the strongest case so far offered that U.S. heavy bombers could have destroyed or caused significant damage to the four major gas-chamber/crematoria complexes.

The critics of Rice and of Erdheim will likely respond that they have constructed elaborate counterfactual cases far from the reality of 1944 and based on optimistic readings of the evidence. Yet it is becoming clear that the often bitter technical debate over the feasibility of bombing, although it has been productive, may well be nearing a dead end in its arcane discussion of aircraft specifications and hypothetical scenarios. While the two sides remain far apart, they do seem to minimally agree that the crematoria complexes could have been bombed one way or another (railroad bombing is another matter). The unanswerable questions—unanswerable because they are in part counterfactual, in part ethical—are whether such action would have slowed the Nazi murder machine, and whether it would have been a justified diversion of Allied resources from an all-consuming war if it did not.

Michael J. Neufeld

5

THE CONTEMPORARY CASE
FOR THE FEASIBILITY OF BOMBING
AUSCHWITZ

Martin Gilbert

I HAVE BEEN asked to address the theme, "the contemporary case for the feasibility of bombing Auschwitz." That case was made twice: first by those Jews in German-occupied Europe who received the first detailed accounts of the killing at Birkenau, and then by some of the American and British officials who were asked to bomb the camps and the crematoria.[1]

Let us look first at the Jewish appeals from inside Europe. A detailed account of the killing process at Birkenau had been smuggled out of Birkenau itself by two Jewish escapees, Alfred Wetzler and Rudolph Vrba, on 10 April 1944. Their report reached the Slovak capital, Bratislava, fifteen days later. It made clear that the fate of up to a million or more Jewish deportees to Birkenau between the summer of 1942 and the first months of 1944 had been death.

A month after the full and terrible truth about Birkenau reached Slovakia, the first deportations began from Hungary to Birkenau. By joining the escapees' description of the nature of the camp with the new fact of the Hungarian deportations, it was clear that the mass slaughter of deportees was to take place upon their arrival at Birkenau. The escapees had described in detail the gas chambers, and the process of selection and killing. Their report made it clear, by inference, that the fate of most of the Hungarian deportees was to be immediate death.

The surviving Jewish leadership in Bratislava, who knew from 14 May, when they received the escapees' report, that Jews were at that very moment being deported to Birkenau but had not yet reached the camp, sent a telegram to the West urging action, including bombing. This telegram, and a follow-up telegram sent from Bratislava on 24 May, reached the Agudas Israel World Organization (of Orthodox Jewry) in New York a month later. The two telegrams were then sent on from New York to the War Refugee Board in Washington, by the organization's president, Jacob Rosenheim, on 18 June.

It was clear that more than 400,000 Hungarian Jews were in danger of being murdered, or were even in the process of being murdered, at Birkenau. That was confirmed when a second pair of Jewish escapees from Birkenau, Arnost Rosin and Czeslaw Mordowicz, reached Bratislava. They had been in Birkenau for the first ten days of the daily arrival of the Hungarian deportees, and their murder. They were eyewitnesses to the renewed and accelerated slaughter.

The telegram that reached the War Refugee Board in Washington on 18 June asked for "prompt disturbance of all transport, military and deportation" by the Royal Air Force, and recommended bombing the deportation railway (between Kosice and Presov). The aim of such a bombardment, the telegram explained, would be "to save also Jews not yet deported." The message ended: "We expect Royal Air Force to act very carefully."

From that moment, the fate and scale of the deportations was known in Washington. From that moment, the route of the deportations was also known to the War Refugee Board, whose specific, and indeed presidentially ordered, task was to do what it could to help the Jews. From that moment, therefore, the case for examining the feasibility of bombing existed, with the request that such action should be done "very carefully." Thus, on 18 June, both the appeal to bomb and the realization that bombing could have negative results were on the table in Washington.

Delay is a feature of many urgent messages transmitted in wartime. It was not until six days later that the head of the War Refugee Board, John W. Pehle, took any action. Although his task since the creation of the board six months earlier had been to find means of helping Jews, Pehle took it upon himself to give this particular request a low priority. Indeed, in putting the urgent Jewish request to the assistant secretary of war, John J. McCloy, on 24 June, the head of the War Refugee Board pointed out that "I had several doubts about the matter." He then listed these doubts:

1. whether it would be appropriate to use military planes and personnel for this purpose;
2. whether it would be difficult to put the railroad line out of commission for a long enough period to do any good; and
3. even assuming that this railroad line were put out of commission for some period of time, whether it would help the Jews in Hungary.

Having expressed these doubts, Pehle went on, as he himself noted at the time, to make it "very clear to Mr. McCloy" that he was not, "at this point at least, requesting the War Department to take any action on this proposal, other than to appropriately explore it." That exploration was not suggested as a matter of urgency. Nor was it given any urgent, or detailed, attention. Indeed, on 26

June, before any detailed study could be made, the operations division of the War Department recommended the form of words that should be used in reply to the Jewish request.

These words were chosen carefully, and were subsequently repeated each time the request was made, and it was to be made four times. The words to be given in reply were: that the suggested air operation was "impracticable" and "that it could be executed only by diversion of considerable air support essential to the success of our forces now engaged in decisive operations."

As a general point, this was true of all air operations outside the current strategic policies. It was also true that, if the will was there, examination could be carried out, and activities initiated, that were indeed outside the scope of the current policies. Urgency and improvisation were the hallmark of the Allied air forces, as had been demonstrated by the successful attack, six months earlier, on a German prison at Amiens, which enabled one hundred fifty prisoners to escape.

On 24 June, two days before the War Department's first negative response, the Czech government representative in Geneva, Jaromir Kopecky, went to see the War Refugee Board representative there, Roswell McClelland. With him was a member of the World Jewish Congress, Gerhart Riegner. Riegner had with him a full text of the report of both sets of escapees, the two who had described the killing process up to April, and the two who had described the first ten days of the destruction of Hungarian Jews in May.

Six proposals were submitted to Washington that day, 24 June. Two were proposals for public warnings, including warnings of reprisals against Germans and Hungarians. One was for the widest radio and newspaper publicity "so that the Germans should know that the outside world is fully informed about their atrocities." Another proposal was for the Pope to issue a strong condemnation; the Vatican had been liberated by the Allies three weeks earlier. Two more proposals, of the six, were for the bombing of the gas chambers and of the railway lines.

McClelland's telegram also listed the routes of the deportation trains, giving, accurately, the names of the towns through which the trains were passing. Unlike the telegram from Jacob Rosenheim, the telegram from McClelland made an immediate impact. But it did so, not on the head of the WRB, but on one of the members of his staff, the forty-year-old Benjamin Akzin, a Jew, who had been born in Riga. In an interoffice communication on 29 June, Akzin argued that the destruction of the "physical installations" at Auschwitz and Birkenau "might appreciably slow down the systematic slaughter at least temporarily."

Akzin's letter was a sustained attempt to argue in favor of the bombing of the gas chambers and crematoria. The "methodical German mind," Akzin believed, would require some time to rebuild the installations, "or to evolve elsewhere equally efficient procedures of mass slaughter and of disposing of the bodies." During this time, some lives at least might be saved. But the saving of lives might also be "quite considerable," because, as he wrote, "with German manpower and material resources gravely depleted, German authorities might not be in a position to devote themselves to the task of equipping new large-scale extermination centers."

Akzin also argued in favor of the bombing "as a matter of principle," as it would constitute, he wrote, "the most tangible—and perhaps the only tangible—evidence of the indignation aroused by the existence of these charnel-houses." One other factor was raised by Akzin in favor of bombing Auschwitz and Birkenau: that during the bombing there would also be many deaths "among the most ruthless and despicable of the Nazis."

In bombing Auschwitz, Akzin added, there would be no "deflecting" of U.S. aerial strength from any important zone of military objectives. Auschwitz itself was in just such a zone, the "mining and manufacturing centers" of Katowice and Chorzow, "which play an important part in the industrial armament of Germany." Akzin ended his note of 29 June:

> Presumably, a large number of Jews in these camps may be killed in the course of such bombings (though some of them may escape in the confusion). But such Jews are doomed to death anyhow. The destruction of the camps would not change their fate, but it would serve as visible retribution on their murderers and it might save the lives of future victims. It will be noted that the inevitable fate of Jews herded in ghettoes near the industrial and railroad installations in Hungary has not caused the United Nations to stop bombing these installations. It is submitted, therefore, that refraining from bombing the extermination centers would be sheer misplaced sentimentality, far more cruel than a decision to destroy these centers.

Nothing came of Akzin's appeal. "It wasn't my job to write this sort of memorandum," he later recalled.

On 29 June, the day that Benjamin Akzin made his plea for the bombing of Auschwitz and Birkenau, his superiors on the War Refugee Board sent a copy of McClelland's telegram of 24 June to John J. McCloy. McCloy's executive assistant, Colonel Harrison A. Gerhardt, had been involved in the rejection of Jacob Rosenheim's railway bombing request only three days before. He at once noted for McCloy: "I know you told me to 'kill' this but since those instructions, we have received the attached letter from Mr. Pehle. I suggest that the attached reply be sent."

The attached reply, duly signed and sent by McCloy on 4 July, turned down the request, using reasons similar to those of the operations division in turning down Rosenheim's proposal.

What exactly did McCloy mean by telling the Colonel to "kill" the bombing request? When we met in New York in the early 1980s, he told me how much he had been bothered generally by Jewish requests throughout the war, and particularly at this time.

Through McCloy, Washington had been unresponsive to the appeals for bombing. But the deportations had continued without respite. The story now turns to London.

On 26 June, the senior Jewish Agency representative in Geneva, Richard Lichtheim, sent a telegram to London with full details of the reports of the four escapees, and with six requests. The first was to give the facts the "widest publicity." The second was a warning to the Hungarian government that its members would be held responsible for the fate of the Jews being deported from Hungary. The third was reprisals on Germans being held in Allied hands. The fourth was "bombing of railway lines leading from Hungary to Birkenau." The fifth was precision bombing of the death-camp installations. The sixth was the bombing of "all Government buildings" in the Hungarian capital: target bombing of all collaborating Hungarian and German agencies in Budapest.

The telegram gave the names and addresses of seventy Hungarian and German individuals said to be most directly involved in sending Jews from Hungary to Birkenau. This telegram was read by Hungarian intelligence and shown to the Hungarian regent, Admiral Horthy, and to his prime minister.

The Geneva request for bombing was followed six days later with a quite unconnected U.S. air raid on Budapest. This was an unusually heavy bombing raid, not only on the marshaling yards (the raid's target), but, in error, on many government buildings and private homes. This seeming direct and rapid response to the Geneva telegraphic appeal of 26 June caused consternation in Budapest at the highest level.

Within hours, the Germans were presented with an official Hungarian demand for an immediate end to the deportations. The Germans bowed to this demand. Within four days, the deportations had ceased. Thus it was that, unknown to the Allies and through no deliberate Allied action, American bombing had been effective in stopping the deportations, and as many as 300,000 lives were saved.

This ironic and dramatic turning point illustrates that the mere threat of bombing could be decisive in saving lives. The Birkenau camp did not even have to be hit: as it happened, Budapest proved to be the key target, even if it was struck, from the Birkenau point of view, by accident.

The question of the bombing of Birkenau was not over, however. Neither the British, the Americans, nor the Jewish organizations yet realized that the deportations had been halted. On 6 July, the day after what was in fact the final deportation from Hungary, and with the Jews of Budapest now spared deportation, a further Jewish bombing request reached London. It had been brought by the head of the Jewish Agency, Chaim Weizmann, and his foreign minister, Moshe Shertok.

On 7 July, Anthony Eden put this new bombing request to Churchill. If there was any single, overriding, contemporary case for examining the feasibility of bombing Auschwitz, it was Churchill's response. He was not only prime minister of an all-party government, but also minister of defense. Churchill's immediate written instruction, when the bombing request was submitted to him, was: "Get anything out of the Air Force you can and invoke me if necessary."

The case for examining the bombing request had been made at the top. Eden passed on the request to the Air Ministry that same day. In the course of his letter to the secretary of state for air, Sir Archibald Sinclair, Eden wrote: "Dr. Weizmann admitted that there seemed to be little enough that we could do to stop these horrors, but he suggested that something might be done to stop the operation of the death camps by (1) bombing the railway lines leading to Birkenau (and to any other similar camps if we get to hear of them); and (2) bombing the camps themselves with the object of destroying the plant used for gassing and burning."

"Could you let me know," Eden asked Sinclair, "how the Air Ministry view the feasibility of these proposals?" He added, "I very much hope that it will be possible to do something. I have the authority of the Prime Ministry to say that he agrees."

On 11 July, while the Air Ministry was still considering the Weizmann-Shertok request, the Jewish Agency sent a follow-up note, in which it referred to the "many-sided and far-reaching moral effect" of the bombing that it had requested. The note read:

> It would mean, in the first instance, that the Allies waged direct war on the extermination of the victims of Nazi oppression—today Jews, tomorrow Poles, Czechs, or whatever race may become the victim of mass murder during the German retreat and collapse. Secondly, it would give the lie to the oft-repeated assertions of Nazi spokesmen that the Allies are not really so displeased with the work of the Nazis in ridding Europe of Jews. Thirdly, it would go far toward dissipating the incredulity which still persists in Allied quarters with regard to the reports of mass extermination perpetrated by the Nazis. Fourthly, it would give weight to the threats of reprisals against the murderers by showing that the Allies are taking the extermination of Jews so seriously as to warrant the allocation of aircraft resources to this particular operation, and thus have a deterrent effect. Lastly, it would convince the German circles still hopeful of Allied mercy of the genuineness of Allied condemnation of the murder of the Jews, and possibly result in some internal pressure against a continuation of the massacres.

The Jewish Agency note ended:

The first report that the RAF or the American Air Force had bombed the death camps in Upper Silesia is bound to have a demonstrative value in all these directions.

For eight days, the Air Ministry examined the possibility of high-altitude bombing. Its conclusions were not entirely negative, as Sinclair wrote to Eden on 15 July:

Bombing the plant is out of the bounds of possibility for Bomber Command, because the distance is too great for the attack to be carried out at night. It might be carried out by the Americans by daylight but it would be a costly and hazardous operation. It might be ineffective and, even if the plant was destroyed, I am not clear that it would really help the victims. There is just one possibility, and that is bombing the camps, and possibly dropping weapons at the same time, in the hope that some of the victims may be able to escape. We did something of the kind in France, when we made a breach in the walls of a prison camp and we think that 150 men who had been condemned to death managed to escape. The difficulties of doing this in Silesia are, of course enormously greater and even if the camp was successfully raided, the chances of escape would be small indeed.

Sinclair's letter concluded:

Nevertheless, I am proposing to have the proposition put to the Americans, with all the facts, to see if they are prepared to try it. I am very doubtful indeed whether, when they have examined it, the Americans will think it possible, and I do not wish to raise any hopes. For this reason, and because it would not be fair to suggest that we favoured it and the Americans were unwilling to help, I feel that you would not wish to mention the possibility to Weizmann at this stage. I will let you know the result when the Americans have considered it.

In the margin of Sinclair's comment that "even if the plant were destroyed, I am not clear that it would really help the victims," Eden noted, "He wasn't asked his opinion of this; he was asked to act."

As far as I can determine, neither Eden, nor any of his Foreign Office officials, took up Sinclair's suggestion that weapons might be dropped to help the Jews escape from Birkenau. Sinclair's proposal to have the bombing request "put to the Americans" effectively ensured that the request was now at the mercy of the U.S. War Department, which had already rejected it twice: twenty days earlier and eleven days earlier.

Even after the halting of the Hungarian deportations had become known, there was information that Jews were being deported from Paris. The Air Ministry, meanwhile, had continued to approach the Americans in an effort to seek a means of carrying out the Churchill-Eden request. On 26 July, the air minister's assistant private secretary had reported that the vice-chief of the air staff was to raise the matter with U.S. general Spaatz "when he is next in the Air Ministry."

A week later, on 2 August, Spaatz was reported by the deputy chief of the air Staff, N. H. Bottomley, to have been most sympathetic. But it was "necessary," Bottomley informed the acting chief of the Air Staff, "to know more about the precise location, extent and nature of the camps and installations at Birkenau." It was "particularly necessary," Bottomley noted, to have "photographic cover." He added, "Will you please have this produced as early as possible, so that the operational possibilities of taking some effective action from the air can be studied by the operational Commands and the Deputy Supreme Commander. I need not emphasize the need for absolute secrecy in this investigation."

This request for photographic intelligence was passed on to the Foreign Office. But despite a telephone call from the Foreign Office on 5 August, the Air Ministry heard no more. On 8 August, the World Jewish Congress asked the War Refugee Board to request the bombing of the gas chambers, crematoria, and railways leading into the camp.

Five days later, McCloy rejected the appeal, explaining that the operation "could only be executed by the diversion of considerable air support essential to the success of our forces now engaged in decisive operations elsewhere and would in any case be of such doubtful efficacy that it would not warrant the use of our resources." These were the same phrases that McCloy and his assistant, Gerhardt, had used a month before.

McCloy added, in a new line of argument. "There has been considerable opinion to the effect that such an effort, even if practicable, might provoke even more vindictive action by the Germans." This latter was not, of course, a technical reason for declining to bomb. It is not entirely clear what could be more vindictive than what had already happened at Birkenau. McCloy was later to reject a fourth bombing appeal.

Inside the British Air Ministry, however, efforts were still being made to work out some means of bombing the gas chambers. Churchill's instruction to Eden—"Get anything out of the Air Force you can and invoke me if necessary"—was still being used as a spur to action. In order to make further progress, the Air Ministry needed a topographical map of Birkenau itself, and asked the Foreign Office for one. The Foreign Office asked the Jewish Agency, which in turn asked the Polish government in London. A map was found. It was surprisingly accurate with regard to much of Birkenau. On it were located "SS barracks, square, kennels, concentration camp for women, gas chambers in a wood west of Brezinki/Birkenau" and "crematorium in a wood probably west of the barracks."

The general layout of the plan was correct, and the hutted area of the women's camp was particularly detailed and accurate. The Jewish Agency gave the topographical map to the Foreign Office on 18 August. But the Foreign Office did not send it on to the Air Ministry. Three weeks later, when the bombing issue had been dropped, partly through lack of the map, a Foreign Office official wrote to his superior: "We are therefore technically guilty of allowing the Air Ministry to get away with it, without having given them (tho' we had it) the info they asked for as a prerequisite." The official continued, "I think, perhaps (tho' I feel a little uneasy about it) we had better let this go by."

Not only did the bombing request "go by," as the official phrased it, because of lack of the map, though this was of central importance, but it was also dropped for political reasons. As an Air Ministry expert noted, after talking to a Foreign Office official, Roger Allen, "In his conversation Allen hinted that the Foreign Office were tending to reconsider the importance that they had placed upon the liberation of the captives at Birkenau."

Roger Allen himself understood that the reason for turning down the bombing request was no longer technical. It no longer had to do with whether Auschwitz was a possible target or not. As he explained in a departmental note on 21 August, "We cannot now shift the responsibility to the Air Ministry, by asking them to say that for technical reasons they are opposed to the whole venture. If the political situation has changed, and we no longer wish, on political grounds, to proceed with this project, it is up to us to tell the Air Ministry. . . ."

The political situation related to the growing British fear of a flood of Jewish refugees who, once the war was over and the camps liberated, would seek entry into Palestine. The phrase "fears of a flood" had begun to appear in the secret files. When, on 22 August, the topographical plans reached the Foreign Office, an official there noted, "I take it that we do not intend to pursue the camps bombing scheme." He was right. All that remained was for the Foreign Office to answer Weizmann's request of 6 July. The answer was sent on 1 September— by a junior minister. No copy was sent to Churchill: because it came from a junior minister and not from Eden, it would not normally have been marked for the prime minister to see.

The long-awaited answer read: "I am sorry to have to tell you that in view of the very great technical difficulties involved we have no option but to refrain from pursuing the proposal in present circumstances."

Looking back over the whole period that the request to bomb the railway lines and the camp was active, it is clear that there were enough officials in both London and Washington who failed, at a practical level, to put the request with necessary vigor and sense of urgency to those who had the ability to examine it for feasibility, or to carry it out. In early August, while the Jewish request was still being put to them, these same officials responded quite differently to another, more distant, appeal. This came from the Polish insurgents in Warsaw, who pleaded with Britain and the United States for help in dropping them arms and supplies.

Air flights far longer than those to Birkenau and back (in all, four hundred miles longer) were organized from southern Italy, to the very limit of the Allied air range; they began on 4 August. These flights actually flew over the Birkenau region on their way out, and again on their way back. Volunteer pilots were sought, and found, for the dangerous missions. For a whole month, these missions flew, despite heavy losses. In the attempt to help Warsaw, much was tried. There was a sense of anguish that nothing more effective could be done.

With regard to bombing Birkenau, nothing was tried. As far as the archives reveal, there was no anguish. Worse than the lack of anguish, there was no sense of probing to the utmost for a means to help. Professor Zuckerman, Air Marshal Tedder's adviser on air strategy, whose expertise was bombing railway lines, was not consulted. Leonard Cheshire, leader of the squadron that carried out many remarkable special tasks beyond the regular bombing missions, was upset in later years to learn about the Birkenau bombing request. He too had not been consulted. He was convinced that had he been asked to carry out a low-level precision attack, he could have been successful.

In 1981, at his desk, with the spring 1944 photographs and the topographical plan in front of him, he explained how he would have mounted the raid, what bombs he would have used, and soon. Here are Cheshire's words in full.

CHESHIRE: We had to devise a means of eliminating the forthcoming threat of the V3, an underground gun in the Pas de Calais—three of them—under fifty feet of reinforced concrete capable, roughly, I think, of putting five-hundred-pound shells once a minute into London, and the thing is nobody could get under fifty feet of reinforced concrete. So we had to be equipped with the bomb to do it and devise a means of dropping a ten-thousand-pound bomb from sixteen thousand feet with an accuracy of twenty yards.

QUESTION: What happened?

CHESHIRE: Well, we succeeded in doing that, but it took us seven months to perfect the technique, so all that time we were perfecting this technique, but using it against important targets, but always hitting the target and not the civilians nearby. For instance, when we attacked the Michelin works—the rubber tire factory—we destroyed two of the factory blocks but left out the canteen that was between them because our instructions were not to touch the workers' canteen.

QUESTION: Can you tell me the date of that particular raid?

CHESHIRE: It must have been March or April '44. I think what I would have done—it's a small target—it is not all that easy to identify. It would have been rather difficult to hit in our normal method, which consisted of my going in at low level, ground level, and dropping a marker, and the others bombing it from sixteen thousand feet, the reason being they had a deep penetration bomb. In this case, I think I would have selected six aircraft to go in low and use a dive-bombing technique because I don't think that building was strong enough to withstand ordinary bombs dropped at low level. You have to dive into it, of course, or the bombs will skip and jump. I'd have the rest of the squadron either doing a diversionary attack, or somewhere in the vicinity ready to be called in, in case we failed.

QUESTION: There were four main crematoria. Do you think you could have destroyed them without killing thousands of people?

CHESHIRE: Your first question is, "Could we have destroyed them?" I should think we might have destroyed three. We might not have destroyed all of them. You are asking a lot at this extreme range in knowing we have to get ourselves out without full cover of night—because it's summer now. I think we could have done three. I do not think we would have many miss-hits because we did not drop bombs unless we knew we were aiming on the target. When you are at that low level, you know. I don't feel I can be the man who judges its effectiveness. I'd question its effectiveness, but I state that as a pilot, and as a member of Bomber Command, and in the name of the pilots of Bomber Command, we would have been willing, have done it whatever the risks, whatever the difficulties, if we had received the request, if we had known it came from the victims themselves.

These were Cheshire's reflections thirty-seven years after the event. He was a man of probity, and his words merit careful study. They are not black and white, and yet, in the moral sense, they are not gray either.

We will never know if Birkenau was, or was not, as Kitchens asserts, extremely difficult to hit successfully. It was never tried, and the multitudinous, tantalizing "ifs" of history will, by their very nature, always elude us. One must also ask, difficult to hit for what end? for success against crematoria and railway lines (however defined)? or for morale and perhaps even morality? These latter two were often at stake during World War II as well.

I would like to end with the words of a young Hungarian deportee to Auschwitz, Hugo Gryn, who survived the war. He recently recalled how, in the summer of 1944, he and his friends would look up into the bright blue skies above Birkenau, and see nothing. These are his words: "It was not that the Jews didn't matter; they didn't matter enough." From the tone of some of the documents that survive, and from the general sense of lack of urgency in the passing of requests from one government office to another in both the British and American capitals, that is, I think, as near to self-evident as a moral judgment can be.

6

THE ALLIES AND AUSCHWITZ:
A PARTICIPANT'S VIEW

Gerhart M. Riegner

My role during the war was to observe what was happening all over Europe to the Jews and to report to the Jewish leadership in America and in Britain. We were very well informed in Geneva. We followed events from day to day, from week to week, from month to month. When you see some of our reports today, you might be astonished at how accurate they were. My most important contribution was in 1942, when I informed the American and British governments about the plan for the Final Solution. This was the first authentic news, coming from a German source that had access to Hitler's headquarters. The tragedy is that it was not believed. But the files are there and show that the governments knew it all.

My task, however, is to discuss my involvement in the request to bomb Auschwitz. First, let me say that this was not an idea that came from us; it came from the Jewish leaders in Bratislava and Budapest. It was they who asked us. They asked us to ensure that the communication lines to Auschwitz would be bombed and that the gas chambers and ovens in Auschwitz would also be bombed. Whatever loss to human life this would cause, at least it would bring the machinery of Auschwitz to a halt, which at certain times and for long periods killed six thousand Jews every day. It would have stopped this process. It would have saved tens of thousands, maybe hundreds of thousands, of Jews.

The first copy of the report on Auschwitz arrived at the office of the Czechoslovakian minister in Geneva, Dr. Jaromir Kopecky, around 10 June. It was brought to Geneva by the Slovakian underground. The report contained a detailed description of the camp in Auschwitz and of the process of extermination, transport by transport. It originated from two Slovakian Jews who had escaped. When the report arrived—a text of nearly thirty pages—the Czechoslovakian minister called me in, gave me the report, and asked me to make a summary for his government and for the British and American governments, which I did.

A week later, a second copy of the report arrived from Budapest, which contained the request for bombing.

Now, what did I do? I went to the American legation and to the British legation in Berne, and I supported this idea, and asked them to relay the reports to the competent authorities. I, of course, knew nothing of the aerial intelligence. I said to myself, "I have to give them something to help them," and I remembered that in 1921 there was a plebiscite in Upper Silesia, where Auschwitz was situated. This plebiscite, organized by the League of Nations, created detailed geographical maps of this region, and I got copies and gave them to the American and British legations in Berne.

Nothing happened. We were told, and this was the crux of the problem, "It cannot be done. It is too far away. We have no aircraft which can go to Auschwitz, and come back." We were not told that the Allies had virtual air superiority over the whole of Europe during the entire year of 1944. We were not told that five kilometers from Auschwitz, the Allies had bombed Monowitz and its Buna works several times. It was about the same period. We were simply told "It cannot be done."

I must say, I have never understood why they lied to us. Because what we were told were clear lies. I have never understood it. I know, and we know today, that Churchill had supported the idea. Eden, not the greatest friend, impressed by Churchill's signature, said, "Okay." Then the request went to the British air minister, Mr. Sinclair. From there, it went back to the general staff, because the British thought they could not do it alone and the Americans might do it. The whole matter kept circulating, and nothing happened.

It is interesting to note that the responsibility for this policy does not lie with political leaders, but with the bureaucracy. There were men like Churchill who after all was one of the great leaders of the Allies, and who expressed the opinion that the bombing should be attempted, and yet despite this, nothing happened. But it shows that the Allied bureaucracy played a major role in the whole extermination process. We also know that on the other side—the Nazi side—the bureaucracy played a fateful role as well.

When I saw the pictures of the air intelligence at the symposium, I was struck. I had never seen these pictures, but I had seen the report of Vrba and Wetzler, the two Slovakian Jews. This report was not simply a report; it included sketches of how Auschwitz and Birkenau were organized. It showed on these sketches the same barracks as we see in the photos—the same long rows of barracks. It showed the places where the crematoria were, where the ovens were situated. I gave the report to the British and the Americans, and it was relayed to Washington. We knew. If they had wanted to act, they could have done it. There were very clear indications of where to strike and what should be done.

But what happened? It was always said, "We have to win the war." We told the military leaders and the political leaders we shouldn't only aim to win the war, but we should also try to help those who were condemned to death. There was a kind of moral insensitivity that prevailed, and it was terribly difficult to accept. I pleaded many times with the American and British authorities who were accessible to me, "We not only want to win the war; we want to save the people. We don't want to win the war only to find that all our people will be dead." But it did not help.

I want to make another remark with regard to the dangers. We were very conscious that the bombing would have its consequence and many people would be killed, but the machinery would be stopped—the machinery that produced six thousand dead every day. The fact that the very leaders of the Jewish communities who were inside Europe under the German occupation asked for it, gave us the right to insist.

But there was another proposal. I was surprised that nobody has mentioned it. My predecessor as secretary-general of the World Jewish Congress, Dr. Kubowitzki, made another suggestion. When the objection, "but you will kill thousands of people," was raised, he said, "Why don't we send a commando with arms and ammunition and explosives and parachute them in by plane and tell them to blow up the ovens from inside?" This was an idea that was clearly put forward as an alternative.

It is true that we did not know all the details about Auschwitz, but we knew that Auschwitz was a death camp. We knew it from the people in Theresienstadt, a camp in Czechoslovakia from which many transports went to Auschwitz. Theresienstadt was presented as a camp for old people, German Jews mostly, whom the Nazis said they wanted to preserve. All of this was a deliberate lie. We were in constant contact with the leadership, both in Theresienstadt and in Prague, through all kinds of underground communications. We were warned by them, "Do not believe that Theresienstadt is a stable camp and is not moving. There are all the time people going to Auschwitz and that means death." We did not know the details, but we knew for certain that those who were going to Auschwitz were condemned to death.

One question I want to raise for historians is, Why was no reliance placed on the reports that came from the Jewish organizations? I conveyed in 1942, among other things, a report to both the American and British governments, about the destruction of the Jews of Riga in two nights in November and December 1941. We heard about this nine or ten months later in Geneva, by pure accident, because one of those who had survived these two nights—a young man—was saved and came to Geneva where he had some relatives. I questioned him for eight hours. What he reported was completely new to us: the extermination of the whole Jewish population in Riga—thirty-six thousand people in two nights. But later I learned that the British intelligence had confirmatory reports. We were never told they had them. My request to the historians—after all, it is more than fifty years now—is that they should try to get these reports of Allied intelligence services, because they make they the responsibility of those who did not act even greater.

It was one of the saddest periods of my life. I know many people think that six million Jews could have been spared. That was not in the cards. One could have stopped Hitler before—in 1933; in 1934; in 1936, when the Rhineland was occupied; perhaps even in 1938, during the Czechoslovakian crisis. But certainly not during the war. I am certain, however, that hundreds of thousands of people, if not more, could have been saved if there had been a greater determination to save them and a greater concern for their lives.

7

THE BOMBING OF
AUSCHWITZ RE-EXAMINED

James H. Kitchens III

ONE OF THE most curious—even bizarre—legacies of the Holocaust is the question of whether the Allies could, and should, have used their air power to destroy the gas chambers and crematoria at Auschwitz and the rail net feeding them. For a decade or so, it has been argued that the camp's location and layout were well known and that the installations and rails vital to its operations could have been easily and precisely neutralized from the air, had not insensitivity, indifference, and even antipathy prevented it. Critics, on the other hand, argue that aerial bombing of Auschwitz or its vital railroads was technically infeasible and militarily chimerical. So where in the cross fire does the truth lie? Though the past cannot be changed, the answer is consequential because the alleged failure to act inculpates the Allied high commands, governments, and even peoples in collective guilt for the deaths of innocent millions. Professional historians, too, have a stake in the answer, because dissection of the bombing problem reveals unsettling deficiencies in the investigation, determination, and assignation of this culpability. Indeed, few dialogues in modern historiography have been so charged with subjectivity and so encumbered by irrelevancies; few have suffered so much from intellectual insularity and from ineffective colloquy. The following comments explore the genesis of the bombing idea and its seminal expressions, identify its premises, and demonstrate that operational constraints rather than prejudice prevented Allied authorities from bombing Auschwitz.

The initial inspiration for bombing of concentration camps or railroads to counter the Holocaust may be traced to early summer 1944, when the dimensions and import of Hitler's "Final Solution" first began to be appreciated in the West.[1] In mid-May 1944, the Slovak Orthodox rabbi Dov Weissmandel, horrified by the incipient deportation of hundreds of thousands of Hungarian Jews to Auschwitz, begged the Allies to block the movement by bombing the Košice-Prešov rail line.[2] Sent surreptitiously from Bratislava to Switzerland and thence to Jewish leaders in New York, Weissmandel's message reached the U.S. War Refugee Board on 18 June. On 2 June Yitzak Gruenbaum, Chairman of the Rescue Committee of the Jewish Agency, independently sent an analogous suggestion to the War Refugee Board.[3] Later in June, the World Jewish Congress in Switzerland proposed that "The camps at Auschwitz and Birkenau and especially the buildings containing the gas-chambers and crematoriums, . . . as well as the sentries around the railings and the watch-towers and the industrial installations should be bombed from the air."[4] Despite explicit first-hand descriptions of Auschwitz's horrors received later in the summer, however, the Allies turned a deaf ear to pleas for aerial intervention. In late June 1944, the U.S. War Department rejected the Košice-Prešov rail bombing plea on the grounds that it was impractical and would require diversion of too many essential resources; in August, the British Air Ministry also refused aerial rescue operations, citing poor intelligence, hazards and high casualties, and dubious results.[5] Thus, no German concentration camps were deliberately attacked from the air before war's end, and no discernible efforts were made to single out deportation railroads for special attacks.

Following the war, whatever questions there may have been about Allied inaction long lay inchoate, in part because of popular satisfaction with victory, in part because of document classification, and in part because even those who had urged bombing during World War II had recognized it as a desperate, symbolic gesture at best.[6] At the same time, however, the Holocaust's dimensions not only became fully known but increasingly became the focus of conscience-wrenching inquiry. This inquiry did not always produce satisfaction, especially where causation and responsibility were concerned. Within this context, the possibility that air power could have saved thousands of innocent lives may occasionally have made cocktail chitchat during the late 1940s and the 1950s, but it remained nothing more than grist for casual speculation until a school of collective guilt began to emerge in the late 1960s. The new tilt toward global responsibility for Nazi atrocities was signaled by Arthur D. Morse's *While Six Million Died* (1968), which asserted that American authorities had been apathetic bystanders to the Holocaust.[7] Eight years later, historian John Morton Blum adopted a more temperate, dispassionate, and scholarly version of this theme in his *V Was for Victory*.[8]

Against this backdrop, in May 1978 David S. Wyman, professor of history at the University of Massachusetts, published a startling article entitled "Why Auschwitz Was Never Bombed" in the American Jewish Committee's magazine *Commentary*.[9] The title told all: Wyman proposed to disclose how the camp could have been bombed but was not. Two months later several letters pro and con turned up in the July issue, thus igniting a controversy which spread to other periodicals in the ensuing months. Some of these commentators went even further than Wyman. For example, Roger Williams's article "Why Wasn't Auschwitz Bombed?" in the 24 November 1978 issue of *Commonweal* was sub-

origins of debate

titled "An American Moral Tragedy," which phrase epitomized its theme.[10] Williams, then senior editor of *Saturday Review*, wrote that "At Auschwitz alone, almost half a million Jews died after the U.S. had acquired the ability to prevent their deaths there" and that, since the inmates were doomed anyway, "the bombing should have been done for larger symbolic reasons."[11] For the next five years the issue bubbled like the mud pots of Yellowstone, percolating but not quite erupting into the national arena. In 1981, for example, Martin Gilbert presented his *Auschwitz and the Allies,* a sober and professional essay which carefully chronicled Allied intelligence about Auschwitz but which also uncritically deduced that the camp could, and should, have been bombed.[12] Two years later, the American Gathering of Jewish Holocaust Survivors in Washington, D.C., prompted Morton Mintz to again ask in the *Washington Post,* "Why Didn't We Bomb Auschwitz?"[13]

Despite spasmodic publicity in the early eighties, the bombing question really did not catch the public eye until late 1984, when Wyman incorporated a refined and annotated version of his *Commentary* article into a weighty monograph titled *The Abandonment of the Jews.*[14] Here Wyman argued that during World War II the U.S. had neglected several potential rescue measures such as earlier establishment of the War Refugee Board; greater pressure on Germany to release the Jews; a freer refugee policy in the U.S. and abroad; support for a Palestinian homeland; concentrated broadcast warnings; and offers of ransom. The failure to energetically pursue such measures amounted to deliberate and callous abandonment of the Jews.[15]

In Chapter XV of *Abandonment,* "The Bombing of Auschwitz," Wyman integrated the camp and railroad bombing question into his larger thesis by positing that the Allies had contributed to the Holocaust's toll by refusing to smash the Nazi genocide apparatus at Auschwitz from the air. Essentially, the nineteen-page chapter was a footnoted version of the author's earlier *Commentary* article. As early as April 1944, Wyman postulated, the Allies had aerial photographs of the Auschwitz-Birkenau concentration camp, and additional evidence became available during May and June through the detailed report of two escapees, Rudolf Vrba and Alfred Wetzler.[16] When combined, these sources supposedly made clear the exact location, number, and dimensions of the camp's gas chambers and crematoria. Despite this intelligence, American bombing of the nearby I. G. Farben works at Monowitz,[17] and the repeated entreaties of European and American Jewish leaders to attack the facilities and the railroads feeding them, however, the U.S. War Department and British authorities did nothing. According to Wyman, American heavy bomber flights over the camp, Frantic shuttle missions to Russia,[18] and relief missions to Warsaw demonstrated that heavy bomber attacks on Auschwitz were eminently feasible without diversion of military resources; even if not, he reasoned, B-25 medium bombers, P-38 fighter-bombers, or British D.H.98 Mosquitoes could have performed the mission. Yet in June 1944 the U.S. War Department declared such attacks would be an impractical diversion:

> The War Department is of the opinion that the suggested air operation is impracticable for the reason that it could be executed only by diversion of considerable air support essential to the success of our forces now engaged in decisive operations. . . . It is considered that the most effective relief to victims of enemy persecution is the early defeat of the Axis, an undertaking to which we must devote every resource at our disposal.[19]

This no-bomb policy permitted the killing at Auschwitz to continue unhindered, costing tens of thousands, even hundreds of thousands of lives until the camp ceased operations late in 1944. Wyman had, it appeared, amply documented these points in eighty chapter footnotes and supported them with appropriate bibliographic references.

The Abandonment of the Jews received considerable attention and wide acclamation following its release by Pantheon in November 1984. On 6 November and again on 24 December, the *New York Times* published plausive articles about Wyman and his research, and on 16 December A. J. Sherman favorably reviewed *Abandonment* for the paper's book review supplement. Perhaps boosted by this publicity, *Abandonment* made the *New York Times Book Review*'s "Best Sellers" list on 17 March 1985 and on four ensuring dates, rising to number thirteen of fifteen nonfiction titles on 31 March.[20] Subsequent reviews were almost universally positive,[21] the History Book Club later made it one of its monthly selections, and it was released in a paperback edition. Total sales ran to over eighty thousand. In short, the book became everything that an academic could dream of.

Largely because of its scholarly trappings and popular reception, but also in part because of its spectacular inferences, Wyman's thesis quickly gained a broad following. In fact, a veritable school of opinion predicated on his views and nurtured by brooding retrospection has arisen since 1984. Thus entrenched, Wyman himself has shown no inclination to revise his thinking on the subject, as his final words on the bombing of Auschwitz in Macmillan's 1990 *Encyclopedia of the Holocaust* indicate. The U.S. War Department's June 1944 refusal to bomb Auschwitz was, he concludes, "no more than an excuse for inaction."[22] Today this conviction is widespread and has been incorporated into several recent Holocaust histories.[23] The United States Holocaust Memorial Council subscribes to it—Wyman has served as advisor to the group[24] and in mid-April 1990, just when the issue was again being debated in letters to the *Washington Post,* a pseudo-judicial proceeding in Israel found the USAAF guilty of failure to save thousands of innocent lives by not bombing the death camps.[25]

As early as 1978, however, Wyman's bombing thesis excited some challenges.

A few weeks after publication of the professor's initial *Commentary* article, Milton Groban, a former Fifteenth Air Force B-24 navigator-bombardier,[26] wrote the magazine to point out why gross inaccuracy made using heavy bombers against Auschwitz impractical without enormous casualties within the camp. Moreover, Groban asserted, bombing the facility would have been very costly in men and machines and might only have distracted, but not significantly impaired, the Nazi killing. Viewing the matter only from his own combat experiences in B-24s, Groban did not comment on sending medium, light, or dive bombers against Auschwitz, nor did he elucidate the requirement for, and costs of, a systematic anti-camp and rail campaign.[27]

After the initial exchanges in *Commentary* faded, further criticism of the Wyman thesis was muted until after publication of *The Abandonment of the Jews* in 1984. Even then the rigorous review process that often sieves out errors in historiography failed Clio's cause when academic specializations and disciplinary insularity among reviewers permitted marked deficiencies in Chapter XV to slip through without notice. On one hand, most reviewers of *Abandonment* were schooled in refugee or religious history or Holocaust studies and apparently knew little about air power;[28] on the other hand, none of the country's handful of professional air power historians seem to have noticed the book or to have publicly critiqued its camp bombing thesis. Thus it was that the Holocaust studies community and that of air power history passed like ships in the night, and thus it was left to Richard Foregger, M.D., a Minnesota anesthesiologist and amateur historian, to become the first to systematically controvert Wyman's propositions. The physician's "The Bombing of Auschwitz," a well-documented thirteen-page article in the Summer 1987 issue of *Aerospace Historian*, refuted most of Wyman's assertions about camp and rail bombing.[29] This quarterly, however, was published by the Air Force Historical Foundation, which to some may have tainted its objectivity. It was also something less than a formal academic forum, and it had a readership of less than five thousand, mostly aviation enthusiasts. Despite Foregger's evident scholarship and critical thinking, therefore, there is no evidence that his rebuttal penetrated the Holocaust studies community; if it did, it prompted no perceptible responses from that community in either *Aerospace Historian* or the national press[30] and has not been cited in many, if any, post-1987 Holocaust histories. Since 1978, therefore, the Wyman thesis has remained for many a convincing explanation of why the Allies did little or nothing to derail the Holocaust from the air.

As conceived by Wyman and adopted by Gilbert and other historians, then, the camp-bombing proposition originated in the groves of academe, and a critical analysis of it properly begins with its chief disciple's perspective and sources. A member of the Society of Friends and a 1966 graduate of Harvard, Wyman joined the University of Massachusetts history faculty in the same year. In 1968 his doctoral dissertation was published as *Paper Walls: America and the Refugee Crisis, 1938–1941*, a study of the United States' prewar Jewish immigration policies.[31] This essay explored the nation's prewar attitude toward Jewish refugees, finding it was shaped by unemployment, nativistic nationalism,[32] and anti-Semitism, factors which found expression in executive and legislative policy such as limited immigration quotas.

Wyman's second book, *The Abandonment of the Jews*, built on these perspectives, themes, and conclusions and extended them through the World War II period. In particular, Wyman carried forward his view that public policy, presumably fashioned and driven by democratic process, was responsible for abandonment of the Jews between 1941 and 1945. He neglected, however, a crucial difference between the prewar era of *Paper Walls* and that of *Abandonment*: a state of total war not of the Allies' choosing. Prior to 1941, though war was clearly on the horizon, the U.S. was ostensibly neutral; American diplomatic and public policy options were unfettered by overt hostilities. After December 1941, America had to focus on mobilization of her wealth, manpower, allies, and world opinion in a global struggle to bring down the Axis powers. Her shipping, for example, was stretched to the limit to meet the needs of war; her foreign policy had to take into account the posture of the Arab world vis-à-vis any Zionist settlements in Palestine. In such a setting, ultimate victory depended almost exclusively on mustering, then applying, brute force to break the Hitlerian regime; military options for rescuing large numbers of Nazi victims from fortress Europe before its fall were severely circumscribed. Given the irrational character of Nazism, its intransigence, and the occupation of most of Europe until after mid-1944, air power assumed overwhelming importance in any effective construct for salvation of the Jews. Air power, after all, was the sole means of projecting military power deep into the enemy's heartland. For these reasons, the camp-bombing question is highly germane to Wyman's overall thesis. Yet it is exactly here in the realm of air power, far from prewar mores, immigration quotas, socioeconomic attitudes, public debate, or legislative mandate that the public policy perspective carried over from *Paper Walls* dramatically changes character.

Not surprisingly, Wyman based *Abandonment* largely on ethnic and sociopolitical sources and personal papers, and considering the criticality of the bombing question to the book's thesis, its air power bibliography is astonishingly anemic. Of five books on air power, two are elderly USAAF and RAF official histories, the first thirty years old, the second twenty years old in 1981.[33] The age factor is particularly significant in such sources because over time the declassification of documents makes them obsolete; one instance of this is mentioned below in connection with the AZON bomb. Of other books cited, one is a buff's book,[34] one an examination of the Poltava affair,[35] and one a 1963 mélange of unannotated articles and extracts about diverse aspects of the European air war.[36] Not a single reference to the B-17, B-24, B-25, or P-38 is listed, even though the combat capabilities and tactical employment of these machines are quintessential to the bombing dialectic.[37] Wyman's remarks about the

D.H.98 Mosquito are scarcely better supported, resting on nothing but Birtles's pictorial history—a far cry from Bowyer and Sharp's definitive 494-page treatment of the machine[38]—and on one apparently misunderstood letter from an RAF Air Historical Branch archivist. Some tangible consequences of this faulty documentation of the Mosquito will be seen shortly. *Abandonment*'s bibliography includes nothing on German air defenses, nor are any works on Ploesti raids listed, even though Fifteenth Air Force experiences against this target usefully illuminate the camp-bombing problem. Finally, not a single article entry out of fifty-eight seems to relate to aircraft, air power, air leaders, or air operations per se, although two essays do address aerial photo intelligence about Auschwitz. Of ten unpublished works, none treat air power; of twenty-four pamphlets and booklets, just one, the Fifteenth Air Force's *Historical Summary: First Year of Operations* (1944) documents that Air Force's operations.[39]

Primary sources are even weaker. The bibliography, for example, simply lists the USAF Historical Research Center as an institution, and nothing indicates which of the facility's files were actually examined. In fact, there is strong inferential evidence that the author never visited the Center, or that if he did, dozens of entries in its finding aids were overlooked or ignored.[40] Nowhere does one find citations to the Center's vast holding of original unit histories, intelligence reports, operational analyses, bombing accuracy studies, airfield files, and orders of battle that are critical to analyzing the camp-bombing problem.[41] The Center's 250-roll microfilm collection of Mediterranean Allied Air Force (MAAF)[42] operations and intelligence files are nowhere cited. Some vague references to mission reports on microfilm are scattered among Chapter XV footnotes, but these are not clarified in the bibliography, and one is left to guess what and where these are. Moreover, no mention is made of the National Archives' immense RG 18, Records of the USAAF, which contains perhaps 80 percent of mission reports surviving today. *Abandonment*'s bibliography does list the National Archives' RG 243, Records of the Strategic Bombing Survey, but readers are not told that the USBSS says nothing about bombing Auschwitz or that in fact the Survey's reports offer solid evidence against the feasibility of such attacks. In any case, there are but four citations to the USSBS in Chapter XV, all to area maps or photo interpretation reports of the I. G. Farben works. Similarly, Wyman cites no materials from the RAF's Air Historical Branch or to AIR files at the Public Record Office, even after Gilbert pointed the way to these in *Auschwitz and the Allies*, nor are air power-related citations from the Imperial War Museum; Bundesarchiv-Militärarchiv; Hoover Institute for War, Peace, and Revolution; or other repositories included. Fewer than ten references to the Carl Spaatz Collection in the Library of Congress do not offset these deficiencies.[43] Taken together, Wyman's scholarly interests, research foci, and superficial documentation go far toward explaining the formulation of his bombing thesis. For the historian of refugee policy, the failure to bomb Auschwitz comfortably fits a pattern of prejudice he believes existed before 1941 and persisted in 1944; pervasive indifference, insensitivity, and antipathy within the cabinet, the War Department, and even the American people are sufficient to explain why Auschwitz was never bombed, especially since American aircraft were over-flying the camp and could have struck it with few, if any, collateral casualties. Gross misconceptions about air-power—common among those out-side the military sciences—together with an uncritical reliance on Wyman's work, help explain how post-*Abandonment* Holocaust historiography has per-petuated the bombing idea. An objective look at targeting possibilities, available intelligence, operational constraints, and the realistic allocation of military re-sources, however, shows that the effective use of air power against Auschwitz is a chimera having little to do with War Department policies, indifference, military ineptitude, or negative ethnic attitudes. Immediately it must be pointed out that from Wyman's 1978 article onward it has never been clear exactly what targets should be included in the camp-bombing question. Wyman himself os-tensibly focused on destruction of the four gas chambers and crematoria at Auschwitz-Birkenau but did not mention the gas chamber/crematorium at Auschwitz I ("Main Camp").[44] The Birkenau buildings were relatively soft tar-gets of brick construction, each about a story or a story and a half high with large portions sunk below ground level. Their narrow aerial profile, however, made them quite difficult targets. The largest pair, Crematoria II and III, each measured 321 feet (99 m) long by 32 feet (10 m) wide,[45] about the size and proportion of a highway bridge. Dispersion and proximity to camp housing posed even graver problems. The four Birkenau buildings were grouped in two loose pairs along the camp's western edge. About 800 yards (750 m) separated the northwestern pair from the nearer of two at the southwestern corner. All four gas chambers and crematoria were within 300 yards (275 m) of camp housing.[46] About a mile and a half southeast of them was the older single gas chamber and crematorium of Auschwitz I, making a total of five discrete, widely spaced objectives within the Auschwitz complex whose destruction could have conceivably impeded the extermination process there.[47]

Adherents of camp bombing from Wyman onward have consistently main-tained that Allied leadership possessed enough, and sufficiently exact, intelli-gence about these five Auschwitz buildings to mount the kind of attack necessary to safely destroy them. Two types of evidence for this are usually cited: photos derived from USAAF reconnaissance over the I. G. Farben Mon-owitz complex ("Buna") near Auschwitz and the report of escapees Vrba and Wetzler. It is true that images of Birkenau appeared on aerial photographs as early as April 1944, but as Brugioni and Foregger have pointed out, the death camp appeared only accidentally and was wholly incidental to the interpreters' work.[48] None of them was tasked to look for concentration camps; their prints and viewing equipment were primitive; none of them had the experience or interpretation guides to make the images speak intelligibly; few, if any, of them had access to other types of intelligence or to Fifteenth Air Force's overall air

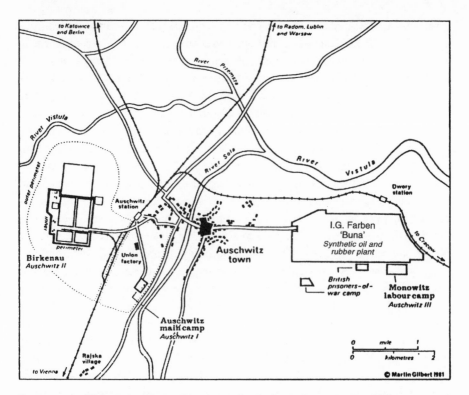

Labels on map:
to Katowice and Berlin
to Radom, Lublin and Warsaw
River Przemsza
River Vistula
River Sola
River
Vistula
Dwory station
Auschwitz station
outer perimeter
inner perimeter
I.G. Farben 'Buna' Synthetic oil and rubber plant
to Cracow
Birkenau Auschwitz II
Union factory
Auschwitz town
British prisoners-of-war camp
Monowitz labour camp Auschwitz III
Auschwitz main camp Auschwitz I
Rajsko village
to Vienna
mile
kilometres
© Martin Gilbert 1981

FIGURE 7-1 Birkenau concentration camp, Auschwitz main camp, Auschwitz town, and the I. G. Farben synthetic oil and rubber plant at Monowitz, with its satellite labor camps. *(From* Auschwitz and the Allies *by Martin Gilbert. Copyright © 1981 by Martin Gilbert. Reprinted by permission of Henry Holt and Company, Inc.)*

campaign. Brugioni has further noted that during May–August 1944, the Mediterranean Allied Air Forces' strategic assets were concentrated on the oil campaign, meaning that MAAF photo interpreters were concentrating on known oil-producing facilities such as Monowitz and Blechhammer at the expense of other types of targets. During July and early August, MAAF's focus also shifted to the forthcoming invasion of southern France. Under these circumstances, it is not surprising that Auschwitz's true nature passed unnoticed under the photo interpreters' stereoscopes. In the context of overall intelligence appreciation, it also should be noted that there was no historical precedent for genocidal installations like Auschwitz and that before the end of 1944, at least, the Allies lacked enough solid intelligence about the "Final Solution" to adequately comprehend its hideous import.[49]

Bombing advocates maintain, however, that when combined with aerial photographs the Vrba-Wetzler report should have precipitated immediate and decisive action from Washington or London. Close analysis reveals why the report's timing and contents prevented this from happening. As Gilbert depicts them, Vrba and Wetzler were both young men whose administrative duties and lengthy survival within Birkenau gave them an extraordinary perspective on the camp's horrors, which they were determined to preserve through memorization and eventual escape. On 7–10 April 1944 their determination succeeded, and on 25 April their report reached Jewish underground figures in Slovakia who tried to get it out to Budapest, Switzerland, the Vatican, and Istanbul. For various reasons the text was delayed, and a telegraphic summary did not reach the War Refugee Board in Washington until 24 June and the British Foreign Office until 4 July. The full twenty-five-page text with a five-page summary did not get to London until 26 July, by which time it was too late for any action to save the Jews of Hungary.[50]

Even after 26 July, the full Vrba-Wetzler report had minimal utility for military intelligence purposes. On the surface, the report appears to be a sickening revelation about what was going on in Auschwitz, and so it was. But in fact, as intelligence collateral for analyzing the camp as a precision bombing target, the report had severe limitations. Neither escapee was a trained observer, and their page-and-a-half description of Birkenau's crematoria was almost exclusively concerned with the ghastly details of operation rather than militarily useful targeting data such as building structural design, materials, foundations, and the like necessary for the selection and placement of ordnance. Potential low-flying hazards such as high tension wires and radio transmission towers were nowhere mentioned, and chimneys and forested areas were only vaguely indicated. Flak guns—Birkenau itself had none—were nowhere mentioned. The escapees' report did not even estimate the gas chambers and crematoria's outside dimensions, nor did it reliably locate them on the ground. Maps included with the report contained at least one error which could have puzzled those seeking to correlate the report with aerial photographs: the summary stated that the northeast end of the camp could be distinguished by the high smokestacks of four crematoria, when in reality these chimneys were located at the opposite or western side of the camp.[51] Moreover, as Foregger relates, a sketch map of the Auschwitz area which reached the British Foreign Office on 22 August was grossly inaccurate: "Neither the Auschwitz II camp at Birkenau [sic] nor the gas chambers and crematoria could be located with the map. A Plaster of Paris model to show the relative size, shape, and location of the gas chambers and crematoria [necessary for attacking air crews] could not be correctly constructed with this sketch map."[52] Finally, expert photo interpreters might, with enough time and effort, have correlated aerial photographs with the Vrba-Wetzler report, but the authors themselves remained in Slovakia, inaccessible for person-to-person debriefing or clarification of the information they had provided.

In sum, the militarily useful intelligence available to the Allies about Auschwitz came late and was much shakier than Wyman suggests. Photo interpreters could not have reasonably been interested in the camp before being alerted to it, and this alert could not have been put out before receipt of the summary of the Vrba-Wetzler report on 4 July. Even under utopian conditions, with an instant appreciation of Auschwitz's vulnerability from the air and a resolute determination to attack, it would have taken another two to three weeks for the Central Intelligence Unit in England to be notified, then for photographs to be retrieved, studied, and related to whatever other data could be had. A comparison with the complete Vrba-Wetzler text, of course, could not have been started before about mid-July. Further photo reconnaissance to verify and refine target assessment, probably at low altitudes, then would have been ordered, consuming a further week or more, depending on weather, availability of photo aircraft and crews, and losses or failures. With the best will and under optimal conditions, then, it is unreasonable to think that sufficient intelligence to properly assess the Auschwitz-Birkenau buildings as targets could have been in hand before early to mid-August 1944. The next step, planning and training for, and execution of, an exacting combat operation with forces on hand in the Mediterranean could not have reasonably consumed less than a week; transfer of specially qualified units within, or to, the theater for the raid would have taken longer. As a comparison, the spectacular 18 February 1944 Mosquito attack on Amiens prison—an infinitely better known, simpler, and closer target than Auschwitz with unmistakable life-and-death urgency—had taken approximately three weeks from receipt of French resistance request to execution; bad weather had delayed the mission by only one day.[53]

Presuming adequate intelligence about Birkenau and Auschwitz I, their nature and location still presented insurmountable obstacles for precision bombing. One major problem was sheer range. The Auschwitz complex lay about 620 miles from Fifteenth Air Force heavy bomber bases around Foggia and approximately 525 miles from the Adriatic island airfield on Vis, operational after 2 May 1944. Thus, Auschwitz was barely within the theoretical range of B-25 medium bombers, P-38 fighter-bombers using an external drop tank, and D.H.98 Mosquito light bombers. Simple distance, however, was inseparably intertwined with factors of terrain, tactics, winds and weather, useful bomb load, air defenses, and crew performance. Sweeping in a great crescent from Albania to Switzerland, the Alps and Carpathian ranges presented tremendous obstacles to the penetration of central Europe from Italian bases. To attack Auschwitz via a direct route out of either southern Italy or Vis required crossing the Dalmatian Alps, ranging above five thousand feet, and the Tatras of Slovakia-Slovenia, also ranging over five thousand feet. Flying heavily escorted in formation above the highest ridges, heavy bombers had no difficulty with the mountains, but a low-level attack by medium or light bombers or fighter-bombers would have been much more difficult. To avoid detection by German air defenses, total radio silence and very low altitude would have been necessary. What would today be termed a med-lo-hi or a lo-lo-hi mission also would have demanded a zig-zag approach through treacherous valleys racked with navigational hazards and wind shear. Such an approach raised fuel consumption, precluded tight defensive combat box formations, and fatigued crews. Long range demanded extra fuel, and extra fuel came only at the expense of bombload and thus more aircraft; in the case of P-38s, for example, just one bomb per aircraft could be carried with one drop tank.

Using Vis Island for staging as Wyman suggests also had grave limitations. Built under German noses, the three-thousand-foot Vis airstrip[54] was a primitive, precarious, and clandestine toehold created as an advanced landing ground for close fighter support and supply of Yugoslav partisans. It had only one runway and eighteen hardstands; fuel, maintenance, ground support, and air defenses were minimal; and it did not even receive all-weather pierced steel planking until October 1944. A handful of aircraft might have used the island for refueling on a return to Italy, but any number would have meant dangerous congestion and a tempting target. Worst of all, any landing or takeoff accident could have blocked the single runway and closed the field to following aircraft.[55]

German air defenses have received relatively little attention in the bombing debate.[56] There were no flak guns at Auschwitz I and Birkenau, but seventy-nine heavy guns defended the I. G. Farben works at Monowitz, four and one-half miles away, and wheeling formations of heavy bombers over Birkenau could hardly have avoided this defensive umbrella.[57] Even small arms fire from the guards could have been effective against low-level attackers, especially P-38s and Mosquitoes with liquid-cooled engines. The Luftwaffe's fighter defenses in the Balkans were not nearly as strong as in Germany, but Y-stations and at least three early warning radars directly opposite Bari provided *Jagdfliegerführer Balkan*'s headquarters in Belgrade with ample electronic intelligence.[58] Located directly under any bomber attack directed northward, *Jagdfliegerführer Balkan* in mid-1944 could have called on a minimum of thirty Bf 109G fighters from II./JG 51, III./JG 77, and II./JG 301 for interception. Another twenty-five Bf 109Gs of Hungarian Fighter Group 101 were based at Veszprém, north of Lake Balaton and directly under the approach to Auschwitz.[59]

On arriving in the target area, attackers faced a dispersed, dauntingly complex objective consisting of five widely spaced buildings (four at Birkenau, one over a mile away at Auschwitz I) which had to be identified and attacked in concert with little loiter time and no release error. In making such attacks, weather also played a part. The atmosphere over mountainous Balkans terrain was likely to be more turbulent than over the sea or northwest European plain. Accurate precision bombing required perfect visibility, yet over southern Poland such weather was unusual and its prediction problematical. How, then, have bombing adherents proposed to attack the Auschwitz complex?

One proposal, high altitude raiding by four-engined heavy bombers of the Fifteenth Air Force based around Foggia, can immediately be discounted. It is true that some of these aircraft could have been diverted from formations attacking the Monowitz synthetic fuel/rubber plant during August 1944, or they could have been sent on a dedicated raid. B-17s and B-24s, however, cruised at 180 to 190 mph and were designed to bomb from fifteen to thirty thousand feet. Unfortunately, from these heights the pickle barrel placement required to hit chosen buildings without collateral damage was utterly impossible, a fact made crystal clear by the USSBS (which Wyman cites) and countless other sources. Normal bomb patterns from the heavies extended hundreds of yards from the aiming point, and it was quite common for bombs to fall a mile or more away from the target.[60] On 15 April 1945, for example, the Eighth Air Forces's 467th Bombardment Group achieved that air force's most accurate bombing of the war. In striking a coastal artillery battery in France—a pinpoint target not unlike the gas chambers or crematoria—B-24s from the 467th managed to put just 50 percent of their bombs within a five-hundred-foot radius around the guns. This was accomplished only with long experience, a fifteen-thousand-foot drop altitude, near-perfect weather, and with no resistance. If this was the best that heavy bombers could do, what would average bombing have done to the extermination camps' inhabitants?

Bombing advocates have consistently minimized the casualties that might have resulted from bombing Auschwitz. Wyman avoided any estimate, but in 1978 Williams ventured that "there would have been inmate deaths, *perhaps dozens of them*" [italics mine].[61] In fact, without too much speculation, it is possible to calculate what casualties a heavy bomber raid on Birkenau would have caused. In November 1944, the 1st Operation Analysis Section of Fifteenth Air Force reported on the relationship between altitude and bombing accuracy based on Mediterranean Theater experience. The Fifteenth's calculations showed that under good conditions the Circular Error Probable (C.E.P.) at 15,000 feet for B-17s was 500 feet and that for B-24s about 515 feet. Put another way, *under absolutely optimal conditions*, one-half of bombs dropped would have fallen at distances greater than 500 feet from the aiming point. The northern pair of gas chambers and crematoria at Birkenau were about 650 feet from the nearest huts; the southern pair were about 300 feet away. Using Gilbert's scale diagram of Birkenau with aiming points in the center of each target building,[62] it can be conservatively estimated that 25 to 30 percent of bombs dropped from 15,000 feet would have fallen within camp housing areas. According to the Paskuly edition of commandant Höss's memoirs, Birkenau held about 36,000 people on 5 April 1944 and upwards of 135,000 in August.[63] If, then, one hundred B-17s and B-24s bombed and each dropped eight five-hundred-pound bombs, approximately 160 to 200 of the 800 would have exploded in densely populated housing areas, within which there was no air raid protection whatsoever and no place to flee. Assuming five deaths by each errant missile, a minimum of 500 to 1000 deaths could reasonably have been expected, with a realistic possibility of as many as 2,000 to 3,000 under adverse circumstances.[64] One does not have to rely on theoretical modelling, however, to know what a heavy bomber raid on Auschwitz might have done. On 24 August 1944 the USAAF's Eighth Air Force carried out Operation No. 568 against a V-2 guidance works and an armament factory adjoining Buchenwald concentration camp at Weimar, Germany. The setting was as analogous to Auschwitz as history permits:

the grounds of one target ran along the camp fence; the other was a few hundred yards away. Backed by precise intelligence, including the factory shift schedule, 129 B-17s dropped 303 tons of bombs in near-perfect conditions, obliterating the objectives. Despite good knowledge of the target and much-above-average accuracy, however, 315 prisoners were killed, 525 seriously wounded, and 900 lightly wounded.[65] Neither *The Abandonment of the Jews* nor any subsequent Holocaust historiography mentions this Buchenwald attack.

A more attractive variation on four-engine bombing that Wyman did not mention, quite possibly because his old and inadequate sources did not suggest it,[66] was employment of the VB-1 AZON bomb, an early type of guided weapon. The 301st Bomb Group of the USAAF actually tested such devices in the Mediterranean Theater between April and July 1944, finding better overall accuracy than with conventional bombs. Unfortunately, the 301st also found that the AZON was quite unreliable: half of the bombs went wild, some hitting 850 feet from their mark.[67] Other guided weapons of the time were no more successful and would have offered no significant advantages over conventional bombing techniques.

Dismissing the possibility of accurate high altitude raids, would it have been possible to send B-17s and B-24s at very low levels to achieve surprise and accuracy? Presumably, such a mission would have been of the hi-lo-hi variety,[68] with the aircraft maintaining defensive formations and high altitudes on the way to Auschwitz, then descending to a few hundred feet north of the Tatras to run in to their targets, then climbing back to altitude for the return to base. Even with strict radio silence, however, it is doubtful that such tactics would have achieved surprise owing to radar and visual observation during the approach over the Adriatic. Moreover, USAAF heavy bomber crews lacked the specialized doctrine, experience, and training necessary to execute the precise bombing of designated buildings from very low altitudes. Used in such a way, the elephantine Fortresses and Liberators would not only have failed, they might well have been decimated, as in fact happened on the low-level Ploesti raid of 1 August 1943 when plane losses reached 30 percent; on the day after, Brigadier General Uzal Ent, Chief of IX Bomber Command, had just 33 B-24s fit to fly, out of 178 sent to Ploesti.[69] Not surprisingly, the USAAF never again tried using large formations of heavy bombers at low levels.

Lest the 1 August 1943 Ploesti operation be thought an aberration, a fluke of bad luck, one should also consider RAF Bomber Command's strike against the M.A.N. diesel engine works at Augsburg. This raid, in fact, bears the closest resemblance to a hypothetical low-level Auschwitz raid of any actual mission of the European air war. On 17 April 1942 the RAF dispatched twelve Lancasters in daylight across northern France to attack a single building, the main engine assembly shed within the M.A.N. diesel engine factory complex. Like Wyman's theoretical Auschwitz raid, planning for the M.A.N. mission was partially based on the interrogation of a prisoner who provided details for a sketch map of the

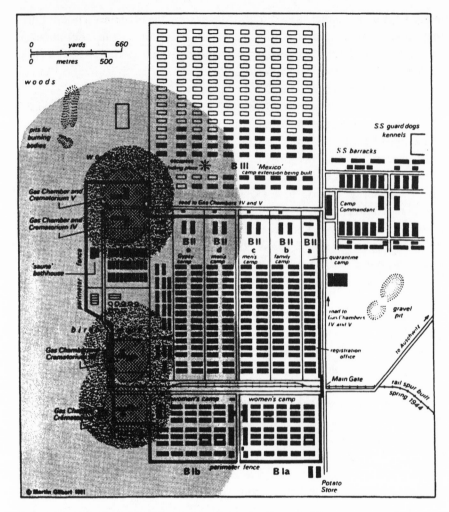

FIGURE 7-2 Strategic Bombing against Auschwitz: B-17s and B-24s at 20,000 ft.

war's best bombing: 500-foot Circular Error Probable (CEP) (from 15,000 ft.)

15th Air Force average bombing, 1944: 1000-foot CEP

"normal scatter": 2600-foot radius (one-half mile)

(Base drawing from Auschwitz and the Allies by Martin Gilbert. Copyright © 1981 by Martin Gilbert. Reprinted by permission of Henry Holt and Company, Inc. Bombing overlay by J. H. Kitchens III.)

plant; unfortunately, the engine construction building was marked in the wrong position. The raid involved a round trip of 1,250 miles, almost exactly the same distance as from Foggia to Auschwitz and back; it was conducted in daylight and at treetop height; there was even some mountainous country between Mulhouse and Lake Constance. Of the strike force of twelve, only five bombers, all damaged, returned to their bases; eight bombers dropped seventeen bombs, five of which failed to explode. Two buildings, neither of which was the intended target, were substantially damaged.[70] The miserable results of this raid helped persuade the RAF that the Lancaster should be used exclusively in high-altitude night operations, which remained the pattern for the rest of the war.

Though again conjecture precludes surety, B-25 medium bombers likely would have suffered the same fate and achieved the same results as heavies. Normally operating from six thousand to fifteen thousand feet, these aircraft were markedly faster than the heavies (but much slower than single-engine fighters) and had a bombing accuracy that was somewhat better. With modest bomb loads and ideal conditions the aircraft might have reached Auschwitz at the very limit of their endurance.[71] But like the Fortresses and Liberators, B-25s wholly depended on swarms of fighters and the mutual defense found in tight combat box formations for protection. With these mass formations, surprise was highly improbable; without them, prohibitive losses could have resulted. In either case, considerable resources would have been tied down. MAAF's Twelfth Air Force never had more than three groups of B-25s,[72] and after mid-April 1944 all three were concentrated in Corsica in support of operations in central and northern Italy and especially for the forthcoming invasion of southern France.[73] Even assuming technical and tactical suitability, utilization of these B-25s for an Auschwitz raid would have required deployment of at least one group with support equipment and personnel to southern Italian bases, a withdrawal from other missions of about sixty aircraft for a minimum period of a week, depending on weather and other factors.

Wyman's suggestion that "a small number of Mitchell medium bombers, which hit with surer accuracy from lower altitudes, could have flown with [one of the heavy bomber] missions to Auschwitz"[74] manifests an ignorance of B-25 characteristics and tactics: the airplane's engines had only two-stage mechanical superchargers, giving their best performance at about thirteen thousand feet with a practical operating ceiling of about eighteen thousand feet. Moreover, the thirty miles per hour cruising speed differential between heavy bombers and B-25s would have imposed impossible problems of station keeping, fuel consumption, and fighter cover while accompanying B-24s and B-17s. Had B-25s been tasked for Auschwitz, they would have had to fly independently, with whatever fighter escort was available; that the Twelfth Air Force never used these aircraft for long-distance raids into southern Germany and Austria is a strong indicator of their unsuitability for such missions.

It is true that the Allies were occasionally able to carry out surgical stabs at well-known, high-priority targets, and bombing advocates have usually cited this kind of operation as optimal for raiding Auschwitz. Typically, it is suggested that twin-engined Lockheed P-38 fighter-bombers or De Havilland D.H.98 Mosquitoes could have bombed selected camp buildings with precision and surprise. The P-38 model is based on an actual Fifteenth Air Force operation against the Ploesti oil refinery on 10 June 1944, when the USAAF's 82nd Fighter Group sent forty-six of its planes covered by another forty-eight from the 1st Fighter Group some six-hundred-plus miles to dive bomb selected buildings in the Romana Americana works. Each plane carried one thousand-pound bomb and one three-hundred-gallon drop tank. The 82nd's pilots reported that they had had to dive through dense smoke—artificial cover thickened by bomb blasts—and had had considerable trouble in locating their targets. Ultimately the raid achieved modest success, with about half of the objectives being damaged or destroyed, but the refinery resumed operations eight days later.[75] The raid's cost was appalling: eight aircraft, or 17 percent, of the 82nd's planes were lost as compared with an average Eighth Air Force heavy bomber loss at this time of about 5 percent. The escort lost an additional fourteen planes, or 28 percent.[76] Perhaps pondering this sobering box score, the Fifteenth Air Force never again tried such a long-range dive-bombing mission, though it continued to hammer the Ploesti refineries with heavies until August 1944.

Of all tactics for camp attacks, however, it is a daring surgical strike by De Havilland D.H.98 Mosquito bombers that has attracted the most attention. In 1984 Wyman wrote that "the most effective means of all for destroying the killing installations would have been to dispatch about twenty British Mosquitos to Auschwitz."[77] In comments on Foregger's article in *Aerospace Historian*, ex-USAAF pilot Robert H. Hodges claimed that the author had "distorted the history of D.H.98s on low-level missions" and went on to assert how several of these raids demonstrated the potential for an Auschwitz operation.[78] On the surface, the Mosquito's potential indeed might seem impressive. Capable of carrying a ton of bombs at nearly three hundred mph close to the ground, the all-wood Mosquito was one of World War II's wonder planes. Highly versatile, it was built in over two dozen versions and performed well in many roles. Its most impressive—though not necessarily most important or successful—operations were a handful of split-second treetop attacks on high-priority pin-point targets in Western Europe conducted between September 1942 and March 1945. The five most daring of these were undoubtedly that of 18 February 1944 against Amiens prison; that of 11 April 1944 against the Dutch Population Registry in the Hague; that of 31 October 1944 against the Aarhus, Denmark, Gestapo headquarters; that of 31 December 1944 against the Oslo, Norway, Gestapo headquarters; and that of 21 March 1945 against the Gestapo headquarters in Copenhagen, Denmark. In the famous Amiens operation, nineteen D.H.98 F.B. Mk.VIs flying as low as fifteen feet breached the prison walls and released 258 resistance fighters, many of whom were later recaptured and shot; over 100 others were killed by the bombs or while escaping.

The similarity of the dramatic Mosquito operations to the problem of attacking Auschwitz's gas chambers and crematoria, however, is vague at best, and in a close comparison, Auschwitz emerges as a well-nigh invulnerable target. All of the notable low-level Mosquito raids from England were conducted across the North Sea or relatively flat northwestern Europe, and none had to contend with navigating long mountainous stretches while flying at maximum range. Few, if any, of the special Mosquito raids attacked more than one building, while there were five discrete objectives at Auschwitz. Mosquito fighter-bombers had no defensive armament and could not dogfight with interceptors; flying unescorted they relied solely on surprise and lightning speed for success. These advantages would have been very hard to achieve and maintain while attacking multiple objectives with a force of perhaps forty aircraft, and in fact even the later special low-level Mosquito operations in Western Europe were escorted by P-51 Mustangs. Thus, flying over 620 miles in radio silence, crossing the Alps in some semblance of cohesion at low altitude, then sneaking through German air defenses with enough fuel to make a coordinated precision attack on five targets and return home beggars belief.

Ironically, the astonishing standards of flying that characterized special Mosquito operations put further limitations on the possibility of such operations out of Italy. In the *Abandonment of the Jews*, Wyman asserts that "At least 44 Mosquitos (and probably more) were stationed at Allied air bases in Italy in July 1944."[79] His authority for this is a letter from archivist Eric Munday of the RAF Historical Branch. But in fact, as MAAF orders of battle at the USAF Historical Research Center show, all forty-four of these Mosquitoes were N. F. Mk.XII and XVI night fighters (108 and 256 Squadron) and Mk.IX and XVI photo reconnaissance aircraft (60 South African Squadron) which could carry no bombs.[80] Furthermore, no Mosquito fighter-bombers were stationed in the Mediterranean in the summer of 1944, and none could be moved there. There were good reasons for this. The USAAF had no Mossie fighter-bombers, and though after mid-1944 the RAF had six or seven squadrons available in Great Britain, it entrusted only four squadrons with the most exacting missions against Gestapo headquarters and prisons.[81] These units, all concentrated in 140 Wing, were Nos. 21, 464, 487, and 613 Squadrons. Their elite crews were priceless human assets, made all the more so by continuous demand and high losses.[82]

During 1944–45, 140 Wing typically employed from six to twenty aircraft against single-building targets on its most demanding low-level strikes. About one-third of the force was usually launched as a reserve. If one assumes a strike force of just eight aircraft to destroy each target at Auschwitz, a strike force of forty aircraft, or two full squadrons, would have been required. In 1944–45, this amounted to one-half of the very best Mosquito fighter-bomber crews in Britain. Had such a force been transferred to the Mediterranean Theater for a death camp raid, numerous sorties against NOBALL (V-1 rocket) sites, barges, petroleum-oil–and–lubricant depots, roundhouses, airfields, power stations and other German military installations would have been sacrificed, and some of the special pinpoint humanitarian missions might have been delayed or given up. How many innocents in occupied countries—some of them Jews—would then have perished because Gestapo headquarters or the Dutch Central Population Registry might have gone unattacked? Such agonizing questions of asset allocation lay at the heart of military science, and Allied air leaders probably had them in mind when they responded negatively to pleas for an attack on Auschwitz-Birkenau in mid-1944.

Diversions of heavy bombers, B-25s, P-38s, or Mosquitoes with attendant losses could perhaps have been justified had the probability of success been higher. No one then could, or can now, accurately predict how much damage might have been inflicted on the gas chambers and crematoria at Auschwitz, or how much effect the destruction would have had on the "Final Solution." Based on parallel USAAF and RAF experiences during the war, however, the author believes that in any type of operation, destruction or heavy damage to 50 to 60 percent of the structures would have represented the most that could be hoped for on one mission; thus follow-up raids—a mini-campaign—would have been required to assure complete success.

The tragic side effects of bombing on the camps' populations are much easier to envision. Dazed, debilitated, and disoriented, most escapees would have quickly been rounded up. While the able-bodied were forced to pick up the casualties and repair the damage, trains destined for the two camps would have been sent to Mauthausen, Belsen, Buchenwald, or any of the Reich's twenty-odd other camps. The rate of genocide at Auschwitz might have been slowed for a few days or a few weeks, but no one can calculate what impact this might have had on the Holocaust. More certainly it can be said that any low-level air raid on Auschwitz-Birkenau would have been a one-shot proposition because the camps would have been easy to defend against precise low altitude strikes. Cheap passive defenses like decoy buildings, barrage balloons, and smoke pots, together with a few 20mm flak guns, would have sufficed to prevent any further intrusions.

Although Wyman hesitates about trying to bomb railroads serving the extermination camps, other bombing adherents have advocated it.[83] But as Foregger pointed out in 1987, a successful line-cutting campaign requires day-in, day-out attacks over the entire system that serves a selected area—in this case, all of occupied Europe. Unless all routes are simultaneously interdicted and remain out, alternative routes, repair gangs, and make-do will largely negate the effort. Thanks to their operations analysis sections, Allied air staffs knew this resources-results equation with great exactitude.[84]

In fact, despite the immense difficulty and modest rewards of strategic rail-cutting, the USAAF did try repeatedly to disrupt the Reich's transportation system, contrary to some assertions that rail lines and rolling stock were never attacked.[85] Freeman's *Mighty Eighth War Diary* lists no fewer than 145 missions by the Eighth Air Force that included attacks against marshaling yards from the Franco-German border eastward.[86] In addition, the Fifteenth Air Force's effort from Italy, though as yet untabulated, probably nearly doubled the Eighth's pounding. Even though the marshaling yards at Bingen, Hamm, Frankfurt, Munich, Salzburg, Linz, Landshut, and elsewhere were turned into moonscapes, the Germans, relying heavily on forced labor, managed to keep some lines open. What happened in the camps and on the battlefronts, therefore, occurred in spite of bombing, and what might have happened with different priorities remains entirely speculative.[87]

Two other vital observations about the bombing question cannot be overemphasized: attacking Auschwitz might have been illegal under international law, and it would certainly have been morally dubious. Under the Hague Convention of 1907 (Hague, IV), Article 25, "the attack or bombardment, by whatever means, of towns, villages, dwellings, or buildings which are undefended is prohibited."[88] The U.S. War Department's Basic Field Manual FM 27-10, *Rules of Land Warfare*, issued in 1940, quoted the Hague rule verbatim and specifically noted that "by whatever means" signatories meant that bombardment of these undefended localities from balloons or airplanes was prohibited. It also gave three examples of "defended places."[89] Only by torturing the third example, "a place that is occupied by a combatant military force," could Auschwitz-Birkenau have qualified as a legitimate target for bombardment.

Legality aside, bombing Auschwitz also becomes a radically different problem if casualties within the camp are disregarded. This would have made operations by B-17s and B-24s technically feasible, for example. Yet, the underlying dilemma is as plain today as fifty years ago: Would it be moral to kill a minimum of several hundred internees in trying to save others—with no assurance of success—and if so, what tragic ratio would have been acceptable? Ultimately, this is a philosophical or theological dilemma, not a historical one, and it is not the historian's duty to resolve it. Arguments, however, that camp inhabitants would have died anyway, or that the symbolism of bombing would have justified it, or that some within Auschwitz might have welcomed death from the air appear specious. In general, Allied leaders were convinced that the innocent should be spared if possible and, weighing out the possibilities, acted accordingly.[90] When Ultra intelligence officer and later Supreme Court Justice Lewis F. Powell was questioned on this specific point in 1985, he stated that "I am perfectly confident that General [Carl] Spaatz would have resisted any proposal that *we* [italics Powell's] kill the Jewish inmates in order temporarily to put an Auschwitz out of operation. It is not easy to think that a rational person would have made such a recommendation" [to bomb Auschwitz].[91]

Looking back from 1992, the bombing of Auschwitz emerges as a peculiar, and peculiarly difficult, historical conundrum. No bombing took place, and asking why decades later has as yet produced only conjecture. The Wyman thesis attributes the Allied avoidance of death camp bombing to callousness, insensitivity, and even anti-Semitic prejudice in high circles. These attitudes were, Wyman believes, evident in prewar America and persisted after 1941, ultimately producing the abandonment of the Jews to their fate. Clearly, a major part of any historian's task is to find and describe meaningful patterns in the chaos of events and, if possible, to establish causative links between possible motives and observed facts. The writer is not expert in refugee and immigration policy, modern anti-Semitism, or Holocaust studies; it is in nowise his purpose here to debate *Abandonment*'s overall thesis. To date, however, the Wyman school has adduced only inferential and circumstantial evidence that Auschwitz remained inviolate because of indifference or outright antipathy for the plight of European Jews. Corollary proof derived from social attitudes, refugee policy, or diplomatic posturing is wholly insufficient to establish the contentions in *Abandonment*'s Chapter XV and of the bombing school in general. This is especially true considering the poverty of documentation offered in *Abandonment*, as well as that of subsequent commentators. More—much more—than inference is required. It is incumbent upon bombing advocates to describe precisely how Auschwitz might have successfully been attacked, given the capabilities of aircraft and airmen in mid-1944; their availability for the mission(s); the anticipated losses; the probable results; and implications for conduct of the war. The most convincing pro-attack argument would be a hypothetical raid scenario analogous to operations which actually occurred, or a credible model based on operational realities. No bombing advocate has yet constructed such a paradigm, and available evidence indicates that one cannot be.

The author suggests that whatever was said or not said, felt or not felt, about camp bombing among Allied politicians and bureaucratic organs in 1944 was, and is, largely irrelevant to what happened, or could have happened. In the instance of Auschwitz, military policy was driven by availability of intelligence, operational possibilities, by asset allocation, by the rules of war, and by conventional morality. Any Allied option to frustrate the Holocaust from the air was illusory, a fact so unmistakably obvious to contemporary commanders that it was taken for granted and warranted little policy discussion. Inaction may have been colored by ethnic attitudes, but it was ultimately dictated by the immutable exigencies of intelligence, operational considerations, weapons system performance, and available resources. From their own experience and that of their staffs, senior air commanders knew that attempting to bomb Auschwitz would have diverted resources from vital military, industrial, and even humanitarian targets; might have entailed heavy Allied casualties; would have had vague or ephemeral success; would have posed grave legal and moral questions; and would to some degree have prolonged the war. Target committees, the Joint Chiefs of Staff, the War Department, and senior civilian officials also knew that their air power assets were finite and imperfect, and they acted accordingly, even if some of their justifications were not always highly articulate. The author believes, therefore, that an awareness of operational limits, not ethnic motives, best explains the failure to bomb Auschwitz. Allied leaders made the mistakes that all humans do, but the available evidence suggests that avoidance of death camp bombing out of prejudice was not one of them.

8

THE BOMBING OF AUSCHWITZ
REVISITED: A CRITICAL ANALYSIS

Richard H. Levy

THE POSSIBILITY OF bombing Auschwitz was widely discussed in the summer of 1944, but after the war it attracted broad public attention only in 1961, when a draft note prepared by the Jewish Agency (JA) in London in July 1944 was introduced into the Eichmann trial in Jerusalem.[1] The note recommended bombing on moral but not on practical grounds. Though unsigned, unaddressed, and apparently never delivered, the note had been intended for the British Government; its disclosure in 1961 resulted in several articles in the British press,[2] though apparently none in the USA. After a short discussion in Parliament,[3] the Prime Minister promised to consider publication of other relevant documents. Criticism of the non-bombing, however, was rare until 1978, when David Wyman's article "Why Auschwitz Was Never Bombed" appeared.[4]

In Wyman's view, the failure to bomb the gas chambers, crematoria, or Hungarian railways was merely one aspect of a larger American and British culpability. For reasons which we cannot consider here, this proposition fell on fertile soil and produced numerous expressions of righteous indignation, outrage, and shame. A few scholars did subject the issue to serious analysis, including its technical aspects.[5] The following expands this analysis and integrates it with the broader issues.

THE EARLY PROPOSALS

The Nazis must have used virtually every railway line in occupied Europe to deport Jews to the extermination camps in the East, especially Auschwitz, from the beginning of 1942. Yet the suggestion that the deportations could be stopped by bombing railway lines does not seem to have surfaced until mid-May 1944, by which time more than five million of the ultimate six million murders had already been committed. On 16 and 23 (or 24) May two short coded telegrams were sent to Isaac Sternbuch, the representative in Switzerland of the Union of Orthodox Rabbis.[6] They relayed urgent appeals originating in Hungary for the bombing of the Hungarian railways.[7]

Among a host of contributory reasons, conditions in Hungary and the increasing power of the Allied bomber offensive in particular, help to explain why the railway bombing suggestion surfaced only at that particular moment. In April, Hungary contained the last intact Jewish community in occupied Europe, amounting to some 750,000 souls. Starting in mid-April, the Hungarian Jews were subjected to a systematic concentration, to be followed by deportations. While the destination of the deportees was at first known only to be somewhere in Poland, the meaning of deportation was all too clear to the authors of the railway bombing appeals. Capital of a nominally independent state, Budapest still hosted many foreign legations, and neutral diplomats could communicate freely with the outside world.

At the same time, the Allied bomber offensive was finally in full swing. The RAF and the USAAF had reached essentially full strength and were pounding targets in Germany and occupied Europe. The USAAF in particular had, since about the turn of the year, established bases at Foggia in southern Italy from which it was able to attack many hitherto unreachable targets in southern and eastern Germany, Austria, southern Poland, Rumania and, of course, Hungary. The most important were the oil and aircraft industries. Beyond their tangible accomplishments, the bomber fleets over all parts of the Nazi empire had become the clearest harbingers of Allied victory. There was, however, a very large gap between what the bombers did in fact achieve and what various parties imagined their capabilities to be. No effort was made in public to play down the power of the bombers; on the contrary, contemporary USAAF propaganda stressed the precision of their attacks. If some air force officers with access to the best available intelligence exhibited a notable propensity to exaggerate the capabilities of their bombers, who can blame the Jews of Hungary or their friends abroad for believing that bombing could help them?

The routes by which the earliest appeals to bomb the Hungarian railways reached the British and American governments were many and varied. The telegram of 16 May referred specifically to the RAF, and its message should obviously have been delivered to the British Government. While it is not known whether this happened, it is certainly the case that the JA was in frequent contact with the British government at this time. On 2 June, at the request of Isaac Gruenbaum (of the Jewish Agency Executive, JAE), L. C. Pinkerton (U.S. Consul General in Jerusalem) sent a telegraphic message to the War Refugee Board (WRB) in Washington; it reached the State Department on the same day.[8] Chaim Weizmann, President of the JA, was at the Foreign Office on June 2, and met Anthony Eden, British Secretary of State for Foreign Affairs, on June

7.[9] On June 18 Jacob Rosenheim of the New York office of Agudas Israel, upon receipt of a message from Sternbuch in Switzerland, addressed letters to high American government officials; his appeals were relayed to the WRB.[10] Wyman claims that the message from Sternbuch to Rosenheim was delayed by American censorship. This claim is irrelevant since Gruenbaum's telegram of 2 June carrying a similar appeal had long since reached Washington. Wyman does not comment on the apparent lack of action in response to Gruenbaum's appeal.

Martin Gilbert has shown that the fact that Auschwitz was the only destination of the deportees was not known until the end of June. Thus the message sent by Pinkerton to the WRB referred only to "the railways between Hungary and Poland." Rosenheim also referred only to "Poland." Wyman misquotes this proposal when he wrongly refers to "Rosenheim's proposal to bomb rail points between Hungary and Auschwitz."[11] Toward the end of June however, and from that time forward, all appeals sought the bombing of the gas chambers and crematoria at Auschwitz, usually in combination with the Hungarian railways. There could be no clearer indication of the exact time at which wholly credible details of the extermination camp at Auschwitz precise enough to support a bombing appeal reached the West. The first such appeal to reach the United States government came on 24 June, addressed to the WRB in Berne.[12] A similar appeal reached the Foreign Office in London on 27 June.[13] Moshe Shertok, Head of the Political Department of the JA, and Weizmann repeated this request on 30 June,[14] and to Eden himself on 6 July.[15] The Czech Government-in-exile relayed appeals which reached the British Foreign Office on 4 July and the WRB in Washington on 14 July.[16] Wyman says only that "starting in early July, appeals for Air Force action to impede the mass murders increasingly centered on destruction of the Auschwitz gas chambers."[17]

INITIAL REACTIONS

Under its Executive Director, John W. Pehle, the WRB seems to have acquired a virtual monopoly on the transmission of appeals to the War Department, where its designated contact was Assistant Secretary John J. McCloy. Pehle's attitude was therefore critical. Pehle apparently did nothing with Gruenbaum's appeal of 2 June, but Wyman recounts his reaction to Rosenheim's appeal of 18 June as follows: "On June 21, Pehle transmitted the request to the War Department. Three days later, he discussed it with McCloy. Pehle himself expressed doubts about the proposal, but asked that the War Department explore the idea. McCloy agreed to look into it."[18]

This is inadequate to judge contemporary considerations of the feasibility and efficacy of the requested operations. In a Memorandum for the Files,[19] written on the same day (24 June) that he saw McCloy, Pehle noted that he had told McCloy "that I wanted to mention the matter . . . for whatever exploration might be appropriate by the War Department." But he added "that I had several doubts":

> (1) whether it would be appropriate to use military planes and personnel for this purpose; (2) whether it would be difficult to put the railroad line out of commission for a long enough period to do any good; and (3) even assuming that these railroad lines were put out of commission for some period of time, whether it would help the Jews in Hungary.

Pehle had made it "very clear to Mr. McCloy" that he was not, "at this point at least, requesting the War Department to take any action on this proposal, other than appropriately to explore it."

This was no ringing endorsement of the appeal to bomb the Hungarian railways, a fact which Wyman fails to bring out. Pehle's first doubt raised a question that both he and McCloy must have known could be settled only by President Roosevelt. His second and third doubts, however, could receive professional consideration at the War Department.

The WRB was established by President Franklin D. Roosevelt on 22 January, and functioned with some success in a number of spheres. These included the facilitation of negotiations at the fringes of occupied Europe, bribery of corrupt Axis officials, handling of messages, transmission of funds, and many other useful activities. It is understandable that the bombing appeals originating with Jewish and other organizations in Europe were passed to the WRB. It is less clear that the WRB was the appropriate governmental agency to respond to them, and Pehle's doubts underline the point. Wyman quotes a legalistic discussion about the language of the executive order establishing the WRB.[20] The paragraph in question charged the War Department (among others) with executing WRB programs. Wyman seems to suggest that the War Department was required to bomb the Hungarian railways or Auschwitz, merely because the WRB had a program calling for it. Pehle certainly knew better. Such an interpretation of his mandate would have prejudiced Eisenhower's operational command in the European Theater and would have been roundly rejected. Neither McCloy nor anyone else at the War Department had the authority to order Eisenhower to undertake specific operations. In operational matters Eisenhower was subject only to orders from the Commander-in-Chief.

With the arrival in Washington of the earliest appeals for the bombing of the gas chambers and crematoria at Auschwitz, Benjamin Akzin of the WRB wrote an interoffice memo dated 29 June arguing in its favor.[21] But the strongest statement he felt able to make on the likely efficacy of the bombing was that the destruction of the "physical installations" at Auschwitz and Birkenau "might appreciably slow down the systematic slaughter at least temporarily." Wyman has changed Akzin's "might" into "would."

Dr. Leon Kubowitzki, head of the Rescue Department of the World Jewish Congress, met with the WRB on 28 June, and wrote to it on 1 July.[22] He was opposed to the bombing of Auschwitz, arguing that the destruction of the "death installations cannot be done from the air, as the first victims would be the Jews who are gathered in these camps." Dr. Kubowitzki also argued that "such a bombing would be a welcome pretext for the Germans to assert that their Jewish victims have been massacred not by their killers, but by the Allied bombing." As an example of editorial opinion in the New York Yiddish-language press, the Zionist leader and columnist Jacob Fishman wrote a long, agonized article on 27 June, reviewing what might be done to help the Hungarian Jews. Three sentences were devoted to the question of bombing Auschwitz.[23] He considered an argument against the bombing (most of the victims would be Jews), and an argument for it (after the revolt in Treblinka, hundreds of Jews succeeded in escaping to the woods and joined the partisans). He was unable to reach a conclusion: "I am still thinking about the idea. . . ."

The JAE in Jerusalem was opposed, and even suppressed an appeal for the bombing of Auschwitz.[24] Gruenbaum reported on 7 June that when he met with Pinkerton on 2 June he asked the latter to transmit to Washington an appeal to bomb "the death camps in Poland." Foreshadowing Dr. Kubowitzki's arguments, Pinkerton asked, "Will this not cause the deaths of many Jews? And will not German propaganda claim that the Americans are participating in the extermination of the Jews?" He then declined to transmit the request unless it was made in writing. In Gruenbaum's words:

> I was forced to consult with the colleagues and they all expressed their opinion that we should not request a thing like that because Jews might get killed in the death camps! I explained to them that in such places all the Jews are about to be killed. They didn't listen to me. They do not want to take such a responsibility upon themselves. They prefer not to prevent mass murder for fear that Jews will be killed by bombs.

Gruenbaum was a member of the JAE, and there can be no doubt that "the colleagues" refers to this body. The minutes of its meeting on 11 June show that after Gruenbaum presented his case, Ben-Gurion (then chairman), Rabbi Fishman, Dr. Schmorek ("We cannot take upon ourselves the responsibility of a bombing which would cause the death of a single Jew"), Dr. Joseph ("He too opposes the suggestion to ask the Americans to bomb the camps, and so to murder Jews") and Dr. Senator ("It is regrettable that Mr. Gruenbaum spoke of it with the American Consul") all spoke against the idea. Kaplan, Schapira, Ben-Tzvi, Hantke, Granovsky, and Eisenberg voiced no disagreement. Ben-

Gurion summarized: "The view of the board is that we should not ask the Allies to bomb places where there are Jews."

Gruenbaum's disgust at this position is plain, but he seems to have remained a minority of one in the Executive. Apparently no appeal to bomb the death camps was transmitted from Jerusalem to Washington. Indeed, having appealed on 2 June for railway bombing, nothing further on the subject of bombing was heard from the JA in Jerusalem until 13 September. On that date, with or without the concurrence of his colleagues, and acting in response to reports that more deportations from Budapest to Auschwitz were imminent, Gruenbaum telegraphed Shertok in London suggesting that five Hungarian railways and Auschwitz itself should be bombed.[25] Shertok evidently passed this telegram on to the British Government. There were in fact no renewed deportations from Hungary to Auschwitz (though deportations from many other places did continue), and two of the five railways that Gruenbaum listed were already largely in Soviet hands. In 1961 Gruenbaum told a reporter that he had sent telegraphic appeals for bombing to Stalin, Churchill, and Roosevelt.[26] Any such telegrams would have been sent over the objections of the JAE. It does not appear that copies have been found in Churchill's papers, Roosevelt's papers, or the Zionist Archives. The Jewish Agency in London would, however, revert to the subject of bombing, as will be seen.

Even though the views of Dr. Kubowitzki, Fishman, and eleven out of twelve members of the JAE might, with hindsight, be judged wrong, they were obviously sincerely held. In his paper, however, Wyman relegates Dr. Kubowitzki's opinion to a footnote, and in his book it doesn't appear at all. But he does say[27] (without citing sources) that unidentified "Jewish leaders in Europe and the United States, assuming the use of heavy bombers and the consequent death of some inmates, wrestled with the moral problem involved. Most concluded that loss of life under the circumstances was justifiable."

On the JAE (to which Wyman makes no reference), Gruenbaum was a minority of one in reaching this conclusion. Were Wyman's unidentified "Jewish leaders" aware that "some inmates" might mean many thousands? Does "most" refer to a large or a small majority? The issue was still divisive in 1978.[28]

Here then are a number of contemporary views: Pehle had serious doubts; Akzin approved but was extremely cautious about the bombing's probable efficacy; Fishman couldn't make up his mind; Dr. Kubowitzki and all Gruenbaum's colleagues on the JAE were opposed. It appears that no one was willing and able to argue that the bombing would be feasible, effective, and proper.

THE FEASIBILITY OF RAILWAY BOMBING

In London, Weizmann and Shertok read an Aide-Memoire to Eden on 6 July.[29] The last paragraph contained five suggestions. The last of these was that the railway from Budapest to Birkenau, and the death camps at Birkenau and else-where, should be bombed. It is not clear why Weizmann and Shertok took a position opposed to the JAE in Jerusalem. There is no indication that the JAE ever changed its collective mind, and some indication that it did not.

In any event, the request was made, and Eden reported on the meeting to Churchill the same day. On the next day, 7 July, Churchill responded favorably to the bombing request, writing "Get anything out of the Air Force that you can." Accordingly, still on the seventh, Eden wrote to the Secretary of State for Air, Sir Archibald Sinclair, asking him to examine the feasibility of stopping the operation of the death camps by bombing the railway lines leading to Birkenau.[30] Sinclair was also asked to examine the feasibility of bombing the camps themselves. On 15 July he replied, in part:

> You wrote to me on 7th July to ask if anything could be done by bombing to stop the murder of Jews in Hungary. I entirely agree that it is our duty to consider every possible plan [but] I am advised that [interrupting the railways] is out of our power. It is only by an enormous concentration of bomber forces that we have been able to interrupt communications in Normandy; the distance of Silesia from our bases entirely rules out our doing anything of the kind.[31]

After Rosenheim's railway bombing appeal was delivered by Pehle to the US War Department, McCloy replied, on June 26: "The War Department is of the opinion that the suggested air operation is impracticable for the reason that it could be executed only by diversion of considerable air support essential to the success of our forces now engaged in decisive operations."[32]

Wyman is persuaded that this language constitutes an evasive brush-off. Yet Sinclair and his advisors clearly supported McCloy's opinion. McCloy was not free to provide still classified detail from experience in Normandy to Pehle. Among many other authorities who could be cited in support of these profes-sional opinions is Marshal of the Royal Air Force Sir Arthur Harris, wartime head of RAF Bomber Command. Harris was never consulted about bombing Auschwitz or its railways during the war, but in a 1962 interview (clearly un-aware of Sinclair's letter) concluded: "In the light of all these factors, I personally fail to see how the cutting of the relevant rail lines to Auschwitz could have achieved any effective result except for a few days, unless a totally impracticable (numerically) effort was applied virtually continuously to that end."[33] Wyman himself essentially accepts the same point of view:

> In the case of railroad lines, the answer is not clear-cut. Railroad bombing had its problems and was the subject of long-lasting disputes within the Allied military. Successful cutting of railways necessitated close observa-tion of the severed lines and frequent rebombing, since repairs took only

a few days. Even bridges, which were costly to hit, were often back in operation in three or four days.[34]

The only question, indeed, is how Wyman can describe the situation as "not clear-cut." Preventing the Hungarian deportations by bombing railways was quite simply beyond the power of any conceivable force that the Allies could have brought to bear. To understand more clearly that this was so we need only to study the furious debates (Harris participated actively) over the use of air power against the railways in Northwest France.[35] After protracted and heated arguments, a very large part of the air forces (strategic and tactical, American and British) based in Britain was committed to the so-called Transportation Plan. Devised by Solly Zuckerman, this plan called for attacks not only on key lines and bridges, but also on rail yards, sidings, stations, sheds, repair shops, roundhouses, turntables, signal systems, locomotives, and rolling stock. Such attacks took place continuously for many weeks before and after the invasion. The prevailing view at the time was that anything less than a program as broad as this was a waste of time and effort. This view would certainly have been familiar, if not to McCloy personally, then at least to his advisers. Post-war hindsight fully vindicated the contemporary views.[36]

The discussions leading up to the Transportation Plan were naturally carried on in secret. The conclusions could not have been known to Gruenbaum, Stern-buch, Rosenheim and others. Nor in all probability were they known to Pehle. The desperation of the prospective victims in 1944 is wholly understandable, as was the eagerness of those not in danger to consider all possible means of assistance. The professional evaluations of Sinclair and McCloy were nevertheless correct, as Wyman himself is forced to acknowledge.

THE END OF THE HUNGARIAN DEPORTATIONS

It is useful to set the chronology of the Hungarian deportations against the discussions of the railway bombing proposals. The facts are indeed tragic. The deportations started on 15 May 1944. By 7 June, 289,357 Hungarian Jews had been deported and the Carpathians and Transylvania cleared.[37] By 17 June the total had risen to 340,162 and the region north of Budapest from Kosice to the Reich frontier cleared. By 30 June deportations had risen to 381,661 and the region east of the Danube without Budapest cleared; by 9 July deportations had risen to 437,402 and the region west of the Danube without Budapest cleared. Pressure on the Hungarian Government halted the deportations on 8 July, the last transports arriving at Auschwitz on 11 July. When the deportations stopped, the Hungarian provinces had lost virtually all their Jews, but in and around Budapest there remained over 300,000, according to the contemporary estimate of the JA.

On 18 July the news that the Hungarian deportations had ceased reached London, where it was widely publicized.[38]

It can be seen that the discussions between Rosenheim, Pehle, and McCloy (18–26 June), and still more the discussions between Shertok, Weizmann, Eden, Churchill, and Sinclair (6–15 July) were far too late to affect the outcome, even if anything had been possible. In addition, the timing of these discussions vividly indicates the complete absence of any up-to-date intelligence on which particular railways out of Hungary were being used at any given moment. This problem alone would have made it very hard to conduct effective military operations.

Wyman concedes some merit to the argument that railway bombing after 8 July would not have helped,[39] but then highlights a further appeal for bombing the railways in late August when renewed deportations from Budapest appeared imminent.[40] He suggests that the "War Department could have agreed to stand ready, if deportations had resumed, to spare some bomb tonnage for those two railroads, provided bombers were already scheduled to fly near them on regular missions." He does not reconcile this suggestion with his own detailed explanation of the difficulties of railroad bombing. Since the "previously scheduled war missions" would have had to be abandoned if the deportation railways were attacked, the routing of these missions were irrelevant. He apparently believes that only two railroad routes connected Budapest to Auschwitz. The vague reference to "some bomb tonnage" avoids the hard question of the minimum tonnage required to do any good and the maximum that might have been "spared." Finally, no one at the War Department had the authority to make operational agreements of this kind.

In this vein, Wyman continues, "the United States could have demonstrated concern for the Jews even if the bombing had to be sporadic." Wyman does not explain why the concern of the United States would have been demonstrated by standing ready to bomb two Hungarian railroads while doing nothing about the numerous other railroads which were bringing victims to Auschwitz from all of occupied Europe (except Hungary) until November—50,000 were gassed there between 7 July and 20 August. Wyman observes that on September 13, 324 American heavy bombers flew within six miles of one of the railways which might have been used for deportations, and that a total of 2,700 American heavy bomber missions were carried out within easy reach of both railways between July and October. But Wyman fails to distinguish between the undoubted ability of the bombers to fly over a railroad and their very limited ability to interrupt it. Even if every one of the 2,700 missions had been redirected to the railways, the average of 27 a day would have been wholly inadequate to the purpose of interrupting them.

In any case, the Hungarian Government had already stopped the deportations on 8 July. Many efforts had been made to achieve this aim, among them pressure from the Swedes, the Swiss, the Vatican, and others[41] (all encouraged by the British and the Americans). Formidable warnings were broadcast by the BBC on 5, 6 and 11 July to all those involved in the deportations,[42] and Gilbert appears to credit these broadcasts with saving more than a hundred thousand.[43] But according to Hilberg,[44] the strongest point made by the Hungarian Prime Minister Döme Sztójay in a meeting on 5 July with the German Ambassador and Plenipotentiary to Hungary Edmund Veesenmayer was the following: Hungarian counterintelligence had intercepted and deciphered three secret teletype messages from the US and British missions in Berne to their governments dealing with the fate of the deported Jews and suggesting the bombing of destination points and railroad lines, including "target bombing of all collaborating Hungarian and German agencies—with exact and correct street and house numbers in Budapest." This kind of bombing was, of course, well beyond the power of the Allies. Nevertheless, Hilberg noted the irony: "History plays strangely with its participants. The Jewish relief committee in Budapest had sent these requests to Berne to be transmitted through diplomatic channels to the Allied capitals, where no action was taken on them. But fate had intervened. The Hungarians in their eagerness had intercepted the messages and had thereupon frightened themselves to death."

A different interpretation is given by Gilbert,[45] who suggests that these telegrams, which were sent from Berne on 26 June, may have been deliberately leaked to the Hungarians. He also says that the leakage was accomplished by the simple device of sending the messages *en clair*,[46] thus offering the amusing picture of Hungarian counterintelligence claiming to have deciphered decoded messages. If Gilbert is right, the individuals who authored the "leaks" should be remembered as unsung heroes. Wasserstein says that it was the Germans who intercepted the British message and that they drew it to the attention of the Hungarians.[47]

The perceived threat was greatly strengthened by the Allied bombing campaign in general, and the bombing of Hungary in particular. Hilberg refers to only two raids on Budapest at the end of June, but Fenyo notes that Hungary was raided on 13 and 17 April; 5 and 11 May; 2, 13, 14 and 26 June; 2 July; "and so on."[48] The raid on 2 July compared in scale to the major raids directed against German cities in the same period. Additional massive raids took place on 14 and 30 July. Gilbert describes the raids of the second as "an unusually heavy American bomber attack on the marshaling yards of Budapest"; John E. Fogg observes that more than 700 B-17s and B-24s bombed Budapest's oil refineries, aircraft factories, and railway targets.[49] Clearly, the effect of the leaked telegrams would have been much less without the actual bombing, especially the raid of 2 July on Budapest.

That the railways were not bombed as or when requested does not constitute proof that "no action was taken." The actual bombing of Hungary helped bring the total cessation of deportations. Thus the 300,000 Jews in Budapest were spared from deportation to Auschwitz and certain death. This in turn provided

the opportunity for Raoul Wallenberg to perform his g\
arrival in Budapest in July. In terms of lives saved, this was ᵢ
result than any that could possibly have resulted from the ten
tion of a few provincial railway lines. It can be argued that (ever
consequence was wholly unintended) the most effective possi\
power was made. The indirect character of this episode lends su\
view, often expressed at the time, that the most effective way to he   ,ews
was to win the war as soon as possible.

OTHER REACTIONS

We have seen how, when the first appeals to bomb the gas chambers and
crematoria at Auschwitz were made, a sympathetic Akzin was able to offer only
a highly conditional view of its likely efficacy, while Kubowitzki and all of
Gruenbaum's colleagues on the JAE opposed the idea outright. Fishman could
not make up his mind. Wyman misquoted Akzin, omitted Kubowitzki from his
book, and made no reference to the JAE or Fishman. He also made little or no
reference to the contemporary evaluations of Weizmann and Shertok, Sinclair
(who had a reputation for sympathy with Zionism),[50] or of the Czech
Government-in-exile, all of which we shall now examine.

Weizmann and Shertok made their bombing proposal to Eden on July 6.
Eden[51] wrote to Sinclair on 7 July, saying "Dr. Weizmann admitted that there
seemed to be little enough that we could do to stop these horrors, but he
suggested that something might be done to stop the operation of the death
camps by bombing. . . ." Five days after the meeting, on 11 July, the JA in London prepared a Note[52] that expressed a rather different view about the proposed
bombing of the death camps. This note represents the most closely argued
contemporary Jewish viewpoint available to us. It said:

> The bombing of the death camps is . . . hardly likely to achieve the sal-
> vation of the victims to any appreciable extent. Its physical effects can
> only be the destruction of plant and personnel, and possibly the hastening
> of the end of those already doomed. The resulting dislocation of the
> German machinery for systematic wholesale murder may possibly cause
> delay in the execution of those still in Hungary. . . . This in itself is val-
> uable as far as it goes. But it may not go very far, as other means of
> extermination can be quickly improvised.

This is certainly consistent with the view ascribed by Eden to Weizmann. But
the Note then went on to say that "The main purpose of the bombing should
be its many-sided and far-reaching moral effect."

The Note itself, which concentrates exclusively on the Hungarian Jews, is

...ed to anyone in particular, nor is it signed. But Hausner describes Weizmann's urgent plea to bomb Auschwitz." Eban also ascribes it to Weizmann. Wasserstein quotes Barlas, who says that it was a "Memorandum from M. Shertok to the British Foreign Office," but does not say how he knows this. Rose quotes from the Note, and ascribes its views directly to Weizmann and Shertok.[53] On the other hand, Gilbert does not offer any opinion as to who prepared the Note, nor who approved it, nor to whom it was sent. The document has apparently not been recovered from British files. There is no indication that the British ever seriously considered an operation expected to achieve little more than a "many-sided and far-reaching moral effect." It is of some interest to know whether Weizmann and Shertok kept their view of the "main purpose of the bombing" to themselves; they might have done this in the belief that it would be much harder to persuade the British to undertake an operation whose main purpose was to be its "moral effect." Perhaps, with Kubowitzki, they feared the use that Nazi propaganda would make of the bombing. Indeed, it seems entirely possible that neither the Note nor its position on the main purpose of the bombing were ever transmitted to the Foreign Office!

The Note itself says that "a detailed description of the two camps [Auschwitz and Birkenau], contained in a report submitted to Allied Governments and published by the Jewish Telegraphic Agency, is attached. It is understood that this report (received since the original suggestion for bombing was made) emanated from Czech underground sources." Since the report itself is not attached to the copy of the Note in the Zionist Archives, and since no other information on this report is available, it is impossible to identify it with certainty. But the timing strongly suggests that it was derived from the "Vrba-Wetzler" report which was translated and distributed by unknown hands at about this time. One version of this report was received at the Foreign Office from the Czechoslovak Government-in-exile on 4 July and contains appeals to bomb the crematoria and the railways leading to Auschwitz.[54] Whatever was done with the Note, however, Sinclair held the same view that it expressed. On the 15th he replied to Eden's 7 July note that "even if the plant was destroyed, I am not clear that it would really help the victims."[55]

Another appeal to bomb the camps was transmitted by the World Jewish Congress to McCloy at the War Department on 8 or 9 August at the request of Frischer of the Czech Government-in-exile in London. Frischer wrote, "I believe that destruction of the gas chambers and crematoria in Auschwitz by bombing would have a certain effect now. . . . Germans might possibly stop further mass exterminations. . . . Bombing of railway communications in this same area would also be of importance."[56] The individual who forwarded this request was the same Kubowitzki who had argued against bombing the camps on 1 July. There is evidence to suggest that he still opposed the idea as late as November after the gassing had stopped.[57] His letter forwarding Frischer's proposal lacks any hint of an endorsement; indeed, the language suggests that he was taking care of an obligation to Frischer in the most perfunctory way.

McCloy replied on 14 August in a letter which has been much quoted. McCloy's general attitude toward the Jews has been much criticized, but the texts of his letters are quite reasonable. To his previous comments on the same subject, he now added doubts about its efficacy.[58] In expressing such doubts, he joined Akzin, Kubowitzki, Shertok, Frischer, Pehle, Fishman, Ben-Gurion and all but one of the members of the JAE in Jerusalem.

It is not known if McCloy was aware of Kubowitzki's opposition to the bombing. He might have been informed by Pehle after 1 July, or he might have inferred it from the tone of Kubowitzki's letter. Presumably, if McCloy had responded that he favored the proposal and planned to put it up for consideration to FDR, Kubowitzki would have taken immediate steps to see that both McCloy and FDR clearly understood his opposition.

BOMBING AUSCHWITZ—LIKELY EFFECTIVENESS IN HINDSIGHT last main point?

Clearly, many people thought about the efficacy of bombing the gas chambers and crematoria in 1944. However, nearly all the written material now available is limited to expressions such as "might appreciably slow down the slaughter, at least temporarily," or "Germans might possibly stop further mass exterminations" or "even if the plant was destroyed, I am not clear that it would really help the victims." But we must now examine the question of efficacy from the entirely different standpoint of hindsight. Based upon what is now known, does it appear that the bombing would have been more effective than believed at the time?

As good a place as any to start is to note that Wyman has failed to enumerate the gas chambers and crematoria correctly. He says that there were four of each.[59] He quotes Olga Lengyel but seems to have overlooked the title of her book, *Five Chimneys*.[60] Uwe Dietrich Adam says that two gas chambers and one crematorium were located in Auschwitz I (Main Camp), at some distance from Auschwitz II (Birkenau); one of the chambers is described as experimental, having been used as early as 3 September 1941; the other was used until October 1942.[61] Yahil says that in May "the pace of the extermination process was set at an unprecedented level, using all five crematoria" (four built only in 1943, the other somewhat older).[62] To complicate matters further, Adam lists a total of ten gas chambers active at various times in Auschwitz II. Of these, four were in "Bunker 2" and were kept in service until the autumn of 1944. According to Pressac, between May and the beginning of July 1944, some 200,000 to 250,000 Hungarian Jews were annihilated in the gas chambers and incineration furnaces of Crematoria II and III, the gas chamber and five incineration ditches of Crematoria V, and the gas chamber and incineration ditch of Bunker 2/V.[63] The facility at Bunker 2/V was formed from the original four small gas chambers of Bunker 2 by removing the internal walls. This made the total seven, the number Foregger cites.[64] The remaining two gas chambers at Auschwitz II, according to Adam, were in Bunker I; these were "subsequently demolished," he says, without giving a date. Confusion remains: is Yahil's "No. 1" to be identified with the gas chamber at Auschwitz I, or with the modified gas chamber in Bunker 2/V? Pressac is clear that main gas chamber IV was not used at this time, but this contradicts Yahil. Still, the confusion cannot alter the fact that the four main gas chambers were not the only ones available and in use at this time.

Reports reaching London in 1944 identified only the four main gas chambers and crematoria in 1944. I have found no contemporary reference to the others. One of the sketches reviewed by Foregger shows Auschwitz I (Main Camp), but the one or two gas chambers are missing.[65] Hausner quotes Weizmann informing Eden "Four crematoria are active daily in Auschwitz."[66] If Weizmann's mistake was excusable in 1944, Wyman should not have repeated it in 1978, although he is not alone. The entire post-war literature on the subject appears to contain only one paper in which the author does not assume without discussion that Gas Chambers and Crematoria II, III, IV and V constituted a complete list of the relevant targets. The exception is Foregger, who says without further comment that "the target was the four installations containing gas chambers and crematoria at the west end of the Birkenau camp."[67] An air raid destroying only the four main gas chambers and crematoria at Auschwitz II would have left intact the gas chamber and incineration ditch of Bunker 2/V, as well as up to four additional gas chambers divided between Auschwitz I and Auschwitz II.

This is no mere quibble. The gassings of Hungarian Jews at a rate of 10,000 or even 12,000 a day, ran from mid-May until the abrupt termination on 8 July of the Hungarian deportations (which was known in London on 18 July). The last Hungarian transport arrived on 11 July. According to Wyman,[68] from 7 July until gassing stopped in November, deaths by gas amounted to about 150,000— that is, an average of perhaps 1,300 a day, little more than 10 percent of the previous rate. Thus, before 7 July, when killing operations were at full capacity and even fell behind, bombing Gas Chambers and Crematoria II, III, IV and V would have caused some disruption. After 7 July the same bombing would scarcely have inconvenienced the murderers, leaving untouched several other operable gas chambers at Auschwitz I and II. Pressac has estimated the capacity of the gas chamber at Auschwitz I as 500 to 700 persons at a time, that in Bunker 1, or the "red house," as 450 to 600 and that in Bunker 2, also known as Bunker V, or the "white house," as 700 to 900.[69] The last of these was in operation in the summer of 1944, when the status of the others is less clear. The facility at Auschwitz I is still being shown to tourists. These gas chambers were quite capable of performing their function several times per day.

How soon after the first appeals could an attack have bee[n] executed? Knowing that there was an extermination camp at Aus[chwitz] thing; locating the gas chambers and crematoria with sufficie[nt] bomb them was quite another. Foregger has analyzed the topo[graphic] mation in various sketches, one of which was made available Office on 22 August, the others published by the WRB on 7 November.[70] These sketches vary so greatly that targeting even the four main gas chambers would have been very doubtful. They were based on escapees' reports, but none of the escapees was available in England, and the original reports had been copied and translated by an unknown number of hands. One sketch mislocates the camp with respect to the river Sola, and leaves out the main line and spur railways. According to Hodges, one of the escapees disavowed one of the sketches supplied to Foregger.[71] Photographs of Auschwitz II[72] were available, but could not be identified at the time for what they really were. At the very least, aerial reconnaissance would have been needed, and even then it is hard to see how the exact targets could have been pinpointed without the aid of escapees. Kitchens[73] concluded that "it is unreasonable to think that sufficient intelligence to properly assess . . . targets could have been in hand before early to mid-August." Besides adequate intelligence, the bombing would also have required the authorization of President Roosevelt. There never was the slightest chance that the gas chambers could have been bombed before the second half of August.

But even if by some miracle all of the gas chambers had been destroyed, including those whose existence was *unknown*, Groban has pointed out just how easy it would have been to improvise more.[74] He also reminds us that at Babi Yar, the Nazis shot 33,000 Jews in just two days (29 and 30 September 1941). At Majdanek, on 3 November 1943, during what the SS euphemistically called a "harvest festival," 18,000 Jews were machine-gunned in front of the ditches that the victims were made to dig.[75] In a 1972 interview Albert Speer said that if Auschwitz had been bombed, the SS would have reverted to the system of shooting-commandos which the Einsatzgruppen had used in Russia.[76] Factual details are given by Pressac and Nyiszli.[77] The latter describes the scene which he witnessed at Auschwitz in which the victims were pushed directly into cremation ditches after being shot in the back of the neck, or even still alive. When both ditches were operating, the "output" varied from 5,000 to 6,000 a day, "better" than the crematoria. He says that this method was used on the "surplus," i.e., those for whom there was no room in the crematoria. Pressac suggests that the method may have been used at a time during the summer when there was a shortage of Zyklon-B. Referring to the same facts, Hilberg says that to cope with the bodies when the transports exceeded the capacity of the gas chambers and crematoria:

Oberscharführer Moll was working full steam. He employed four Jewish Sonderkommandos in four shifts, a total force of between 1500 and 2000

[115]

en. . . . Eight pits were dug, each about four by sixty yards in size. . . . Although the corpses burned slowly during rain or misty weather, the pits were found to be the cheapest and most efficient method of body disposal.[78]

Wyman asserted in 1978 that "bombing the gas chambers and crematoria would have saved many lives." In response to Groban's criticism he conceded that he "did not claim that mass killing would have been impossible without Auschwitz," but nonetheless continued to maintain that "without gas chambers and crematoria the Nazis would have been forced to reassess the extermination program in light of the need to commit new and virtually non-existent man-power resources to mass killing."[79] Is this reassessment the best he could have urged upon McCloy, or Roosevelt? Most observers, including Dawidowicz,[80] agree that the Nazis gave a very high priority indeed to the Final Solution, even when labor and transport were desperately short. The Nazis' reassessment might, of course, have required some improvisation, as the JA suggested, but only to the extent of perhaps 10 percent of the original capacity for gassing. The roughly 1,300 murders a day after 8 July represented only a quarter of the capacity of the shooting and incineration method already in use. This method was invulnerable to bombing. But Wyman's 1978 retreat is nowhere to be found in his book, published six years later.

As noted, Wyman says that some 150,000 Jews were gassed at Auschwitz after 7 July, and he adds that if:

the earliest pleas for bombing the gas chambers had moved swiftly to the United States, and if they had drawn a positive and rapid response, the movement of the 437,000 Jews who were deported from Hungary to Auschwitz would most likely have been broken off and additional lives numbering in the hundreds of thousands . . . saved.

Here Wyman implies that the 150,000 Jews gassed after July 7 would have been saved by bombing the chambers at that time, and that an additional 437,000 might have been saved by still prompter bombing of the gas chambers. This new claim is chronologically impossible by a wide margin.[81]

BOMBING AUSCHWITZ: OPERATIONAL CONSIDERATIONS

The weakest part of Wyman's work still remains to be analyzed, the operational aspect of bombing the gas chambers and crematoria. First, however, we must dispose of two more details from Sinclair's letter to Eden of 15 July, where he wrote, "Bombing the plant is out of the bounds of possibility for [RAF] Bomber

Command, because the distance is too great for the attack to ⬚
night."[82] Its aircraft, all based in England, were quite lightly ⬚
pended on darkness to penetrate German defenses. The distan⬚
covered at night ruled out bombing beyond a range correspon⬚
that of Berlin. In addition, Bomber Command's ability to hit s⬚
night was practically nil, especially beyond the range of the ra⬚
aids then in use. Harris agreed with Sinclair when, in a 1962 inter⁄iew, he said
that his responsibility for the selection of targets from the limited group laid
down in their strategic directives was governed almost entirely by the weather,
tactical feasibility, and the extent of darkness as affecting range.[83] Group Captain
Leonard Cheshire V.C., a highly decorated hero of Bomber Command, said, in
a 1961 interview "It would have had to be done by Lancasters, and so would
have had to be a night operation. . . . On a moonlit night, going in low, we
could have bombed it accurately.[84] This seems to contradict Sinclair and Harris,
but it appears that when Cheshire made this statement he was not aware that
the raid was requested in the summer of 1944. In a 1982 interview, told that
bombing Auschwitz would have taken place in the summer, he said, "You are
asking a lot at this extreme range in knowing we have to get ourselves out
without full cover of night—because it is summer now."[85]

Although the British could not attack Auschwitz, and the USAAF operated
only by day and in clear weather, there is a controversy over whether the camp
could have been located at night by the light of its own installations. Loebel
writes that in fact the crematoria, going full blast, emitted bright red fiery
plumes which might have been visible at night from 75 miles away.[86] But Wasserstein says that, "The danger of an air attack on Auschwitz later led to a
cessation of the burning of bodies in open trenches at night as a consequence
of protests by anti-aircraft units at the camp."[87] Brugioni and Poirier examined
aerial reconnaissance photographs taken on 4 April, 26 June (when mass gassings of the Hungarian Jews was under way), 26 July, 25 August, and 13 September, finding no indication of smoke or flames emanating from the chimneys.[88]
Pressac[89] considers the absence of smoke or flames in the photographs of 26
June, 25 August, and 13 September coincidental, since all three dates corresponded to temporary lulls in the activity. In any event, nothing was known on
this subject where it counted, and even if the chimneys had been emitting smoke
and flame, it would still have been a very difficult job indeed to strike them
with the required precision.

After ruling out the use of the RAF, Sinclair pointed out that a daylight
attack on Auschwitz by the Americans:

would be a costly and hazardous operation. It might be ineffective and,
even if the plant was destroyed, I am not clear that it would really help
the victims. There is just one possibility, and that is bombing the camps,
and possibly dropping weapons at the same time, in the hope that some

e victims may be able to escape. We did something of the kind in
rance, when we made a breach in the walls of a prison camp and we
think that 150 men who had been condemned to death managed to escape. The difficulties of doing this in Silesia are, of course enormously
greater and even if the camp was successfully raided, the chances of escape would be small indeed.[90]

Sinclair refers to a raid on a prison at Amiens in February using 19 RAF De
Havilland D.H.98 Mosquito bombers. This raid,[91] coordinated with the French
resistance, aimed at breaching the walls of a small prison to free partisans being
held by the Gestapo for execution. It was known even when Sinclair wrote that
the raid had achieved only mixed results. At Auschwitz no local coordination
was possible, and knowledge of at least some of the extremely elaborate arrangements[92] put in place by Himmler in February 1943 to guard against mass
breaks during air raids would have been discouraging.

Sinclair did not suggest that Mosquitoes could be used against Auschwitz,
but in a letter to the editor, Lawrence Blum argued that the Mosquito might
have been capable of success.[93] Wyman accepted this with alacrity, commenting
that "requests for bombing the gas chambers and the deportation railways were
also made of the British government, which, like the US government, refused
without giving any real consideration to the proposals."[94] This assertion cannot
be reconciled with Sinclair's reasoned letter of July 15. Following Blum's suggestion, Wyman obtained[95] a letter from the Air Historical Branch of the Ministry of Defence in London, assuring him that at least 44 Mosquitoes were
stationed at Allied air bases in Italy in June. Thus reinforced, he wrote in his
book:

> The most effective means of all for destroying the killing installations
> would have been to dispatch about twenty British Mosquitoes to Ausch-
> witz, a project that should have been possible to arrange with the RAF.
> This fast fighter-bomber had ample range for the mission, and its tech-
> nique of bombing at very low altitudes had proven extremely precise.[96]

In his 1961 statement quoted above, Cheshire, who flew Mosquitoes as well as
Lancasters during the war, ruled out the use of Mosquitoes for an attack on
Auschwitz.[97] Unfortunately, he did not give a detailed reason, and the subject
has attracted much uninformed comment. The use of Mosquitoes for an attack
on Auschwitz was also discussed by Dawidowicz, Foregger, Hodges, Kitchens,
and others,[98] who noted various arguments against the idea. But none of these
authors seems to have noticed the elementary point that, notwithstanding Wyman's statement to the contrary, the Mosquito did not have sufficient range to
bomb Auschwitz. The whole discussion is entirely beside the point. The Mos-

quito's inadequate range was probably why Cheshire ruled out its use. Two versions of the Mosquito interest us here, and Wyman has confused them.[99] The photo-reconnaissance version carried 760 gallons of fuel, giving it a still air range of 1,500 or 1,600 miles. It carried cameras, but neither bomb racks nor bombs. Using Italian bases, it was used for several high-altitude reconnaissance missions over Auschwitz in 1944. The bomber version had a maximum fuel load of 539 gallons "with a useful operational load" (i.e., bombs), but could carry two 50-gallon drop tanks at the expense of its bomb load. This gave it a still air range of 1,430 miles, but a maximum *operational* radius of only 535 miles. Mosquito bombers based at Foggia could not reach Auschwitz, 620 miles away.[100] How did Wyman know that the Mosquito "had ample range for the mission" and that "about twenty" was the right number? Is it possible that he correctly estimated attrition on the way to the target? Bomb loads? Bomb dispersions? The number of targets? Since he has got the most basic facts about the Mosquito wrong, this seems unlikely.

Wyman offered two other operational possibilities. He proposed that North American B-25 Mitchell medium bombers might have flown with one of the missions to Auschwitz.[101] The Mitchell was, however, by the standards of the day, lightly armed and obsolescent. It was not used in 1944 on deep penetration daylight raids. But Wyman wrote that the Mitchell could have "hit with surer accuracy from lower altitudes." The heavy bombers, we are informed, operated from 20,000 to 26,000 feet, whence "complete accuracy was rarely possible." Why does Wyman think they stayed so high, if it affected their accuracy? Could it have been the flak, deadly at lower altitudes? Were the Mitchells immune to flak? Wyman stated that an even more precise alternative would have been to use "a few" Lockheed P-38 Lightning dive-bombers, which "could have knocked out the murder buildings without danger to the inmates."[102] His basis for this claim is the Lightning raid against Ploesti on June 10. On this occasion 36 Lightnings were used as dive-bombers, and a further 39 as escorts.[103] But of 75 planes, 23 were lost. Do 75 planes constitute more or less than "a few" for Wyman? Three refineries suffered only partial damage, and the experiment was therefore not repeated. The refineries, however, were much larger than the proposed targets at Birkenau. Wyman gives the distance for this mission as 1,255 miles, but the straight line distance from Brindisi to Ploesti is 515 miles. This may well indicate confusion between straight-line and operational-track distances. The loss of 23 P-38s on June 10 reminds us that German air defense was not as weak as Wyman suggests. While it certainly varied from day to day and place to place, the claim that it was negligible as of summer 1944 is certainly inaccurate.[104]

Forty years after the fact, Wyman offered three operational solutions (Mosquito bombers, Mitchell bombers at moderate altitudes, Lightnings), all of them seriously flawed. The gas chambers and crematoria at Auschwitz could hardly have been the only group of small targets worthy of attention. Wyman's solutions could be accepted only if he were able to point to other successful operations of the same type at comparable ranges. This he has not done.

There was in fact just one way in which the Allies could have destroyed the four known killing installations at Auschwitz, the same one available for the destruction of its industrial installations—namely, the use of the heavy bombers of the U.S. Fifteenth Air Force, based in Italy, with fighter escorts, for good-weather daylight raids. Such flights might have combined raids on nearby industries with details against the gas chambers and crematoria. Their number would have had to offer a good probability of achieving the desired destruction while bombing from the usual high altitudes even though "complete accuracy was rarely possible from such heights."[105] Groban describes the technique in use at the time, which it would not be unfair to describe as plastering the targets with bombs.[106]

A very rough estimate of the number of bombs needed can be made as follows: the fraction of the bombs dropped by the Fifteenth Air Force that fell within 1000 feet of target grew from 32 percent in June to 50 percent in August.[107] From Gilbert's layout of Birkenau, the gas chambers and crematoria numbered II to V each occupied about 35,000 square feet,[108] roughly 1 percent of the area of the circle 1,000 feet in radius within which half the bombs fell. Thus it would have required 200 bombs to obtain a good probability of at least one direct hit. The buildings were of solid construction, and the gas chambers were largely underground,[109] suggesting that 500-pound bombs would be required. If one direct hit was enough, about 50 tons of bombs would have been required to put out of action each gas chamber and its associated crematorium. This makes 200 tons for all four (gas chambers IV and V were only 500 feet apart, so some reduction might have been possible). In comparison, the synthetic oil plant at Auschwitz absorbed 1,336 500-pound bombs (300 tons in all) on 20 August. The intelligence report on the results of this raid was disappointing: "The damage received is not sufficient to interfere seriously with synthetic fuel production, and should not greatly delay completion of this part of the plant." A further raid was judged necessary, and 235 additional tons were dropped on the same plant on 13 September. Bombing the four known gas chambers at Auschwitz would have diverted resources equivalent to one or both of these raids.[110] Essentially similar calculations would apply to a railway bridge, or any other small target, which perhaps is why heavy bombers were not used against such targets. Goldmann's estimate of a few dozen bombs is far too low.[111] Wyman seems never to have estimated the weight of the bombs that would have been required.

If 200 tons of bombs had been aimed at the four gas chambers numbered II to V, about 100 tons would have landed more than 1,000 feet away. A glance at the layout provided by Gilbert suggests that many of the barracks housing the inmates would have been hit.[112] If we recall how crowded these were, there can be no doubt that many inmates would have been killed or injured.[113] This was why Kubowitzki and Ben-Gurion objected to the whole idea, and it is why Field-Marshal Sir John Dill worried about the deaths of "thousands of prisoners."[114] Weapons analyst P. M. Sprey estimates that 135 bombers delivering 1,350 500-pound bombs would have destroyed half the targets but that a third of their bombs would have hit the prisoner barracks area; that bombs would have fallen on the railway spur where hundreds of freight cars packed with prisoners sometimes sat; and that bombs would have fallen into the "Canada" storage warehouse where prisoners worked.[115] Williams's 1978 estimate of "perhaps dozens" of inmate deaths is far too low.[116] The question plainly worried Wyman too, as he favored the P-38s precisely on the grounds of diminished danger to the inmates.[117]

After the war, some survivors (including one inmate in the Gypsy Camp, only 600 feet from one of the crematoria[118]) indicated with great feeling that they wished the camp had been bombed. Paradoxically, we probably owe our knowledge of this opinion to the fact that it was not. In any event, as this opinion could not have been known at the time in London, Washington, or Jerusalem, it seems very hard to castigate the participants in the debate (Kubowitzki and Ben-Gurion's colleagues, for instance) for not assuming it.

BOMBING AUSCHWITZ: COMMAND CONSIDERATIONS

If Wyman feels that the failure to bomb Auschwitz or its railways was a culpable error, he remains reluctant to say precisely who was to blame. His favorite target would appear to be McCloy. Yet, as we have seen, McCloy was not in the chain of command, and had no authority to order operations. Although McCloy was undoubtedly a man of considerable influence, his subsequent claim[119] that only the President could order such an operation ("I couldn't order a soldier from A to B) is entirely accurate. Lerner concludes that Wyman has told a story without the main characters—Roosevelt was mentioned only in passing.[120] To fill the gap, the chain-of-command issue needs to be reviewed.

The Fifteenth Air Force, based in Italy, was, as we have seen, the only weapon capable of striking at Auschwitz. The chain of command for the Fifteenth ran from its commander, General Eaker, through General Spaatz, Commander-in-Chief of United States Strategic Air Forces in Europe, to General Eisenhower, Supreme Commander. General Eisenhower received broad directives from the Combined Chiefs of Staff, sitting as a committee, but was subject to direct operational orders only from the Commander-in-Chief, President Roosevelt.

At what level might an order have been issued for the highly political operations favored by Wyman? Eaker was too far down to order such a thing on his own authority. An example from June (when the Allies were struggling in the Normandy beachhead) shows how much latitude Spaatz and Eisenhower felt they had.[121] Concerned about what he saw as numerous mistaken diversions imposed on his bombers, Spaatz requested that Eisenhower release his bombers from operations against the V-1 launching sites in France "on the few days [when the weather is] favorable over Germany." Eisenhower directed his deputy to inform Spaatz that the priority for the launching sites would stand regardless of the weather. Spaatz clearly lacked the authority to target Auschwitz. Had it reached him, Eisenhower would almost certainly have referred the matter to Roosevelt as a political question.

The proposal to use large military forces for a political operation belonged properly on Roosevelt's desk and nowhere else. In his book, Wyman cites an exhaustive search by Mintz which showed that the bombing proposals almost certainly did not reach Roosevelt.[122] Wyman does, however, cite one letter of 24 July calling upon Roosevelt to bomb the deportation railways and the gas chambers.[123] Nothing came of this overture. Roosevelt was never pressed. But the problem was surely not one of access.

Akzin of the WRB understood the chain-of-command problem.[124] Better late than never, he urged Pehle on 2 September to go directly to Roosevelt with the proposal. Pehle did not do this. We are not told why; it might have been the natural disinclination of a civil servant to go outside the normal chain of command, which tied him to McCloy in the War Department. Then again, perhaps Pehle still had the doubts he had expressed on 24 June, and could not urge the operation in unequivocal terms.

If McCloy is to be faulted, his fault must lie in having failed to go to the President himself. If his judgment was wrong, however, the omission need not have been fatal since many other people and organizations had access to the President. In fact, the operation would have had the best chance of being carried out if it had descended from the political to the military level with an accompanying expression of enthusiasm, as in the query Churchill inspired Eden to send Sinclair on 7 July, qualified only by concern about its feasibility. Among others who could have addressed the President were all those who had urged him to create the WRB. Perhaps the very creation of this non-military organization made it harder for them to go round it on the bombing question. With Kubowitzki opposed to the bombing, however, the World Jewish Congress could hardly have joined such a lobbying effort.

The JA in Jerusalem sent two telegrams to Roosevelt[125] on 11 July, once again using the facilities of Consul-General Pinkerton. The proposal to bomb Auschwitz was being most actively considered at just this moment. But the action the JA desired from President Roosevelt had nothing whatsoever to do with bombing Auschwitz, for these topics appeared in neither telegram. The JA wanted Roosevelt to approve of negotiations with the SS concerning ransom of Hungarian Jews. This lack of interest in bombing Auschwitz was entirely consistent with the position taken a month earlier by the Executive. But the fact that the telegrams were addressed directly to Roosevelt shows that the JA knew perfectly well which decisions were outside the authority of the WRB. Coincidentally, the telegrams were sent on the same day that the JA in London prepared its discouraging Note on the proposal to bomb Auschwitz.

Churchill might have addressed himself directly to Roosevelt; we have seen that he took a favorable view of the operation, if shown feasible, on 7 July. But Sinclair's finding that the operation, though impossible for the RAF, might be possible for the USAAF does not seem to have reached him, and he played no further part in the matter.

There was thus no shortage of people who could have placed the bombing question before Roosevelt, but not one, Jew or non-Jew, civilian or military, believed in the proposed operation with sufficient conviction to see that it was in fact considered by the President.

Sinclair's finding, however, did reach Spaatz, but not Eisenhower or Roosevelt: neither the JA in Jerusalem (for reasons of policy) nor Weizmann in London (for unknown reasons) ever requested the Americans to bomb Auschwitz. But Weizmann's request to the British did reach Sinclair, who concluded his letter to Eden of 15 July by stating that he would have "the proposition put to the Americans, with all the facts, to see if they are prepared to try it. I am very doubtful indeed whether, when they have examined it, the Americans will think it possible, and I do not wish to raise any hopes."[126]

Sinclair was as good as his word, and after the matter was raised with him, apparently on 2 August, Spaatz was reported to be "most sympathetic."[127] But it is unlikely that the geographical information given him went beyond the words "death camps at Birkenau in Upper Silesia."

Weizmann and Shertok evidently did not provide whatever precise details on the "death camps at Birkenau" they may have had when they placed their bombing requests before Eden on 6 July, or at any later time for that matter. In particular, the JA Note of 11 July refers to a detailed description of the two camps (Birkenau and Auschwitz) in a report emanating from the Czech underground and "received since the original suggestion for bombing was made." The reader will recall that there is no indication that either the Note or the attached report was ever delivered to the British. Could Weizmann, a scientist by training, have failed to understand that before Auschwitz could be bombed, more intelligence than "death camps at Birkenau in Upper Silesia" would be needed? Is it possible that he failed to support his own "urgent plea to bomb Auschwitz" with all the information in his possession?[128] In the circumstances, the proposal seems to have been placed before Spaatz with almost no supporting detail, and it was entirely natural for him to ask the British to provide the additional intelligence without which a "most sympathetic" attitude could not possibly have been turned into a military operation. Thus, on 3 August the Chairman of the Joint Intelligence Committee noted that:

The Air Staff are anxious to obtain more precise details regarding the locality of this "death camp" at Birkenau. It may be within ten miles or more of that place. Unless the Air Staff can be given an exact pinpoint of this camp the airmen will experience difficulty in finding it.[129]

If the Chairman knew that the Air Staff wanted this intelligence in order to assist with the evaluation of an American operation (a British one having been ruled out on 15 July), he did not say so. Subsequently, several British bureaucrats dealt with the matter, but the memoranda that they left behind show they wrongly assumed that a British operation was contemplated. Writing long after the war, Wasserstein and Gilbert both missed this error. Wasserstein assumes that a British operation was still being contemplated, and was undermined by these bureaucrats.[130]

Even though the best intelligence available in London at that time, based upon escapees' reports, is now known to have been confusing and inaccurate, it should have been supplied by Weizmann (in July) or the British bureaucrats (in August).[131] In the event, Spaatz never received even this inadequate intelligence. But if he had, and if his staff had succeeded in interpreting it, the most that could have happened was that in mid- or late August the proposal to bomb Auschwitz would have gone from him to Eisenhower, and from Eisenhower to Roosevelt. It would likely have carried a sympathetic note and a negative recommendation.

OPERATIONS IN RELIEF OF WARSAW

Operations were undertaken by both the RAF and the USAAF in August and September in a vain attempt to relieve the Polish Home Army, which had risen against the Nazis in Warsaw. These operations have been cited by Wyman and many others as an example of what should have been done at Auschwitz.[132] There is indeed a rough parallel, but both the operational and the political details need to be taken into consideration.

Some 200 miles farther away from the Italian bases than Auschwitz, the RAF had only a relatively small number of planes capable of reaching Warsaw with useful loads. These were used on night missions to parachute supplies to the Polish Home Army, usually at prearranged drop zones marked by light signals in open country behind the lines. The operations cost 31 heavy planes out of 181, and, according to Slessor, "achieved practically nothing."[133] The planes were not equipped and their crews were not trained for bombing missions. On parachute supply missions, missing the target by half a mile would hardly have mattered. By contrast, in a night bombing attack on Auschwitz, missing the target by more than twenty yards would have amounted to total failure.

The bombers of the USAAF (which did not conduct night operations) could reach Warsaw from either Italy or England, but the essential escorting fighters could not. It was therefore necessary to make arrangements to refuel the bombers and fighters in territory controlled by the Russians. The Russians did not hurry, but they did finally agree, and the USAAF mounted an operation from England on 18 September. Though not expensive in terms of bombers lost, this operation did tie up a considerable fleet for some time, and like the RAF operations before it, "achieved practically nothing." Since it in no way endangered the lives of those it was intended to help, there were no objections to the Warsaw operation comparable to those of Kubowitzki or Ben-Gurion and his colleagues to the Auschwitz plan.

Churchill was pressed most vigorously by the Poles to help out and he felt a strong political imperative to assist.[134] Warned that the RAF could accomplish little, he nevertheless ordered it to make the attempt. Told that only the USAAF could do more, Churchill persuaded Roosevelt to approve operations. (He didn't address Spaatz or Eisenhower: this was a political matter.) Spaatz advised that "notwithstanding the humanitarian aspects of the problem in Warsaw, it was clear that aerial drops could never be massive enough or accurate enough to promise much relief to the Poles."[135] His biographer notes that even though Spaatz had argued against the efficacy of the Warsaw airlift his political superiors ordered it carried out. If ordered to do so, the military had to undertake missions whose purpose was entirely political.

As in the Warsaw operation, Churchill also favored using the RAF to relieve Auschwitz if this was at all possible. It turned out that the RAF was unable to do anything but that the USAAF could at least reach the area. Here, however, the Warsaw and Auschwitz stories diverge, as Churchill never seems to have been informed of the technical difficulties, and did not return to the subject. Had he known, would he have vigorously urged Roosevelt to intervene as he did in August on behalf of the Poles? We can never know for sure, but two facts bear on the question. First, the general war situation was much less tense in August after the Normandy victory and the liberation of Paris and most of France. Second, the only organization to raise the question of bombing Auschwitz with the British was Weizmann's JA. Relations between Weizmann and Churchill were cordial, contacts between the JA and the British Government frequent. The bombing of Auschwitz was at no time vigorously pressed by the JA, which had a different agenda.

CONCLUSIONS

It was beyond the power of any force the Allies could possibly bring to bear to interrupt the Hungarian railways by bombing. This conclusion was reached by responsible British and American officials acting with the benefit of professional military advice. In spite of this, Allied bombers did play a significant though indirect role in persuading the Hungarian Government to end the deportations on 8 July.

The British were unable to bomb the gas chambers and crematoria for sound technical reasons. From about the end of August (two months before the Nazis themselves stopped the gassings at Auschwitz), the Americans could have bombed these installations, but only by diverting substantial resources to the task, and in a manner that would likely have resulted in death or injury to thousands of camp inmates. Among those who opposed bombing the camps for the latter reason were the head of the Rescue Department of the World Jewish Congress, and all but one of the members of the JAE.

The bombing would also have required the approval of President Roosevelt, but he was never seriously asked. It is likely that widely expressed doubts about the efficacy of the proposed operation discouraged many individuals from pressing the issue at lower levels, or raising it with Roosevelt directly. Hindsight has confirmed these doubts were well founded.

The issue was resurrected in 1978 when Wyman wrote "there is no question that bombing the gas chambers and crematoria would have saved many lives." This assertion struck an extremely responsive chord in many quarters. In the same article, Wyman also made the less definite statement that "without gas chambers and crematoria, the Nazis would have been forced to reassess the extermination program." Pressed, Wyman disavowed the stronger statement: "I did not claim that mass killing would have been impossible without Auschwitz." But this did not prevent him from repeating both claims, and omitting the disavowal in 1984. Wyman's version has received wide exposure on television, at several Holocaust museums, and in scholarly and popular literature, but almost no competent criticism. Widespread popular acceptance, however, obliges historians to reconsider the issue and to be certain that their accounts are based on meticulous research.

ACKNOWLEDGMENTS

The author acknowledges the encouragement of Professor Sir Martin Gilbert, C.B.E. Additional thanks go to the Franklin and Eleanor Roosevelt Institute and to the Franklin D. Roosevelt Library, which published an earlier and longer version of this study in Verne Newton, ed., *FDR and the Holocaust* (New York: St. Martin's Press, 1996). I thank Peter Novick for bringing to my attention the minutes of the Jewish Agency Executive meeting of 11 June.

9

COULD THE ALLIES HAVE
BOMBED AUSCHWITZ-BIRKENAU?

Stuart G. Erdheim

SEVERAL WORKS DATING from the late 1970s onward have explored the question of whether the Allies had the knowledge and technical capability needed to bomb the killing facilities at Auschwitz-Birkenau. Beginning with a 1978 article in *Commentary* (later incorporated into a 1984 book, *The Abandonment of the Jews*), David Wyman argued that the failure to bomb the death camp did not result from any cogent assessment of military infeasibility, but rather was yet another example of Allied indifference to the ongoing destruction of European Jewry. More recently, two critics have sought to undermine Wyman's thesis by focusing on the operational obstacles that confronted a potential bombing mission over Auschwitz-Birkenau (hereinafter Birkenau). In separate chapters in this volume, James H. Kitchens III and Richard H. Levy deflect criticism from the Allies by examining such military complexities as intelligence, target distance and placement, bomber availability and accuracy, and defenses. This chapter is a direct challenge to their assessment as to the military practicality of bombing the death camp. Although the operational issue is clearly a complex one, the research presented below will show that, at least from a military standpoint, bombing Birkenau itself was no more complex than numerous other missions undertaken by the Allied powers during the Second World War.[1]

Undisputed is the fact that, despite numerous bombing missions in the vicinity of Oswiecim (Auschwitz) in Upper Silesia, the Allies never attacked the Birkenau crematoria from the air. With regard to the logistical obstacles to such a raid, Allied communiqués and letters from 1944 are less than candid. Still, both Levy and Kitchens cite these communications as clear evidence of the operational impracticality of bombing this particular target. Upon closer review, we will see that these statements actually reveal more about the Allied mindset than any elaborate military consideration that might have justified inaction.

An underlying premise of this chapter, then, is that Kitchens and Levy have distorted the boundary of the debate from whether Birkenau *could* have been bombed to whether it *should* have. Since they both argue that it *should* not have been bombed, Kitchens and Levy immediately cast Birkenau as a no-priority target. As such, the first step in military procedure for assessing targets (i.e., obtaining and analyzing photo-imagery and correlating it with available ground intelligence) does not apply. Without the necessary intelligence, an appropriate feasibility study cannot be undertaken. And where there is no feasibility study, there can be no genuine target assessment or operational planning, without which there can be no bombing.

Only by assuming that Birkenau was a potentially valid target can we answer the "could have" question and objectively examine the prospect of a hypothetical bombing mission over Birkenau. But this is precisely the point that Kitchens dismisses. By claiming that "any Allied option to frustrate the Holocaust from the air was illusory, a fact so unmistakably obvious to contemporary commanders that it was taken for granted," Kitchens ignores all questions of an operational review for such a mission.[2] The incorrectness of this assertion is evident when one considers the reactions from Air Marshal Norman H. Bottomley, Deputy Chief of the Air Staff, and General Carl Spaatz, Commander-in-Chief of the U.S. Strategic Air Forces in Europe, concerning a proposal to bomb Birkenau. In a minute to the Assistant Chief of the Air Staff dated 2 August 1944, Bottomley wrote:

> 1. I have discussed this subject with General Spaatz, who is *most sympathetic*. Before we can consider any action, however, it is necessary to know more about the precise location, extent and nature of the camps and installations at Birkenau. *It is particularly necessary to have some photographic cover.*
> 2. Will you please have this produced as early as possible, so that the *operational possibilities* of taking some effective action from the air *can be studied* [my emphasis].[3]

Bombing Birkenau, according to this August 1944 memo, was clearly not out of the question as long as the usual target assessment procedures were applied.[4]

This chapter seeks to answer the "could have" question by examining the most critical operational factors in any World War II bombing mission: (1) photo reconnaissance and intelligence; (2) German defenses; and (3) Allied bombing tactics. By treating Birkenau as the Allies would have handled any other potential target, as Bottomley attempted to do, we can properly assess whether operational considerations nullified or supported the possibility of bombing Auschwitz-Birkenau.

PHOTO RECONNAISSANCE AND INTELLIGENCE

Aerial Reconnaissance and the Vrba-Wetzler Report

If the Allies had considered Birkenau a potential target, they would have immediately ordered aerial reconnaissance in order to determine the capacity of the air forces to bomb the camp effectively. Photo intelligence was indispensable to the planning of bombing missions, and Birkenau would have been no exception. In order to make any operational assessment, then, we must first apply the same photo reconnaissance techniques to Birkenau that the Allies would have applied to any other target.

Any photo reconnaissance efforts might have been requested on the basis of earlier intelligence about the camp, but certainly by June 1944, when it became available to the Allies, the Vrba-Wetzler report established itself as the most crucial source. The testimony provided by Rudolf Vrba and Alfred Wetzler, who escaped from Auschwitz in April 1944, contained detailed information about the camp, including sketches of its layout. Yet Kitchens dismisses this evidence out of hand, arguing that it "had minimal utility for military intelligence purposes," did not "reliably locate" the gas chambers and crematoria, and that the "maps included with the report contained at least one error which could have puzzled those seeking to correlate the report with aerial photographs. . . ."[5] Moreover, he quotes Richard Foregger who insisted that the sketch map was so inaccurate "Neither the Auschwitz II camp at Birkinau [sic] nor the gas chambers and crematoria could be located with the map."[6] Foregger added that a plaster of Paris model (an important aid for low-level precision raids) could not have been constructed from this map.

But the point missed by Foregger, Kitchens and Levy is that the normal procedure for model making required aerial photography, with requests for the models made at the C.I.U. (Central Interpretation Unit) at Medmenham, England.[7] These authors also play down the more important question of correlating the intelligence on hand, i.e., the report and sketch map from Vrba and Wetzler, with aerial photography, which was no less than standard military procedure when ground intelligence was available.[8] Indeed, even when there was a good deal of reliable ground intelligence, as in the Amiens raid, obtaining aerial imagery was considered essential.[9] The critical nature of this practice is expressly stated in the Aiming Point Report for the I. G. Farben synthetic rubber (Buna) plant at Auschwitz:

> The buna plant should not be attacked until cover has been received: the preparation of this provisional aiming point report does not eliminate the necessity for photographs. Upon receipt of photographs, EOU-CIU-MEW in either the Mediterranean area or England will be in a position to judge whether the ground intelligence reporting . . . is valid. If the photographs bear out the ground intelligence, the present report may be

useful should immediate action be desired. . . . All that is available at the present time is a rough plan drawn from memory.[10]

The point is, the existence of the sketch map and detailed ground intelligence did not mitigate the need for photo reconnaissance, but rather helped to validate it.

Kitchens only grudgingly concedes that "with enough time and effort," photo interpreters "*might*" [my italics] have been able to correlate aerial photos with the Vrba-Wetzler report. He hastens to add, however, that since the authors remained in Slovakia, they could not be questioned, thus implying the necessity of further debriefing to validate their report. Levy takes an even less sanguine approach, writing that ". . . aerial reconnaissance would have been needed, and even then it is hard to see how the targets could have been pinpointed without the aid of escapees." Using Foregger's analysis of the sketch maps as his sole proof (and ignoring the report altogether), Levy distinguishes between "knowing that there was an extermination camp at Auschwitz" and "locating the gas chambers and crematoria with sufficient precision to bomb them."

Have Kitchens and Levy made an effective case? Was it really necessary to interview the escapees again before being able to locate the gas chambers and crematoria with any confidence? Instead of turning to Foregger (a retired medical doctor), Kitchens and Levy could have looked to one of the pre-eminent experts in photo-analysis, Dino Brugioni.[11] Regarding the correlation of the Vrba-Wetzler report with photo-imagery, Brugioni states: "It is my professional opinion that had such information been provided to the photo interpreters, they would have *quickly* located the gas chambers and crematoriums."[12] Unlike Foregger, Kitchens or Levy, Brugioni does not think the sketch maps would have "puzzled" anyone. Yet referring to the article from which this quote was taken, Kitchens asserts that it, along with an earlier article by Brugioni, is "indispensable for understanding the problem of interpretation and intelligence appreciation of the Auschwitz aerial photographs made in 1944." If he thinks so highly of Brugioni, why doesn't he quote him instead of Foregger?[13]

The intelligence which Kitchens claims was not forthcoming from the Vrba-Wetzler report, such as the outside dimensions of the crematoria, flak gun emplacements, forested areas, and the identifications of low-flying hazards like high tension wires and chimneys, could all be detected with photo-imagery. The target intelligence organization, A.I.3(c)1, aided primarily by photo-interpreters (hereinafter 'P.I.s'), determined exactly how many flak gun emplacements there were, as well as their "pinpoint" positions.[14] With this information, a "Flak Clock," and E Section Flak Map and Amendment Reports were drawn up for the Farben industrial plant at Auschwitz, and the airmen were briefed on the course, approach and rally routes that best avoided the flak defenses.[15] The P.I.s could also have determined the outer dimensions of the crematoria, whether there were any low flying obstructions, and the height of high tension pylons and the crematoria chimneys.[16] The imagery additionally distinguishes between forested areas and the level farmland that mostly surrounded the camp and was "conducive to a good shallow run-in [for fighter bombers] to the drop point."[17] This open terrain also provided less ground "interference" to distract high altitude bombardiers trying to locate the aiming point. The Vrba-Wetzler report, in short, was not necessary for any of the above intelligence, which was available from the imagery if P.I.s had only been tasked to look for it (as they were, in fact, in preparation for the attack on the Farben plant, which would have also been useful for an attack on Birkenau).[18]

Kitchens also criticizes the Vrba-Wetzler report for not including intelligence on the "structural design, materials, foundations," of the crematoria, adding that such construction details were "necessary for the selection and placement of ordnance." This prompts us to ask two questions: (1) How was this information normally acquired? and (2) How necessary was it? In other words, were precision targets successfully bombed without such detailed knowledge, and were structural plans available for every Gestapo and Wehrmacht headquarters attacked? The latter does not appear to have been the case.[19] Structural information was generally obtained by target intelligence personnel using whatever sources they had at their disposal, including "ISTD (Inter-Services Topographical Department), CIU (Central [photographic] Interpretation Unit), POWs, refugees, learned societies and professional associations, technical journals, insurance companies and other private firms."[20] The choke points at oil plants, for example, were ascertained by consulting petroleum industry experts. Similarly, companies experienced in the construction of crematoria and industrial furnaces could have provided sufficient information about the design and structure of such a facility to help plan an attack.

While Kitchens openly criticizes the Vrba-Wetzler report for not providing detailed information on the size and design of the crematoria, he fails to discern valuable information that the report did provide. The escapees indicated, for example, that Birkenau prisoners worked outside the camp, thus lowering estimates of potential collateral deaths from a bombing raid.[21] Their report also contained relevant corroborating material for several 1943 reports on gas chambers and crematoria.[22] Finally, as indicated above, there was enough intelligence in the report that experts would have had little difficulty locating the extermination facilities, if only they had aerial imagery with which to correlate it.

Another argument that Kitchens offers, making an attack on Birkenau appear more difficult than it would have been, concerns the actual layout of the target area. He describes the "dispersed" target areas as "dauntingly complex" and "consisting of five widely spaced buildings (four at Birkenau and one over a mile away at Auschwitz I . . .)."[23] There are several problems with this reasoning. First, by the second half of 1943 Crematorium I at Auschwitz I was no longer available, rendered useless through overuse, it had been "converted into an air raid shelter for SS personnel."[24] Besides, aerial photographs would have shown that there were no large buildings with tall chimneys at Auschwitz I which compared to those at Birkenau anyway.[25] Additionally, the four large crematoria at Birkenau—II, III, IV, and V—were hardly "dispersed," but rather lined up in a row on the periphery of the camp, the two mirrored pairs only slightly offset.

The crematoria in question, moreover, were situated at the westernmost part of the camp, with barbed wire fences and watchtowers their only separation from the woods beyond. Unlike Gestapo headquarters buildings which Mosquito fighters daringly picked out from crowded city streets, the crematoria stood alone, in a large fenced-in area, and could easily be distinguished from nearby barracks.[26] Longer than a football field, Crematoria II and III were amongst the largest buildings in the camp and the only ones with such tall chimneys, making their identification far less complex than Levy and Kitchens suggest (and the aerial imagery affirms).

In the end, Levy's and Kitchens's arguments come down to the same point: how much destruction would have been necessary to make a significant impact on the killing process? Kitchens's scenario implies that unless all five crematoria were destroyed, an attack would be pointless. Similarly, Levy argues that there were other facilities like Crematorium I (which in fact was not functional in 1944) and the gas chamber and incineration pit of Bunker 2/V that would have had to come under attack. Yet neither acknowledges that the four Birkenau crematoria buildings were responsible for the incineration of the vast majority of Auschwitz's victims. The possibility that a gas chamber or undamaged crematorium might remain in operation after a raid was hardly a cause to reject an attack out of hand. With that logic, how many World War II bombing missions might have been aborted?

Obtaining Photo-Reconnaissance

Since we have established that photo reconnaissance (PR) was crucial to any major bombing raid, we must now ask whether there was enough intelligence for the photo reconnaissance pilots to locate the Birkenau camp and obtain the proper imagery. What exactly would have been required—precise coordinates or the approximate distance from a known locale? Or would a vague report suggesting the existence of a target within the appropriate parameters of dozens or even hundreds of square miles have been adequate? The examples below will allow us to examine what was accomplished by the photo-intelligence gathering units and, consequently, what might have been achieved at Birkenau.

In early 1942, a British intelligence officer reading a smuggled German petroleum industry journal noticed a classified ad for jobs at a new oil plant near Brüx, a town in the Sudetenland (Czechoslovakia). Solely on the basis of this advertisement, intelligence officials decided to send a PR aircraft to reconnoiter the area.[27] As the ad obviously did not mention that the plant was situated three miles northwest of Brüx, the pilot was on his own. Using a lens with a 36-inch focal length and flying at 25,800 feet, he succeeded in bringing back imagery of a worksite that P.I.s identified as the new oil plant under construction.[28]

In 1944 the Polish Intelligence Service informed the British that missile trials were being conducted in the vicinity of Blizna. While intense German security in the area precluded them from learning any more than this, PR pilots based in Italy obtained imagery of various sites in the area on 5 May 1944. In Medmenham, P.I.s were able to identify a flying bomb ramp on one of the photos, but felt that the surface coverage was incomplete and requested another mission. This time they located a compound that was part of the installation; and later turned out to be the first V-2 testing site uncovered in Blizna.[29]

Finally, in a massive effort to locate the V-1 launching sites in northern France, over 4,000 PR sorties were flown covering hundreds of square miles. P.I.s painstakingly but successfully combed through tens of thousands of photos to locate the tiny V-1 sites camouflaged in vast wooded areas, all the while trying to distinguish them from decoys. This imagery provided the only intelligence for sites whose locations were otherwise unknown.

The three cases above are indicative of the kind of procedure commonly employed by PR units. In those instances where intelligence was vague or non-existent, aerial reconnaissance proved an effective means of locating obscure potential targets. So the question begs: At the time of Air Marshal Bottomley's 2 August request for cover, was specific intelligence available that could have helped PR pilots to identify Birkenau?

The answer, as we have already begun to see, was a resounding "yes." Not only did the Allies possess detailed summaries of the Vrba-Wetzler report, but also at their disposal was a British War Office report entitled "List of Concentration Camps" (30 June 1944), which accurately located Birkenau at thirty kilometers south-southeast of Katowice.[30] Furthermore, we now know that from 26 February (not 4 April, as has previously been asserted) numerous reconnaissance missions were being flown in the Upper Silesia area in preparation for the strategic bombing of oil targets there. When General Spaatz, the architect and main proponent of the "oil war," wrote to Lt. Gen. Ira Eaker, commander of Mediterranean Allied Air Forces (MAAF), inquiring as to the feasibility of an attack on the Blechhammer refineries, Eaker replied (8 May) "that not only were such strikes possible, but that war industries at Auschwitz and Odertal 'might also be attacked simultaneously.'"[31] Responsible for target selection, Spaatz and his staff were therefore aware that Upper Silesia, including the synthetic oil plant at Oswiecim, were in the midst of a major bombing campaign necessitating photo-imagery. It would thus have been perfectly logical for him to request either a search at the integrated Anglo-American photo libraries at the Allied Central Interpretation Unit (ACIU) in Medmenham or Mediterranean Allied Photographic Reconnaissance Wing (MAPRW) in San Severo, Italy, for existing cover, which by 2 August would have revealed the entire Auschwitz complex, including Birkenau. By then, PR missions had flown on 26 February, 4 April, 31 May, 26 June, and 8 July. Before the 20 August raid on Auschwitz, two more were dispatched on 9 and 12 August. In other words, additional photo reconnaissance would not have required any special missions: planes already surveying the area needed only to be briefed on finding and photographing the camp.

With extensive photographic coverage of the area already available and the Vrba-Wetzler report released to the press in June, what became of Bottomley's request? The response came on 3 August from a senior Foreign Office official, William Cavendish-Bentinck, Chairman of the Joint Intelligence Sub-Committee (JIC):

> Air Staff are anxious to obtain more precise details regarding the locality of this "death camp" at Birkenau. It may be within ten miles or more of that place. Unless the Air Staff can be given an exact pinpoint of this camp the airmen will experience difficulty in finding it.[32]

In light of both the available intelligence and the skill of PR flyers in locating obscure targets, these remarks were completely unjustified. Precise details of Birkenau were in the Foreign Office by 4 July. The Czech Government-in-Exile had provided the British with an eight-page summary of the Vrba-Wetzler report, which indicated that Birkenau was four kilometers (2.5 miles) from the town of Oswiecim, in a district known to the Poles as "Rajsko." The camp itself could hardly be missed, consisting as it did of three blocks covering the enormous area of 1,600 × 850 meters. The report also mentioned the four crematoria, "two large and two small in the camp of Birkenau itself," adding that "the crematoria can be recognized from the outside by their lofty chimneys."[33] On 26 July, just eight days before Cavendish-Bentinck's memo, the Foreign Office received a complete version of the report. Finally, the Foreign Office informed the Jewish Agency that planning could not proceed until they received more topographical information, which was then procured from the Polish Ministry of the Interior-in-Exile and forwarded to the Foreign Office the very same day.[34]

Auschwitz bombing critics have seriously overstated the difficulty of obtaining imagery for ten miles around. With a commonly used scale of 1:60,000, *one nine-inch-square negative provided coverage for 8.5 × 8.5 miles, or 72.25 square miles. Each camera magazine held 500 negatives. A photo from the June 26th imagery of Oswiecim clearly shows all of the Farben industrial plant, Auschwitz I and Birkenau with room to spare.[35] As chairman of the Joint Intelligence Sub-Committee (JIC), which was responsible for the Joint Photographic Reconnaissance Committee (JPRC), Cavendish-Bentinck was certainly aware of this technical capability as well as of the highly organized photo libraries at Medmenham and in Italy. Besides searching these libraries, the Foreign Office or

JIC could also have asked Lt. Gen. Ira Eaker, Commander of MAAF, to order a debriefing of MAPRW pilots who had sortied in the area. Southern Poland was under such continuous aerial reconnaissance that Charles Barry, the PR pilot on the April 4 mission to Oswiecim, writes that he and his two tour navigators "became so used to the area that we could find our way round it without a map."[36] And Col. Roy Stanley, a photo-interpretation expert, states that: "Allied intelligence—certainly at the operational level—knew about the camps [at Auschwitz-Birkenau] but had no idea what was going on in them."[37] Seeing the sizable camp on the imagery in hand, photo experts could have ordered the camp covered in greater detail either on the scheduled 9 or 12 August missions or on a special mission.[38]

Was the failure in early August 1944 to utilize ground and photo intelligence from the Vrba-Wetzler report, the Polish Ministry of the Interior-in-Exile, and other Allied operational sources due to a lack of common sense, incompetence, or willful evasion? Whatever the answer, by 2 August at the latest, locating and obtaining aerial imagery of Birkenau was well within the means of Allied PR aircraft flying out of either England or Italy.

More difficult to assess is the possibility of locating the camp and crematoria prior to the Vrba-Wetzler report. Would an intelligence officer assigned to collect and analyze the information being received on genocide, as Professor Richard Breitman suggests, have been able to piece together a coherent picture of Birkenau? Breitman concludes that "[prior to 1944] there was enough generally accurate information [obtained through the Polish underground] about Auschwitz-Birkenau to preclude the argument that the Allies did not bomb the camp because they got the necessary information too late."[39] If this information had evoked enough curiosity, if not horror, to have justified just one PR sortie, Birkenau could have been photographed much sooner.[40] Indeed, as early as 6 October 1942 and 20 August 1943, photo reconnaissance Mosquitoes obtained imagery of the oil refinery at Blechhammer, Germany, forty-seven miles from the death camp.[41] When the Joint Chiefs of Staff received reports of crematoria at Oswiecim in May 1943 from Polish Military Intelligence, for example, the area could have been included on the 20 August 1943 Blechhammer mission.

Photo-Interpretation

A further example of how Auschwitz bombing critics have distorted the historical record with respect to Allied knowledge about the death camp concerns the actual analysis of available photo intelligence. Kitchens quotes Brugioni that "the death camp appeared [in photographs] only accidentally and was incidental to the interpreters' work. None of them was tasked to look for concentration camps." Clearly Kitchens has misunderstood this. Brugioni's statement was merely one of historical fact as to why the P.I.s did not analyze the Birkenau imagery, i.e., they were not tasked to do so since bombing the camp was never seriously contemplated. If it had been targeted, and procedure followed, then the P.I.s would have found the accidentally obtained photographs. In this instance, Kitchens seems to have inadvertently supported the case against himself.

Kitchens also criticizes the quality of the prints and viewing equipment, and refers to the deficiency of interpretation texts that could "make the images speak intelligibly." In his understanding of the situation, P.I.s were either lacking in experience or were too busy concentrating on other targets, which is yet another refrain of the no-priority theme. We also learn that there was "no historical precedent for genocidal installations."

Of course, when P.I.s analyzed imagery for target assessment, or to confirm reports of new German radar, or "flying bombs," they used the same "primitive prints" and equipment. They had no interpretation guides for radar aerials, and there was no historical precedent for the V weapons. The politicians and military commanders needed information, not excuses, and the P.I.s found a way to "make the images speak intelligibly." The point is not whether Birkenau had as high a priority as radar or V weapons, but rather that the state-of-the-art photo-interpretation equipment and the trained P.I.s were as applicable to Birkenau as to any other target under review. Had they been tasked for the job, the P.I.s might well have noticed such clear clues as the separate rail spur running directly into the "labor" camp, the "obvious lack of industrial installations within the camp" (especially in view of the "large number of boxcars on the Birkenau sidings"), and the "four separately secured extermination areas," each containing one lone building with suspiciously tall smokestacks. These are exactly the kinds of anomalous clues to which P.I.s were trained to be sensitive.[42] There is no question whatsoever that P.I.s were often capable of spectacular analysis far more challenging than finding "separately secured" buildings with lofty chimneys.[43]

Allied Intelligence on the Final Solution

Another important issue concerns the level of military intelligence on the Final Solution in general. On this point Kitchens argues that intelligence authorities were not alerted to look for gas chambers and crematoria since genocide was still unknown. Kitchens writes that "before the end of 1944, at least, the Allies lacked enough solid intelligence about the 'Final Solution' to adequately comprehend its hideous import."[44] In support of this, he quotes a 10 October 1944 British War Office Report which, he informs readers, was an attempt to "summarize the concentration camp intelligence then in hand" and indicates that the Allies "had no exact knowledge of the number of the camps the Germans were operating, where the camps were located, how many internees there were, or to what overall purpose the detainees were being held." Kitchens also cites F. H. Hinsley's *British Intelligence in the Second World War*, the official history of British intelligence, to support his position.[45]

In the case of the 10 October report, Kitchens completely ignores what it had to say about Auschwitz, which is important not only in an informative sense, but as to the quality of this report itself. For starters, it provides a great deal of information on the concentration camp system (including identifying and locating all six death camps) and gassing facilities. It correctly locates the Auschwitz camp, states that it had been "mentioned frequently since 1939," and lists the estimated annual population since 1940. The report notes too that the "Birkenau camp is definitely connected, as Auschwitz makes use of Birkenau's gas chambers, though it is said to have ten crematoria and four lethal gas chambers itself." Moreover, the report identifies the leading SS personnel by rank for December 1943 and March 1944 and classifies Birkenau as a "Special KL (*Konzentrations-Lager*) and annihilation camp for women," where the inmates are said to be "mostly Hungarian Jews." Under the "remarks" section, it asserts bluntly: "Most likely controlled by AUSCHWITZ, where Jews are sent to keep the four crematoria busy." In short, though they did not get each and every fact exactly right, Allied Intelligence knew the location of an extermination camp that utilized gas chambers and crematoria to murder human beings and efficiently dispose of their remains.[46]

As for Kitchens's use of Hinsley to support his position on the minimal amount of Allied intelligence available on the death camps, he states that in the British decrypts of German wireless telegraphic messages known as ULTRA, there were "scarcely any references to concentration camps." The basis for this conclusion is a footnote on page 736 in Vol. II, part 2, which Kitchens paraphrases as follows:

> "There were," the authors write, "no Sigint [signal intelligence] references to the extermination camps" before April 1945 apart from "a few Police decrypts in the second half of 1944 and early 1945. . . ."

In his own footnote, Kitchens explains why concentration camps were not mentioned in the decrypts: "The reason, of course, was that for clarity and security the Germans used land lines not subject to eavesdropping wherever possible." Yet here is an unedited version of what Hinsley actually says about SS concentration camp decrypts:

> Apart from a few Police decrypts in the second half of 1944 and early in 1945 about the movement into concentration camps of Jews from France, Hungary and the Baltic States and about the use of camp inmates as forced labour, the above decrypts were the first Sigint references to concentration camps *since the cessation in February 1943 of the daily returns referred to in Volume II, p. 675* [sic] There were no Sigint references to the extermination camps. [my emphasis]

The decrypts that were available ran from spring 1942 until February 1943 and specified exact prisoner and death counts for each of the camps mentioned, including Auschwitz, known even at that time to be the largest. Yet according to Kitchens, there were "scarcely any references to the concentration camps."

Kitchens's contention that the decrypts did not provide "solid intelligence" about the Final Solution ignores completely a related source of information on mass executions: German Order Police intercepts that were received by the British as early as July 1941.[47] In August 1942, Churchill also learned from decrypts that 8,000 men and women had died in one month at Auschwitz. Although unable to reveal that they were all Jews (that would have exposed the intelligence coup of Ultra), Churchill nonetheless announced in a radio broadcast to the British people (25 August 1942) that "whole districts are being exterminated," and that the Germans were perpetrating "the most frightful cruelties." "We are in the presence of a crime without a name," the great wartime leader concluded, leaving no doubt that he understood all too well the "hideous import of the Final Solution."[48]

This "crime without a name" was officially denounced by the Allied Declaration of 17 December 1942, signed by the United States, Britain, the Soviet Union, and the governments of eight occupied countries. It condemned the German government's "intention to exterminate the Jewish people in Europe," and denounced "in the strongest possible terms this bestial policy of cold-blooded extermination." Putting its prior hesitations to believe the reports on genocide aside, the Allied governments now publicly confirmed what they had known for over a year.[49]

Why did the Allies wait so long? According to William Casey, the former head of the CIA and an OSS agent during the war, the numerous reports on the Jewish genocide "were shunted aside because of the official policy in Washington and London to concentrate exclusively on the defeat of the enemy."[50] Yet many of these reports contained reliable information on the gas chambers and crematoria at Birkenau. One of them, which came from Polish military intelligence in London, reached Washington by diplomatic pouch in May 1943 and the Joint Chiefs of Staffs by June. Updating information for Auschwitz-Birkenau, the report noted that: "A huge new camp crematorium consumes 3,000 persons daily."[51] A summary of this and similar reports was made public on 21 March 1944, when the Associated Press in London released a report from the Polish Ministry of Information confirming that "more than 500,000 persons, mostly Jews, had been put to death at a concentration camp at Oswiecim, southwest of Kracow." The report also stated that "three crematoria had been erected inside the camp to dispose of 10,000 bodies a day." The *Washington Post* published the AP release on the following day on page 2 under the banner, "Poles Report Nazis Slay 10,000 Daily." On 24 March 1944, five days after the Nazis installed a puppet government in Hungary and less than two months before the deportation of Hungarian Jews was to begin, Franklin Delano Roosevelt declared: "In one of the blackest crimes of all history . . . the wholesale systematic murder of the Jews of Europe goes on unabated every hour . . . [the Jews of Hungary] are now threatened with annihilation. . . . All who knowingly take part in the deportation of Jews to their death in Poland . . . are equally guilty with the executioner."[52]

What about those who knowingly stood by while this wholesale slaughter took place? Are they also to be counted among the guilty? Based upon the evidence presented above, there can no longer be any question as to what the Allies knew and whether or not they had enough time to act upon it. We must now turn to the question of what they might have done.

GERMAN DEFENSES

Antiaircraft at Auschwitz

An important aspect of the bombing of Auschwitz question on which there has been much misinformation concerns the defenses which surrounded the camp. According to Kitchens, "There were no flak guns at Auschwitz I and Birkenau, but 79 heavy guns defended the I. G. Farben plant at Monowitz, four and a half miles away. . . ." But this does not correspond to the April 4 aerial imagery, which clearly shows a battery of heavy AA guns (no. 2) one-half mile southeast of Auschwitz I, with another battery (no. 1) less than one-half mile east of the northeast corner of Birkenau.[53] Moreover, Kitchens fails to indicate that most of the 79 heavy guns were added in the weeks immediately preceding the 20 August raid on the Farben plant.[54] Between April and July, there were actually 29–33 heavy guns, only about 20 of which (flak batteries 1, 2, 5, and 12) were capable of reaching bombers attacking Birkenau.[55] Clearly, a raid carried out in this period would have encountered considerably less enemy flak than one in August or September.

With regard to the 79 heavy AA guns, Kitchens states that ". . . wheeling formations of heavy bombers over Birkenau could hardly have avoided this defensive umbrella."[56] For the 13 September raid on the Farben plant, bombs were released at 24,000 to 26,000 feet while the planes were directly over the western portion of Birkenau, about five miles from the Aiming Point. This is confirmed by dramatic photos taken at "bombs away," which show one of the crematoria encircled by a group of 500-lb. bombs.[57] What Kitchens completely misses here is that in order to bomb the death camp, the "wheeling formations" would take place five miles south of Birkenau at "bombs away," not directly over the camp as he suggests (see fig. 11-1).[58] The critical bomb run was even farther to the south, putting the bombers out of range of batteries 5, 6, 7, 8, 9, 10, 11 and part of 12.[59] Attacking from the south, the bombers would rally left (west) after dropping their bombs, carrying them away from the flak and never coming closer than five miles to Birkenau. With the flak considerably lighter

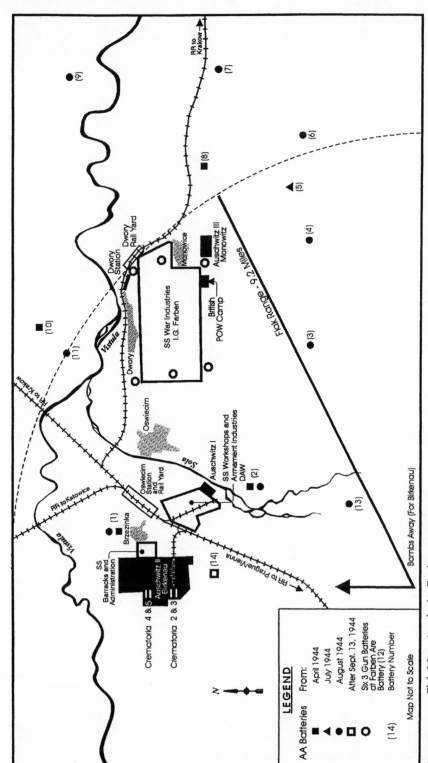

LEGEND

AA Batteries   From:

■	April 1944
▲	July 1944
●	August 1944
☐	After Sept. 13, 1944
○	Six 3 Gun Batteries at Farben Are Battery (12)
(14)	Battery Number

Map Not to Scale

FIGURE 9-1. Flak Map, Auschwitz Environs, 1944.

than in Kitchen's scenario, one would expect the bombing to be more accurate and with minimal Allied losses. In any case, it is clear from the aerial imagery that an attack on Birkenau any time through August 1944 would not have encountered nearly as much flak as an attack on the Farben plant for which the defenses were designed.

Small Arms Fire

Kitchens writes that small arms fire from the guards could have been an effective deterrent against low-level P-38s and Mosquitoes. This seems tantamount to saying that infantrymen in battle can be injured or killed. The statement is true of every low-level fighter bombing and strafing mission in the war. Yet if we are to respond to Kitchens directly, it behooves adding that the SS guards at Birkenau, used to policing half-starved defenseless prisoners, would be far less of a threat to Allied planes than front-line troops constantly on the lookout for an air attack. (By the spring of 1944, over a year had passed since Himmler instituted escape prevention measures, during which time there had been no attacks on the camp.) The camp guards were more likely to run for cover (as many former prisoners reported seeing them doing during air raids) than stand and fire at attacking fighters.[60]

Luftwaffe Fighter Defenses

Before even reaching the death camp, Allied planes en route to Poland had to pass through fighter defenses in the Balkans. While Kitchens admits that these defenses were "not nearly as strong as in Germany," he could have presented a more nuanced picture by using mission reports and other primary sources. Instead, he settles on a discussion of Freya (a type of German radar) sites and an estimate of enemy fighters available (which rarely corresponded to actual fighter sorties).[61] What Kitchens overlooks is the observation on German radar made in the Intelligence Report for the 20 August raid on the Czechowice oil refinery near Auschwitz: "It is believed that enemy reporting system is not as effective in this Eastern area of penetration."[62]

In Upper Silesia, German Air Force activity tended to be limited and un-aggressive. A useful example in this regard is the 7 August 1944 attack on the Trzebinia oil plant thirteen miles northeast of Auschwitz. In this "Frantic"[63] shuttle mission from and back to Russia, excellent weather allowed for visual bombing. One bomber group observed four Me 109s out of range, two of which then made a sweeping circle to attack. Yet a bomber in the low squadron reported that the enemy broke off the attack at 500 yards. One enemy plane was even seen spiraling to the ground. The Allied crews reported that the pilots of the enemy aircraft were "unaggressive [sic] and inexperienced." The second bomber group observed only one enemy aircraft, possibly an Fw 190, which made "only one aggressive pass and crews believe a P-51 shot it down."[64] A total of five enemy aircraft were spotted but only three actually encountered, far below the "maximum fighter reaction" (within 100 miles of the target) of 75 that the Intelligence Annex Report on this mission had predicted.[65]

Another example comes from the 22 August 1944 mission to the Odertal Oil Refinery ten miles northwest of Blechhammer. According to Operations Order Nr. 672, the number of German fighters that could be put up to oppose this mission consisted of the following: 60 to 70 single engines from the Vienna-Budapest area; 35 to 40 Me 109s and Fw 190s from the Munich area; 30 to 40 single engines in the target area. The report adds, however, that "Negligible fighter opposition on recent missions may be due to a shortage of gasoline." The five heavy bombardment groups flying from Italy encountered eighteen enemy aircraft, with reports of seven downed.[66]

During the 20 August 1944 raid on Auschwitz, the 2nd Bombardment Group (BG) reported two Me 109s attacking a B-17 straggler just after "bombs away." They made several passes, "after which the enemy aircraft broke off attack and disappeared," while the B-17 went down with no chutes observed. Out of 127 bombers, this was an unusually light loss rate of 0.78%, especially in view of the 79 heavy antiaircraft guns.[67] The 483rd BG reported 20 to 25 enemy aircraft ten miles south of Budapest, of which "approximately 15 Me 109s made one pass at the lead box . . . our escort intercepted them." One Me 109 was destroyed, one probably destroyed, and one damaged.[68] The 99th BG reported that two enemy aircraft made "very unaggressive" passes in the Budapest area, while the 301st BG and the 97th BG reported no encounters at all.[69] The Intelligence Report stated: "B. FIGHTERS: Enemy could not put up 100 sorties in BUDA-PEST/VIENNA area if reinforced by 30 to 35 MUNICH area fighters. . . . No strong opposition expected on withdrawal. . . . C. ESTIMATE OF TOTAL SCALE OF EFFORT: a. 50 to 60 single engine fighters."[70] The actual number of encounters was only about nineteen.

In the 13 September raid on Auschwitz, the 96 B-24 bombers observed a few enemy fighters but encountered none. Except for the P-38 escort engaging three enemy fighters, it was a relatively quiet day. The five groups of B-24s lost three planes to flak (which the Germans had increased since the 20 August raid) for a total loss rate of 3%, well below average for the Fifteenth Air Force. In this case, the Intelligence Annex Report had predicted that the total number of enemy fighter sorties would probably be less than 100. They were not even close.[71] Indeed, we must conclude from the above examples that even if the Freya Radar sites were in operation in 1944, the Germans were not sending many Luftwaffe fighters at the bombers attacking the Upper Silesian oil plants. And on those occasions when the German Air Force chose to fight, they faced Allied air forces that were quantitatively and qualitatively superior.[72]

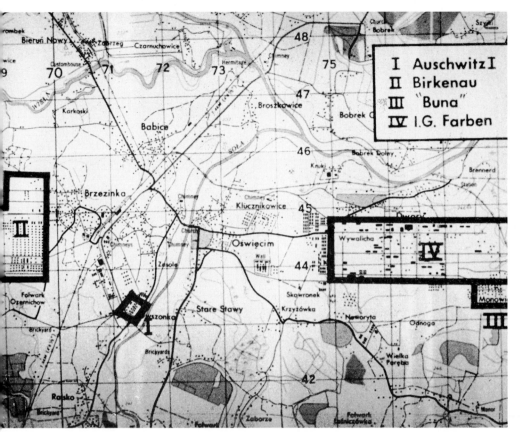

Figure 4-1. This map shows Auschwitz II-Birkenau camp on the left (II) in relationship to the original main camp I, the Auschwitz III-Monowitz labor camp for I. G. Farben, and the Farben industrial zone itself, which was due east of Birkenau. *Courtesy of Dino A. Brugioni*

Figure 4-2. This aerial photo from 26 June 1944, labeled by Dino A. Brugioni and Robert G. Poirier in 1979, again shows the spatial relationship of the various Auschwitz camps and industries. *Courtesy of the National Archives and Dino A. Brugioni*

Figure 4-3. The Auschwitz I main camp and the related industrial area is shown in this photo from the first successful photo-reconnaissance mission over Auschwitz on 4 April 1944. In 1979 Brugioni and Poirier noted on the far right the construction of the rail spur into Birkenau that would take Hungarian Jews directly to the extermination complex. *Courtesy of the National Archives and Dino A. Brugioni*

Figure 4-4. Hungarian Jews being "selected" on the ramp at Birkenau, 1944. Most will shortly be murdered in the gas chambers. *Courtesy of Yad Vashem and Dino A. Brugioni*

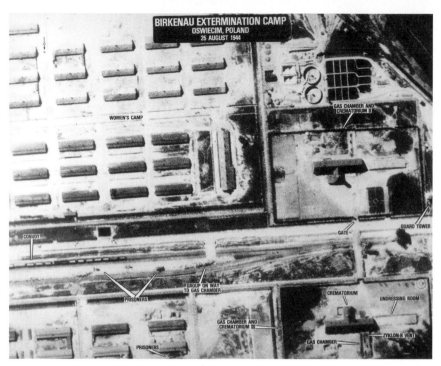

Figure 4-5. With much higher magnification than was available during the war, in 1979 Dino Brugioni and Robert Poirier were able to detect what appears to be a column of new arrivals on 25 August 1944 being marched to their death in Crematorium II. *Courtesy of the National Archives and Dino A. Brugioni*

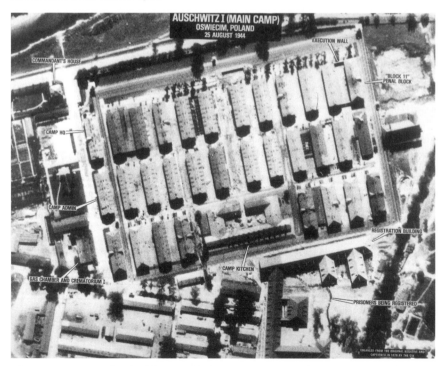

Figure 4-6. In another highly magnified 25 August 1944 photo, Brugioni and Poirier found a line of new prisoners being registered at Auschwitz I. *Courtesy of the National Archives and Dino A. Brugioni*

Figure 4-7. USAAF B-17 Flying Fortresses of the 20th Bombardment Squadron, 2nd Bombardment Group, 15th Air Force, are accompanied by a P-38 Lightning escort fighter on the first deep penetration mission against the Blechhammer synthetic oil complex on 7 July 1944. *Courtesy of the National Archives*

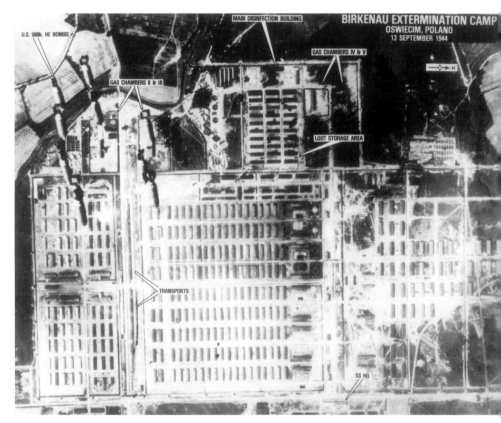

Figure 4-8. In this photo taken during the 13 September 1944 American heavy bomber raid on the I. G. Farben complex, U.S. 500-pound bombs encircle Birkenau Crematoria II and III. Because of the momentum of the aircraft, the bombs will fall much farther east.
Courtesy of the National Archives and Dino A. Brugioni

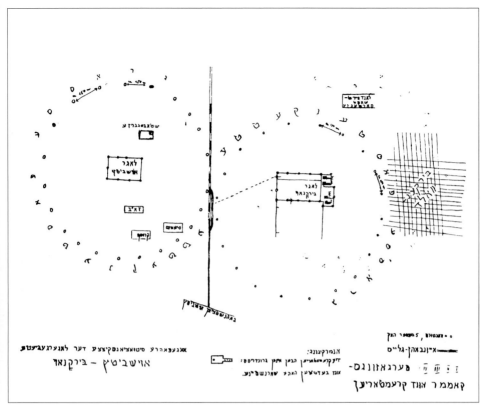

Figure 4-9. Original Yiddish version of the sketch map of the Auschwitz camps prepared by Rudolf Vrba in Zilina, 25 April 1944. *Reproduced with permission of Rudolf Vrba. Source: Franklin Delano Roosevelt Library*

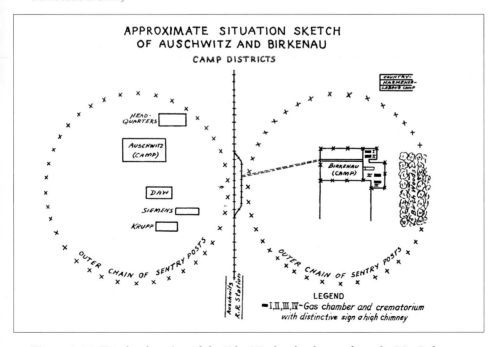

Figure 4-10. Translated version of the Vrba-Wetzler sketch map from the War Refugee Board report "The Extermination Camps of Auschwitz (Oswiecim) and Birkenau in Upper Silesia," released 26 November 1944. *Executive Office of the President*

Figure 4-11. A 21 December 1944, reconnaissance photo of Birkenau shows *Reichsführer-SS* Heinrich Himmler's attempt to cover up Nazi crimes by dismantling the gas chambers and crematoria after he ordered the gassing program stopped in November. The photo also shows the destroyed Crematorium IV, which was blown up during a suicidal but effective revolt of the Jewish *Sonderkommando* in October. *Courtesy of the National Archives and Dino A. Brugioni*

Weather Factors

The extent to which the weather could have hampered a bombing mission over southern Poland has also been overstated by the critics. While an issue that is as relevant to Birkenau as it is to any other target in Europe need not take up more space than necessary, it is important to clear up an error by Kitchens with regards to the weather in southern Europe, Upper Silesia and the Balkans. In contrast to Kitchens's assertion that northern Europe had better weather, General Doolittle argued for the formation of the new Fifteenth Air Force in southern Italy, citing better weather conditions in Foggia as one reason.[73] In fact, during the summer of 1944, Allied air crews encountered clear visibility for their missions in Upper Silesia. For the period of April through September 1944, official statistics indicate that, except for September, the Fifteenth Air Force experienced fewer aborted bomber sorties due to bad weather than did the Eighth Air Force based in England.[74]

ALLIED BOMBING SCENARIOS

High Altitude Bombing

BUCHENWALD ALLIED AIR RAID. A common argument long marshaled by bombing of Auschwitz critics is that any concentrated high altitude air attack on the death camp would have killed many prisoners in the process. We can never know for sure the extent of the prisoner casualties that would have resulted. But by comparing such an attack to raids like that on Buchenwald, we can judge the degree to which this factor should have played a role in any potential bombing decision.

While Kitchens cites the 24 August 1944 raid on Buchenwald as proof that the inaccuracy of heavy bombers would have killed many Birkenau prisoners, the mission itself proves the exact opposite. The Buchenwald raid was, in fact, an extremely accurate one, successfully avoiding the concentration camp during a bombing of the Gustloff Works adjacent to it. According to the *Buchenwald Report*, the attack "completely destroyed the 'industrial development work' of the SS in Buchenwald in one single, well aimed blow."[75] The *Report* further stated that "there were only two large fires caused by incendiary bombs,"[76] and an inmate wrote that "no [heavy] bombs struck the camp itself; only one bomb fell adjacent to the crematorium."[77] The 384 prisoners killed were working in the factory areas at the time of the raid and were not allowed to retreat to the camp or to use bomb shelters during an air-raid alarm or attack,[78] prompting another inmate to write: "The sole responsibility for the unfortunate deaths of several hundred prisoners in this attack falls on the SS, which at the time forbade prisoners to evacuate into the camp during an air raid alarm. . . ." The same prisoner also made it a point to note the effort of the Allied pilots to avoid collateral damage: "The Allied pilots in particular did all they could in order not to hit prisoners. The high number of prisoners killed is to be charged exclusively against the debit accounts of the Nazi murderers."[79]

Striking aerial imagery shot during the raid shows bomb bursts clustered in the factory areas, while the concentration camp clearly remains untouched. Notation on the photos indicates that two of the attacking groups reported 90% of bombs falling within 1,000 feet and 50% within 500 hundred feet of the target area, an achievement rivaling the April 1945 raid Kitchens mentions as being the most accurate of the war.[80] And though Kitchens is forced to concede this "above average accuracy," he does not make the critical distinction that the prisoners' deaths came about directly because the SS prevented inmates from returning to the concentration camp.[81] In the case of Birkenau, since many of the prisoners were used as forced labor outside of the camp (as the Vrba-Wetzler report indicated and Colonel Stanley confirms[82]) and far away from the crematoria, the argument weakens further still. We now know that estimates by Kitchens and others for collateral deaths can be reduced by 40–50% based on the approximate number of inmates living in Birkenau and used as slave labor outside of the camp.[83]

The Buchenwald raid sheds light on a hypothetical Birkenau bombing scenario in other ways as well. Since 80 SS men died in the attack, it made, according to the *Report*, "an extraordinarily deep impression on the SS. From then on they were rather intimidated, fleeing to the shrapnel trenches at the slightest air raid alarm." It goes on to say that the SS "viewed the camp as a place of refuge and protection for themselves," ironic testimony to the accuracy of Allied pilots.[84] In the event of a low-level fighter attack at Birkenau, the concentration camp guards would most likely have been cowering in their trenches than firing on the planes. Their "courage," in any case, was reserved for beating and killing their defenseless prisoners.

Despite the inadvertent killing, the collateral effects of the raid included lifting the spirits of the inmates. "Every visit by Allied planes encouraged a mood of confidence among the prisoners."[85] If anything, the Buchenwald raid gives us an intriguing glimpse of what might have been achieved at Birkenau.

There is a final aspect of this raid which is also useful in conceptualizing what might have happened at Birkenau. The Buchenwald factories were believed by the Allies to be producing V-2 rocket parts and were thus attacked as part of the CROSSBOW offensive, despite the fact that the Allies knew well of the adjacent concentration camp.[86] Whether they knew too that over 82,000 inmates were there is unclear, though even assuming a far lesser figure the decision to bomb was made with full knowledge that numerous prisoners could be killed if accuracy was below average (and this for a questionable strategic and tactical objective).[87] Indeed, if the accuracy had not been up to standards, it is conceivable that more inmates would have been killed in this one raid than the total number of British civilians killed by all V-2 rocket attacks.[88] To be consistent in their reasoning, then, those opposed to high altitude bombing of Birkenau because of collateral deaths would have to consider this raid unconscionable. The British government, however, had its own priorities.

HIGH ALTITUDE BOMBING ACCURACY. In his discussion of possible raid scenarios, Kitchens dismisses any attack by heavy bombers, arguing that their limited accuracy would have killed too many prisoners, thus resulting in unacceptable collateral damage.[89] The problem, in this case, is not so much Kitchens's argument as his reasoning. He ignores, for example, the fact that most of these prisoners would be killed anyway, focusing only on how many Jews might have been killed by the bombing, rather than how many could have been saved.[90] Kitchens manifested no similar concern with collateral killing of innocent civilians in the various Gestapo headquarters raids or the non-condemned prisoners at Amiens by the Royal Air Force (RAF), which was an expected and accepted part of that risky mission. As for the Jews, it was common knowledge that they were all condemned to death; Roosevelt made that clear in his 24 March speech. The only valid question was how soon and by whom the sentence would be executed.

Furthermore, one way to ensure that potential collateral deaths were kept to a minimum was to use more accurate crews. In the Fifteenth Air Force, "the [heavy bomber] Wing with the smallest aiming errors was 40% more accurate than the Wings with the highest aiming errors."[91] Use of medium bombers, which also enjoyed higher accuracy, was another option.[92] On 18 August 1944, for example, the 321 BG attacked Toulon harbor in a raid that shares some similarities with a hypothetical raid on Birkenau. Thirty-six B-25Js using 1,000-lb. bombs were assigned to destroy four precise, narrow-profile targets—the battleship *Strasbourg* (214m long × 31 m wide), the cruiser *La Gallisoniere* (179 m × 17.48 m), a submarine (approx. 70m × 6.5m) and a destroyer.[93] Bombing from 13,000 feet, the planes met 82 heavy AA guns protecting the harbor. Despite the "extremely intense" flak on the run up, the 321 BG destroyed the battleship, cruiser, and sub with direct hits (the destroyer had departed prior to the attack). Eleven men were wounded and 27 planes received some damage, but none were lost.[94]

Accuracy was also dramatically improved when bombing conditions such as a good run up to the target, clear visibility, and positive target identification were met. In most cases, when these conditions were not optimal, secondary or tertiary targets were chosen. The 19 July 1943 raid on the marshaling yards in Rome provides a good illustration of this. For this particular mission, air crews received special, detailed instructions to avoid cultural and religious shrines, and famous churches and historic building were clearly marked on the aerial maps with bright red squares and the warning: "MUST NOT BE HARMED." General Lewis Brereton wrote that "Bombardiers were instructed that if there was any doubt about where their bombs would land they were not to release them."[95] Post-raid PR revealed "precision bombing of the highest order" with "only one religious shrine" in the whole city receiving any damage.[96]

Another example of the ability of air commanders to influence bomber accuracy occurred in the spring of 1944, when General Spaatz was faced with the possible deaths of French and Belgian civilians resulting from the planned destruction of local rail centers. He answered this threat by ordering that "the best lead bombardiers would be used, no indiscriminate bombing would be permitted ... and crews must be impressed with the need for air discipline in order to avoid needless killing of French personnel." Conrad Crane writes that through Spaatz's efforts, "civilian casualties were considerably reduced."[97]

Those who advocate bombing Auschwitz, Kitchens writes, "have consistently minimized the casualties that might have resulted." While it is true that high altitude bombing was not a precise weapons delivery system, Kitchens's arguments for heavy collateral casualties are just too simplistic and misleading.

Kitchens and Levy have further confused the bombing of Auschwitz question by making use of an inaccurate map of the camp and giving an imprecise analysis of bombing accuracy. Camp BIIf, the section closest to the crematoria, shows barracks in the middle and southern part of the camp which are within the 1,000 foot overlay of Crematoria III. Photo-imagery and more faithful postwar maps, however, show this area to be completely devoid of any buildings. And most of the barracks indicated to be within 1,000 feet of the four aiming points (on the map Kitchens adapted from Gilbert's *Auschwitz and the Allies*) do not even exist! Further, Crematoria IV and V are placed directly north of Crematoria II and III, instead of further west and away from the closest barracks area, reducing the number of barracks within 1,000 feet of IV and V even more.[98]

As for Kitchens's and Levy's analysis of bombing accuracy, the averages they quote are imprecise, as any statistical averaging will be when used without careful analysis and comparison of raw data with a specific mission. Operations analysts during the war noted that the smaller the bomber force and size of each combat box (a bombing formation where all planes drop their bombs after the lead bombardier releases his), the more accurate the bombing. While either a single stream or three plane front would have been used at Birkenau, the average is weighted more with the less accurate 6-, 9-, and 12-plane fronts.[99] While anything more than 50 to 100 bombers would have been untenable at Birkenau, the raw data is composed of formations of hundreds of bombers whose inaccuracy would be measured not in feet but in miles.[100]

With the more accurate three-aircraft front, bombs fell in patterns most resembling rectangles, with the larger dimension parallel to the track of the formation over the target.[101] If at Birkenau the track is south to north, errors in range would *not* result in bombs falling in the barracks area, but rather in: (1) open fields north or south of the crematoria; (2) the second crematoria of each group; and (3) the "Canada" loot storehouse area between the two pairs of crematoria.[102] Easterly errors in deflection would land in barracks areas, while those on the west would land in open fields. Since large errors were greater for range than deflection, the barracks area would more likely receive a smaller proportion of errant bombs outside the 1,000-ft. radius than the areas long or short of the Aiming Point.[103] (See fig. 9-2.)

In sum, accurate crews ordered to bomb under optimal conditions and using the most advantageous bombing formations, while not capable of pickle-barrel placement, could have achieved significantly higher accuracy averages than those cited by Kitchens and Levy.

American Low-Level Scenarios: P-38 Raid on Ploesti

The Allied raid on the Ploesti oil fields of Romania (10 June 1944) provides another comparative scenario for a potential bombing mission over Birkenau.[104] It was David Wyman, in fact, who first suggested that low-level P-38 fighter bombers could have been effective on the death camp, while both Kitchens and Levy were quick to point out the "appalling" losses suffered by the Allies flying P-38s over Ploesti. As we will see below, the Ploesti raid may have had its problems, but these problems in no way indicate what one would expect using P-38s with the very different target conditions presented by Birkenau.[105]

The most glaring fault of the Kitchens/Levy argument is that they make no attempt whatsoever to differentiate the defenses of Ploesti with those of Birkenau. Kitchens writes, for example, that the pilots of the 82nd FG "had to dive through dense smoke—artificial cover thickened by bomb blasts—and had considerable trouble in locating their targets."[106] At Birkenau, however, we know that smoke screens were not a problem. On the photo-imagery for the 20 August and 13 September raids, the smoke screens for the Farben plant did not affect Birkenau at all.

As for the enemy opposition at Ploesti (barrage balloons, fighters and flak defenses, in addition to well armed and trained troops), it was significantly greater than Auschwitz ever was. According to the official US Army Air Force history, in June 1944 ". . . Ploesti by now had become the third best defended target on the continent," just behind Berlin and Vienna.[107] And the United States Strategic Bombing Survey reported that "During April, May and June [1944] there were more enemy aircraft encounters per 100 sorties over the Ploesti area than over any other area attacked."[108] The Farben plant at Auschwitz, although certainly an important target, did not command the kind of fighter defenses that Ploesti did. Levy's point that "German air defense was not as weak as Wyman suggests" simply fails to distinguish the obvious priority that the hard-pressed Germans placed on defending Ploesti over other targets.

In order to avoid the intense ground fire from 237 light AA guns and numerous heavy machine guns defending Ploesti, the mission was conceived and executed as a dive bombing raid rather than an attack from the "deck."[109] In

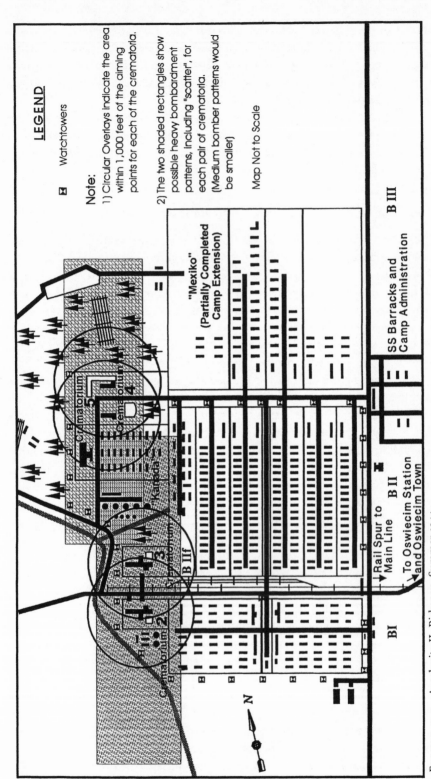

FIGURE 9-2. Auschwitz II, Birkenau, Summer 1944.

other words, the P-38s began to dive at 7,000 feet, releasing their bombs at 3,000 to 2,500 feet. This technique, in short, is not nearly as accurate as diving from lower altitude or attacking from the deck, which were the approaches used at Amiens and various Gestapo headquarters in the absence of light and medium AA. It is also the approach, as Cheshire suggests, that would have undoubtedly been employed at the lightly defended Birkenau.

Both Kitchens and Levy ignore the positive operational model that the Ploesti raid provides for Birkenau. They fail to mention that P-38s were able to carry a 1,000-lb. bomb, in addition to a full load of ammunition, a distance of 650 miles over the "turbulent air" of the Balkans, returning 650 miles to base for a total of 1,255 miles.[110] (This is Wyman's figure. Levy's statement that Allied bases at Brindisi were at a direct distance of 515 miles from Ploesti ignores the fact that to achieve tactical surprise a circuitous route around Bucharest was selected.) Kitchens and Levy also fail to comment on how well Allied fighter escorts would be expected to function in air space considerably less well defended than Ploesti.[111] Further, while Kitchens is silent about the minimal collateral damage expected in a precision low-level raid by P-38, he is quick to emphasize possible heavy collateral damage from a high altitude attack. Nor is there any mention that the handful of heavy aircraft guns at Birkenau and Auschwitz I would have been ineffectual against fast low-level fighters.[112] When Kitchens speaks of Birkenau as being a "well nigh invulnerable target," one wonders what hyperbole he might suggest for Ploesti.

Royal Air Force Scenarios

Since Wyman's book concentrates on America and the Holocaust, he does not consider the potential role of the Royal Air Force (RAF) in a raid on Birkenau, and Kitchens, ironically enough, follows this lead. Fortunately, Bernard Wasserstein's *Britain and the Jews of Europe, 1939–1945*, carefully analyzes the circuitous paper trail left by British political and military leaders involved in the decision over the bombing of Birkenau.

On 7 July 1944, British Foreign Secretary Anthony Eden wrote to the Secretary of State for Air, Sir Archibald Sinclair, inquiring "if anything could be done by bombing to stop the murder of Jews in Hungary." Sinclair and his staff replied on 15 July that due to various operational problems, the RAF could do nothing. And though he did propose bringing the question up with the Americans, Sinclair added that "I am not clear that it would really help the victims." Next to this remark, Eden scribbled: "He wasn't asked his opinion of this; he was asked to act," and then summed up the letter as "characteristically unhelpful."[113] Richard Levy, however, took Sinclair's response at face value and labeled the letter "reasonable." What was the exact nature of the operational obstacles that Sinclair mentioned, and how valid were they?

First, Sinclair argued that bombing the camp was "out of bounds of possibility for [RAF] Bomber Command, because the distance is too great for the attack to be carried out at night."[114] Levy quotes Air Marshal Harris (a.k.a. "Bomber" Harris) for confirmation that "the extent of darkness" affects range. In other words, the major operational obstacle for the RAF in attacking Birkenau was the inability of British bombers to return to their bases in England under cover of darkness. Yet this same inability of airlift bombers to leave from and return to Italian bases at night did not prevent them from being sent in August and September to Warsaw, 150 miles farther than Birkenau was from Allied bases in Italy.

In a further clarification of Sinclair's statement, Levy writes that RAF aircraft were "all based in England . . . ," implying that they were too far from Birkenau to return home before the first light of day. If, then, we assume that such a raid would have been possible as long as British bombers were based close enough to the target to return before dawn, it is difficult to understand why Sinclair and later Levy say nothing about RAF 205 Group and the Balkan Air Force based in southern Italy (a British bombardment group is the equivalent of an American bombardment wing and vice versa). The 205 Group consisted of three wings of Wellington Mk. X medium bombers, one wing of American-made Liberators (B-24 heavy bombers), and one squadron of Halifax target-finder aircraft.[115] The official history of the RAF states that the Wellington Mk. X could carry 4,500 lbs. of bombs 1,470 miles, or 1,500 lbs. of bombs 2,085 miles, giving it the capacity to attack Birkenau with an effective bomb load and return to base while it was still dark.[116] As evidence, Wellingtons and Liberators played an important part in the "oil war," attacking Ploesti five times between 5 May and 17 August with 924 sorties and mining the Danube River to prevent oil-laden barges from reaching the Reich. And while Sinclair and Levy seem to have conveniently forgotten about this force, the British air staff also called upon it to fly the Warsaw airlifts that began on 4 August.

Second, Sinclair's claim that the distance to Birkenau precluded an RAF raid is disputed by Leonard Cheshire, V.C., a highly decorated RAF pilot. In a 1961 interview that he gave, Cheshire stated: "It would have to have been done by [heavy bombers] Lancasters, and so would have had to be a night operation . . . going in low, we could have bombed it accurately."

However, to support Sinclair's claim, Levy implies that Cheshire had a change of heart when he learned in a 1982 interview that the raid would have occurred during the short nights of summer, preventing the bombers from returning to their bases under the cover of darkness. In the same 1982 interview, however, Cheshire clearly remained convinced that an effective raid was possible, even giving details of such a precision raid: ". . . I would have selected six aircraft to go in low and use a dive bombing technique. . . . I'd have the rest of the squadron either doing a diversionary attack, or somewhere in the vicinity ready to be called in, in case we failed." When asked in the same interview if the four crematoria could have been destroyed without killing thousands of prisoners nearby, Cheshire replied:

> I should think we might have destroyed three. We might not have destroyed all of them. You are asking a lot at this extreme range in knowing we have to get ourselves out without full cover of night—because it's summer now. I think we could have done three. I do not think we would have many miss-hits because we did not drop bombs unless we knew we were aiming on the target.[117]

While acknowledging Sinclair's claims of extreme range and short summer nights, Cheshire nevertheless believed the crematoria could have been successfully attacked by the RAF with minimal collateral damage.

Because Cheshire's 1961 statement called for Lancasters in the bombing of Birkenau, Levy concludes that Cheshire "ruled out the use of Mosquitos for an attack on Auschwitz." The reason for this, he writes . . . lies in the simple fact missed by Wyman, Kitchens, Foregger, Robert H. Hodges, and Lucy Dawidowicz: Mosquitoes "did not have sufficient range to bomb Auschwitz." Was this indeed the case?[118]

Figures from the official history of the RAF indicate the following Mosquito bombers as operational aircraft in 1944.[119]

	BOMB LOAD (LBS)	STILL AIR DISTANCE (MILES)	OPERATING RANGE
Mosquito Mk. XVI	2,000 lbs.	1,795 miles	1,346 miles
Mosquito Mk. XX	2,000 lbs.	1,870 miles	1,402 miles
	3,000 lbs	1,620 miles	1,215 miles

Mosquito variant listed as operational aircraft in 1942–43 are as follows:[120]

	BOMB LOAD (LBS)	STILL AIR DISTANCE (MILES)	OPERATING RANGE
Mosquito Mk. IV	2,000 lbs.	1,620 miles	1,215 miles
Mosquito Mk. IX	1,000 lbs.	1,870 miles	1,402 miles

The Mk. XVI and Mk. XX, each with a 2,000-lb. load, and the earlier Mk. IX with a 1,000-lb. load are within the 1,240 mile round-trip to Auschwitz. The Mk. IV with a 1,000-lb. load could also have made it. Based on precision raids against various Gestapo headquarters and the Amiens prison, we can assume that only 2 × 500-lb. bombs would be carried per plane, giving an additional cushion of about 200 miles to the Mk. XVI, XX, and IV aircraft. Further, another 110-mile buffer was available by using the Allied base on the Adriatic island of Vis, as Wyman suggests. Kitchens, while describing the manifold potential problems with Vis, ignores the simple fact that up to 120 planes were refueled daily at this forward base.[121]

Though the above aircraft were clearly capable of a mission to Birkenau from US and RAF bases in Italy, they would not have made it from England, 840 miles away (1,680 miles round-trip). This is why Cheshire, referring only to British based operations in the 1961 interview, singled out Lancasters, which as early as 1942 had flown missions of up to 1,700 miles round-trip.[122]

A clear instance of the low-level precision bombing of which RAF Mosquitoes were capable is the Amiens prison raid of February 1944, which Wyman referred to as a model for a mission to Birkenau.[123] Though Kitchens called it an "infinitely better known, simpler, and closer target than Auschwitz with unmistakable life-and-death urgency," the prison at Amiens (northeastern France) was actually a far more complex target than Birkenau would have been, primarily because of the mission's objective: to pry open the prison gingerly (rather than simply destroy it) with bombs in order to allow for the escape of resistance leaders slated for execution. As difficult as using just the right amount of precisely placed explosives to break thick prison walls and locks without also killing the very people they were attempting to save was, there was the additional consideration of 24-hour manned machine gun emplacements, German anti-aircraft coastal defenses, and the Luftwaffe forces at the nearby Abbeville base.[124] So complex and fraught with peril was this mission, in fact, that several RAF commanders as well as the Air Ministry questioned its practicality, and the contingency plan called for the complete destruction of the prison (and therefore death of numerous prisoners not scheduled for execution) should the attack look like it was going to fail.[125] Still, despite a driving snowstorm that sent back four of the nineteen planes, the mission proceeded with good results.[126]

What is unquestionable is that the purpose of the Amiens prison raid had been clouded in the military bravura of a job well done. Perhaps there are classified files that would shed light on this complex mission, carried out despite the misgivings of senior commanders and under the most trying operational conditions. But what is known is that the decision to save the doomed inmates was made in full awareness that many people not condemned to death would be sacrificed as a result, and in the face of operational complexities that would have made Birkenau appear routine. To claim that the "unmistakable life and death urgency" of a handful of prisoners could somehow outweigh that of the thousands of innocents perishing daily in the gas chambers just goes beyond all rational and moral thinking and certainly brings us no closer to an answer for why the Allies did not bomb Birkenau.

CONCLUSION

The focus of this chapter has been the narrow but crucial issue of whether the Allies had operational capacity to successfully bomb the killing facilities at

Auschwitz-Birkenau. In addition to this question of whether they could have bombed the death camp, the separate question of whether they should have must also be asked, though we must do so in the correct order. First, from a strictly operational point of view, could the four extermination facilities have been destroyed from the air? If the answer is no, then the discussion is at an end. But if the answer is yes or even maybe, then we can begin to ask the more compelling question of should such a raid have been carried out.

The Allied political and military leaders understood the logic of this order. Both Sinclair and John J. McCloy, the U.S. Assistant Secretary of War, indicated that the target could not be bombed, thus putting an end to any further discussion on the matter. Yet their determination was not based upon standard operational procedure. As we have seen above, neither the British nor the Americans ever deliberately took a single photograph of Birkenau, though it would hardly have stretched their resources to do so. Further, no one ever bothered to make a simple request to the photo library for imagery of the Auschwitz area. The "could not" assessment, in short, appeared the most expedient way to implement the already established policy of not using the military to aid "refugees."[127]

Even if the death camp could have been bombed, as this chapter has sought to prove, the next line of argument against doing so was that it would have required, as McCloy indicated, the "diversion of considerable air support essential to the success of our forces now engaged in decisive operations."[128] This term "diversion" can be applied to those actions which are (1) not directly related to military operations, or (2) not expressly ordered by the proper authority. Thus if Churchill (and the War Cabinet) or Roosevelt or any high-ranking commander had ordered an attack, then that mission would not be considered a diversion. The substantial distraction of the Warsaw airlift from "decisive operations elsewhere" was not considered a diversion for precisely this reason.

Another official Allied response against the bombing was that a mission to Birkenau required the kind of "considerable" military resources that would have seriously affected the prosecution of the war. Viewed against the backdrop of the Fifteenth AF operations, just how "considerable" would one raid of 80 fighters (half for escort) or 100 bombers (with escort) have been? The number of effective fighter sorties in the Mediterranean Theater of Operations (MTO) in 1944 was the following: April—14,908; May—19,652; June—15,568; July—14,768; August—17,538.[129] With the average number of sorties per day between 500 and 650, one mission of 80 fighter sorties represents $\frac{1}{7}$–$\frac{1}{8}$ of one day's total missions. If genuine military considerations are the true test, we are forced to conclude that the scale of such an air attack would not have affected the war effort in any appreciable way.

From a simple comparison with other missions, there can be no question that the Birkenau extermination facilities could have been attacked by P-38 or

Mosquito fighters using low-level precision bombing and causing minimal collateral damage. As we have seen, the route to southern Poland did not have the
same German Air Force priority that Vienna or Ploesti did, and the defensive
measures instituted by Himmler in February 1943 were to prevent prisoner
escapes, not to thwart an air attack. With no light or medium AA or smoke
screens, and with the heavy guns defending the Farben plant ineffective against
fast fighters, Birkenau was quite vulnerable to a low-level attack.

Also indisputable is the fact that both USAAF and RAF heavy and medium
bombers had the range to attack the camp, though the inconsistent bombing
accuracy of the heavies made it necessary to consider the cost/benefit ratio in
human terms. In other words, how many would have to die to prevent the
slaughter of how many others? Such a judgment, of course, was not unique to
Birkenau, but constituted a decision taken even for strictly military operations.[130]

This chapter has made it a point to emphasize the ways in which Birkenau,
had it been considered as a potential target, would have compared favorably
with targets that were actually bombed during the war. What remains is only
to examine whether it should have been given such status, now that we know
it could more than likely have been bombed successfully. Humanitarian missions were not unique to World War II, even when they constituted a greater
strain on Allied resources than bombing Birkenau would have been.[131] The
British government, for example, voted to appropriate £300,000 in order to save
15,000 starving nomadic Bedouin in the southern Arabian district. Forming a
Famine Relief Flight in April 1944, the RAF ME HQ flew six Wellington Mk.X
bombers, "fresh from the UK," to a desert landing strip built especially for the
task. These six aircraft, with their full air and ground crews pulled from England
six weeks before D-Day, were used exclusively to feed the Bedouin at the same
time the Birkenau gas chambers were operating at full capacity.[132]

While this is not to equate the importance of one humanitarian mission
over another, such decisions were regularly made during the war. The airlifts
to the Polish Home Army in Warsaw, for example, represent an operation in
which the political goal of displaying solidarity with the Poles was deemed
worthy of military diversion, even in the face of severe loss of men and material.
Air Marshal John Slessor, one of many field commanders who articulated objections to the dangerous and costly airlifts (31 bombers with air crews were
lost), described his own inner struggle as the RAF Mediterranean commander
during the airlifts: "I was not unconscious of the fact that commanders must
sometimes accept casualties for what are narrowly called 'political reasons' . . .
it was that alone which precluded me from refusing absolutely to send any
more aircraft to Warsaw."[133] The airlift, by orders from the highest levels, became the operational fulfillment of a mission, not a diversion from "decisive
operations" elsewhere. And this mission, despite its enormous costs, was con-

sidered well worth the immeasurable benefit of displaying solidarity with the Polish uprising.

Such a cost/benefit analysis was simply never made in the case of Birkenau. The judgment that many inmates might have been killed was decided upon without any feasibility study and in complete ignorance of the location of the extermination facilities in relation to the camp. For all the Allies knew, the crematoria were situated in a field a mile from the camp and could have been destroyed with a few well-placed bombs, as Cheshire suggests. In short, moral values and political considerations were tragically neglected in the case of the Holocaust.

Finally, the *should have* question must be approached—to the extent possible based upon counterfactual reasoning—from the point of view of the efficacy of the mission. Richard Breitman argues that with intelligence reports received in 1943, enough could have been known about Birkenau to plan a raid in early 1944, had there been the will to act.[134] If we consider a scenario in which Roosevelt ordered an attack at the time of his 24 March 1944 speech and it took place sometime in May (just as the Hungarian deportations were beginning), destroying at least Crematoria II and III (which constituted 75 percent of the killing capacity), would the killing process have been impeded? First, as Wyman points out, it took eight months to build these complex "industrial" structures at a time when Nazi Germany was at the height of its power. To organize the skilled labor and refashion highly specialized parts in the spring/summer of 1944 would have been difficult, if not impossible.[135]

Kitchens's suggestion that the Jews could have been sent to Mauthausen, Belsen, or Buchenwald, none of which were extermination camps (or capable of accepting a few hundred thousand inmates on short notice), shows a certain ignorance of the camp system.[136] Without the extermination facilities, the SS would undoubtedly have been forced to slow or altogether halt the deportations (which in the summer 1944 amounted to 70–80,000 Hungarian Jews a week) while they resorted to other, less efficient means of killing and body disposal. Cremation ditches, like those used for a short period in 1944 for the overflow of corpses, were hardly a practical alternative due to the problems posed by the humidity as well as the threat of disease. It was for these very reasons, in fact, that Himmler had ordered the crematoria built in the first place.

Why the Allies did not bomb Birkenau will always be a subject of controversy due both to the significance of the site in historical memory, and to the built-in complexities of this counterfactual question. Yet we can now say with a good deal more confidence that the reasons put forth by Richard Levy and James Kitchens, based as they are on an "awareness of operational limits," are simply not credible. The truth that we must all face is that which David Wyman first brought to our attention twenty years ago: that the answer to this troubling question lies not in any military feasibility assessment that the Allies never made, but rather in some artificial determination of what constituted target priority. Indifference? Indecision? Disbelief? Anti-Semitism? All of these point to reasons that had more to do with the Allied mindset than its military capabilities.

Doris Kearns Goodwin, a noted Roosevelt historian, once said that she thought bombing Auschwitz would have been worthwhile "if it had saved only one Jew. FDR somehow missed seeing how big an issue it was."[137] With the kind of political will and moral courage the Allies exhibited in other missions throughout the war, it is plain that the failure to bomb Birkenau, the site of mankind's greatest abomination, was a missed opportunity of monumental proportions.

ACKNOWLEDGMENTS

The author is grateful to Professors David S. Wyman and Richard D. Breitman and Dr. Michael J. Neufeld for their comments on an earlier draft of this essay; and Dr. Paul B. Miller for his capable editing.

10

BOMBING AUSCHWITZ: U.S. FIFTEENTH AIR FORCE AND THE MILITARY ASPECTS OF A POSSIBLE ATTACK[1]

Rondall R. Rice

THE ONGOING HISTORICAL DEBATE surrounding the proposed bombing of Auschwitz has yet to provide a detailed analysis of the Fifteenth Air Force and its capabilities. If one leaves political decision-making aside, and examines the status of Fifteenth Air Force and German defenses during a specific, and likely, bombing period, the facts stand out clearly. The Fifteenth Air Force had the technical means and the window of opportunity to bomb the camp with a high probability of success, and with an accuracy that provided an acceptable risk to the prisoners. The only reason the bombing was not conducted was the lack of political will and backing.

David Wyman, Bernard Wasserstein, and Martin Gilbert, among others, have provided an in-depth analysis of the political aspects of why the Allies did not take military measures against the Nazi death facilities around Auschwitz, Poland.[2] These authors, however, only skimmed the surface of the capabilities, constraints, and complexities involved had the Allies decided to attack the four operating crematoria and gas chambers at Auschwitz II–Birkenau. On the other hand, James Kitchens and Richard Foregger have presented arguments against such an attack while ignoring the fact that despite the difficulties,[3] the Allies could have carried out such an attack if the political will existed to do so. An examination of the military's knowledge of Auschwitz's mission, the capabilities of various bombers to bomb the killing facilities, and possibilities of attacking the crematoria reveal that the heavy bombers of Fifteenth Air Force could have indeed bombed these facilities with acceptable accuracy. However, it would have required bombing during daylight and clear weather, and the missions would have to have been flown between July and early October 1944.

BOMBING REQUESTS AND GOVERNMENTAL
INFORMATION FLOW

In order to divert bombers from their priority targets would have required political intervention at the executive level. The military leaders would not, on their own, have diverted assets for what they would have viewed as a militarily nonessential mission. In the September 1944 airdrop of supplies to the Warsaw resistance, precedent demonstrates, however, that political pressure could indeed force the military to conduct a mission they viewed as outside the scope of winning the war as quickly as possible.

David Wyman provides excellent coverage of the relationships and discussions between the War Refugee Board (WRB) and the War Department's Operations Division (OPD).[4] In fact, the WRB's mission was to provide executive oversight and coordinate efforts to "rescue the victims of enemy oppression who are in imminent danger of death."[5] When discussing the possibility of using military forces to carry out its charge, the WRB coordinated with both the War Department's Civil Affairs Division and the OPD, which was in charge of planning the use of military forces to carry out national objectives. Wyman and Gilbert detail the interactions between the WRB and the War Department, but missing are any earnest bombing-related discussions at lower levels of command.

Had the War Department seriously studied the possibility of attacking Auschwitz, or rail lines leading to it from Hungary, during the spring and summer of 1944, it is reasonable to assume that these requests and studies would be in the records of Army Air Forces (USAAF) leaders such as Generals Henry "Hap" Arnold, Carl Spaatz, James Doolittle, Nathan Twining, and Ira Eaker. No such records exist in their official or personal papers until very late in the period, and these documents referring to the possible bombing of Auschwitz were less a request for planning proposals and more afterthoughts for information purposes only. At the very least, a serious inquiry into an important operation using air power would have reached General Arnold, since he was Commanding General, Army Air Forces. In addition, it is also reasonable to assume that Arnold would have approached his theater commanders to ask their opinion, and to request information as to the plausibility of such attacks, available resources, resources necessary for such an attack, and chances of success. Arnold remained in constant contact with the air commanders in Europe—especially with Spaatz—because of the latter's direction of the largest and most important campaign in the young history of the U.S. air forces, the Combined Bomber Offensive. The belated information given on 4 October 1944 (as opposed to a serious request for planning action) demonstrated the lack of impetus behind the request from military and political leaders above Arnold. The lack of planning at the theater and lower command levels indicates that the bombing of Auschwitz was never seriously contemplated or studied. However, had the political will to bomb Auschwitz existed, it would have overcome the objections of the military leaders, as the Warsaw airdrop operations demonstrated.

Polish forces in Warsaw, anticipating the arrival of the Red Army, rose against the Nazis on 1 August 1944. The Soviet forces halted their offensive only 10 kilometers (6.2 miles) from the city. The personal attention of Churchill and Roosevelt ensured that the Allies attempted to provide badly needed supplies via airdrop—despite the objections of military, especially air force, leaders. The discussions, planning, and stated objections of military leaders, particularly General Carl Spaatz, generated a large amount of message traffic.[6]

After much planning and negotiation, the initial missions to assist the resistance fighters occurred on 11 September 1944, and continued for a week, halted only by the refusal of the Soviets to allow further missions. In comparison, the Auschwitz bombing proposals displayed a lack of urgency and political will. Still, the Warsaw operation aptly demonstrates that military leaders, when forced to accept missions with which they did not agree, would salute smartly and carry them out to the best of their ability when urged to do so by the civilian leadership.[7]

INTELLIGENCE AND PLANNING

In order to examine the possibility of bombing, assuming the political will existed and assuming the USAAF had become tasked with planning and carrying out such a mission, its leaders would have needed timely intelligence. First, they would have had to have known about Auschwitz, and its ghastly mission to exterminate Jews and others the Germans deemed undesirable. Then, specific target information would have been needed to plan the attack: the specific camp location, detailed location and construction of the four crematoria/gas chambers, and German defensese. All of this information was available by the end of July 1944, and further detailed information could have been accessed.

Before assessing what information the planners required, one must examine the information available to the air commanders during the summer of 1944. From 1942 to mid-1944, the Allied governments' information on Nazi concentration camps remained fragmentary. Martin Gilbert has asserted that the Allies did not know Auschwitz's secrets until June 1944, when they received the Auschwitz escapees' report.[8] However, taking advantage of recently declassified ULTRA intelligence, Richard Breitman has demonstrated that British intelligence knew about Auschwitz as early as 1942, and could have begun to solidify information from multiple sources, including the Polish underground, by 1943.[9]

Still, with the protection given to ULTRA codes and the Allied leaders' dictum not to act on ULTRA intercepts alone in order to protect the knowledge of the decryption,[10] one must question whether that material would ever have reached the British and American air forces. Information in available intelligence reports, notably in USAAF targeting folders, centered on the I. G. Farben industrial facility, and made little reference to the camps. Even when intelligence sources mentioned the presence of camps, they continually referred to them as prisoner-of-war or labor camps. Moreover, due to the range of the available aircraft, the Allies still could not have attacked Auschwitz prior to the Fifteenth Air Force being established in southern Italy and receiving its combat complement of aircraft. Nonetheless, it remains important to identify the intelligence, ULTRA excepted, that might have been available to the aircrews by 1944.

One of the earliest available official reports on Auschwitz came from the Office of Strategic Services (OSS), the forerunner of the Central Intelligence Agency. The short report, dated 25 August 1942, recorded the number of inmates for Auschwitz at fifteen thousand and describes them as "mostly intellectuals and middle class elements."[11] The report did mention inmate turnover as being "very great" and that two Polish workers had been executed. A separate report, dated 15 October 1943, provided in-depth information on the synthetic-oil and rubber works in the vicinity of Auschwitz. As detailed as the information is on the plant, very little data existed on the nearby camps.[12]

Intelligence information available to flight crews in Europe contained much the same information as the 1943 OSS report. However, the Target Information Sheet for the I. G. Farben complex, used for planning bombing missions, made no mention of the camps (as of 18 July 1944).[13] The file did contain a separate amendment, dated 21 September 1944, covering the labor camp area (Auschwitz III, or Monowitz). It provided a grid reference to locate the camp and said, "[it] is now known to be used as a Prisoner of War Camp."[14] The file also included the reconnaissance photos taken on 4 April 1944 by U.S. aircraft, and a map used by aircrews to show distance and magnetic headings as they approached the target.

The most significant intelligence, the escapees' reports, came to the WRB in July 1944. The WRB representative in Switzerland, Roswell McClelland, sent two messages to Washington, one to the State Department and one to the War Department (annotated "for the WRB"). Although dated 6 July, the messages arrived at their separate destinations on 8 July and 16 July, respectively, according to the stamps on the original messages. Together, they supplied the information on Auschwitz I and Birkenau (Auschwitz II) from the separate escapee reports of two Slovakian Jews who had fled the camp in April, Rudolf Vrba and Alfred Wetzler, and an escaped Polish officer. These reports do not include hearsay, but "actual personal experiences." In addition, McClelland wrote, "Their authenticity seems corroborated by fragmentary reports from different individuals and organizations in Switzerland which have come in the last two years, and particularly as to the composition of transports of Jewish deportees coming from everywhere in Europe."[15] The second message, a summation of all three escapees' reports, provided details on the layout, functions, and operations of both Auschwitz and Birkenau.[16]

Historians disagree on the actual dates that the complete reports were received by these authorities. In any case, the arrival stamp on the messages displays the dates mentioned previously. Therefore, had the political force been behind an effort to bomb the camp, military planners should have been able to access the information from these messages not later than 18 July. Still, as both Foregger and Kitchens wrote in their articles, these messages contained only a summation of the reports, and not the actual reports themselves. The complete reports, and their associated maps, did not arrive in Washington until the beginning of November, confirmed by the date on the WRB report.[17]

It remains unclear how much and what kind of information the military commanders in Europe had about the camp complexes around Auschwitz. As mentioned above, the target information file contained none of the WRB reports' information. Even two months after the WRB reports were in Washington, the target folder still mentioned only a prisoner-of-war camp.

Further down the command line, at the bomber squadrons themselves, crews of the Eighth and Fifteenth Air Forces do not recall ever being briefed about Nazi concentration camps, their location, or their function. In personal interviews with four crew members from the Fifteenth Air Force (727th and 838th Bombardment Squadrons) and one from the Eighth Air Force (339th Bomb Squadron), none remembered knowing about the camps during the war from official sources. They all had heard of possible atrocities from open press sources, but were never officially briefed, or otherwise informed.[18] Milton Groban, a B-17 radar navigator-bombardier, flew with the Fifteenth Air Force both in North Africa and Italy, and also served as a staff officer at Fifteenth Air Force Headquarters in Bari, Italy. He concurred with the other crew members' recollections and added that information regarding treatment of Jews came only via the press. He also said that personnel at the lower levels (group and squadron) took more interest in these press reports than Fifteenth Air Force staff officers. Of major concern was the treatment of downed Jewish fliers (Groban was himself Jewish).[19] This probably explains why those who flew missions tried to keep informed of Nazi treatment of Jews. The concern became a reality when Jewish fliers were ordered to alter the letter *H* on their dogtags (indicating Hebrew religious affiliation).[20] The easiest and least noticeable alteration was to imprint a *B* (for Baptist) over the *H*.[21]

Despite the claims of Kitchens and Foregger, if Washington had ordered the USAAF to bomb the camp, the available information, when compiled, provided sufficient intelligence to begin planning. By pooling the WRB's information, and the available target intelligence photos from 4 April and 26 June (and, depending when the mission planning occurred, the 25 August photos), air planners would have had a significant amount of information immediately at their disposal.

Both Foregger and Kitchens alluded to the inconsistencies between the escapee reports and the reconnaissance photos. Both argued that the reports (and later the sketch maps) did not provide adequate information for accurate bombing.[22] Furthermore, Kitchens asserted that only a personal debriefing of the escapees by Allied personnel could have resolved the inconsistencies between the report and the photos.[23] This statement is farfetched and inaccurate. Intelligence personnel would not have ignored information simply due to small inconsistencies. Trained to know that human intelligence reports can be fallible, they could easily have compared the reports to the photos and identified the correct location of the crematorium. Had clarification become necessary, additional reconnaissance missions could have been flown.

The question now returns to the "diversion of assets" so commonly given as the rationale of the War Department's refusal to bomb. While usually referring only to diversion of aircraft from military targets, the full impact of the effort that would have been required to plan the attack must be considered. Kitchens correctly stated that without the proper information at hand, military personnel in theater, and even military and civilian workers in Washington and London, would have been diverted from their normal war tasks to obtain the required intelligence. Such an effort would have required at least staff personnel, intelligence analysts, photo interpreters, and probably additional reconnaissance sorties. Intelligence resources, especially photo analysts, remained a constant priority throughout the war. Spaatz wrote to Arnold in March 1944 confirming that, in both northwest Europe and the Mediterranean theaters, unless more intelligence, planning, and communications officers arrived, "our air forces will suffer."[24]

Kitchens also wrote that the necessary intelligence gathering, planning, and bombing could not have been done in time to save the deported Hungarian Jews. Even though he did not consider the possibility that, with the proper authorities directing such events, this mission could have taken priority over other tasks, the mass of Hungarian Jewry probably could not have been saved. The final mass deportation of Hungarian Jews took place on 9 July,[25] while the crematoria continued to operate against new deportees from other countries. The Central Construction Office at Auschwitz estimated that crematoria II to V could incinerate 4,415 bodies each day, with two bodies burned in each oven for thirty minutes. Desiring to increase their capacity, camp authorities ordered the time be reduced to twenty minutes, and up to three bodies burned in each, thus almost doubling their capability to eight thousand bodies per twenty-four hours.[26] While perhaps unable to save the mass of Hungarian Jewry (Yehuda Bauer states that the Nazis gassed approximately seventy-five percent of them upon arrival),[27] bombing anytime before November, when gassing operations ceased, carried the possibility of saving many lives. (Bombing accuracy and probability of damage will be discussed later). The population of the Auschwitz camps fluctuated more than usual between the summer and autumn of 1944, due to killings, inflows from other areas and camps, and the beginning of the westward evacuation. Leni Yahil's sources put the 21 August population at 105,168 in all of Auschwitz's areas. By mid-October, the number dropped to around 95,000. At the final roll call on 17 January 1945, the number stood at 66,020 inmates.[28]

Pressure from either Roosevelt or Churchill could have ensured that the effort would have received the proper priority and would have been conducted in a timely manner. Without a doubt, to compile the necessary intelligence and plan the mission would have diverted work and assets being used to prosecute the air war against Germany. The full extent of such a diversion cannot be accurately measured, but probably would have been minimal in relation to the overall war effort.

Examination of available evidence so far suggests that the information existed, or could have been obtained, in order to plan an attack on the Auschwitz killing facilities. Had such an attack been ordered, the effort most likely would have fallen to the Fifteenth Air Force. By operating from air bases in Italy, it was within range to bomb Auschwitz, and it conducted attacks against strategic targets in and around Upper Silesia. The Eighth Air Force, operating from England, did not have the range to reach Auschwitz. For this reason, historians have mainly focused on the possibility of using the Fifteenth Air Force.

FIFTEENTH AIR FORCE: CAPABILITIES AND MISSIONS

Despite being a new command and heavily involved in the Combined Bomber Offensive, by the late summer and early fall of 1944, the Fifteenth Air Force contained the assets necessary to conduct an attack on Auschwitz. In addition, its operational doctrine contained the flexibility necessary to allow air commanders—even without political pressure—to order the attack. When looking at operational directives and capabilities, the timing of planning an attack on Auschwitz must be kept in mind. As shown above, the required intelligence was not available before late June 1944.[29] However, by July and August, enough information was available (or could have been so) to plan and carry out an attack. These two months were the optimum time to attack, and offered the best chance to save deported Jews. While attacks could have taken place from September to December, weather factors decreased the possibility of success. Therefore, this study pays maximum attention to the late summer months of 1944.

The original plans called for the Fifteenth Air Force to fill out its combat complement of units by March 1944. By June 1944, the Fifteenth Air Force controlled five bomb wings (BW) and one fighter wing. The 5th BW included six groups of B-17 Flying Fortresses. The remaining wings (47th, 304th, 55th, and 49th) operated B-24 Liberators. All B-24 wings contained four groups, except the 49th, which included only three.[30]

Although smaller than the Eighth Air Force, the Fifteenth represented a sizable force. On 7 June, the Fifteenth Air Force reported 1,146 heavy bombers on hand, compared with the Eighth's 2,786. Of the Fifteenth's total force, 720 bombers (63 percent) were operational.[31] From 7 June until 30 September, the Fifteenth Air Force averaged 1,204 bombers on hand each day. Of these, an average of 914 (76 percent) were reported as ready for duty.[32] Compared to the Eighth Air Force during the same period, the Fifteenth averaged fewer than half as many bombers on hand, but their operational rate was twelve percent higher. These numbers also reflect an acute shortage of replacement B-17s during the summer of 1944 due to increased B-29 production at the expense of the Flying Fortress.[33]

With such a significant force available, the next question follows: what were they doing? Specifically, the tasking and bombing directives require examination. At the Combined Bomber Offensive's inception, submarine bases topped the list of priority targets due to the Allied concerns over German interdiction efforts in the Battle of the Atlantic. Early in 1944, the attention turned to preparations for Operation Overlord, the D-Day invasion of Fortress Europe, and concern about the strength of the Luftwaffe. The 13 February 1944 directive from the Combined Chiefs of Staff formally placed the Luftwaffe at the top of the bombing list. The first priority became fighter airframe and component production, and installations supporting the German fighter force followed.[34]

As the German fighter threat diminished in the spring and early summer of 1944, Lt. Gen. Carl Spaatz, then the U.S. Strategic Air Force's (USSTAF) commander, viewed oil as the most promising strategic objective. The USSTAF commanded all U.S. strategic bomber forces in Europe, then divided into the Eighth and Fifteenth Air Forces. On 8 June 1944, only two days after the Normandy landings, Spaatz ordered that the USSTAF strategic aim be shifted to denying oil to the enemy. The order remained in force for the war's duration.[35] As a result of Spaatz's order, the Mediterranean Allied Air Force (MAAF) sent a revised bombing directive to its units on 15 June 1944. The information flow for POINTBLANK (the Combined Bomber Offensive's codename) targets flowed from USSTAF, to the MAAF, to the Mediterranean Allied Strategic Air Forces (MASAF), to the Fifteenth Air Force. The directive gave special missions, as required and directed by the commander, to support the land campaign in Italy and air support for OVERLORD as the first two target priorities. The third priority, POINTBLANK targets, had oil as the primary objective, followed by counter-air and communications targets.[36]

Eighteen days after it became effective, MAAF rescinded the 15 July bombing directive and ordered new priorities. The 3 August directive kept oil as the top priority (Auschwitz's oil facilities became target number nine), but remaining sources of ball and roller bearings moved to second, and counter-air came third. Although the revised order no longer incorporated wording regarding special targets as the top two priorities, the directive allowed for variations from the target list. If necessary, tactical uses of strategic bombers to aid the ground forces could replace the strategic priorities. Also, the directive stated, "specific attacks against targets in the above categories or any others may be ordered by this Headquarters from time to time."[37] Throughout the remainder of August and September, only minor changes occurred in this list. Spaatz, then the commander, issued a clarification of target priorities on 1 September. He urged using the remaining good weather to intensify attacks against oil targets, and he changed the second priority from bearings to rocket- and jet-propelled fighters and aircraft-engine factories.[38] A new bombing directive on 13 September duplicated the 3 August directive but added communications targets as the fourth priority.[39]

The evidence clearly shows the Fifteenth Air Force's ability to bomb Auschwitz, in aircraft and in command discretion within the target priorities. By the summer of 1944, the command controlled ample aircraft; those aircraft had sufficient range and payloads necessary for such a mission; and bombing directives allowed commanders the flexibility to direct attacks against special targets.

ANALYSIS OF GERMAN DEFENSES

By the late summer and early fall of 1944, German defenses, like the Nazi military machine overall, displayed signs of weakness but still constituted a sizable threat. The principal danger to any aircrews bombing Auschwitz came from Luftwaffe fighters along the route, and from antiaircraft guns at the target. Although the Germans could have met an attack on Auschwitz, this threat would not in itself have been enough to deter air commanders from planning such an attack. Moreover, as analysis of similar bombing missions shows, Allied losses would not have been significant.

Critics of the failure to bomb the crematoria, led by Wyman, tend to underestimate the German air defenses in 1944, while those who do not support the bombing, most notably Kitchens and Foregger, exaggerate the German threat. The Germans, like all World War II combatants, used two main systems for air defense: fighter aircraft and antiaircraft guns. On the Nazi side, the former was in decline by the summer and fall of 1944, while the latter became the most effective. Each will be examined, in turn, by looking at the threat perceived by planners, as well as at each system's actual bombing missions on and around Auschwitz.

Writers supporting a bombing effort correctly point out that the USAAF controlled the skies of Europe by mid-1944, but they wrongly characterize the notion of "air superiority." While Allied aircraft could fly over the continent with a higher degree of safety than in 1943, this did not mean they could fly with impunity. German fighters still represented a threat, and they continued to attack Allied aircraft. However, due to dwindling resources, especially fuel, the Germans marshaled their forces and attacked only when they saw a possible advantage or when targets they viewed as essential were threatened.

Spaatz, in his weekly summaries to Arnold, mentioned Luftwaffe tactics on two separate occasions in early and mid-1944. On 4 March, he wrote, "The enemy has been unable or unwilling to send his fighters in strength against [operations of the past week]. [I] believe he will withhold them except when weather conditions over Germany indicate good visual bombings over vital areas."[40] Spaatz summarized the enemy fighter tactics in his 8 May message. "German fighter forces," he wrote, "can no longer oppose our attacks indiscriminately but must, for purposes of conservation, select occasions when they have a tactical advantage."[41] Therefore, the time frame and area of attack must be analyzed to make possible an accurate analysis of German fighter opposition.

Among other duties, estimating and reporting on enemy air activity within the Fifteenth Air Force fell to the Assistant Chief of Staff for Intelligence (designated A-2). The A-2 staff produced several reports on enemy fighter defenses for the period in question. A 10 July report analyzed enemy fighter opposition to the Allied 7 July attack on Blechhammer (another important oil target located slightly more than forty miles northwest of Auschwitz, and that included a subcamp of Auschwitz providing slave labor). The Blechhammer attack was part of a concerted effort of the Eighth and Fifteenth Air Forces to attack oil-related targets in the region. The total effort sent more than a thousand B-17s and B-24s, with German fighters downing only twenty-five bombers.[42] Due to the importance of the targets, the Germans sent at least four hundred sorties against the formations (approximately three hundred aircraft, but some landing and attacking again). The intelligence report indicated 225 fighters assembled along the Vienna-Gyor line (Gyor is approximately seventy miles east of Vienna, or halfway between Vienna and Budapest). From Vienna to the target area, from 100 to 125 more aircraft attacked the formations. Finally, forty to fifty fighters, flying for the second time against the mission, intercepted the bombers near Gyor.[43] Although a significant effort by the Luftwaffe, it did not react in the same way when bombers attacked similar targets in the same area only six weeks later.

The first attack on the Auschwitz synthetic-oil refinery occurred on 20 August 1994 as part of a larger attack on oil facilities in the former Poland and Czechoslovakia. The attack plan called for five of the six B-17 groups of the 5th BW to attack Auschwitz with twenty-eight bombers each, for a total of 140.[44] In addition, ten of the twelve groups of B-24s in the 47th, 304th and 55th Bomb Wings would target the refineries Szolnok (Hungary), Dubova (Czechoslovakia), and Czechowice (Poland). The three B-24 groups of the 49th BW would attack Szolnok–Rakoczifalva airfield. The plan included using five groups of fighters from the 306th wing for escort.[45] The intelligence annex estimated that the enemy could oppose the attack with up to 110 sorties in the Budapest–Vienna area, and could reinforce the effort with thirty to thirty-five fighters from the Munich area. In addition, target area opposition could include fifty to sixty fighters, at most.[46] Milton Groban, one of the mission's radar-bombardiers, wrote in his diary, "we were expecting plenty of Luftwaffe because we were going into their stronghold.[47] However, on 20 August, the Luftwaffe disproved his and Fifteenth Air Force's expectations.

The Fifteenth Air Force A-2 report on the attacks called enemy opposition to the 20 August attacks "meager." After analyzing the separate reports from all fighter and bomber groups, the A-2 concluded that the formations saw only twenty-five to forty-five enemy aircraft. Of these, fifteen to twenty-five made a single-pass attack at the bombers as they passed east of Budapest, and the escorting fighters drove them away. Only two Me 109s attacked near the target areas. They targeted a "straggler," but did not succeed in bringing the aircraft down.[48] All bombers from the 5th BW returned to their base, and the remainder of the bombers reported no losses to enemy fighters. In fact, the 97th BG claimed its bomber crews shot down one Me 109, a second Me 109 kill was reported as probable, and a third one was damaged.[49]

The decline in enemy activity from the 7 July Blechhammer attack to the 20 August attacks around Auschwitz should not be interpreted as a trend. Only two days after the attacks on the I. G. Farben facility, the Fifteenth Air Force again attacked targets in Vienna and Blechhammer, drawing a reaction from 150 enemy aircraft.[50] The same complex was reattacked on 13 September when the 55th BW tasked a "normal effort" for all four of its B-24 groups.[51] Of the 115 bombers tasked, 101 arrived over the target area. Two of the groups reported seeing no enemy fighters, one reported seeing nine (six over the target area), and the other reported seeing three. None of the fighters engaged the bombers.[52] The mission and intelligence reports correspond with aircrew recollections. Six crew members interviewed said that although the Luftwaffe was not as aggressive and feared as they were prior to 1944, they remained a threat to be respected. In addition, all agreed that flak was the primary danger to the bombers. While the Luftwaffe threat declined as 1944 wore on, the flak became more numerous and "damned accurate."[53]

The revised A-2 Intelligence Plan assumed that, due to the declining capacity of the Luftwaffe, the Nazis would use antiaircraft (AA) guns to their maximum capacity. A-2 also believed that the concentration of guns could increase due to a fairly steady availability of AA guns conentrated within the Nazis' constantly shrinking territory. The document also noted that, with the Third Reich trying to defend its precious oil supplies and production capabilities, these areas contained some of the heaviest AA defenses. At the time of the report, Blechhammer was the eighth most heavily defended target in Europe.[54]

Flak defenses around the Auschwitz I. G. Farben facility totaled 316 heavy guns in late August. The 20 August tasking order's intelligence annex includes those guns around Vitkovice (thirty-five miles southwest), Krakow (twenty miles east), and Katowice-Gleiwitz (fifteen miles west) as being target area defenses.[55] These guns could target aircraft during their bombing run, during their time in the target area, or during their poststrike recovery prior to exiting the target area.

The mission reports, however, revealed that the flak defenses did not take a toll on the attackers. Two of the groups (99th and 2nd) reported the defensive fire as accurate, but only moderate in intensity. The remaining three groups of B-17s called the flak inaccurate and moderate.[56] The difference in reporting does not constitute inaccuracies by one or the other group. As in all large-scale bombing missions, the formations of aircraft could extend out miles on either side, and appeared over the target area at different times. The groups arrived over the target separately, but all dropped their ordnance between 1030 and 1100 hours. The flak downed no aircraft, but forty-five B-17s received minor damage, and one was severely damaged. In addition, flak wounded one man in the leg.

Less than one month later, the Fifteenth Air Force's visit would meet with a different fate from the German guns. Although not providing a specific count, the 13 September prestrike intelligence annex specified that "heavy guns have been added since [the 20 August attack]."[57] All four B-24 groups reported the target area flak as accurate and intense. Of the 101 aircraft flying over the target area, nine did not return to Italy. Four aircraft went down in the target area, four more made forced landings in Yugoslavia, two headed toward Russian territory, and one ditched in the Adriatic. In addition, eight B-24s recovered with severe flak damage, while forty-four more reported minor damage, and two crewmen were injured. Only thirty-seven of the 101 aircraft returned unscathed.[58]

The crematoria at Auschwitz–Birkenau were slightly more than four miles from the I. G. Farben facility. Although camp commandant Rudolf Höss and the escapees from Auschwitz all mentioned AA guns being in the camp,[59] the distance between Birkenau and the industrial complex would still allow the guns protecting the latter to engage the bombers. German flak guns ranged from the 88-millimeter to the 128-millimeter. The most numerous was the 88-millimeter Flak-36. Its maximum ranges extended 14,860 meters (9.2 miles) horizontal, and 10,600 meters (6.6 miles) vertical.[60] Still, one must consider whether German gunners would have targeted the bombers when they were not attacking the oil refinery. It would be reasonable to assume that if they did, because of the increased range from their positions, the damage would not have compared to the casualties suffered on 13 September.

Clearly, neither the fighter nor flak threat represented such danger to any proposed attack against the Birkenau crematoria that air leaders would have argued against the effort. Bombing accuracy, however, encompassed a large threat—not to the bombing forces, but to those the bombing would have attempted to save.

Before we analyze accuracy, the weight of effort required to destroy the gas chambers and crematoria requires examination. *Weaponeering*, a term used in today's target analysis, defines a target's characteristics and the number of bombs and aircraft needed to achieve probable destruction. Weaponeering will also provide insight into how much of a "diversion of resources" the attack would have demanded. Selecting and defining the target is the first step in weaponeering, followed by examination of target construction. From the type and construction, the targeting officer selects the type and number of weapons best able to destroy the target. These criteria determine the number of aircraft required to carry the ordnance. The expected damage is expressed in a "probability of damage."

By 1944, Auschwitz II–Birkenau contained all of Auschwitz's operational gas chambers and crematoria. Crematorium I at the main camp, and its attached gas chamber, ceased operation in December 1942. In 1942, two small cottages near Birkenau (called Bunkers One and Two by the SS) were relegated the majority of the gassing operations. These small, brick buildings could not have been targeted. Surrounded by woods, Bunker One measured only 49 by 21 feet, and Bunker Two, 56 by 27 feet.[61] In addition, intelligence sources did not know of the existence of these buildings. Being converted houses separate from the main area, they would have received little attention from photographic analysts unless other sources revealed their purpose. Neither Vrba nor Wetzler knew of their operation, and these escapees' report identifies only the four large crematoria at Birkenau as being in operation.[62]

Birkenau's four main killing facilities were located on the camp's west side. Numbers II and III, built to almost identical specifications, contained three parts, two of them belowground. The "undressing room," where victims disrobed, measured 162 by 26 feet; an outside entrance led underground. The gas chamber, also underground, measured 99 by 23 feet. Being underground did not necessarily hide the chambers' existence. Had a photo-interpreter been informed of the chambers' existence and specifically tasked to identify them for pre-strike reconnaissance, he could have located them. Examination of aerial photographs using modern techniques shows the outline of both, and the gas vents of the killing chamber.[63] The aboveground crematorium buildings, 99 by 37 feet, would serve as the aiming point.[64] These calculations, taken from the original plans, differ slightly from those in Richard Foregger's essay, "Technical Analysis of Methods to Bomb the Gas Chambers at Auschwitz." Foregger used figures from the study by Dino Brugioni and Robert Poirier (CIA analysts who published the reconnaissance photos and explanations in 1979). These measurements came from analysis of the aerial photographs. Obviously, personnel of the day could not access the original plans.[65] Therefore, for weaponeering purposes, this study will also use Foregger's figures for facilities II and III. He used

352 by 41 feet as the overall size of each building complex.[66] Like the first two, Crematoria IV and V, located 1,746 feet from III, were a "matched set." Their complexes measured 220 by 42 feet (of interest, here Foregger's figures match the plans).

Foregger used wall and roof thickness to determine bombs and fusing. Assuming any planning effort would have used the Vrba-Wetzler report and reconnaissance photographs, it is doubtful they would have known these precise elements of construction. However, Foregger's analysis finds this construction required five-hundred-pound general-purpose bombs with delayed fuses. This bomb was the standard weapon used by the USAAF, and probably would have been the weapon chosen anyway. The delayed fusing allowed for penetration before exploding. However, even an impact on the crematorium or the above-ground vent area without delayed fusing would have caused damage. In addition, Groban concluded that for a target partially above, and partially below, ground, the ordnance crews would set a mixed fusing. Some bombs would detonate on impact, and others would allow some penetration.[67]

Foregger's calculations (of which he gives no details), for facilities II and III, figured that these two buildings would require four hundred bombs for a 64 percent chance of damaging each complex. Half as many bombs would provide a 50 percent chance.[68] Facilities IV and V, being smaller, gave only a 60 percent probability with four hundred bombs, and 39 percent with two hundred, for each complex. A typical heavy bomber carried ten bombs (as did the raids against the Auschwitz refinery). Therefore, the total effort would require 160 bombers, 40 assigned to each facility, to obtain at least a 60 percent chance of damaging each of the four buildings. As a comparison, the September raid on the I. G. Farben oil refinery tasked 115 B-24s, and only 101 reached the target.[69] The tasking reflected a normal effort for all four groups of the 55th BW.

A comparison can be drawn, again using the oil-refinery attacks as a reference for bombing effort. If the 55th BW used twenty-eight bombers from each of the four groups, each group could target one of the facilities. Only 280 bombs would be targeted for each facility, giving a less than 50 percent chance of a hit.

Since Foregger did not provide details on his calculations, I have done an independent study using three different methods. The first two methods will use the figures for bombing probabilities from the *Handbook for Bombardiers* (the same book Foregger used). A final method will examine numbers produced by modern computer-based software using ballistics for the standard five-hundred-pound bomb.

Starting from scratch, to completely weaponeer a target is a very detailed process. Figures and formulas for ballistic error, bomb and fuse reliability, stick length (distance of bomb impacts on the ground), intervalometer settings (time between release of bombs), and slant range (angular distance from bomber to target) all affect bombing probabilities. From these numbers, a Range Error Probable and Deflection Error Probable can be calculated; these help assess the

Single-Shot Probability (SSP). The SSP gives the number of individually sighted and released bombs necessary to achieve at least one hit with a prescribed degree of assurance.[70] Fortunately, the *Handbook for Bombardiers* provided tables whereby, if certain elements were known, others could be derived from charts.

The first method begins by selecting the probable range and deflection errors. Using a 20,000-foot bombing altitude, the range and deflection errors probable are 201 and 250. Next, the Vulnerability factor (V_f) for each is determined. Using the dimensions of crematoria II and III as the allowable errors (since any error beyond these would miss the buildings), the range $V_f = 0.20$, which translates to a Range Single-Shot Probability (RSSP) of 0.1073. The deflection $V_f = 1.408$ gives a 0.6584 Deflection Single-Shot Probability (DSSP).[71] Multiplying these two figures gives an SSP = 0.07 for the first two targets.[72] Using the same methodology for crematoria IV and V calculates to an SSP of 0.05 (smaller due to smaller buildings).

Using the smaller SSP, the charts show that for each ten bombs dropped (one bomber's load), there existed a 40.131 percent chance of hitting the target one or more times.[73] Furthermore, 105 bombs would give a 99.5 percent chance of at least one hit on one building. If one group of heavy bombers attacked each building with twenty-five bombers each (250 bombs), there was a 99.5 percent chance that five or more bombs would strike each building.[74]

These figures probably overstate the real likelihood of success. The original range and deflection errors probable (from Table I in *Handbook*), when calculated to a Circular Error Probable (CEP), come to a 392-foot radius—far better than any World War II heavy bomber achieved. Therefore, a second method using the charts must be calculated.

Circular Error Probable (CEP) describes the probability of one-half of the bombs falling with a circle of designated radius. During August and September 1944, the CEP of all aimed bombs in the Fifteenth Air Force was 800 feet.[75] Using the width of the smaller crematoria (220 feet), the target radius would be 110 feet. Again using the *Handbook*, these figures correspond to a $V_f = 0.1375$ and an SSP of less than 0.01. This SSP corresponds to the third method's findings.

The final method involved using current targeting software to check the SSP. The program would be valid for such computations since the five-hundred-pound bomb's ballistics remain virtually unchanged. Using various intervalometer settings and altitudes between 18,000 and 20,000 feet, the SSP computed to 0.01, the lowest output available. Using the 0.01 SSP, the *Handbook*'s charts show that every ten bombs, or one fully loaded bomber, will give a 9.56 percent chance of hitting the target at least once. Thus, 220 bombs on each crematorium (dropped by twenty-two bombers—less than the normal Fifteenth Air Force method of using between twenty-five and twenty-eight bombers per group per attack) would give a 90 percent chance of one hit or more.

These calculations consider bombing accuracy in terms of the probability of hitting the target. Many other factors must be considered, including bomber methods and tactics. Different tactics and altitudes could increase the probability of success and decrease the number of bombs possibly striking the barracks areas. Therefore, a further analysis of accuracy and probability for collateral damage remains in order.

BOMBING METHODS, TACTICS, AND ACCURACY

The importance of bombing accuracy has played a central role in the historical controversy surrounding any bombing attempt on Auschwitz. With the noted inaccuracy of World War II bombing, critics discount the idea that bombing would have saved prisoners because Allied bombs would have killed significant numbers of the camp's occupants. However, close analysis of the Fifteenth Air Force's bombing during the period from August through September 1944 displays a high degree of accuracy—by World War II standards. In addition, by using a three-bomber front and bombing only during clear weather with each aircraft's bombardier acquiring the target, Auschwitz's killing machinery could have been hit with a high degree of accuracy while limiting the danger to the prisoners.

What military personnel called "precision bombing" during World War II bears no resemblance to the use of the same term today. Instead, it meant that a specific target was being attacked rather than an area target. The precision arose from planning to bomb a specific target, and selecting a desired Mean Point of Impact (MPI). The alternative was area bombing, or "carpet bombing," in which bombardiers did not select specific targets, but dropped their bombs on geographic areas.

For the most part, RAF Bomber Command conducted the Combined Bomber Offensive's area night bombing while the U.S. strategic force employed daylight, precision bombing. The RAF experimented with attacking individual targets in 1940, but believed the effort too costly and ineffective. Believing that the accuracy of bombing technology and related intelligence lagged too far behind bomber capabilities, the RAF opted to attack German cities and their large industrial areas.[76] The USAAF entered the war believing in the ability of a heavily armed bomber to attack specific installations with "pinpoint" and "pickle-barrel" accuracy. To achieve such accuracy, the attacks had to take place in daylight. However, during battle conditions, and due to technological limitations, such accuracy did not become commonplace. The USAAF adopted a "target area" to define accuracy. It considered bombs falling within a circle with a radius of a thousand feet around the aiming point, or MPI, as being within the target area.[77] As will be seen, the daily and weekly accuracy reports used this circle to establish accuracy.

One important factor requires clarification. Bombing accuracy statistics and analysis beg examination only because of the proximity of the prisoner barracks to the gas chambers and crematoria. Had the killing facilities been detached from the camp, large-scale bombing could have been accomplished without considering the deaths of those whom the bombing attempted to save. Again, reconnaissance photographs and the escapees' reports would have shown planners the necessity of minimizing bomb-deflection errors. Due to this proximity, not only does the accuracy of the bombers require examination, but certain methods of bombing must be excluded because of their gross inaccuracy.

Blind bombing meant bombing without actually seeing the target or any other reference point.[78] Usually, this meant bombing from above cloud cover, but the increase in the Germans' use of smoke generators created additional target-acquisition problems. These generators were used during the August and September attacks on the I. G. Farben complex, and achieved their desired effect. Not only did the smoke partially obscure the target during bombing, but four of the five groups on the first mission could not report accuracy results.[79] Due to the European weather, the military looked for ways to improve upon bombing accuracy when weather (or smoke) obscured the target. As earlier missions against I. G. Farben proved, smoke generators could affect bombing accuracy. However, due to the distance between Birkenau and the oil plant, it is doubtful that any smoke screen could have obscured the camp.

The Massachusetts Institute of Technology's Radiation Laboratory improved on an RAF radar-bombing system, designated H2S. The Eighth Air Force first used the American version, H2X, in November 1943.[80] The system (also known as AN/APS-15, Pathfinder, PFF, or "Mickey") became a valuable tool, but did not provide pinpoint bombing in limited visibility. Both the August and September attacks against the I. G. Farben complex used the Pathfinder as a bombing aid. Milton Groban was closely associated with the introduction of Pathfinder into the Fifteenth Air Force, and wrote a system training manual entitled *Bombs through the Undercast*. The book, and the training he directed, proved so valuable that he received the Bronze Star for his efforts.[81] Although the H2X system aided navigation and allowed the bombers to bomb with improved confidence, it remained unreliable.[82] Using the system effectively required additional training, intelligence support, and operator proficiency.[83] One way to train the operators included using "pictures" taken by the scopes of targets, and having the operators identify the target.

Radar methods, being in their infancy in World War II, represented images that are crude compared to today's systems. To improve on accuracy, the air forces developed a system called PFF-Synchronous bombing. The system required close communication between the radar-bombardier and a visual bombardier, and usually was used when broken clouds or smoke partially obscured the targets. The visual data, being more reliable, supplemented Pathfinder information. The PFF-Synchronous method improved in accuracy as the cloud cover diminished, affording additional visual updates.[84]

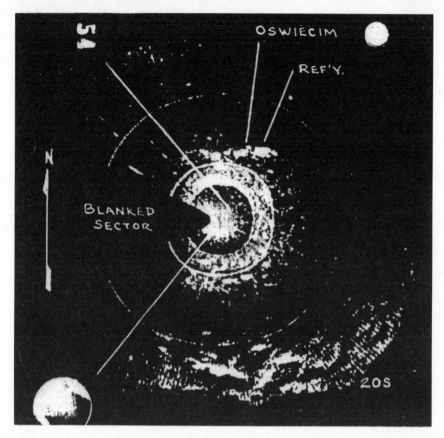

FIGURE 10-1. Pathfinder Radar Image of Oswiecim (Auschwitz), 1944. "Oswiecim" refers to the town, and "Ref'y" shows the radar return of the I. G. Farben facility ("refinery"). Source: Personal files of Milton Groban.

Visual bombing remained the most accurate method. Radar bombing could not have been used to attack a target such as the facilities at Auschwitz–Birkenau. A simple examination of the radarscope view of the Auschwitz area proves this point, as even a trained bombardier would be unable to discern individual targets from the large images projected on a small screen.[85] (See fig. 10-1.) Due to this mission's inherent concern for collateral damage to the prisoners, the bombers would have relied on the most accurate methods. Therefore, the attack would have required good weather.

Bombing tactics greatly affect bombing accuracy. Bomber formations varied from three- to twelve-bomber fronts. Target nature and size, among other factors, determined the formation employed. Using the dimensions and length of the bomb run, the axis of approach and target line presented a target area approximately 350 feet wide and 2,800 feet long perpendicular to the buildings' lengths. The three-aircraft front would not only have minimized the width of the pattern of bombs possibly falling on prisoners' barracks, but would have

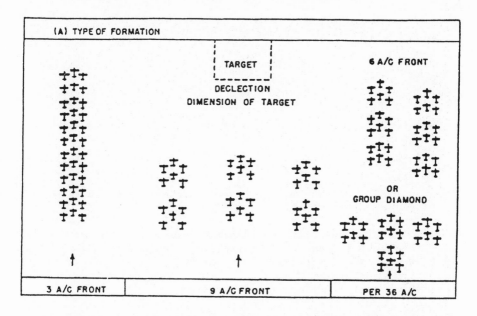

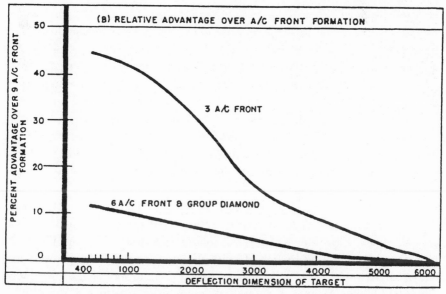

FIGURE 10-2. Bomber Formations and the Advantages of Smaller Front Formations. First Operational Analysis Section, *Optimum Tactics for Current Level of Bombing Accuracy*, 23 October 1944, USAFHRA, Maxwell AFB, Alabama, File Number 670.01–3C Annex 19, 7.

provided the best accuracy for smaller targets. Operational analysis demonstrated that compared to a nine-aircraft front, a three-bomber front would place 46 percent more bombs against a 400-foot-wide target. (See fig. 10-2.) Crossing the targets did not drastically decrease accuracy: for a 400-foot-wide target, attacking down the length improved accuracy by only five bombs per four

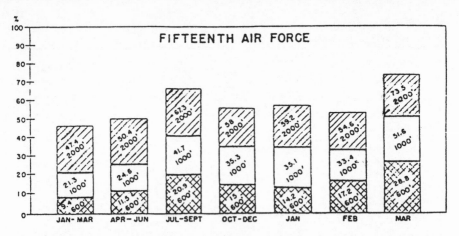

FIGURE 10-3. Bombing Accuracy for Fifteenth Air Force, January 1944–March 1945. For each indicated period, the numbers show cumulative percentages of bombs dropped inside circles of 600, 1,000, and 2,000 feet from the Mean Point of Impact (MPI). Source: First Operations Analysis Section, Fifteenth Air Force, *Bombing Accuracy*, 30 April 1945, USAFHRA, Maxwell AFB, Alabama, File Number 670.56–2.

hundred dropped.[86] The three-wide formation provided the smallest pattern width, 880 feet.[87] Due to the size of the oil refinery, most formations used a six-aircraft front. However, target size and the importance of bomb-width dispersion would dictate a smaller three-front formation when attacking Birkenau.

So far, the evidence demonstrates that any attack against the Birkenau killing facilities would have required a daylight clear-weather attack, by a small-front bomber formation, attacking perpendicular to the target. Although representing the best available tactics, these measures would not have guaranteed that the barracks area would not receive damage. Analyzing the Fifteenth Air Force bombing statistics from the summer and fall of 1944 provides the best means of anticipating collateral damage.

The following statistics do not present a Circular Error Probable (CEP). Kitchens used CEP, and this can cause confusion in the statistical analysis when comparing and measuring accuracy. Therefore, this study will adopt the direct percentage method used by the Fifteenth Air Force. If the Fifteenth Air Force quotes an accuracy rate of forty percent for a thousand-foot circle, then out of a hundred bombs dropped, forty landed within a thousand feet of the MPI.[88]

From July to December 1944, the Fifteenth Air Force averaged putting 40.1 percent of its bombs within a thousand feet of the MPI. In addition, the best months were July to September, with 41.7 percent accuracy. (See fig. 10-3.) The best wing, 47th BW, placed 49 percent within the thousand-foot circle. The worst wing, 304th BW, produced only a 22.4 percent showing. The only period exceeding the accuracy rate for this quarter was March 1945, when the Fifteenth Air Force placed 51.6 percent of its bombs within a thousand feet.[89]

Drawing the circle even smaller, to six hundred feet, the command put 20.9

percent of its bombs "on target" between July and September. In the smaller target area, the 55th BW surpassed the 47th BW in accuracy by 0.2 percent, with 25.2 percent. As with the thousand-foot circle statistics, only March 1945, with 28.8 percent, surpassed the July–September period.[90] The high accuracy rates correspond to the Fifteenth Air Force's most intense flight activity. Bombers flew 20,845 sorties in August 1944, and posted the Fifteenth's highest effective sortie rate (percentage of bombers airborne to those arriving in the target area and dropping their ordnance): 88 percent.[91]

A combination of factors, including the aforementioned dramatic decline in German air defenses and effectiveness, and favorable European weather conditions could have aided bombing accuracy. The relatively stable and complete manning of the Fifteenth Air Force aircrews also warrants mention. June to November 1944 was the Fifteenth's most stable period. Prior to June, the command was still in the process of receiving the manpower to bring it to its authorized strength.[92] After November, due to the reduction in combat losses and turnover, the Fifteenth Air Force had a surplus of aircrews; this actually contributed to its decreased bombing accuracy, due to inadequate training and experience.

Overlaying 600- and 1,000-foot circles on a diagram of Birkenau aids in demonstrating these accuracy statistics when applied to the camp. The 600-foot radius does not include any additional buildings, and the 1,000-foot circle adds nine barracks in Block BIIf, and one-third of the "Canada" loot storage facility. Using the earlier computations requiring 400 bombs to have a 60 to 64 percent chance of hitting the target, this means that, between July and September 1944, a total of 233 bombs would have fallen somewhere outside one thousand feet. If the Fifteenth Air Force had sent one bomb wing to attack Birkenau, with each group targeting one building, then 163 bombs would have fallen outside the circle.

These statistics do not tell the whole story. Using these alone (as Kitchens and Foregger did), one could argue that bombing would have caused serious damage to the camp's housing areas. But one must recall the statistics presented earlier and overlay a three-bomber pattern-width of 880 feet (this also came from August and September 1944 mission statistics). Overlaying this width on the diagram demonstrates a greatly reduced threat of bombs to the prisoners. Also, by analyzing bomb plots from other contemporary missions in the same geographic region, the majority of the stray bombs fell along the flight path. In other words, they would have impacted long or short of the target rather than at great widths from the target.

These statistics demonstrate the feasibility and probability of success while limiting the amount of danger to the inmates. Still, these are only statistics. Any attack on the camp would have carried with it a probability of killing inmates who otherwise might have survived the war (and in some cases did). Only a minor error in deflection aiming (in this case, aiming bombs to the right of the intended target) could lay the pattern of bombs down the center of the camp. Even the tightest pattern would have had stray bombs that could have hit the camp. Even with a good run described previously, the "Canada" storage area would have been in danger. Many prisoners worked there, and the area, although dangerous, provided these inmates, more than any other work detail, with the best chance of securing food and of bartering items.[93]

Above all, however, the four buildings at Birkenau constituted the largest and most apparent danger to all inmates, and to people still arriving. Kitchens and Foregger point out that the bombing would also take out the rail link by which large numbers of prisoners arrived almost daily. But the majority of those arriving, like the Hungarian Jews, went straight to the gas chambers. In addition, these were perceived as the weakest and not fit for work (young, old, and many women). Although the survival rate for the remainder was low, it certainly was higher than for those sent to the gas chambers.

With a political push for action, the air leaders would have carried out the attack. Certainly any such effort would have been a "diversion of assets," but such diversions were not unprecedented. As I have shown, the total effort would have required one mission by one wing of heavy bombers. In order to minimize collateral damage to Jewish prisoners, Birkenau could not have been attacked at night or in bad weather. Most of the targets it would have replaced could have been attacked in less than optimum weather with systems such as Pathfinder.

Authors who have considered the military aspects of a possible attack tend to generalize all aspects of any such operation. Kitchens and Foregger use broad representations and generalities to portray the mission as impossible or foolhardy. They used bomber accuracy statistics and information on German defenses from various dates and regions. However, as this study has demonstrated, analyzing the situation under specific probable circumstances provides the most effective means of defining the possibilities and characteristics of any possible attack.

When narrowed to the period between July and October 1944, the historical record reveals that German defenses rarely took a heavy toll on attacking bombers, and strategic bombardment accuracy reached a high level. During these months, the Luftwaffe mustered its resources, yet did not seriously adversely affect the bomber missions against the Upper Silesian oil facilities. German flak guns, while ever-present and with improving accuracy, did not significantly reduce attacking formations, and these months also saw the second-highest level of the Fifteenth Air Force's strategic bombing accuracy. The command's statistical analysis unit detailed how lower altitudes and varying formations could offer increased precision.

Regardless of the bombing platform used or the statistical accuracy then available, there existed a chance that the attack would kill Jewish inmates. In order to minimize the collateral damage, the military leaders would have had to pick the best asset available under the existing time constraints. Using the Fifteenth Air Force would have been the easiest means to attack the gas chambers and crematoria, but it also would have required a large effort with questionable accuracy.

If the Fifteenth Air Force had been selected, the mission could have been performed only within a rigid set of circumstances to limit the possibility of killing large numbers of prisoners. The bombers would have had to use a three-bomber front under clear weather, with each bombardier acquiring the target. Only these tactics and conditions could have helped limit stray and inaccurate bombs from hitting the barrack areas. Under these criteria, and in view of the Fifteenth Air Force's bombing accuracy for August and September 1944, the Allies stood a very good chance of destroying or damaging the Birkenau facilities while limiting the possibility of harm to those their efforts were designed to spare.

In the absence of decisive political intervention from Washington to order an attack on the crematoria, however, such a mission was unlikely ever to have taken place. Even if it had been ordered, the German reaction to either temporary or permanent disabling of their high-capacity industrial killing machinery cannot be accurately gauged. It could have included using older, less efficient methods requiring additional manpower—e.g., firing squads and trenches. Or, with the ever closer approach of the Red Army, the SS might have begun the death marches back to the Reich a few months earlier. Whereas bombing offered only a possible reprieve for Jewish prisoners, destroying Hitler's grip on Europe was a guaranteed means for saving the remaining Jews.

Part III

NEW

PERSPECTIVES

on the

CONTROVERSY

———

A SINGLE-MINDED FOCUS on the technical feasibility of various bombing missions, or on the degree to which Jewish groups advocated bombing Auschwitz-Birkenau, often has led the participants in the debate to neglect the larger contexts of World War II, the Holocaust, and the Jewish role in Allied countries. The newly commissioned essays in this part all attempt to step back and look at the larger picture. In the process, they raise some new perspectives on why the debate has been useful, what alternatives and viewpoints may have been forgotten, and why the debate is so interesting to us in the first place.

Chapter 11, "Auschwitz," by the well-known historian Walter Laqueur, opens with a defense of the value of counterfactual history and proceeds to provide a brief for the feasibility and necessity for attacking Auschwitz. As the author of *The Terrible Secret* (1980), Laqueur is well qualified to comment on how much the Allies knew about Auschwitz, and to what degree something could have been done earlier. But he also looks at the larger context of the disinterest in the West in rescuing Jews, in the process shooting some pointed barbs at recent authors who have said little or nothing could have been done. Although he does not say so, his chief target appears to be William D. Rubinstein, whose 1997 book *The Myth of Rescue* integrated the antibombing arguments of Kitchens and Levy into a larger framework transparently indicated by the book's title. Laqueur notes that a single gunboat might have stopped the deportation of the Jews of Rhodes and Kos in the summer of 1944, and asserts that, in the larger scheme of things, devoting a small amount of money, personnel, and resources into rescue would hardly have affected the Allied war effort.

Why the Allies had so little interest is explored at greater length in chapter 12, "Bombing Auschwitz and the Politics of the Jewish Question during World War II," by a leading historian of American Jewry, Henry L. Feingold. As he makes plain, there were multiple reasons why the Holocaust was not central to the Allies' agenda in World War II. Anti-Semitism at home was certainly part of why Roosevelt and Churchill did not act more energetically, especially as prejudice among Allied populations interacted with the Nazi propaganda strategy of attempting to exploit anti-Jewish feeling in the West. As for Stalin's Soviet Union, Feingold notes how much a combination of Communist ideology and Nazi "Judeo-Bolshevist" propaganda made the Soviet leadership unwilling to acknowledge that the Jews' fate was significantly worse than that of other ethnic groups among the millions of USSR and Eastern European war dead.

In this chapter, Feingold also reintroduces an alternate bombing strategy he discussed as long ago as 1970: retaliatory or retributive bombing.[1] The Allies, notably the British, could have announced that their attacks against German cities were partly in retaliation for the genocide of the Jews, thereby emphasizing an interest in the issue that, as he goes on to show, unfortunately scarcely existed. Feingold also discusses some of the reasons why an open policy of retaliation met resistance from the air forces and military bureaucracies; however, he may not emphasize enough how much Allied military and civilian leaders wanted to avoid initiating tit-for-tat actions with the Germans, or publicizing the reality of indiscriminate air attacks on Germany.

In chapter 13, "Monday-Morning Quarterbacking and the Bombing of Auschwitz," the distinguished military historian Williamson Murray provides yet another contextual perspective: that of the overall military situation of the Allies in the spring, summer, and fall of 1944. Allied military and civilian leaders in the West were overwhelmingly preoccupied with the preparations for, and the course of, the invasion of France. Working up to fifteen hours a day, seven days a week, to defeat an able, heavily armed, and desperate foe, these leaders naturally saw all requests to divert military forces to rescue missions as a questionable distraction—unless political realities intruded enough to force them to act. In this context, Murray takes the view that has been most typical among military historians: that bombing of Auschwitz is essentially ahistorical, because it represents our concerns, not those held at the time. Moreover, as a historian of air power, Murray endorses James Kitchens's belief that a raid was likely to miss the gas chambers and cause many casualties among the prisoners.

His opinion is not shared by the second commentator from the military history community, Richard G. Davis, author of an authoritative work on Gen. Carl Spaatz, commander of the U.S. Strategic Air Forces in Europe. In chapter 14, "The Bombing of Auschwitz," Davis provides some expert commentary on the technical debate, noting that, while specialized raids by B-25s, P-38s, or Mosquitoes might have been feasible, these scenarios are questionable in their effectiveness, or at odds with the way the air forces normally operated. Under the circumstances, American air leaders would, if tasked with a raid on Birkenau, have simply done the obvious and diverted Fifteenth Air Force B-17s and B-24s to the task. By his estimate, it would have taken multiple raids, extending over perhaps a six-week period, to destroy the four gas chamber/crematoria complexes. However, because it was feasible, in hindsight he is willing to state that it should have been done. But Davis does not venture how many lives such an effort would have saved, or cost.

In the final chapter, Deborah E. Lipstadt, author of *Beyond Belief*, an important account of reluctance in the American press to report the persecution of the Jews, steps back from the events of 1944 altogether to look at the deeper reasons why the bombing-Auschwitz debate has struck such a chord in the American Jewish community. She believes that it is part of a larger fascination with the failure to rescue that arose since the 1960s, and it has led to many moralistic distortions of the historical record. Finger-pointing about the failure of Franklin D. Roosevelt and his administration, or about the failure of American Jewish groups to do much about the Holocaust, has set the tone. This has been met, she states, by often equally emotional responses from the other side.

As Lipstadt notes, this reaction is part of the larger cultural fascination in American society and the media with the role of ourselves and others as bystanders to the Holocaust—a role in which we can much more easily imagine ourselves than that of victim or perpetrator.[2] (Ironically, this fascination with our potential guilt for doing nothing about the European Jews seems to have generated no significant public pressure on the politicians when the Cambodians, Rwandans, or Bosnians were being slaughtered.) If Lipstadt's contribution does not move much beyond the debate among American Jews (with a sideways glance at Israel), her contribution does help to explain why the thesis that Auschwitz should have been bombed has become so influential in our museums and textbooks, and has since the 1970s received so much attention from American Jews and Gentiles alike.

Michael J. Neufeld

11

AUSCHWITZ

Walter Laqueur

MILITARY HISTORIANS, MORE perhaps than others, have frequently chosen as their motto Leopold von Ranke's most famous dictum, that it is the task of the historian to find how it essentially was (*wie es eigentlich gewesen war*). But as often as not, this has given rise to misunderstandings, for Ranke certainly did not mean that historians can be no more than chronologists, accounting on the basis of their sources what happened and when. They must be equally interested in the "how," and this leads them inevitably into questions about why a certain situation arose, why a certain decision was taken. In other words, they have to engage all along in a certain amount of counterfactual history. They have to ask whether alternatives existed, and what would have been the likely outcome if these alternatives had been adopted by the decisionmakers. True, they must also take into account the uncertainties, the "fog of war," and the benefits of hindsight. But in the final analysis, their judgment must be based not only on what happened but also on what might have happened. But for this, history becomes a chain of inevitabilities with one thing inexorably leading to another, and everything happens because it is predestined, as in a Greek tragedy or the Song of the Nibelungen.

To choose at random two examples: Various courses of action were open to Western governments at the time of the Great Depression, but to gain a fuller understanding of the alternatives open to them, one ought to go back well beyond Black Friday in 1929 by which time the disaster had already occurred. In a similar way, a consideration of the alternatives open to Britain and France at the time of the Munich crisis cannot possibly begin with Chamberlain's first meeting with Hitler in Bad Godesberg; it has to go back a year or two or perhaps even three, considering the state of affairs in France and Britain in the thirties and the policy of appeasement.

How far should one go back to discuss the question of whether Auschwitz should and could have been bombed in 1944? And is it legitimate (and even if it is legitimate, is it helpful) to discuss the bombing of Auschwitz in isolation from other actions that could have been taken to slow down the massacre of European Jewry? "Bombing Auschwitz," as I see it, does not pertain only to the question of the destruction of the gas chambers; it also concerns the destruction of the railway lines leading to Auschwitz, and this, by necessity, leads also to the question of bombing targets in the countries where the deportations originated.

It could be argued that only in the case of Auschwitz was the issue of bombing raised on the diplomatic level. But it was not only in Auschwitz that Jews were killed, and there were ways and means other than bombing to slow down the deportations that could have been tried. In the case of Auschwitz, there is fuller documentation concerning possibilities of rescue, but should historians be guided in their overall perspective only by the availability of archival material?

Thus, seen in a wider perspective, would it not be more helpful to regard the Auschwitz discussion as *pars pro toto*, in the wider framework of possible military and diplomatic efforts to stop or slow down the massacre, or at the very least to gain time? Analyzing the specific circumstances of the Auschwitz debate is still of interest, but so is the analysis of the number of bombers available at the time, the distances to be covered, intelligence available, probable weather conditions, accuracy of bombing, and so on. But it is less certain whether such an investigation should start on a certain day in May or June of 1944 when, as some historians have told us, it first became technically feasible to bomb Auschwitz in view of the Allied advance in Italy. The question of technical feasibility seems controversial to this day, but even if it were crystal clear, it is still a minor issue. For it is leaves open the wider question of whether it might have become feasible earlier, if higher priority had been given to saving Jewish lives.

Against this, it might be argued that it is unrealistic to pose the question in these terms simply because no higher priority was given. But the question confronting us is not whether bombing Auschwitz was likely in the given circumstances, but whether it was at all possible. It is my contention that this argument cannot be accepted without some further investigation. How much political pressure would have been needed, and how extensive a diversion of resources from the general war effort?

Some historians argue that only in June 1944 was sufficient information available and only then could the Allied air forces based in Foggia in Italy reach targets in eastern Europe. This argument leaves out of sight that Kiev had been in Russian hands since November 1943, that Chernovtsi (Czernowitz) had been reoccupied by the troops of the First Ukrainian Front by mid-March, and that Ternopol had been reoccupied by 14 April 1944. A look at the map shows that the distance from Auschwitz to Ternopol and Chernovtsi is less than three hundred miles, not as much as the distance from London to Hamburg or Frankfurt, which were bombed with devastating effect well before the summer of 1944. Auschwitz could have been bombed from these bases. But would the Soviets not have opposed this? They were less than enthusiastic, but they had accepted "shuttle bombing" on a few occasions. However, considering the strong position in which the western Allies were at the time vis-à-vis Moscow (the Lend-Lease Act was then in full swing), there is no doubt whatsoever that Stalin would have relented when faced with a determined Western demand.

But for London and Washington, these targets in eastern Europe were of no particular importance, and following some routine requests and representations, they desisted. Perhaps they were afraid of putting additional strain on the alliance with the Soviet Union. But it can be said with certainty that the alliance would not have broken up if Roosevelt and Churchill had been more insistent and Stalin had accepted (probably for a price) the bombing of Auschwitz and the railways leading to it.

The story of the shuttle bombing reflects the general dilemma in a nutshell. It all depended on how much priority was given to a certain project. If it was thought to be of little or no importance (like the bombing of Auschwitz), even a small investment seemed too risky and unwarranted. If, on the other hand, it was deemed essential, no expense was spared, and the technical difficulties were overcome in no time.

Every military operation involves some risk. If the Germans had used poison gas on D-Day (a scenario for which the Allies were unprepared), the invasion of the continent might have ended in disaster. It would not have changed the outcome of the war, but the first nuclear bombs might have been used against Cologne and Berlin. Military leaders usually adduce technical reasons when asked to undertake missions that are not to their liking. If the decision had been left to the military, it is doubtful that the nuclear bomb would ever have been built; the Manhattan Project, after all, cost two billion dollars in 1945 (and the nuclear arms race from 1940 to 1995 cost four trillion). Could one not have produced a lot of hardware instead? There are difficulties and risks in war, as in peace. But there were few technical difficulties that could not be solved by a power that during the war produced 296,400 aircraft, 86,330 tanks, and 6,500 naval vessels.

Other arguments seem to me equally unconvincing, such as the alleged lack of knowledge about Auschwitz among the Allies. When I wrote about this subject in *The Terrible Secret*,[1] I took a conservative line; as subsequent discoveries in the archives have shown, I erred on the side of excessive caution. The Allies did not need the Vrba-Wetzler report to learn about Auschwitz. If Prof. Victor Klemperer, totally isolated in his *Judenhaus* in Dresden, without access to either radio or newspapers or useful contacts, had heard about Auschwitz in 1942, it stands to reason that the Allied intelligence services had also heard about it. But again, it was not a matter of crucial importance how many Jews were killed and where, and for this reason the people in intelligence no longer passed on these items to their masters. Unfortunately, it appears in retrospect that the question of sufficient information was not really relevant. Even if the most detailed facts about Auschwitz had been available in 1942 or 1943, even if the most accurate maps had been published in American and British newspapers, it would have made no difference as far as the strategic planners were concerned.

But what about the destruction of railway lines, bridges, and tunnels? Is it not true that such damage can be easily repaired? It is correct, by and large, with regard to railway lines, but it is much less true with regard to bridges and tunnels. The arguments against bombing rail lines also do not take into account that the whole purpose of a bomb attack would have been to slow down the deportation of Jews. And, as far as the deportation of Jews from Hungary is concerned, such bombing did succeed to a certain extent; thus, if the bombing had been more intensive, it would have had an even greater effect. It was certainly not beyond human ingenuity and the resources available to pick the right targets and to cause more delays.

It was a race against time; the millions of Jews who had been killed in 1941–43 could not be brought back to life. But there was a chance to save many of those who remained. What were the technical difficulties that could have delayed or prevented the deportation of the Jews of Rhodes and Kos—one of the most tragic and bizarre incidents in that summer of 1944? These two islands in the eastern Mediterranean are located a few miles off the shore of neutral Turkey, which can be seen with the naked eye and reached with a rowboat or, in the case of Kos, even by a good swimmer. There was a small, forgotten German garrison on the island, and following instructions, the commanding officer published an order that all Jews had to assemble within three days for deportation. There was no secret at all about the operation, but no warnings were given over the Allied radio. As the deportation took place on 23 July 1944, Rome was in Allied hands, the Allied armies were in France, Germany was in disarray following the attempted assassination of Hitler, and the Allied bombing raids were in full swing. The Allies had full air and naval control in the eastern Mediterranean, and British intelligence knew all there was to know on the islands. Allied aircraft in Cyprus (less than two hundred miles away) and in Egypt were underemployed and could have taken off at a moment's notice. But neither sophisticated aircraft nor precision bombing would have been needed to intercept and divert the convoy of eighteen hundred Jews on three slow oil barges making their way, at a snail's pace, to Athens (it took them almost ten days). A motorboat or two, with twenty or thirty Allied soldiers equipped with a Bren gun or two, would have been sufficient to intercept the barges that, for all we know, did not even have a military convoy. There might not have been a fight, and if the British did not want to be burdened by yet another group of Jews, Turkey was gravitating toward the Allies by that time and would have given them temporary abode. (In fact, the only individual to do something to save Jews was the Turkish consul in Rhodes, who extended protection to a few dozen.)

It took this miserable convoy twenty-four days to make its way over the Mediterranean, through Greece and other Balkan countries and Hungary to Auschwitz, where it arrived on 20 August. Most of the new arrivals were killed within a day. Nor was it the only such case; on 31 July 1944, a transport of Jewish children left Paris and made its way slowly through war-torn Germany toward Auschwitz.

If the bombing of Auschwitz, the railways, the tunnels, and the bridges would have meant the diversion of some aircraft and bombs, how could it have been justified in strategic-military terms? This question takes us closer to the real dilemma: the Jews had no political influence at the time, much less than the Polish or Czechoslovak governments-in-exile. The official line was that everything had to be subordinated to defeating Hitler, and once this aim had been achieved, the Jews (or whatever remained of them) would be saved too.

There is no certainty that even from a purely military point of view such a distraction in eastern Europe would have been a total waste. It is frequently argued that Allied bombing attacks suffered heavy losses against industrial and similar targets in west and north Germany precisely because German fighters and antiaircraft artillery were concentrated there. By increasing their air attacks in eastern Europe, the Allies would have compelled the Germans to withdraw some of these forces and disperse them, which would have made Allied attacks in the West less risky.

The question of bombing Auschwitz boils down not to issues such as types of aircraft, accuracy of bombing, and the distance from Foggia. Stuart Erdheim shows convincingly, I believe, that bombing would have been feasible, even though no one can say with any confidence how many inmates would have been saved.

The decisive question is, of course, what could have been achieved if greater priority had been given by everyone concerned to rescuing Jewish lives? World War II was not fought in order to save Jews from Hitler, even though the Nazis in their propaganda often suggested this and even though Allied officials were unduly apprehensive of the potential of anti-Semitic propaganda in their own camp. But what if, for argument's sake, one percent of the Allied war effort in 1944 had been devoted to this end? Or, to be more realistic, one-half of one percent? The war effort in 1944 accounted for about forty percent of the American GNP, rather more in Britain, and it is easy to translate this into dollars, pounds sterling, sorties flown by bomber aircraft, and the number of Allied broadcasts devoted to the massacres, naming names, warning, and threatening. Deflecting one-half of one percent would not have fatally undermined the Allied war effort, but it would have made, in all probability, a difference with regard to the chances of saving people from certain death. We know with what minute sums the emissaries who engaged in rescue work in Switzerland and Turkey had to operate. What if millions had been at their disposal—say the budgets now allocated to the memory of the victims of the Shoah (to which one could add the production costs of the books now published arguing that nothing could have been done). Would more money and more bombing and more publicity have made no difference at all?

It is unlikely that the SS and Gestapo could have been bribed in 1942, but it is by no means impossible that they would have been more amenable in 1944. Hungarian and Rumanian officials almost certainly would have shown interest. Those engaged in rescue work firmly believed that more lives could have been saved if they had had at their disposal the sums that began to arrive from Jewish and non-Jewish sources after the war had ended. Perhaps they were overly optimistic, but to claim that there was no chance whatsoever in 1944 is unbelievable.

Most of the Jews of Poland, the Baltic countries, the Ukraine, and White Russia (to repeat once again) were dead by early 1944, but the inmates of the Lodz ghetto had not yet been deported to Auschwitz, Hungarian Jewry still survived, and so did tens of thousands of Jews in Slovakia and other parts of Europe, from France to Terezin (Theresienstadt) to the island of Kos.

Those claiming that nothing more could have been done to rescue Jews underrate the profound change that had taken place in Nazi-occupied Europe as the result of the German military setbacks and the retreat in the East. They also underrate the fall of Mussolini and the general dislocation caused by the bombing campaign on Germany. The fanatics still believed in the *Endsieg* (final victory), but a majority of people in Germany seemed to have doubted it. A great majority of people among Germany's satellites were convinced that the war was lost. Inside Germany, the Gestapo was losing control because so many offices issuing identification papers had been destroyed and because Germany was flooded by millions of foreign workers. Hiding and even escaping became far easier than before. If even Nazi officials inside Germany could be bribed to let Jews escape to Switzerland, the Nazis' helpers in countries such as Slovakia, Hungary, and elsewhere could have been made to work a little slower, to delay the deportations, to show less enthusiasm.

Once the deported Jews had reached Auschwitz, rescue attempts became exceedingly difficult. But what could have been done to prevent the transports from reaching Auschwitz? It is wrong to claim that such thoughts can only arise with the benefit of hindsight. On 21 December 1942, a four-page article entitled "The Massacre of the Jews" written by Varian Fry was published in the *New Republic*. It shows how much was known even outside government and the intelligence services by those who wanted to know. The article had been written in all probability in October 1942, more than a year and a half before the events discussed. It gave a fairly accurate description of the extermination centers, even though it did not mention names, and an equally accurate estimate of the number of people already killed. Toward the end of his account, Fry suggested a number of steps that should be taken to prevent total annihilation. Above all,

President Roosevelt and Prime Minister Churchill "could and should speak out against these monstrous events." Even if this would not influence Hitler, it might have an effect on some other Germans. There should be a joint declaration in the most solemn terms by the Allied governments of the retribution to come: "Tribunals should be set up now to amass the facts." Diplomatic warnings should be conveyed through neutral channels to the governments of Hungary, Rumania, and Bulgaria, which might save at least the 700,000 to 900,000 Jews still in their borders. Pius XII should threaten with excommunication all Catholics participating in these frightful crimes; the Protestant leaders should do the same. The news about the crimes should be broadcast day and night to every European country. Fry decried the fact that the Office of War Information had allegedly banned mention of the massacres. The fact that the crimes were committed not in Western Europe but in the East, showed that the Nazis feared the effect on the local population of the news of the crimes. Why play into their hands? Fry made several other suggestions and also proposed that asylum should be offered to those succeeding in escaping. He quoted a correspondent from Marseilles who had written him that little Switzerland, by accepting nine thousand refugees since July 1942, "had done more for the cause of humanity that than the great and wealthy United States with its loud declarations about the rights of the people and the defense of liberty notwithstanding."

There were no military suggestions in Fry's article: this would hardly have been apposite in an article in the open press, nor might it have been practical at the time. It is known what happened—neither Roosevelt nor Churchill, let alone the Pope or the bishops, spoke out loudly and clearly; there were no threats; no resolutions; and radio broadcasts were kept to a minimum. No funds were allocated for rescue missions, and no military operations were planned. Two years passed, and next to nothing was done. The fatalists may still claim that nothing could have been done. All we know is that it was not even tried.

12

BOMBING AUSCHWITZ AND THE POLITICS OF THE JEWISH QUESTION DURING WORLD WAR II

Henry L. Feingold

Bᴇᴛᴡᴇᴇɴ 1938 ᴀɴᴅ 1945, there were numerous proposals about ways to save the Jews. Some, like the Rublee-Schacht and the "Blood for Trucks" ransom proposals that bracket the Holocaust like bookends, never seemed very feasible. Others, like the omnipresent plea to revoke the British White Paper restricting settlement in Palestine, or the numerous proposals to resettle refugees in places like Alaska or Mindanao, were perhaps slightly more so. Even before the implementation of the Final Solution, getting Jews out of Nazi clutches was beset with difficulties of no ordinary kind. The proposal to save Jewish lives by bombing Auschwitz and the rail lines, which first appeared in the final phase of the Holocaust when there was knowledge of the gruesome death camps, has received special attention by researchers. This interest is not necessarily related to its greater feasibility, but to the fact that by 1944 what was happening in the camps was known, and it was apparent that the war would end in an Allied victory. For students of the Holocaust, the indifference to this rescue opportunity, no matter how remote, has become more unforgivable than the others with which it should be compared. The remnants of European Jewry, the Jews of Hungary, the remaining Jews of Slovakia, those clinging to life in the camps, and those in hiding all over occupied Europe, had after all survived for four years. It is the very closeness of the rescue possibility for families like the Franks hiding in an Amsterdam attic that gives the bombing question its special poignancy.

Yet when the possibility of rescue through bombing is closely scrutinized, its possibility of saving lives seems remote. Some argue that it would itself have been costly in Jewish lives. Bombing did not address what would cause a greater loss of life in the final phase of the war, the breakdown of the rudimentary sanitation and nourishment system that allowed some *kazetniks*, concentration-camp prisoners, to cling to life. Nor could bombing do much to stop the bloody death marches that would take additional thousands of lives. But such lack of specificity is not the basic reason why Auschwitz was not bombed. Behind the technical reasons presented, the absence of the right kind of aircraft, the speed with which rail lines could be repaired, the imprecision of "precision bombing,"[1] Roosevelt's unawareness of the bombing proposal,[2] the opposition of the Jewish leaders of the World Jewish Congress and the Jewish Agency, and the numerous other reasons given by researchers, is the problem of determining what World War II was all about for the Allies. Clearly, it was not about saving European Jewry.

In the fullness of time, as new information becomes available, researchers should be able to reach some agreement on what the lifesaving possibilities for bombing Auschwitz and the rail lines were. I suspect that the verdict will be that there was a possibility of saving lives, but bombing Auschwitz would have involved the willingness to expend lives and aircraft; that in turn required an open recognition that what was happening in Auschwitz required an Allied response. But the Allies did not recognize, much less speak of, a separate need to rescue Jews. There was within the war a "politics" of the "Jewish question" in which the Nazi government held all the cards. When historians ask why Auschwitz was not bombed, they are really asking, why was there not more concern about the industrial murder of European Jewry? To answer that question, we need to know more about the causes of the war and the role the "Jewish question" played in it, especially in the bloody character of that war in the East.[3] It was not simply a lack of will in Washington, London, and Moscow that lay behind the failure to bomb or to implement other proposals for rescue. It went beyond abandonment.

The possibility of retaliatory bombing and of shuttle and direct bombing of Auschwitz via and by the Soviet Union—the former rejected by the Allies and the latter by the Soviet Union—provides insight into the historical context in which the resistance to becoming involved in the Jewish aspect of the war occurred. They are used in this discussion as a prism through which to view the "bombing problem."

A fact rarely mentioned by researchers who seem ignorant of the historical context is that the rejection of bombing follows a long line of rejections of other opportunities to help save Jewish lives. They fall into two categories. The first period, before the implementation of the Final Solution became known, was marked by the reluctance of receiving nations to accept the penniless refugees extruded from the Reich.[4] There was indifference (with the exception of Rafael Trujillo's Dominican Republic) at the refugee conference held at Évian-les-Bains in July 1938. That indifference to the refugees came to a tentative end only in July 1944 when the Roosevelt administration adopted the policy of temporary havens. There were also those rescue opportunities that developed when knowledge that the Reich had embarked on a policy of genocide became known. As the depredation grew more intense, rescue advocates experienced difficulty in getting Allied governments to issue a warning that there would be retribution.[5] Jewish delegations were told that a quick victory over the Axis would save the Jews and all the occupied people of Europe. No distinction was made. The opposition to the Rublee-Schacht ransom offer in 1939 and to the "Blood for Trucks" offer of 1944 was based partly on the fact that implementation would require recognition of the existence of—and possibly negotiations over—what Berlin called the "Jewish question."

For rescue advocates, therefore, John J. McCloy's rejection of the 9 August 1944 request for bombing could not have come as a surprise. It came after much evidence that there was little interest in singling out the Jewish plight for special attention. Bombing, rescue advocates were told, required a diversion of aircraft and, more important, the willingness to absorb casualties and aircraft losses.[6] It was possible to allow such an expenditure for a demonstrative raid on Tokyo, led by Gen. James (Jimmy) Doolittle in April 1942, that had no objective other than to raise the morale of the American people. But Tokyo was not Auschwitz, about which the American people knew little during the war.

Strangely, the bombing alternative, which had been suggested by the Polish government-in-exile as early as 4 January 1941, and which had been rejected by RAF Bomber Command as "not a practical proposition," was not included in the rescue resolutions sent to the Oval Office in March 1943.[7] The suggestion was not repeated until it was raised by the London Poles on 24 August 1943. The request included a suggestion that an effort be made to liberate the inmates of Auschwitz by bombing.[8]

Also unmentioned in the rescue resolutions was retaliatory or retributive bombing. Such bombing simply entailed announcing that the massive raids by the RAF on Cologne or Essen in March 1942 or Hamburg in June 1943 were in retaliation for what was being done in the East in the name of the German people. It was not necessary to mention Jews; that would have been understood. A request for just such an action "on a large scale, of non-military objectives in Germany . . . in retaliation for German savagery" was made by Gen. Sikorski of the Polish government-in-exile on 22 June 1942.[9] Churchill, who supported retaliatory bombing, went as far as suggesting the "elimination" of a small German town, as the SS had eliminated Lidice in Czechoslovakia.

Such a propaganda policy was certainly possible after the RAF had chosen a strategy of nighttime blanket or area bombing of German cities in mid-1942. But Bomber Command was reluctant to abandon the moral high ground that ruled out attacks on civilians for reasons of revenge. An attack on the enemy, even if the goal was to break civilian morale, had to have a direct military purpose. As late as February 1943, after Churchill requested that the projected raids on Berlin be accompanied by leafleting emphasizing retaliation, and again in July 1944, when the indiscriminate use of V-1 buzz bombs again prompted Churchill to call for reprisal raids, the middle echelon of the RAF bureaucracy blocked the proposal on the same grounds. Although, with the breakdown of German air defenses in mid-1944, German cities were becoming more vulnerable, there was also a fear that Berlin would escalate the terror against captured British air crews, which Goebbels's Propaganda Ministry had begun calling "terror fliers."[10]

Paradoxically, the link between the bombing of German cities and retaliatory bombing for what was vaguely called the "atrocities in the East" had already been made in the German public mind. To this day, many Germans consider the devastating fire raid on Dresden in February 1945 as a payback for Auschwitz. It was the only way they could make sense of it. German propaganda emphasized a direct link between Jewish control of the war and the bombing of German cities that caused the loss of a half million civilians. Yet the opposition in the British Foreign Office and the Air Ministry to linking the savaging of German cities from the air to the savagery of German policy toward occupied peoples, not only Jews, was never dissipated.

In retrospect, retaliatory bombing was far more practical than was bombing Auschwitz. It required no change in war priorities; one could not argue that it was "of doubtful efficacy," because the cities were in any case being bombed. An open Allied statement by the Office of War Information broadcast to the German people and the satellites would have alerted them to what was being done in the death camps. It would not have taken much because many people in occupied Europe had already heard stories about what was happening. Had that been done, it would have broken the curtain of silence that concealed the operation of the Final Solution. It had been the opposition of German public opinion that brought the euthanasia program to a temporary halt in 1941. It may be, as some maintain, that an intense anti-Semitism held sway in the German public mind, but that did not include the processed murder of millions in the death camps, assuredly not if the cost of such public policy was the lives of their sons and their neighbors, and the destruction of their homes.

Retaliatory bombing circumvented all the technical objections presented against bombing Auschwitz. German cities were being "Coventryized" in any case. Losses of planes and lives were being absorbed to implement a strategy aimed at destroying German civilian morale. That the Nazi *mentalité* was attuned to retaliation was evidenced by the fact that Goebbels, perhaps fully expecting such a linkage in Allied propaganda, took care to prepare a counter-atrocity campaign. When protest about what was being done to the Jews rose in December 1942, German broadcasts suddenly showed much concern about British mistreatment of colonials.[11] Prone to a direct and sometimes brutal application of military power, the sensibility that held sway in Berlin seemed better attuned to retaliation than moral suasion. From the war's outset, the fettering (chaining together) of prisoners taken by the Germans had been an issue. The British government protested and requested intercession by the ICRC (International Committee of the Red Cross), to no avail. Only when photos were shown of German POWs similarly fettered was it possible to reach an agreement to end the practice. The Führer, himself a veteran *Frontsoldat*, interceded, but only after a large number of German soldiers had fallen into Allied hands.[12]

In the satellites, the mere threat of retaliation could reverse cooperation with the deportations, especially after it became clear that victory would go to the Allies. A cable sent to London by Richard Lichtheim, the agent of the Jewish Agency in Geneva, fell or was put into the hands of Hungarian intelligence. In the cable, Lichtheim urgently requested that a stern warning be given Hungarian authorities that they would be held accountable for the fate of the victims should deportations be restarted. In addition, the cable contained the location of government agencies and the names of seventy officials believed to be involved in the deportations. A fortuitous raid on Budapest followed. That proved sufficient to assure the safety of the surviving Jews of Budapest for a while. Had the regimes in Slovakia, Vichy, and Rumania been made aware in 1943 that the cost of cooperation with the deportations would be the targeting of their cities for raids, and had that actually been followed up by a token raid, many more lives might have been saved.

Retaliatory or retributive bombing was eminently feasible and held out the possibility of saving more lives because it could have started as early as 1942. It would have made the implementation of the Final Solution more difficult and costly. Involved was the mounting of a major propaganda campaign alerting the people of occupied Europe to Berlin's heinous mass-murder operation, which many already suspected was happening. Some of the Nazi officials directly involved in the Final Solution undoubtedly shared Goebbels's view that "at bottom . . . both the English and the Americans are happy that we are exterminating the Jewish riff-raff."[13] But most "ordinary Germans" were probably not fully aware of what was being done in their name. Merely informing the people of Germany and occupied Europe that part of Allied war aims was the resistance to genocide would have compromised its cloak of legitimacy.

Like the bombing of Auschwitz, the more feasible retaliatory bombing was not seriously considered by the Allies. Apparently, something other than feasibility and priorities was blocking such ideas from being realized. The more one probes, the more one senses that more than mere indifference or moral obtuseness was involved in the failure.

Allied reluctance to bomb Auschwitz is usually hidden behind technical reasons. For most of 1943, it would indeed have been very difficult, considering the distance involved and the estimated cost in lives on the ground and in the air. But in the case of retaliatory bombing, where the heavy cost of bombing German cities was already being absorbed, opposition was couched in terms of the legality of such raids. In the midst of a mass-murder operation, middle-echelon British officials argued against such raids, and they continued to do so when British lives were being lost due to Berlin's indiscriminate use of its V-bombs against civilian targets in mid-1944. Rescue advocates may have sensed the irony involved. In order to hold the moral high ground, they had to forego assigning a mission to bombing that the Allies were doing anyway and which might have saved thousands of innocent lives. It is difficult to comprehend such obtuseness even today unless another explanation is involved relating to the unmentionable "Jewish question" that Berlin talked about endlessly.

Retaliatory bombing also raised the possibility of negotiating with the Germans through neutral nations or agencies, a proposal raised by the Madison Square Garden petition delivered to Roosevelt in March 1943. But again there were difficulties. If retaliatory bombing were to be linked to the Final Solution, then any negotiation would be tit for tat: the ongoing bombing would stop if the killing would stop. But such a proposition placed the initiative in Berlin's hands. It would have allowed them to shape British air-war strategy by using the Final Solution as a bargaining chip. The British, who had opted for night area bombing of German cities in 1942, leaving daylight bombing to the USAAF, had no intention of halting the raids, which they were convinced, despite contrary evidence in their own backyard, would eventually break the morale of the German home front. In addition, between the invasion of North Africa (November 1942) and D-Day (June 1944), with the exception of the comparatively bloodless African campaign and the desultory war in Italy, there was little direct confrontation with the Wehrmacht, as on the bloody Russian front. Much to the chagrin of Moscow, the bombing of German cities and the comparatively minor Italian campaign were the only real combat contribution the Allies were making to defeating the still formidable Nazi war machine. Stopping the bombing of German cities in exchange for abandoning the Final Solution would have further weakened the Allied bargaining position vis-à-vis the Soviets at the peace negotiations that were surely coming.

Viewed through the prism of retaliatory bombing, a deeper reason for Allied reluctance to acknowledge what was happening in the death camps becomes discernible. There was fear that making the fate of Europe's Jews central to the Allied war effort, as Berlin had done, would interfere with the mobilization of the requisite passion in the public mind to defeat the enemy and absorb the loss of lives that required. It is not that Allied leaders were anti-Semitic, as some would claim; they were probably less so than the general public, in whose mind Jews were not winning medals for popularity. But to allow German propaganda to make points by arguing that it was a Jewish war and that Allied soldiers were being asked to sacrifice their lives to save the Jews might have had a deleterious impact on the Allied war effort. Instead, the Jewish aspect of the war was fudged. Rescue advocates were repeatedly told that a quick victory would save the Jews, together with all people who suffered under the Nazi heel, and nothing should be done to interfere with that goal. The destruction of European Jewry took its place as merely another atrocity in a war full of atrocities. No recognition was made in the Allied camp that the Nazi genocide meant something different was happening to the Jews of Europe, who, without some form of intercession, would not survive the war.

The Soviet government had a more urgent reason to bomb the death camp. In the Russian war, no quarter was asked for or given. The *Vernichtungskrieg* (war of annihilation) waged by the Wehrmacht in Russia had been particularly barbaric and left millions of casualties and utter devastation in the wake of the Nazi retreat. The eastern war's ferocity was related to the same racial ideology that marked the Jews for death by the *Einsatzgruppen* that followed behind the advancing German front. Berlin's master plan saw the Ukraine as the Reich's breadbasket and the Slav people generally to be subjected and held to a deliberately low level of education. The derivation of *Slav*, German children were reminded, stems from the word *slave*.

The linkage between the Holocaust and the war in the east had ideological roots embodied in the term Judeo-Bolshevism. The link between communism and Judaism embodied in that term was a mainstay of far right-wing ideology the world over. Nazi ideologues considered communism to be but the last in a series of Jewish ideas, including Christianity itself, intended to subvert Western civilization. A murderous response to these two great threats, Judaism and communism, was imbedded in the 1941 Commissar order that commanded the execution of the political officers who served down to the battalion level in the Red Army, and Jews, wherever found. It is the only written order we possess that actually ordered the murder of Jews.

The Soviet link to the death camps and Auschwitz directly is more visible than the American and British connection. The invasion of the Soviet Union in June 1941 unleashed a war that in destructiveness and loss of life differed radically from the kind waged in Africa, Italy, and later France. In its bloodiness, it seemed related to the Final Solution. The link was sometimes a direct physical one. The uniforms of the over two million Soviet war prisoners who were brutalized and literally starved to death after the initial collapse of the Red Army, were worn by the earliest inmates of Auschwitz, including the Jewish women of Slovakia. The first *kazetniks* were not Jews but German communists. Ernst Thaelmann, the communist martyr of the former German Democratic Republic, and many of his colleagues were imprisoned in Buchenwald, one of the most notorious camps. Most important, after Stalingrad, the Soviets were increasingly in a better position than the Allies to respond to Auschwitz directly. Yet Moscow's silence was if anything deeper than that of London and Washington.

In Moscow too, the desire to avoid the linkage with the Jewish aspect of the war was strong and continued well into the postwar period. In the Soviet Union and its satellites, Jewish Holocaust victims became in death what they were never allowed to be in life: esteemed citizens of that country. In its war memorials, the fate of the Jews was simply not mentioned. The Soviet Union coped with the growing interest in the Holocaust by claiming that it had saved over a million and a half Jews who fled eastward after the German invasion of Poland and found a precarious haven in Soviet Asia. Films showed how Soviet troops liberated Auschwitz on 27 January 1945. Unmentioned was the information vacuum that kept Jews in the path of the invading German armies and the *Einsatzgruppen*, in total ignorance of what fate had in store for them, though there was ample evidence in German-occupied Poland of the beginnings of the Final Solution.

The possibility of shuttle bombing, having the planes fly through from liberated Foggia in Italy to airfields near Kiev, which could have solved the technical problems related to range, is detailed elsewhere in this volume.[14] As the Soviet army rolled westward, this strategy became increasingly practical, as was the simpler alternative of direct low-level bombing by the Soviet air force. Yet, except for an unanswered request by the Board of Deputies of British Jews in September 1944, that the Soviets be asked to conduct raids on Auschwitz, and some discussions among the leaders of the Jewish Agency, the matter did not come up. It may be that the idea of bombing Auschwitz by USAAF shuttle raids was a casualty of Moscow's general reluctance regarding shuttle bombing. Yet we know of no evidence that Moscow ever considered bombing Auschwitz directly.

Moscow rarely talked about the fate of its Jewish population, which suffered such a massive bloodletting. It is, of course, true that for a patriotic Russian, Babi Yar and the numerous other killing grounds for Jews were viewed in the context of the massive loss of life endured by all Russians. But there was something else in that eerie official silence. The Soviet regime was after all no stranger to the world of the concentration camp. It had organized one of its own camp systems, which easily rivaled the one to which Auschwitz belonged. Nor was the regime a stranger to massive deportations of entire ethnic groups like the Crimean Tartars, or to mass murder, as with its Kulaks or the Polish officers at Katyn. The shock of death camps and special killing units may simply not have been felt as deeply by an inured Soviet leadership. Most important, the Soviet government had special reason to fear Nazi propaganda, which repeated over and over again that Judaism and communism were linked. To counteract that, the Soviet regime risked reviving Russian nationalism and even allowed the Russian Orthodox church to function again in order to present itself to the Russian people as a purely Russian phenomenon worthy of their sacrifices.

Washington, London, and Moscow, each for its own reason, had little interest in addressing the "Jewish question." Their silence, which seems deafening today, could not have gone unnoticed at the time, if only by contrast to Nazi propaganda. By 1943, seventy to eighty percent of German broadcasting was focused on the Jewish issue.[15] But in the Allied camp, especially in the Soviet Union, the order of the day was silence. Even today, the approach of Russian

Jewish leaders wishing to memorialize the Jewish victims must be circumspect lest they arouse anti-Semitism.[16]

It is in this context that the bombing question is best viewed. In a sense, the destruction of European Jewry was concealed by the exigencies of the politics of the war itself. It is that cruel fact that gives the bombing-of-Auschwitz question and all other missed opportunities to save Jewish lives an accusatory aspect. It seemed so easy to pay heed. But that is only true outside the context of history and what people were thinking and feeling during the war.

The current debate about the bombing question is largely a dialogue of the deaf. The question of whether it should have been done is replaced by a debate about its feasibility. But the primary reason why it was hardly considered should not be simply related to the possibility of carrying out such air attacks. Retaliatory bombing was far more easily done. There were no problems of range of aircraft and pinpointing the target. Yet it too was rejected. The resistance to bombing and to other strategies to save Jewish lives can better be found in the low priority given to the rescue of Jews during World War II. That in turn was related to the refusal of Allied leadership to succumb to Berlin's insistence that the war had something to do with the "Jewish question." If the problem of saving Jewish lives was on the consciences of Roosevelt, Churchill, and Stalin at all, we have found no evidence of it. Bombing Auschwitz required a sense of concern that was not present in the minds of the people or the leadership of the Allied lands. All the rest is commentary.

The destruction of European Jewry is so horrendous and the passivity of the witnessing nations and agencies so difficult to reconcile with our sense of what humanity should be, that the temptation to write a post hoc brief to indict them before an imaginary bar of justice is almost irresistible. Such briefs contain much truth but their objective is to accuse—a far cry from the historian's task, which is to reconstruct the past in as complete and balanced a manner as possible.

Clearly, the issue of bombing Auschwitz, was given currency by David Wyman's 1978 *Commentary* article and by his book *The Abandonment of the Jews*. In neither case did he offer what I consider a balanced account, but rather a convincing brief based on impeccable research to demonstrate that bombing could have been done. But in plucking the bombing-of-Auschwitz case out of its historical context, a distortion occurs. It is given a historical weight and an urgency not felt by actors in the historical drama. A similar twist occurs when one considers the far more likely case of retaliatory bombing that was also rejected. The fate of the Jews was viewed as a minor problem not differentiated from the often cruel treatment of subject people under German occupation, especially in the East. The actors in the historical drama simply did not think as much about what was happening to the Jews as we do today. Those few who were aware of the genocide sensed that to focus on it, to make it a war to save the Jews, would mean fighting the war on Nazi terms.

Those who are unaware of the otherness of Jews in European history may rue the absence of a moral imperative or moral outrage about the Final Solution. That is more keenly felt when one realizes that such moral obtuseness did not apply to all victims of the war. There was a will to feed the Greeks despite wartime blockade prohibitions. There was also a will to supply thousands of starving Arabs in the remote Saudi desert by air during the landings on the Normandy beaches. A will existed to expend the costs in material and lives to supply the beleaguered Polish Home Army during the uprising in Warsaw in August 1944. The difference was that the rescue of Jews was more problematic. In these other cases, there was not a powerful nation-state totally committed to their destruction. The high priority given in Berlin to the realization of that goal was not matched by the Allies, and there can be doubt that it ever could be in the midst of the war for their own survival. In fact, it was barely recognized by them.

There remains the puzzle mentioned at the outset: Why is the bombing-of-Auschwitz problem receiving such attention from researchers? Clearly, it has become the "silver bullet" for those who want to demonstrate an Allied failure as moral witness during the Holocaust. It declares that there was a quick and practical opportunity to save Jewish lives in this late moment of the Holocaust, but it was not seized.

The other historical problem, determining what role the "Jewish question" played in World War II that would place the bombing in its historical context, is more difficult. There is no evidence that I have seen that the "Jewish question" or "problem" played any role in Allied decision-making. It was never discussed in the several strategy planning conferences with Allied leaders and the Combined Chiefs of Staff—in Casablanca in January 1943, in Cairo in November and again in December 1943, in Moscow and Teheran in December 1943, or in Yalta in February 1945—through which the Allied war effort was coordinated.[17] There is no record that Roosevelt ever discussed the question with Churchill during the several protracted visits to the White House and Hyde Park in 1942 and 1943. Like most requests concerning the fate of European Jewry, the request for retaliatory bombing and later the direct bombing of Auschwitz never reached the Oval Office. They were screened out, probably because they were not considered important enough to warrant the president's attention.

Those seeking to indict Allied leaders can find ample evidence of their refusal to directly confront the Final Solution, of which the bombing-of-Auschwitz question is part. But to see it *only* as evidence of moral indifference does not encompass all that was involved in the rejection. It was also a reaction to Berlin's effort to foist a "Jewish question" that occupied the central place in its demonology onto the Allies. While the reasons for resisting that effort were different in Moscow as compared to Washington and London, they had in common a fear that allowing Nazi propaganda to image the war as one to save the Jews would have meant handing Berlin a great propaganda victory.

Allied refusal to deal with the Final Solution led to a standoff. Berlin denounced the bombing of German cities as evidence of Jewish control of Allied leadership. But the Allies refused to consider an announcement that such bombing was indeed retaliation for what was being done in the name of the German people in the East. Had that step been taken, the effect would have been to inform the German people that their lives were being sacrificed for the elimination of a supposed Jewish threat that had become meaningless by 1944.

But in Berlin, where Hitler ruled with a power unprecedented in modern history, the "Jewish question" continued to reign supreme until the final days of the war.[18] Hitler began by declaring in his Reichstag speech (30 January 1939) his intention to annihilate the Jews, and he ended the war still fuming over his obsession in his last political testament, written in his Berlin bunker on 29 April 1945. In contrast, the Atlantic Charter (August 1941), which embodied the first ideas of Allied war aims, spoke of freedom from fear and want and of liberating the nations that had fallen under the Nazi yoke. But throughout the war, the idea of also liberating the Jews was not discussed. The several special appeals for the saving of Jewish lives in the death camps were rejected the way the bombing of Auschwitz proposal was rejected. The Jews would be liberated like everyone else through a quick victory. Nothing would be allowed to interfere with that goal. It was almost unpatriotic to suggest that the Final Solution was a special case that required a special response.

Beyond the question of whether or not the bombing of Auschwitz was feasible, or whether the bombing of rail lines would have appreciably slowed down the killing process, lies the unanswered, perhaps unanswerable, question of why the destruction of the Jews of Europe was largely ignored. The answer has to do with the role the "Jewish question," as viewed in Berlin, could be allowed to play in the Allied war aims. The story might have been different had Hitler been obsessed with liquidating the Dutch. The difference was that the Jews of Europe were not fully part of the "universe of obligation" that informs the Western world. Had they been, there would have prevailed a sense that that world, founded on Christian and democratic principles, was also burning in Auschwitz.

13

MONDAY-MORNING QUARTERBACKING AND THE BOMBING OF AUSCHWITZ

Williamson Murray

History is an alluring discipline. The past lies before us in an almost infinite number of documents, memoirs, accounts, and, of course, histories. We can examine the actions, decisions, and conduct of leaders and participants from every angle; we have great expanses of time to study alternative courses of action and suggest how leaders might have responded more effectively and efficiently to the harsh challenges of war, politics, and strategy. Yet for this very reason, the study of history is a profoundly misleading discipline, for the world does *not* provide world leaders, politicians, or soldiers an infinite amount of time to examine the implications of their decisions.

Instead, those who make decisions of life and death at every level in war must do so under unbelievable pressure. Theirs is a Clausewitzian universe of chance, ambiguity, and uncertainty. They must always act with incomplete information. And each decision is only one of many that compete for attention. As the British general James Wolfe said before Quebec, "War is an option of difficulties." The higher the level of government, the greater the pressure.

A reading of the diaries of Field Marshal Lord Alanbrooke (Sir Alan Francis Brooke), chief of the Imperial General Staff for the last three and a half years of the war, underlines this point.[1] As Alanbrooke's exhausted commentary on the conduct of strategy, operations, and policy makes clear, the British leadership, Churchill, his political advisers, the cabinet, and his generals and admirals worked fifteen hours or more a day, seven days a week for virtually the entire war.

It was no different for those in charge in Moscow or Washington. There was rarely rest or time for reflection, and even the most important decisions crowded in on each other in endless numbers. There was no time for careful, thoughtful analysis; they acted as best they could. For the most part, their decisions have stood the test of time. But the world of decision-making in which they lived had no moments for reflection. Exhausted, their minds and bodies drained of energy, they had to work at a killing pace until it was over.

And it was a killing pace for civilians as well as military. It drove Roosevelt and Harry Hopkins to early graves. It drove many generals and admirals over the edge. And the terrible responsibility hanging over political and military leaders in the democratic nations was that they were responsible to their electorates and their own souls for the lives of the men and women entrusted to their leadership.[2] That was a terrible responsibility that most took with greatest seriousness, as they should have.

We, however, with the advantage of over half a century of history and analysis, can search for the perfect solution. We know the full extent of the Holocaust. We know in endless detail the hideous machine of terror that the Germans created and then used to destroy six million Jews as well as countless others who had the misfortune to fall afoul of the dictates of Nazi Germany's pernicious ideology.

And we are *not* responsible for the lives of our fellow men and women—at least not the ones who lived in those days. We also know how the battles of 1944 will turn out. We know that the Western Allies will launch a great amphibious invasion of Normandy in June 1944. We know that instead of breaking out onto the plains of central France in the first month, Anglo-American armies will remain firmly bogged down in Normandy for nearly two full months until the end of July.

Only in August will they finally break out into the open, and then in a wild charge sweep across France and into the Low Countries, threatening for a short period of time to topple the Wehrmacht. And we know they will fail because of miscalculations and the incapacity of senior generals to make Allied forces work together to the extent they might have. And yet the thrill of the onrush across France and the collapse of German forces in front of Mortain, then the Seine, then Paris, and finally at Antwerp suggested to generals and privates alike that the battle had finally been won. But in fact the desperate Germans, partially motivated by fear of what punishment their crimes would bring down on their heads, mounted a last-ditch desperate resistance that brought the Allied advance to a halt and prolonged the war into spring 1945.[3]

It is a similar story on the eastern front. We know that there will be a massive Soviet offensive, beginning on the third anniversary of the start date for Barbarossa (22 June 1944). We know that Soviet forces will destroy an entire German army group and roll forward to the gates of Warsaw and East Prussia.[4] We also know that there, the iron law of logistics will bring Soviet armies to a halt. Busily engaged in launching their forces into the Balkans to establish Stalin's empire in that region, the Red Army will not return to the offensive in Poland until January 1945, well after Auschwitz had completed its grim business.

What then was the overall military situation as it unfolded, and what would have been the most probable response of Allied commanders had they been approached about the possibility of bombing Auschwitz? The crucial points for this chapter will not be the tactical and technological issues that Allied commanders would have raised in objection to such an effort. The realities of a bombing effort against Auschwitz have been thoroughly laid out by James Kitchens in chapter 7.

This chapter will instead address the operational issues that Allied commanders would have raised to such an effort. In other words, it will discuss why the military situation, as it was occurring in spring and summer 1944, would have made it appear unwise to most Allied military commanders and airmen to devote any substantial resources to the bombing of either the rail lines leading to Auschwitz or to the actual gas chambers or crematoria themselves.

THE MILITARY SITUATION

The military decisions and operations occurring from May through September 1944 were crucial to the eventual defeat of Nazi Germany. As suggested above, what happened on the operational level in both the air and ground campaigns possessed none of the clarity that history books suggest. For the first portion of this period, the issue of the campaign appeared to be very much in doubt. In the second portion—from August through September—it appeared that Allied forces might, if everything worked, tumble the Germans into defeat. Above all, the minds of Allied commanders focused on the business of defeating the Germans in as short a period as possible and at the least cost to the millions of soldiers, sailors, and airmen under their charge. But there is another side to their efforts: the sooner their military forces accomplished the destruction of Nazi Germany, the larger would be the numbers of Jews, Dutch, Russians, Ukrainians, French, Danes, Czechs, Serbs, gypsies, and others who would survive the war.

We might begin with the operational situation in the air. Over the preceding three years, Allied strategic bomber forces had waged a costly campaign against the industry and cities of the Reich. In summer and fall 1943, the American Eighth Air Force had flirted with absolute defeat in the skies over Germany. Against the formidable fighter defenses of the enemy's Bf 109s and Fw 190s, it had lost over thirty percent of its crews nearly every month. In the winter of 1943–44, the British Bomber Command had suffered even more terrible losses in the Battle of Berlin.

From January through May 1944, the Eighth Air Force in England and the Fifteenth from Italy had waged a great battle of attrition against the Luftwaffe. This effort had been supported by long-range fighter escorts not available the previous year. But it was a close-run contest, and not until May 1944 did U.S. bomber losses begin to drop significantly. For a three-month period from February through April, the Eighth Air Force lost approximately thirty percent of its bomber crews each month; the battle for air superiority over the European continent—on which a successful invasion of the continent depended—remained quite literally up in the air almost to the last moment.

Against the tenacious opposition put up by the Luftwaffe in winter 1944, American bombers had first targeted the German aircraft industry; while those raids inflicted great damage to the aircraft factories, the Germans still managed to increase production. But the attack on its production base had forced the Luftwaffe to come up and fight, and the resulting battle had decisively crippled the Luftwaffe's fighter force by killing and maiming its pilots. But the extent of the German defeat in the air was not entirely clear to either side, and Allied air commanders would continue to fear a resurgence of German air power, if they were not to keep the screws on the enemy's defenses.

In April 1944, in addition to their efforts against the Luftwaffe, Allied strategic and tactical air forces turned to the business of destroying the railroad network in central and western France. The aim was to prevent the Germans from bringing up reserve divisions faster than the Allies could build up their forces across the beaches of Normandy. By the beginning of June, but only the beginning of June, the *full* weight of the Allied air forces, strategic as well as tactical, had finally achieved the aim of breaking the weight of the French transportation network in western France. Again, the critical nature of this effort raises the question as to what resources could have been spared for a bombing of Auschwitz—at least in terms of what was known at the time.

With their access to Ultra, Allied commanders were able to watch and weigh the effect of their bombing campaign against the transportation network on which the coming invasion would depend.[5] Throughout June and July, Allied air forces had the new responsibility of not only assuring that the Germans did not carry out significant repairs to the transportation network, but of waging a relentless effort to shut down the French roads to German supply traffic supporting the defenses against the Normandy beachhead.

Along with the attacks on the transportation network in western France, the Allies confronted a serious threat from German plans to launch a massive attack of V-1 cruise missiles on the British Isles. Specially designed and built ramps in France would launch these relatively cheap, pulse-jet missiles at area targets—such as London, or the southern British ports where the invasion forces were gathering. Alerted by intelligence, Allied bombers began attacking these sites in Operation Crossbow. In the end, a sufficient number of these sites were destroyed so that the V-1 never threatened the invasion, nor did it damage British morale to any great extent. Yet the V-1 sites constituted one more major commitment to the strategic and tactical air forces over the spring and summer.

By mid-May 1944, Generals Jimmy Doolittle and Carl Spaatz were confident enough in the success of their efforts to request permission to begin attacking the great synthetic-oil plants in the Reich itself. The Fifteenth Air Force out of

Italy had already begun its attacks on the Rumanian natural-oil complexes around Ploesti, where those attacks had run into ferocious opposition from Rumanian and German fighters. On 12 May, the Eighth Air Force struck the major synthetic-oil plants at Zwickau, Merseburg-Leuna, Brüx, Lutzkendorf, Bohlen, Zeitz, and Chemnitz. The damage was extensive but not crippling; within two weeks, the Germans had gotten the production almost back to what it had been before the raid. But unlike the previous year, the Eighth Air Force had the bomber strength to return to attack the same target sets, while Ultra provided intelligence indicating that the Germans were desperately worried by the initial attack on their oil plants.[6]

In two massive raids on 28 and 29 May, the Eighth and Fifteenth Air Forces lost eighty-four bombers to enemy fighters and antiaircraft fire—over eight hundred airmen were killed, wounded, or prisoners of war in German hands. But the results were graphically clear from Ultra decrypts in the hands of senior commanders almost within the week:

> Following according to *OKL* [Luftwaffe high command] on fifth. As a result of renewed interference with production of aircraft fuel by Allied action, most essential requirements for training and carrying out production plans can scarcely be covered by quantities of aircraft fuel available. Baker four allocations only possible to air officers for bombers, fighters, and ground attack, and director general of supply. No other quota holders can be considered in June. To assume defense of Reich and to prevent gradual collapse of readiness for German Air Force in east, it has been necessary to break into *OKW* (the German high command) reserves. . . . Only very small quantities available for adjustments, provided Allied situation remains unchanged. In no circumstances can greater allocations be made. Attention again drawn to existing orders for most extreme economy measures and strict supervision of consumption, especially for transport, personal and communications flights.[7]

The U.S. strategic bombing force in Italy as well as in England had struck pay dirt. This second raid on the synthetic-oil plants had forced the Germans to break into their strategic reserves of aviation fuel, shut down their training program for pilots, and limit transport flights severely. Over the summer, an increasing number of raids on synthetic-oil plants would bring the entire synthetic-oil industry to its knees. But the Germans desperately made every effort to repair the damage and prevent the complete collapse of oil and gasoline production. The attacks on the German oil industry with such enormous impact on the fighting capabilities of the German military would have raised objections from American airmen that any diversions away from this effort might prolong German resistance and raise the number of Allied soldiers killed or wounded.

Again we confront the issue of what was known at the time, not what we know today.

Heavy raids in early June knocked production back severely, but by mid-July the Germans had managed to quadruple production. Another series of heavy raids at the end of July, supported for the first time by Bomber Command, managed to knock out ninety-eight percent of the German capacity to produce aviation fuel.[8] By August, the numbers were down to forty-six percent of oil production (all fuels), but repair work had increased the level of aviation gas production back to sixty-five percent of the prebombing rate.

The following month, those numbers were forty-eight percent for all fuels and thirty percent of normal aviation gas production.[9] What was required was a constant repetitive cycle of heavy raids against the large number of synthetic-oil plants throughout the Reich and the Rumanian oil fields and refineries—raids that faced enormous opposition not only from the remaining fighters the Germans possessed, but by the heavy concentrations of flak surrounding all the major refineries and synthetic oil plants.

These raids on the German synthetic-oil plants had immense long-term consequences. The destruction of so much of the productive capacity meant that neither Luftwaffe nor Army (nor *Waffen-SS*) were able to train replacement pilots or tank crews with sufficient tactical proficiency to stand up to their Allied opponents. But it also meant that the army and Luftwaffe could not make the kind of defensive effort that had marked their operations before mid-May 1944. For example, the German forces that attacked in the Ardennes in December 1944 possessed only sufficient fuel to get to their initial objectives on the Meuse River; their only hope of achieving their objective was to capture American fuel dumps, which they never did. When the great Bomber Command raid on Dresden took place in February 1945, most of the Luftwaffe's night fighters were on the ground, immobilized by a lack of fuel.

Similarly, the month before, in January, the province of Silesia had fallen to Soviet forces in less than a week despite the Germans having over a thousand tanks in the area; but the panzer forces had virtually no fuel, and consequently no mobility. They were no more than immobile, aboveground bunkers, of little use in the fighting. In every respect, the oil campaign shortened the war and saved lives; but only in the long term, with a payback that lay much farther in the future than American airmen had calculated.

While Allied air forces were waging their great air campaigns to wreck the French transportation network, destroy the V-1 launching sites, wreck the Luftwaffe, and begin the destruction of the petroleum industries on which the Wehrmacht depended for its mobility, the Allies were about to mount the most ambitious amphibious assault ever attempted. On this effort depended whether the military power of the Western Allies would regain the continent, destroy the German army, move on to occupy the Reich, and finally bring the war to a close. On the great assault and the subsequent campaign depended whether the merciless killing unleashed by Nazi Germany's ferocious ideology would end.

The airmen could do great damage to Germany's industry and even its military forces, but they could not end the killing. Only the success of troops on the ground could do that. The invasion's success would depend on two crucial stages: first, the ability of the Allies to gain a toehold on the Normandy coast; and second, the ability of the Allies to build up faster than the Germans so that they could eventually break out into the plains of central France.

The first day of the invasion—the amphibious assault on 6 June—succeeded only by the narrowest of margins.[10] Steven Spielberg's terrifying movie, *Saving Private Ryan*, suggests the nightmare that was Omaha Beach—an assault that cost the U.S. Army far more casualties than the Marine Corps suffered on the first day at Tarawa. And had the assault on Omaha Beach not succeeded, the entire assault on Normandy might have failed. However, the gaining of a lodgment in Normandy was only the first problem the Allies confronted in Normandy. As they fought their way inland, they discovered that the *bocage* country of Normandy—the thick, almost endless series of hedgerows that had separated Norman fields since time immemorial—provided the Germans with a series of outstanding defensive positions.

Instead of breaking out into Brittany within the first month as planned, Anglo-American forces were bogged down in a minuscule strip of Normandy that expanded only at great cost. Not surprisingly, the Germans fought with all the ferocity and tactical effectiveness that had marked their battlefield performance in two world wars. For June and July, the Allies fought desperately to break out from the narrow confines of Normandy.

Again, the air forces confronted a multiplicity of tasks, from the suppression of the German oil industry to the continued effort to ensure that the fewest possible supplies got through to the German troops resisting in the *bocage* country. Casualties among infantry and armored units reached a level previously reached only in the worst fighting of World War I, and the focus of the entire Allied senior leadership was on what was happening on the battlefields of western France.[11] As the fighting teetered on the brink of stalemate (at least from the Allied perspective), one doubts whether any Allied commander would have supported taking even the slightest pressure off the Germans.

For a period in mid-July, senior Allied commanders, including Gen. Dwight Eisenhower, worried that the stalemate in Normandy would continue into the fall and perhaps into the winter. So desperate was the situation in July that ground commanders on four separate occasions called on Bomber Command and the Eighth Air Force to launch massive raids on German defensive positions that were holding up their advances. In the first two cases, Bomber Command dropped huge numbers of bombs on German positions around Caen, but in the end did more damage to the French countryside and buildings than it did to the Germans.[12]

But in late July, the Eighth Air Force launched a major bombing effort to help U.S. forces break through German defenses. Operation Cobra got off to a bad start as the threat of bad weather canceled the mission, but not before a number of the bombers had bombed short, killing 25 U.S. soldiers and injuring a further 131. The next day, the full weight of the Eighth Air Force went in against German positions, and again there was even worse fratricide; this time, 111 American soldiers died, including Lt. Gen. Leslie McNair, while 490 were wounded. The heavy casualties suffered by American ground troops on the second day suggest how problematic "precision" bombing could be. However, this time the bombing had done its job. The German defenses were shredded.[13] Gradually, over the course of the next two days, American troops broke out into the open.

Thus, at the very end of July, U.S. troops reached Avranches, and the exploitation phase of the landing finally began—over a month later than Allied planners had forecast. But the exploitation of the victory in Normandy now took place at a far faster pace and involved far more territory than any of the Allied leadership had expected—with the possible exception of the irrepressible George Patton. Over the first two weeks of August, American spearheads reached deep into the Breton peninsula, drove south and to the east of Normandy, and threatened to surround the German Seventh Army in the Falaise pocket. By the third week in August, British, American, and Canadian forces were across the Seine, while Jacques Leclerc's Free French armored division had achieved the liberation of Paris.

The Allied drives continued at full speed into the beginning of September: Brussels fell; Patton's spearheads approached Metz in the east; American forces, which had landed in southern France on August 15, drove up the Rhone valley and approached Alsace; and British troops captured Antwerp on September with all its dockyards and port facilities in full operating condition. There was every prospect that the Allies would be able to open the port of Antwerp to relieve their growing supply problems, while at the same time trapping the German Fifteenth Army, which had been guarding the Pas de Calais over the summer, in southern Holland.

But Field Marshal Bernard Law Montgomery, commander of the Twenty-first Army Group, consisting of British and Canadian forces, inexplicably disobeyed Eisenhower's instructions to open Antwerp. Instead, he concentrated his forces on the ill-fated Operation Market Garden, a combined paratroop-armored effort to bounce the Rhine.[14] But for all of August, well into mid-September 1944, it had appeared to Allied commanders that they were on the brink of bringing the war to a successful close. Again, as we suggested previously, they were wrong, but that could not have been apparent to them in the tide of victory, as their armies swept across France.

Consequently, Allied senior military leaders would have resisted any less-ening of the pressure on the Germans in terms of support for the ground fighting or the bombing of the Reich's petroleum industry. From their per-spective, considering what was possible for them to know and what their re-sponsibility to their troops involved, they would have been absolutely right. Their obligation was to end the war as quickly as possible, and such an approach to the conflict would in the end save far more lives than any misbegotten efforts to attack targets that in no conceivable way could have contributed to the ending of the war and to Allied victory.

CONCLUSION

On 23 June 1944, Soviet spearheads reached a small group of Jewish partisans near the Pripet Marshes. A survivor recalled "the tremendous wave of joy that flooded the heart . . . [but it] could not remove the feeling of deep sadness; if only they could have come two years earlier! Now that the day of liberation was here, there was no one left to free."[15]

The grim truth expressed by the sad survivor was that massive bombings could not have saved significant numbers of Jews in 1942, 1943, or even 1944. Strategic bombing could maim and kill hundreds of thousands of Germans; it could severely impair the production of crucial goods and fuels on which the Wehrmacht depended; and it could distort German armaments production in significant directions. But only victory on the ground could put an end to the terrible killing of Jews and other innocent civilians by the Germans that had begun in 1941 on a massive scale.

The harsh truth is that, as far as the fate of a substantial portion of the Hungarian Jews was concerned, their extermination coincided with the prepa-rations for Overlord and the opening round of attacks on German oil produc-tion. Ironically, between 15 May and 30 June 1944, as hundreds of thousands of Hungary's Jews were murdered, the crucial military events were unfolding that would bring the military forces of the Western powers back onto the European continent. No military or political commander could have allowed the diversion of even the slightest force from that task. Thereafter, as it appeared the Wehr-macht would lose in 1944, Allied commanders would have objected that they could not afford any such diversions—particularly given the dubious prospects for success.

Thus, the fate of Overlord proved essential in determining whether any of Europe's Jews at all would survive the Holocaust; in the end, there would be survivors, survivors because the military pressures would force the Germans to concentrate on their terrible predicament rather than on killing Jews and be-cause Allied armies would eventually stand over all German territory. Despite the claims of air-power advocates, bombing could not substitute for victory on the ground. In every respect, the air campaign in World War II supported in the long run the ability of ground forces to defeat the Germans; bombing could no more force the Nazis to desist from the Holocaust than it could force them to desist from producing weapons.

Gerhard Weinberg suggests in chapter 1 of this volume that bombing would most probably not have saved the lives of any of the Jewish victims, but that as a gesture, such as the dropping of arms to the desperate Poles in the Warsaw uprising of August 1944, it would at least have signaled that the Allies had heard. And it would not have cost much to divert a few of the bombers from one of the raids on the Auschwitz chemical plants to attempt to hit the killing machinery. He is right on target from our perspective, but his argument in the end rests on what we know today, not on what was known at the time.

We should have no illusions that any bombing attempt would have significantly damaged the target.[16] In fact, there is every prospect that such bombing, given the inaccuracies of "precision bombing," would have killed a significant number of the Jewish inmates. The terrible irony of "Monday-morning quarterbacking" history, is that, if such a raid had failed and killed a number of innocent Jews, we would now be debating the heartless aerial attack by the Allies on Auschwitz that had only added to the terrible burden of suffering that the Jews endured.

14

THE BOMBING OF
AUSCHWITZ: COMMENTS ON A
HISTORICAL SPECULATION

Richard G. Davis

*All that was needed was to bomb the train tracks. The Allies bombed the targets
nearby. The pilots only had to nudge their crosshairs.*
  *You think they didn't know? They knew. They didn't bomb because at that
time the Jews didn't have a state, nor the political force to protect themselves.*
                                          BENJAMIN NETANYAHU
        prime minister of Israel, at Auschwitz death camp, 23 APRIL 1998[1]

As THE READER of this volume has no doubt discovered, the question of why
the Anglo-Americans did not use their air superiority over Europe to intervene
in the Holocaust has become a matter of intense and emotional debate. How
can anyone with a knowledge of the Nazi death apparatus remain emotionally
detached from its horrific practices or arrive at a completely objective synthesis
of the subject matter of this book? From the perspective of over half a century,
I believe that President Franklin D. Roosevelt and Prime Minister Winston S.
Churchill erred in not ordering the bombing of Auschwitz. It is my judgment
that by July 1944 the Anglo-Americans had the knowledge and capability to
begin the destruction of the Birkenau death camp. This task, which would have
taken several weeks, would have sent an unmistakable message to the Nazis to
halt their genocide and might have prevented the extermination of tens of
thousands of individuals.[2] The fulfillment of that single task, had it been undertaken in the summer of 1944 when the U.S. Army Air Forces (USAAF) had
reached their full European deployment of sixty-two heavy bombardment
groups, would not have constituted a significant diversion of force from the
ultimate Allied goal of winning the war. I also believe the destruction of the gas

chambers and crematoria would have been a gesture toward posterity: it might have lessened the charges that the Allies did nothing to help Hitler's victims and may have provided a precedent for even stronger actions against future examples of human barbarism in Cambodia, Rwanda, and Yugoslavia.

The bombing of Auschwitz is the focus of this work because it is one of the most dramatic examples of the Anglo-Americans' failure to intervene. An analysis of the capabilities of Allied air power, when compared to the course of the Holocaust, further reveals that the bombing of Auschwitz in the summer of 1944 has become the central point of this attention because air power could not have effectively struck Auschwitz or any other death camp earlier.

ALLIED AIR POWER AND THE HOLOCAUST BEFORE 1944

By July 1942, the Nazis had established six death camps in Poland for the extermination of the Jews. The Germans built all these camps far from the prying eyes of Western Europeans and, except for Chelmno, out of range of Allied bombers flying from and returning to airfields in Great Britain. From 1939 to 1945, Royal Air Force (RAF) Bomber Command, stationed in England, hit only one target in Poland, the port of Gydnia: once in March 1942 and twice in December 1944. It could have struck only one death camp, Chelmno, approximately 85 miles south of Gydnia, and then only in the unlikely event that it could have located that camp in a night mission. But there is no evidence that the RAF knew of the camp's existence. Flying from and returning to English bases from August 1942 through May 1945, the U.S. Eighth Air Force struck Gydnia twice (October 1943 and April 1944); Posen, 180 miles west of Warsaw, twice (April and May 1944); and Krzesinski, near Posen, once (May 1944). From 21 June through 18 September 1944, the Eighth conducted Operation Frantic, a series of shuttle bombing missions from English airfields to Soviet bases in the Ukraine. These missions could have hit both Auschwitz and Majdanek, the only death camps operating in that period.

Two of the Eighth's Frantic missions have a particular interest for students of the Holocaust. On August 8, 1944, fifty-five bombers, flying from Soviet fields, dropped 109 tons of bombs on the refinery at Trzebinia, about twenty miles from Auschwitz. On September 18, 1944, a total of 107 B-17s, flying from English fields and landing in the Soviet Union, dropped supplies on Warsaw to aid the Polish Home Army, which had risen against the common enemy. Most of them landed in German hands. This raid, and other supply drops on Warsaw flown by Allied air forces in the Mediterranean, demonstrated that the Anglo-Americans had some capability to aid groups in occupied German territory, if they had had the desire to do so. One might also note that these raids were personally ordered by Churchill and Roosevelt over the objections of their air commanders, who regarded the missions as likely to be militarily ineffective and too costly in casualties.³ The 18 September mission to Warsaw ended Operation Frantic. Stalin refused to authorize any further missions, while the Americans lost interest, in part because of political differences with the Soviets, and in part because the Soviet summer offensive had overrun most of the eastern targets intended for the operation.

Heavy bombers flying from England could have had little impact on the Holocaust before the summer of 1944, but as David Wyman and others have indicated, Anglo-American heavy bombers flying from Italy had the range to reach Auschwitz. However, the American heavy bombers of the U.S. Fifteenth Air Force, created in November 1943, and the medium and heavy bombers of RAF No. 205 Group, did not deploy from North Africa to Italy until December 1943. No. 205 Group would have had the same problem as Bomber Command in locating and attacking Auschwitz at night. Although the Fifteenth had Auschwitz in reach by December 1943, it was not until the end of March 1944 that it had the long-range escort fighters that would enable it to operate deep into enemy territory with acceptable losses.⁴ It began operations against Hungary by attacking the Budapest rail marshaling yards on 3 April 1944. The next day, the Allies flew their first photo-reconnaissance sortie over the I. G. Farben syntheticoil and rubber plant at Auschwitz,⁵ and began sustained operations over Rumania by attacking the Bucharest marshaling yards. By then, all the Polish death camps had discontinued operations, save Majdanek, which was liberated by the Russians in July 1944, and Auschwitz.

On 7 July 1944, the Fifteenth dispatched its first raids to targets near Auschwitz: 448 bombers and 1,150 tons of bombs against the refinery complexes at Odertal and Blechhammer, sixty miles northwest of the death camp. The Americans continued to attack these targets through 26 December 1944, expending almost 4,200 sorties and 9,250 tons of bombs. Six weeks later, on 20 August, the Fifteenth sent the first of three raids against the I. G. Farben industries at Auschwitz, using 127 bombers and 334 tons of bombs. The Americans followed up these raids on 13 September (96 bombers, 236 tons), 18 December (49 bombers, 109 tons), and 26 December (95 bombers, 170 tons). From 29 August through 19 December, the Americans also bombed two Czechoslovakian targets within forty miles of the camp, Moravska Ostrava (286 sorties, 708 tons) and Bohumin (34 sorties, 75 tons).⁶

Birkenau ceased its mass killing operations in mid-November 1944. For each and every day prior to this cessation, the complete destruction of its crematoria/ gas chamber complexes might have saved more than a thousand lives. But this does not alter the fact that ninety-five percent of the 5.8 million Jews and the many thousands of Gypsies and others who died in Hitler's death camps, concentration camps, and ghettos died before those who commanded Allied air power had both the knowledge and capacity to interfere.

THE BOMBING OF BUDAPEST

On 2 July 1944, the U.S. Fifteenth Air Force put 509 heavy bombers and 1,200 tons of bombs over targets in or near Budapest. The raid, the largest single day's concentration of heavy bombers over Hungary during World War II, and the culmination of a weeklong effort against the Hungarian capital, underlined the Allies' ability to bomb any Hungarian target whenever they wished.[7] The Fifteenth's effort that day had an unintended, but extremely beneficial, side effect.

The American B-17s and B-24s not only savaged their assigned targets—the Shell Oil refinery, the city's rail yards, and the airfield at Vecses—but they landed bombs in the midst of the city itself, where they destroyed private homes and damaged government buildings. They also struck the minds of the leadership of the Hungarian puppet regime, installed in a Nazi-approved coup in March 1944. The timing of the mission coincided (apparently quite unintentionally on the part of either Lt. Gen. Carl A. Spaatz, the overall commander of U.S. strategic bombers in Europe, or of Lt. Gen. Nathan F. Twining, commander of the Fifteenth Air Force) with an Anglo-American diplomatic initiative. The Allies had learned of the Hungarian government's acquiescence in and support of the liquidation of Hungary's Jews at the hands of the Nazis. At that moment, both Allied governments, as well as neutral nations and Pope Pius XII, were protesting Hungary's deportation of its Jews to the German-operated death camp at Auschwitz. On 4 July, the Hungarian prime minister, Döme Sztójay, informed the German minister and plenipotentiary in Budapest, Edmund Veesenmayer, that Hungarian intelligence had intercepted Allied plans to bomb rail lines to the death camp and to attack government ministries and individuals in Budapest involved with the shipment of the Jews. This information alarmed his government.[8] On 9 July, the transports stopped, after carrying approximately 435,000 Jews since May 1944, of whom the Germans killed all but 100,000 upon their arrival in Auschwitz.

Three hundred thousand Jews remained in Hungary. Many succumbed from suffering experienced in German-established ghettos, from German-inspired anti-Semitism, and from the fighting between the Red Army and Axis forces, but relatively few met their fate in a death camp—the final lot of most of those who had been deported. As for their brethren already gassed and cremated in Auschwitz, one can only speculate on whether or not a direct threat to the Hungarian government, backed up by a mass raid of all seven hundred of the Fifteenth's bombers on the administrative center of Budapest, would have ended the transports sooner. Since the slaughter at Auschwitz during the Hungarian shipments averaged over 8,300 persons per day, every minute was precious.

The 2 July attack, although flown against military targets and for unrelated motives, was the only bombing raid of the war with a direct and significant effect on the Holocaust. Apparently, it succeeded because it struck the weak government of an Axis satellite. Hungary still retained some autonomy, and within its governmental ranks, there was no consensus of opinion in cooperating with the SS in the destruction of its Jews. For example, Admiral Miklós Horthy, regent of Hungary, had successfully resisted handing over Hungary's Jews until the coup of March 1944 effectively ended his control of the government. Even afterward, Horthy, who remained the titular head of state until October 1944, and other elements within the regime, continued to oppose extermination of Hungary's Jews, perhaps due to principle or perhaps due to fear of postwar Allied reprisals. However, the Allies possessed no such leverage over Hitler's government within Germany or its occupied territories.

THE FEASIBILITY OF BOMBING AUSCHWITZ

Much of this volume has dealt with the feasibility of conducting a bombing raid aimed at the gas chambers and crematoria of the Birkenau death camp. The target was a factory complex, albeit one producing and then disposing of corpses rather than one manufacturing war matériel. In addition to its aboveground facilities, made of modern brick construction designed to support heavy machinery and resist heat and fire, it contained belowground (or slightly aboveground) structures with concrete roofs, of an undetermined thickness, covered with dirt. The target was in close proximity to workers' housing. Consequently, its destruction would require an accurate bombing attack designed to minimize damage to friendly civilians. (The Allied air staff planning raids on Auschwitz would assuredly have been unaware of the psychological outlook of the prisoners, who would have gladly accepted their own deaths at the hands of American or British airmen, as long as the camp was destroyed.) Auschwitz could not be attacked at night because it was too small to appear on the British H2S radar carried in RAF bombers and it was beyond the range of ground-based electronic night-bombing aids such as OBOE and GH. Night bombers would have had a difficult time identifying the target and even greater problems hitting it without destroying some nearby barracks, which would be jammed to overflowing at night. Day bombers attacking Auschwitz in cloudy or overcast conditions would encounter similar problems. The target required a daylight, clear-weather assault.

David Wyman and Stuart Erdheim have suggested that the Allies should or could have employed RAF Mosquito attack aircraft to bomb this target complex. However, I believe the nature of the facilities would tend to rule out attack by such aircraft and their crews, especially by units trained in conventional low-level attacks or by units reserved for "special operations," such as the support of espionage and partisan organizations in occupied Europe. Examples of such operations were the Mosquito attacks on the Amiens prison, the Dutch records facility, and the Gestapo headquarters in Oslo and Copenhagen. These missions, consisting of a few aircraft, struck a single structure from low altitudes, and they followed routes largely over water, where they would not be detected and tracked until they were close to their targets. Such would not have been the case for a long overland route from the Adriatic Sea to southern Poland. The use of forty such fast aircraft to attack several buildings from slightly differing headings at approximately the same time, or in closely coordinated waves, would have presented a daunting, perhaps insurmountable, problem in coordination and mission planning. In addition, a close examination of the tactics employed by low-level Mosquito attacks shows that, with the single exception of experimental tactics unsuccessfully used on V-1 launching sites, only above-ground facilities were attacked and then only with straight-ahead or shallow-dive approaches.[9] Such tactics, although highly accurate against walls and the sides of buildings, would have been less effective against the gas chambers at Auschwitz, which were below or only slightly above ground level. As long as the gas chambers were operational, the SS could dispose of bodies by burning them in pyres composed of rails and ties, such as the Germans used at Auschwitz during the Hungarian transports, when the daily number of individuals killed surpassed the capacity of the crematoria.

As Wyman and Erdheim have further suggested, American P-38 fighter-bombers flying at extreme range could have attacked the death camp. These aircraft employed steeper diving angles than the Mosquitoes and would have had a better chance of landing bombs on the gas chambers. However, what is feasible is not necessarily what is practical. The 10 June 1944 raid of the 82nd Fighter Group, which Erdheim identifies as a prime example of P-38 capability, was a one-time special mission flown to attack the highest-priority target in Europe, a relatively undamaged refinery complex at Ploesti that had escaped many previous heavy bomber attacks. There was no need to fly such a specialized mission to Auschwitz, until other, more conventional, attacks had been tried. In addition, the 82nd Fighter Group's attack on Ploesti assigned one squadron to each of three aiming points, only one of which sustained major damage. Given the substantially weaker defenses at Birkenau, one might have expected a P-38 raid to land bombs on at least two or all three of its aiming points. Even so, the raid would have had to have been repeated at least three times in order to hit all four crematoria and all four gas chambers.

B-25 medium bombers, and B-17 and B-24 heavy bombers, all equipped with the same Norden bombsight, could have attacked with their standard medium- or high-altitude tactics. Their bombs, angled to drop straight down, provided they possessed the necessary penetrative force and weight, could have destroyed both the crematoria and the gas chambers. Although the twin-engined B-25 medium bombers may theoretically have had the range with a minimum bomb load to attack Auschwitz and return, the Americans rarely employed them at such extreme ranges. They were more vulnerable than other craft to flak and to fighter defenses along the route because of their lower operating altitudes. Nor, despite Erdheim's example of the B-25 attack on Toulon, is there any evidence to suggest that American medium bombers were, on average, substantially more accurate then American heavy bombers. Also, the American medium bombers in the Mediterranean belonged to the Twelfth, not the Fifteenth, Air Force. Their use would have required an entirely different chain of command. There is no reason to suppose that going through British Gen. Maitland Wilson, the Allied theater commander in the Mediterranean, and American Lt. Gen. Ira C. Eaker, commander of the Mediterranean Allied Air Forces, would have posed more of a problem than going through Gen. Dwight D. Eisenhower, the Allied Commander for the European Theater, and Lt. Gen. Carl Spaatz. However, no research has yet shown that either Wilson or Eaker was ever approached on the use of the B-25s to bomb the death camp. There would have been no reason to do so.

The four-engined B-17s and B-24s not only carried a heavier bomb load than the B-25s, but with a range of over six hundred miles, they counted Auschwitz as a target well within their capabilities. In addition, the Fifteenth Air Force, as compared to the Twelfth, had substantially greater experience in planning and conducting long-range strikes against industrial targets. The Fifteenth already had prepared a target folder for the I. G. Farben synthetic-rubber complex at Oswiecim supported by the Auschwitz slave labor complex, a mere seven miles from the Birkenau death camp. Had the Fifteenth attacked these targets with one of its bomb wings, composed of five or more groups of heavy bombers (approximately one hundred and seventy-five bombers), it would not have been an insurmountable problem to give two of those groups primary visual aiming points in the death camp. Furthermore, it seems logical that the Fifteenth would have handled the issue of collateral damage (the death of prisoners within the camp from Allied bombs) in the same manner as the American Eighth Air Force dealt with the bombing of transportation targets within French cities in April, May, and June 1944, where General Spaatz instructed his air crews to take all reasonable precautions to avoid hitting friendly civilians.[10] If the Anglo-Americans had chosen to bomb Birkenau, they would have made the American heavy bomber their weapon of choice.

Heavy bomber missions against Auschwitz might have even offered the opportunity to send the strongest possible message to the Nazis. Given the permission of Soviet dictator Joseph Stalin—and who can judge if this would have been granted?—a raid on the death camp could have been conducted as part of Operation Frantic. Such a mission would have sent a combined Anglo-American-Soviet warning to the Germans and given a strong indication of the desire to halt the Holocaust to the people of occupied Europe and to the Allies' own populations.

In any case, it seems unlikely that a single raid by any type of Allied aircraft, such as is apparently assumed by other contributors to this volume, could have destroyed all the facilities at once and halted the exterminations. At least three, if not four, separate strikes probably would have been required. If one of those efforts had encountered overcast conditions at Auschwitz,[11] it would have had to divert to another target, necessitating the scheduling of an additional mission. The history of strategic bombing has shown time and again that targets are often far more resilient than suspected. German industry, for example, maintained production in plants with roofs blown off and outside walls breached. Could the crematoria have continued to function with their chimneys down, or their roofs blown away, or an outside wall collapsed? Were the ovens sturdy enough to survive all but a direct hit? As for the gas chambers, would one or two holes through their roofs, quickly repaired with a steel plate and two feet of earth, make them any less deadly? It is possible that Birkenau might have been far less vulnerable to bomb damage than the proponents of bombing have acknowledged, even to themselves. Furthermore, how quickly could the Nazis repair damage? They had a virtually unlimited supply of slave labor on-site. Nor would the Allies have sent these strikes on consecutive days. Their standard operating pattern would have been to space the raids two or three weeks apart in order to confuse the enemy, carry out other priority missions, assess bomb damage, and wait for optimum weather. Therefore, the destruction of Auschwitz could have stretched over a period of six to eight weeks from the date of the first strike. As already noted, from 7 July 1944, the date of the last of the Hungarian transports, through late November 1944, when Himmler ordered the SS to discontinue exterminations, the camp averaged over a thousand murders per day, a fraction of its daily physical capacity of six thousand. Knocking out excess capacity, which the first raid or two would have done, might not have slowed the process of killing in the least.

If the destruction of the extermination facilities required a minimum of four missions of approximately seventy-five effective heavy bomber sorties each, would those three hundred sorties have constituted a significant diversion of force? In July 1944, the Fifteenth launched 10,716 effective heavy bomber sorties and dropped 27,400 tons of bombs; in August, it sent out 10,708 effective heavy bomber sorties and dropped 26,200 tons of bombs.[12] Three hundred sorties and 900 tons of bombs, or even twice that number, would not have been a substantial diversion of this total effort. Even if one assumes that the three hundred sorties, because of their deep penetration into German-occupied territory, would all have come at the direct expense of the Fifteenth's highest-priority target, the German oil supply, the effort expended on Birkenau would have amounted to about seven percent of that effort. In July and August 1944, a period of very heavy attacks on Ploesti in Rumania, the Fifteenth directed 5,059 sorties and 12,054 tons against oil targets. Although the Anglo-American air leaders would have certainly begrudged any diversion of their forces from their already assigned targets, it would seem that the amount of force required to put Birkenau's gas chamber/crematoria facilities out of action would not have seriously delayed the accomplishment of other goals.

The destruction of those facilities was a limited and attainable task. However, the expansion of that priority into one implementing a systematic bombing campaign against the vast SS organization of camps and industrial enterprises that had metastasized throughout Nazi Europe would have constituted a significant diversion of force. Allied air leaders would have strenuously objected to such an effort, and it seems unlikely that Roosevelt or Churchill would have overruled them.

In order to answer the question, "When could the Anglo-Americans have begun attacks on the death camp?" one must first satisfy two additional queries: "When did the Allies have the physical capability to launch a sustained series of attacks against the camp?" and "When did the Allied leadership (Roosevelt, Churchill, and their Combined Chiefs of Staff) possess authoritative knowledge of Auschwitz's purpose and location?" The first of the additional queries is easily answered. The Fifteenth Air Force, for reasons noted earlier, could not have begun a series of operations against Birkenau until the beginning of April 1944. It is unfortunate that it did not do so, because a series of successful bombing attacks on the death camp at that time would probably have disrupted the mass transports of the Jews of Hungary and saved, at least momentarily, hundreds of thousands of lives.

However, in April 1944, the Anglo-American leadership had not yet come to a complete appreciation of Auschwitz's function and location. Richard Breitman, of course, presents an irrefutable case that portions of the Allied governments possessed all the information necessary to deduce the exact site and role of the camp by mid-1943, if not before. He does not make the case that the Allies had fully analyzed and appreciated this information. For example, the Ultra code-breakers at Bletchley Park had known about and routinely decrypted the series of German police reports that contained detailed data on the course of the Holocaust. However, the Ultra organization had limited resources and other intelligence-collection priorities. Consequently, it concentrated on bomb damage assessment data in the police messages and on other series of messages that had a more direct influence on military strategy and operations. Breitman does not show that those Allied leaders in a position to affect bombing policy were made aware of all the necessary information and were then confronted with a decision whether or not to take action.

Naturally, some of the intelligence about the Holocaust did reach the leadership, and they reacted by authorizing various declarations and radio broadcasts denouncing it. Two additional circumstances, when joined with already held knowledge, finally prodded Churchill to intervene on 7 July 1944. First, the Vrba-Wetzler report, not available to the Anglo-American governments until June 1944, provided explicit, authoritative details of the horrors at Birkenau, and summaries of it actually reached the hands of the highest leadership. Second, the Allied leadership knew of the Hungarian Jewish transports, begun in mid-May 1944, and could now begin to visualize their fate. Hence, Allied airmen could not have been ordered to commence planning the raid until the beginning of July or later, after the decision had worked its way through the British Foreign Office and Air Ministry and the U.S. State Department and War Department. In addition, both Roosevelt and Churchill would have had to have given their approval, probably on the record, to this politically significant change in bombing policy and priorities. Given a minimum of two weeks of planning, which includes prompt access to the necessary aerial photo-reconnaissance, bombing could not have begun until after the Hungarian transports had stopped. As noted previously, the high-priority oil targets near Auschwitz, known to Allied targeteers long before June 1944, were not attacked by the Fifteenth before 7 July 1944. Given the six to eight weeks needed to accomplish the physical destruction of the gas chambers and crematoria, and assuming that the Germans would not invest in an effort to rebuild them, Auschwitz might have ceased to function by 1 September 1944.

Of course, there is no way to calculate how many of the people who would have been spared by bombing Birkenau might have succumbed later in improvised extermination facilities, labor camps, and ghettos before the end of the conflict. Nor is there any way to know what the reaction of the Nazi leadership would have been. After all, a prime rationale for the bombing of the camp was to send a message to the Nazis to cease their policy of genocide. Who can state with assurance that the leveling of that death camp would have halted an insane policy supported by a demented ideology? In this instance, I must agree with Gerhard L. Weinberg, who stated in chapter 1 of this volume, "The idea that men who were dedicated to the killing program, and who saw their own careers and even their own lives tied to its continuation, were likely to be halted in their tracks by a few line cuts in the railways or the blowing up of a gas chamber is preposterous."[13] One might even ask the hard question, "Would an indication that the Allies were willing to devote hundreds of aerial sorties to stopping the extermination have been an incentive for the Nazis to halt the process, or would it have encouraged them to proceed in hopes of diverting yet more Allied air power from oil and armaments plants?" We will never know the answer because the Allies failed to act. Their inaction allowed the tragedy of the death camp to continue.

THE BOMBING OF AUSCHWITZ AND THE SUMMER OF 1944

If a bombing campaign of six to eight or more weeks was to be effective against Auschwitz, it probably should have begun in mid-July—and at least no later than mid-September. Not only would beginning the bombing in October 1944 have been too late to save many lives, but the weather then was so bad that the Fifteenth flew only 5,800 sorties, the least of any month since March 1944. Although this book by its very nature focuses the reader's attentions on a small section of eastern Europe, we should not lose sight of the dramatic sweep of events occurring elsewhere on the continent. On 6 June 1944, only a few days before the Vrba-Wetzler report reached the Allied leadership, the Anglo-Americans commenced the cross-channel invasion from Great Britain to France. The Normandy invasion was the Western Allies' single most important military operation of the war. If it had failed, the war might have been extended for years, as the Germans would have been freed to devote far more resources to the eastern front, where they might have gained a stalemate or possibly have convinced the Soviets to seek a separate peace. At the same time as the invasion, the Anglo-Americans had apparently broken the deadlock on the ground in Italy: taking Rome on 4 June and advancing north. The Eighth Air Force found itself tied to supporting the Normandy invasion until 21 June. For much of the rest of summer, it devoted a substantial effort to combating the German V-1 pilotless bomb menace (of large, perhaps inordinate, concern to the British home front and leadership) or to attacking its prime objective, German oil. The Fifteenth extended some support to ground operations in Italy, but expended its primary effort in the summer of 1944 in attacks on Axis oil installations. The bombing of the German oil industry, in postwar analysis, proved to have been the single most effective Allied bombing campaign of the war. It grounded the German air force and denied the priceless asset of mobility to the German ground forces. Without this campaign, the Nazis might well have extended the war (and genocide) many months. On 25 June 1944, the Soviet summer offensive began. Within a month, it destroyed a German army group of some fifty divisions, and by 19 August 1944, it placed the Red Army at the gates of Warsaw and at the borders of Hungary.

The window of opportunity for bombing the Auschwitz death camp opened just as these actions unfolded. For most of July 1944, the British Air Ministry mulled over its options on Auschwitz, and inexcusably delayed contacting Gen. Spaatz, whose headquarters were only a few miles from the ministry building, until 2 August.[14] Spaatz expressed sympathy for the effort and asked for aerial photography of the camp.[15] As others in this volume have described, Spaatz never received the appropriate intelligence, and on 6 September 1944 (when the opportunity for bombing Birkenau had almost passed), the Air Ministry informed him that he need no longer consider the project.[16] Here again, our focus on the death camp should not obscure the events surrounding it. On 26 July, a week before Spaatz learned of a possible operation against Auschwitz, the Allies broke out of the Normandy beachhead. By mid-August, the Germans were in full retreat from France, and on 25 August, amid scenes of tremendous emotion and excitement, the Allies liberated Paris. At almost the same instant,

Rumania switched sides, trapping a German army and capsizing the entire German position in the Balkans. Bulgaria and Finland surrendered to the Soviets in early September. And finally, on 10 September, spearheads of the U.S. Army reached the Franco-German border.

It appeared to many in the West, especially in light of Germany's collapse under somewhat similar circumstances in World War I, that the conflict might end within weeks. Even as late as 20 October 1944, after the Allied ground forces had stalled in Poland, Italy, and northwest Europe, U.S. Army Chief of Staff George C. Marshall informed Eisenhower that the U.S. Chiefs of Staff contemplated issuing "at an early date" a directive for a supreme effort to end the war in Europe by 1 January 1945.[17]

With the advantage of hindsight, we know that the war would not end until many months later and that the Allies should have attacked Birkenau as soon as they could have accomplished it. I do not offer the above review of events as an excuse for Allied inaction. But I do suggest that the reader should understand that, in the minds of many Allied decision-makers in late July through mid-September 1944, the urgency of combating the Holocaust was subsumed in the larger hope that victory was in the offing.

The Allies could have bombed and destroyed Auschwitz. The Allies should have bombed and destroyed Auschwitz. Why didn't Roosevelt order it done? And why didn't Churchill follow up his interest, expressed to Foreign Minister Anthony Eden on 7 July 1944, when he instructed him, somewhat cryptically, to write the Air Ministry and ask the Air Staff to examine the feasibility of bombing Auschwitz and to "Get anything out of the Air Force you can and invoke me if necessary"?[18]

We cannot know. Roosevelt died before the question arose, and even if he had lived, who can say how the "Sphinx of the Potomac" would have replied? Churchill never followed up his instructions to Eden. That probably was because, given the context of his comments to Eden, Churchill was more concerned with stopping the Jewish deportations from Hungary than in actually bombing the death camp as a statement of policy. Hence, when the Hungarian government halted shipment of its Jews, Churchill had accomplished his objective and saw no need to pursue the matter. After the war, Churchill was apparently never asked why he did not act. (Martin Gilbert, the world's leading Churchill scholar, who would know if this occurred, if anyone would, offers us nothing on this point.)

As a Gentile, I am uncomfortable with the implication that anti-Semitism is the most obvious and leading cause of the West's inactivity. However, as a historian, I must acknowledge that anti-Semitism is a recurrent theme in Western civilization and that during World War II, some decision-makers in both the British and American governments were anti-Semites. If the Holocaust stood alone as the sole instance of genocide in the twentieth century, anti-Semitism might have accounted for the world's inactivity. But anti-Semitism does not explain the world's inaction in the face of the other genocides of the modern era. Benjamin Netanyahu came closer to an answer when he noted that European Jewry lacked political force or leverage in the Anglo-American governments to protect themselves. The Western leaders made decisions affecting the lives and deaths of millions of souls every day. Perhaps, in the midst of the noise of a total war, it was only natural that they listened most closely to those with the closest and loudest voices. This would also appear to apply to the victims of the other mass exterminations of the twentieth century. The Armenians, Cambodians, Rwandans, and Yugoslavs have had no greater constituency within the West than did the Jews of Europe.

15

THE FAILURE TO RESCUE AND CONTEMPORARY AMERICAN JEWISH HISTORIOGRAPHY OF THE HOLOCAUST: JUDGING FROM A DISTANCE

Deborah E. Lipstadt

SWISS GOLD; SECRETARY of State Madeleine Albright's lineage; artwork looted from Jews; Red Cross officials who laundered victims' money; debates about ordinary Germans' role in the Holocaust; the Vatican's 1998 statement on the Shoah; and British detailed knowledge of the murder of European Jewry from secret German radio transmissions. These are some of the stories that captured the American public's attention during recent years. In 1997, sixty-five million Americans watched *Schindler's List* when the Ford Motor Company, whose founder once spread virulent anti-Semitism, sponsored a commercial-free three-and-one-half-hour broadcast on television. The Holocaust, which not long ago some pundits feared would be consigned to the historical storage shelf, seems firmly ensconced in popular culture.

One issue that continues to provoke the interest of scholars and laypeople alike is the American response to the Holocaust. This is particularly so when the topic is the bombing of Auschwitz. As is repeatedly evident in this volume, the conversation regarding bombing is often more intense than is usually the case in historical discussions. But it is not just scholars who are passionate about it. American Jews have shown an intense interest in the topic.[1] This chapter, which sets the bombing of Auschwitz within the larger context of the U.S. response to the Holocaust, argues that for many American Jews this debate transcends history and enters the arena of contemporary behavior and politics. Debate about the war often is actually a debate about an array of contemporary political, religious, and ideological issues.

It is instructive to begin by placing the American response to the Holocaust within the context of aforementioned Holocaust stories, which have repeatedly captured headlines in the American press during recent years. These are not disparate stories that happen to be about the Holocaust. They share a common theme and contemporary relevance. They concern those we have always viewed as bystanders to the Holocaust: neutral governments and agencies, Jews living in relative safety, occupied countries, ordinary Germans, and above all, the Allied governments who ultimately defeated the Nazis. Many of these bystanders have spent fifty years protesting their innocence. But historians have repeatedly demonstrated—and the recent stories reaffirm—that many were not innocent, and virtually no one, including the American public, was ignorant.

Focusing on the bystanders expands our thinking about the Holocaust beyond victims and perpetrators. A myriad of memoirs has given us some sense of what it was like to be a victim; we have wondered and tried to understand what motivated the perpetrators to engage in acts that were utterly devoid of humanity. But we find it difficult to see ourselves in either of those roles. The recent stories ask us to imagine ourselves as bystanders. Stories about bystanders are, in some fashion, *about* us.

The recent spate of Holocaust stories also resonate because they shatter commercial, humanitarian, and artistic icons. Swiss banks may have laundered Nazi gold from the teeth of Jews. The Red Cross had Nazi sympathizers in its employ who may have spirited stolen funds out of Germany to neutral hiding places. French museums have in their possession artworks looted directly from Jews. Spanish, Portuguese, and Dutch opportunists all trafficked in Nazi gold, most of it apparently booty acquired from Nazi victims.

The British learned of the Holocaust almost at its inception when they intercepted German military cables. They did not or would not warn Jews who might have escaped because to do so would have revealed that they had cracked the enemy code. While this decision could be justified on strategic grounds, harder to explain is the satisfaction some British diplomats expressed when Jews were thwarted in their escape attempts. In 1943, a British diplomat expressed relief that a boatload of Jews escaping the Final Solution had sunk because this would prevent other Jews from trying to do the same thing.[2]

For a time in 1997, the least consequential of these Holocaust stories transfixed the American imagination: Madeleine Albright's family history. Suddenly it became as important as her China policy. Some people were indignant that Albright was ignorant of her Jewish ancestry; others accused her parents of abandoning their parents. But Albright was not unlike thousands of Jews in Europe and America whose parents cut themselves off from their roots rather than face painful truths. One could argue she *should* have known—all the evidence was in front of her—but like many others "chose" not to deduce the obvious.

All these seemingly disparate stories are about people and institutions at the margins of the Holocaust. Even Daniel Goldhagen's much-debated *Hitler's Willing Executioners* spotlights those who have comfortably claimed bystander status. These ordinary Germans have long found refuge behind comforting mantras:

"We did not know"; "My father was on the Russian front"; "The Nazis did this."[3] But, as many scholars including Goldhagen have demonstrated, thousands of them participated in the Final Solution.

Stories of bystanders have a particular resonance for post-Holocaust generations. None of us think of ourselves as perpetrators. But we all know we can be—and often are—bystanders. As bystanders, we both distance ourselves from the idea that there is nothing we can do and are captivated by Raoul Wallenberg and Oskar Schindler because they demonstrate that something could have been done. Examples like theirs show that in the face of unmitigated evil, a bystander who takes no action becomes a facilitator. We are drawn to their stories because they are bystanders with whom we want to identify. We assuage any discomfort we have about being bystanders today—to genocide in Rwanda and in the former Yugoslavia—by convincing ourselves that we would have been more like Wallenberg and Schindler.

America's response to the Holocaust is part of this web of bystander stories. But it is more than just that. The often moralistic nature of the conversation about the bombing and the fact that this particular issue "consistently raises public interest" can be attributed, in part, to a form of synechdocical or associational thought: the substitution of the part for the whole.[4] Discussion about the failure to bomb is shorthand for an intricate and complicated web of failures by the British and Americans from 1933 on.[5] It illustrates the utter abandonment of the Jews. Because the debate about the bombing of Auschwitz is in fact often a debate about the larger, more complex, and multifaceted American refugee/rescue policy, this chapter in contrast to the others in this volume, strays from the precise parameters of the question of the bombing and addresses the broader issue of American refugee/rescue policy.

When discussing the bombing issue with Jewish audiences, I find that many people are convinced that bombing the camp would have saved many of the six million Jewish victims. They ignore the fact that a significant number of victims were killed before Auschwitz was in the range of Allied bombers. Moreover, half a million victims were killed by the *Einsatzgruppen,* mobile killing units, far from any camp and *before* the United States entered the war. From 1941 through 1944, when the vast majority of Jews were being murdered by the Germans, there was limited action the Allies could have taken to save Jews already in enemy hands.[6] The ahistorical conclusion about the efficacy of bombing one camp at a relatively late stage of the destruction process reflects how anger about the part—the failure to bomb Auschwitz—is substituted for anger about the whole—the United States' apathetic response to Jewish suffering. Unless the connection between the part and the whole is made, it is hard to fully grasp what a conversation, which ostensibly concerns one particular strategic issue, is really about.

Beginning in the late 1960s and continuing for two decades thereafter, a series of books was published that delineated in painful degree the depths of this betrayal. Arthur Morse's *While Six Million Died: A Chronicle of American Apathy* posited that the U.S. refusal to rescue resulted from deep-seated anti-Semitism. Henry Feingold's *The Politics of Rescue* also accused the Roosevelt administration of betraying the Jews. Saul Friedman's *No Haven for the Oppressed* strongly condemned Jewish leaders for their failures. David Wyman's *Paper Walls* criticized American officials for their blatant anti-Semitism. Other serious historical works appeared during this period. Richard Breitman and Alan Kraut's *American Refugee Policy and European Jewry: 1933–1945,* while critical of the U.S. record, argued that rather than anti-Semitism, bureaucratic indifference was at fault.[7] David Wyman's article on the bombing of Auschwitz appeared in 1978 and was followed in 1984 by his book, *The Abandonment of the Jews,* which sharply critiqued Roosevelt, the churches, and the press. It appealed to, among others, Jews who saw the failure to bomb Auschwitz as a symbol of American anti-Semitism and Jewish complacency. Wyman's conclusions, which are based on voluminous and groundbreaking research, have galvanized many historians and provoked a significant amount of additional research and discussion.[8]

But in addition to the serious historical works that have been produced, there is, however, another body of literature that has differed in tenor and tone. Some of it echoed Wyman's arguments, and some of it went further by depicting the American bystanders as accomplices in the destruction of European Jewry. Typical is the *j'accuse* in Herbert Druks's *The Failure to Rescue,* which was published seven years before Wyman's book: "Roosevelt and the British acted in such a manner as to prevent the rescue of European Jewry. Their policies enabled the Nazi Germans and their European collaborators to slaughter six million Jewish men, women and children."[9] In *The Holocaust Conspiracy: An International Policy of Genocide,* William Perl argued "that it was *not* apathetic inaction of the world's powers which made the Holocaust . . . so tragically effective . . . [but] *deliberate action* on the part of many nations [i.e., the Western Allies] that kept millions of those destined for murder, prisoners in a hostile Europe."[10]

But it is not only Allied political leaders and government bureaucrats who are criticized. Jewish historians, journalists, filmmakers, and writers condemn American Jewish leaders. Druks wanted his students to learn from his book that "many American-Jewish organizations failed to help save the Jews of Europe."[11] Rafael Medoff charges that the primary concern of these leaders was only "how non-Jews would react."[12] Even Eastern European leaders who rose to positions of leadership, Medoff contends, were "more concerned about the need to curtail whichever Jewish behavior might arouse gentile hostility." Medoff claims that American Jewish leaders did not call for the bombing of Auschwitz or increased immigration to the United States because they believed that "anti-Jewish prejudice could be eliminated" if non-Jews were convinced that Jews shared the same concerns as gentiles; hence the Jews' relative silence on this matter.

Some of the critique of Stephen S. Wise and his cohorts comes from people associated with the Irgun/Bergson/Revisionist camp. Many are still fighting the historical battle of sixty years ago. In *Years of Wrath, Days of Glory: Memoirs from the Irgun,* Yitshaq Ben-Ami accuses Stephen Wise and Nahum Goldmann of being satisfied "as long as power remained in their hands," even if only "remnants" of the Jews in Europe were left.[13] William Perl, in *Operation Action: Rescue from the Holocaust,* accuses established Jewish leaders of more than "silence and inaction." They were guilty of "outright interference with rescue efforts."[14] A similar argument is made by Laurence Jarvik in a wildly one-sided film, *Who Shall Live and Who Shall Die?* which purports to be about American Jewry's response to the Holocaust. It is a brief for the "opposition" (i.e., the Bergson group) and makes no effort at balanced analysis.[15]

Saul Friedman, whose *No Haven for the Oppressed* is highly critical of both the government and the American Jewish community, heightened the level of criticism in an essay in the *Goldberg Report,* a study evaluating the role of American Jewish leadership during the war. A terribly flawed effort, which has mercifully been mostly ignored, its objective was to indict American Jewish leaders for not doing enough to rescue their European coreligionists.[16] Friedman's essay blames American Jews' failure to pressure the government to act, ascribing the failure to "ego conflicts" and to their willingness to let themselves be "coopted by the system." Compromised by their "proximity to power," these leaders were "flattered by attention directed their way" from Washington and the White House and were "impressed with their self-importance,"[17] In the initial draft of the *Goldberg Report,* Samuel Merlin, a close associate of Bergson, claimed that "the leadership of major Jewish organizations . . . knew enough to act or rather counteract, had there been enough compassion and a will."[18]

Some of the most searing criticism of the Jewish leadership comes from Jews associated with the far-right wing of the Orthodox movement. They blame the secularism and Zionism of the Jewish leadership during the 1930s, which led those leaders to ignore the cries of their fellow Jews. David Kranzler, in a book on the role of Orthodox organizations published by Mesorah/ArtScroll publications, a publishing house known for its Orthodox theological perspective, savages Stephen S. Wise. Wise, he claims, forsook Torah for "the more popular ideology, the secular religion, of liberalism." He blames Wise's failures on his "assimilationist tendencies" and his commitment to Reform Judaism and Zionism.[19] Wise allowed nothing, not even "Jewish suffering," to interfere with his reverence for the president. Kranzler accuses Wise of preferring that yeshiva students languish in Europe, where they were ultimately destroyed, because he did not want more Orthodox Jews in the United States, where they might arouse anti-Semitism and hostility.[20]

Rabbi Morris Sherer, an ultra-Orthodox rabbi, describes Wise as the "chief architect of an American Jewish policy which resulted in the loss of many thousands of Europe's Jews who could have been saved." Sherer blames this "policy of inaction" on Wise's Zionism. If these leaders had viewed events from "a Torah perspective," the rabbi laments, they would have acted as Jews and engaged in rescue.[21] According to these authors, the only ones who performed admirably were the strictly Orthodox. The message is clear: the enemy was then and today still is liberalism, secularism, assimilation, and Zionism.

How do we explain this literature, which presupposes that if the United States had acted and if American Jews had been more forceful, millions could have been saved? For Americans, this aspect of the Holocaust has a personal resonance because it reflects directly on the nation's mythic self-image as an island of refuge. For American Jews, who have prided themselves on responding to the cries of their oppressed brethren, it has an even greater resonance. Yehuda Bauer believes that this wallowing in "self-pity and exaggerated anti-Allied or, more generally, anti-Gentile accusations" is the result of Jews recognizing the degree to which the Allies, whom they treated as heroes, had, in fact, abandoned them.[22]

But this is not just a debate about the past, as becomes clear if we place this literature in a historical context: that is, What was happening in the American Jewish community when it began to appear? Beginning in the late 1960s with the Arab-Israeli Six-Day War, American Jews experienced some radical changes in the political alliances, communal agendas, and ideological affiliations. The Holocaust and the United States' shortcomings during this period became a prism through which the Jewish community's view of the present was refracted. The Holocaust loomed large in the communal conversation that began in May 1967. In the weeks before the Six-Day War, Jews feared that another Jewish genocide was in the offing.[23] Once again, as had been the case in the 1930s and 1940s, Jews' putative allies—church groups, liberals, and other minority groups—were silent. Reminded of the world's silence during the Nazi period, many Jews concluded that nothing had changed.[24] A few months after the war, Milton Himmelfarb of the American Jewish Committee analyzed the lessons of May 1967. "We learned," Himmelfarb wrote, "the old, hard truth that only you can feel your own pain."[25] During the weeks before the war, Jews had "a sudden realization that genocide, antisemitism, a desire to murder Jews—all those things were not merely . . . about a bad, stupid past. . . . Those things were real and present."[26] These bleak expectations contrasted sharply with the spectacular military successes of the Israeli army. "Alone, unaided, neither seeking nor receiving help, our nation rose in self-defense," Israel's foreign minister, Abba Eban, told the U.N. General Assembly on 19 June 1967.[27] The "betrayals" of May 1967 taught that, as concerned the outside world, nothing had changed. The "unaided" victory of June 1967 taught that, as concerned Jews' behavior, much had changed. Jews seemed to have gleamed the lessons of the Holocaust: they had not put their faith in "princes," and by relying on their own resources, had triumphed over the enemies.[28] This was the message of a United Jewish Appeal fund-raising poster that showed a Hasid praying before the Western Wall. The caption read: "Thirty years ago his back was up against a different wall."

The issue of betrayal and its connection to events in the 1960s and 1970s explains why Roosevelt has become a target of many Jews' anger. While he was in office, and for many years thereafter, Jews showered him with love and revered his memory only to "discover," thirty years later, that this was, at best, an unrequited love affair.[29] More than spurned by their lover, they were duped.

But it was not just the Arab-Israeli war that invested the U.S. response to the Holocaust with symbolic importance. The liberal political alliance that Jews treated as an organic expression of their religious identity tottered during this period. Some African Americans, with whom Jews had assumed they shared both a common history of persecution and a common agenda, began to express anti-Semitism. A series of disparaging references by African Americans about the Holocaust[30] and the bitter 1968 New York City teachers' strike, which positioned Jewish teachers against African American community activists, prompted many Jews to reevaluate the efficacy of such alliances.[31] It was further proof of their aloneness. This was also the time of the affirmative-action debate. Many Jews questioned a policy that they believed worked against Jewish interests.

Jews also watched the political left adopt virulently anti-Israel politics. In the fall of 1967, one of the largest gatherings of political groups associated with the New Left passed a resolution condemning the "Zionist imperialist" war.[32] Students for a Democratic Society, a popular leftist organization, adopted a militantly anti-Israel agenda. During the next two decades, the left was a source of hostile attacks on Israel, complete with comparisons to Israelis as Nazis. Some Jews concluded that, as had been the case in World War II, they had been duped by putative friends.[33]

During this period, a group of Jews who identified themselves as neoconservatives questioned the wisdom of Jews' commitment to liberal causes. The hostility to Israel on the left and the election of a right-wing government in Israel gave this conservative voice added prominence. Jews' liberalism, whether in the 1940s or the 1960s, had yielded few results, these neocons argued. M. J. Nurenberger, in his vitriolic attack on American Jewry, linked the two issues when he asked why "so many young Jews sacrificed their lives for Black rights . . . [but] were not inspired to fight for the Six Million?"[34] Perl went further by simply melding the wartime and postwar policies of the Jewish community and treating them as one. Accusing the American Jewish community of adhering to a "policy of silence . . . with ever increasing ferocity" during the war, he argued that "Jewish organizations had been in the forefront of the fight for the rights of the oppressed everywhere. They continued this tradition after the war when they marched in America for the rights of the oppressed blacks, the underpaid grape pickers, the exploited gravediggers and garbage collectors. But they were so eager to demonstrate their 'objectivity' that the murderous persecution of their own kind evinced no more that meek protests."[35]

But it was not only those who aligned themselves with extreme Jewish groups who engaged in such ahistorical criticisms. The post-Holocaust generation did as well. Many of the members of the first generation to have come of age after the Holocaust were closely aligned with politically liberal causes. In 1967, appalled by the hostility of those on the left to Israel and their inability to relate to an Israel that was a victor and not a potential victim, they reevaluated their priorities. Though they were shocked at being "abandoned" by their former allies, they were even more shocked to "discover" their parents' record during the Holocaust. They seemed intent on demonstrating, to themselves as much as to anyone else, that they had learned the lessons of the past.[36] By acknowledging—some would say judging—the United States' shortcomings, they are saying, "Had I been there, I would have acted differently." Young Jewish activists working on behalf of Soviet Jews proclaimed that they would not repeat their parents' mistakes. These activists, members of the first post-Holocaust generation, were also heavily influenced by the Vietnam protest movement, which attacked the "establishment." Young Jews turned this critique on the Jewish community. Contrasting their behavior with that of the Jews of the 1940s, many in this first post-Holocaust generation advocated a more forceful response to the plight of their Soviet coreligionists. "We," one proclaimed in self-righteous and historically inaccurate fashion, "would not sit silently by as our parents did when their brothers and sisters called out for help."[37] This attitude persists today. In 1993, a young lawyer gave the invocation at a UJA luncheon: "Give us strength to lead our people like Joseph and Esther, and not like Henry Morgenthau and Felix Frankfurter. . . . They could have influenced Roosevelt but they chose not to."[38]

American refugee/rescue policy reminded Jews of both the consequences of powerlessness and why Jews needed that power now.[39] It justified Israel's transformation in the 1970s from a threatened entity in the Middle East to a military power. Ironically, many of the extreme critics of American Holocaust-era leaders are convinced that "if only" the leadership had acted differently, myriads could have been saved. Bauer describes this as internalization of "antisemitic notions by Jews."[40] Jews have power. Therefore, the critics contend, had they wished to save their fellow Jews, they could have. Such is the assumption made by M. J. Nurenberger in *The Scared and the Doomed: The Jewish Establishment vs. the Six Million:* "Thus the question: How could six million Jews be exterminated in Europe with the full knowledge of their brethren . . . in the United States?"[41]

There is much for which to criticize these leaders. They expended great time and energy in internecine warfare. They worried about organizational politics when such considerations should have been irrelevant. It is highly doubtful, despite the claims of postwar critics, that they did not care. Monty Penkower's *The Jews Were Expendable* is a fierce critique of Allied governments. Because of his indictment of Western governments and neutral agencies, Penkower's findings are accepted by many of the critics cited previously. While Penkower posits that established American Jewish leaders feared being charged with dual loyalty, he nonetheless refuses to indict them. He acknowledges that his archival research has indicated "beyond doubt" that Wise and the organizations he led "vainly tried throughout the war to move the Allies to save European Jewry."[42]

Even if these leaders had been united, they would not have been able to move the Allies to act. Even if they had "raised an outcry day after day," it is doubtful whether they could have—as Arthur J. Goldberg and Arthur Hertzberg suggest in their 1984 essay—"pierced the prevailing indifference" or convinced Allied governments that rescue should be the country's top priority. Ultimately, they lacked a critical tool: clout.[43] They were powerless. Postwar suggestions that they should have broken with the Allies and acted on their own or used "the Jewish vote for leverage" are as fanciful as they are divorced from reality.[44] The historical analyses that presuppose that, if Jews had united and exerted political pressure, things would have been dramatically different suffer from a disease that afflicts much contemporary historical analysis: presentism.[45] *Presentism* is the application of contemporary or other inappropriate standards to the past. Prevailing historical conditions are ignored. Hence, it is assumed that because Jews have a great deal of political clout today, they had the same clout fifty years ago. Medoff's charge that they should have used the Jewish vote for "leverage" reflects the contemporary political situation, not that of the 1930s or 1940s. It assumes that, because in the 1980s and 1990s political parties will tailor their platforms to win Jewish support, they would have done the same before and during World War II. Had Jews, therefore, really wanted Auschwitz to be bombed, it would have been bombed.

Before concluding, it is important to note other sources of moralistic criticism that have fallen outside the parameters of this chapter. There are the staunch defenders of Roosevelt and Allied rescue policy. Their absolutist position constitutes a mirror image of the attacks on the president and the Jewish establishment cited previously. The defenders contend that all that could have been done was done. Ignoring any shortcomings of American policy, they take deep umbrage that Roosevelt is subjected to any criticism. Arthur Schlesinger and William Vanden Heuvel, among others, defend Roosevelt against charges of anti-Semitism by noting that he appointed many Jews to public office, surrounded himself with Jewish advisers, and in contrast to any previous president, "condemned antisemitism with . . . eloquence and persistence."[46] They accuse the president's critics of leveling "unsubstantiated calumny against men . . . [who were] honorable, humane and honest."[47] Even more extreme in his defense is William Rubinstein, whose *Myth of Rescue* contends that the critics are "wrong and lacking in merit" as well as "grossly misleading and inaccurate." Wyman's charges are "not merely wrong, but egregiously and ahistorically inaccurate."[48] Rubinstein claims that not one additional Jew could have been rescued. This may be true of Jews caught in the Nazi vise. It was not true of tens of thousands who ultimately became victims. His book suffers from the same blanket ahistorical extremism evidenced by those who believe the United States did nothing right.

There is also a group of critics who target world Zionist leaders, particularly those in the pre-state of Israel's Palestinian Jewish community, the Yishuv. They accuse these leaders of having ignored the Jews of Europe because the former were interested only in building a Jewish state. These attacks, which have been "launched with great bitterness," come in the main from younger Israeli writers on the left. Walter Laqueur posits that these attacks are motivated in part by the current political situation in Israel. It is a form of historical revisionism versus political revisionism.[49] Tom Segev's *The Seventh Million* is a virulent attack on the leadership of the Palestinian Jewish community, Ben-Gurion prominently among them. He argues that Ben-Gurion and his cohorts did not care about European Jewry. The fallacy of many of his charges about the leadership has been exposed by Shabtai Teveth in *Ben-Gurion and the Holocaust* and Dina Porat in *The Blue and the Yellow Stars of David*. Segev is particularly annoyed by Israel's use of the Holocaust as a political justification for statehood. While one can question the validity of his critique, comments such as those made by Prime Minister Benjamin Netanyahu at Auschwitz-Birkenau in April 1998 do not raise the level of the conversation. Netanyahu accused the Allies of knowingly letting Jews be killed. The reason they did not bomb the camp was because "Jews didn't have a state, nor the military and political force to protect themselves." While it is true that had there been a Jewish state, various rescue actions would have been possible, Netanyahu's facile reasoning—that it was simply the absence of a state that kept the Allies from bombing the camps—uses history as a political tool.

The United States—the White House, Congress, the Jewish community, the churches—could have done more to help rescue Nazism's victims. Auschwitz could have been bombed, though the efficacy of this in terms of saving prisoners' lives is still open to debate. Virtually every segment of the American population during the war could be criticized for some degree of apathy.

However, as we have tried to demonstrate in this chapter, while hard-hitting but balanced historical analysis is to be encouraged, moralistic condemnations that attempt to resolve contemporary issues by using a historical period that was dramatically different from today are not. When the "wrath and frustration of the Jewish people turn[s] against itself" in this manner, it results in a "suicidal tendency in historiography."[50]

There are many legitimate lessons to be drawn from the Holocaust. They can and should be drawn without twisting the truth and engaging in vilification and blanket criticism. Invoking the Holocaust for contemporary political purposes—whether it is done by the right or the left—is not only ahistorical, but it will ultimately diminish the memory of those whose lives might have been saved by the bombing of Auschwitz or any one of a myriad of other actions.

Part IV

DOCUMENTS

———

THE DOCUMENTS SELECTED for this section are all from 1944. They represent the most important original sources for the history of the appeals to the United States and Britain to bomb Auschwitz-Birkenau or the rail lines leading to it. These appeals overlapped chronologically, but the British government's discussion of the appeal from the Palestinian Jews was circumscribed within a narrower time span from July to September 1944, whereas the appeals to the United States, the internal government discussions about them, went on from May to November. Thus we have divided these documents into three phases: the first appeals to the Americans, the appeal to the British, and the later appeals to the Americans. Preceding these three sections are two preliminary documents that set the context: (1) the first Allied Aiming Point Report for I. G. Farben at Auschwitz III–Monowitz, and (2) excerpts from the famous Vrba-Wetzler report by two Slovakian Jews, Alfred Wetzler and Rudolf Vrba (the cover name for Walter Rosenberg), who had escaped Auschwitz just as the camp was preparing for the mass annihilation campaign against the Hungarian Jews. These excerpts are supplemented by a short excerpt from the report of the two more Slovakian Jews who escaped at the end of May, Arnost Rosin and Czeslaw Mordowicz. The full text of these two reports did not reach the West from Switzerland until the fall of 1944, because Switzerland was surrounded by Nazi-occupied Europe until the liberation of France in August 1944. Nevertheless, summaries of the reports had a significant impact on the appeals to bomb from late June onward.[1]

Where previous publication of public domain documents is noted, in most cases we have done so so as to afford interested readers an opportunity to consult facsimiles.

PRELIMINARIES

1.1 I. G. Farben Auschwitz Aiming Point Report, 21 January 1944

PROVISIONAL   American SECRET
E.O.U. AIMING POINT REPORT IV.D.4.   British MOST SECRET
21 January, 1944

I. G. FARBEN, OSWIECIM, SILESIA
(SYNTHETIC RUBBER)

I. LOCATION

> Latitude: 50° 2' N.
> Longitude: 19° 16' E.
> Distance from FOGGIA: 620 miles
> Distance from MILDENHALL: 840 miles

The attached G.S.G.S. map section locates the plant with reference to nearby towns.

II. ECONOMIC IMPORTANCE

This plant, on which construction is said to have begun in 1941, has never been photographed. The ground reports make it possible to say the following:

(a) It is certain that a very large chemical works has been under construction here;

(b) It is almost assured that a substantial size synthetic rubber (buna) plant forms part of the complex;

(c) It is uncertain whether the synthetic rubber plant has been completed and is in large scale output.

If there is a synthetic rubber plant producing at the rate of 20,000 tons per year or better (some reports indicate output as high as 40,000 tons), the target is well worth attacking. The rubber blockade about Europe has been tightened to the point where Germany relies for current supplies solely upon synthetic rubber output of somewhat over 100,000 tons per year, and reclaim rubber output about half as large. Oswiecim would thus account for 15 to 20 per cent [sic] of total output, ranking after Schkepau (A.P. Report No. IV-D-1), Hüls

(IV-D-1), and Hannover-Limmer (IV-D-3), and about on a par with Ludwigshafen-Oppau (IV-D-2). The plants comprise an attractive target system. The cessation of rubber receipts through the blockade, the successful bombing of Hüls six months ago, and the fact that three-quarters of rubber production is used for military equipment, principally tires, suggests that successful attack against this system will begin to make itself felt in a decrease of military mobility in about six months. In addition, German High Command anticipations of such impairment of military effectiveness may make itself felt sooner.

The buna plant should not be attacked until cover has been received; the preparation of this provisional aiming point report does not eliminate the necessity for photographs. Upon receipt of photographs, EOU-OIU-MEW in either the Mediterranean area or England will be in a position to judge whether the ground intelligence reporting of large scale buna production is valid. If the photographs bear out the ground intelligence, the present report may be useful should immediate action be desired.

One of the important points to be determined from photographic cover is the extent to which the plant is in operation. The vulnerability of a synthetic plant is greater when it is operating than when idle, owing to the inflammable and explosive nature of the materials. Should it not be operating, however, tactical or strategic considerations might make it worth while to attack it sooner rather than later.

Oswiecim's other activities are said to include methanol production and eventually synthetic oil production. Mention has also been made of production of propulsion fuel for secret weapons.

III. OBJECTIVES

For the reasons given in E.O.U. Aiming Point Report IV-D-1, the primary aiming point is the butadiene plant. Secondary installations are:

The butylene glycol plant,
The acetaldehyde and aldol plants,
The polymerisation plant,
The calcium carbide and acetylene plants,
The boiler houses.

Identification of the foregoing production stages will have to be made upon receipt of cover. All that is available at the present time is a rough plan drawn from memory which describes the location of several main buildings. This plan is attached, the objectives listed above, so far as they have been located, being colored red.

The plant construction office and the plant operations offices have been colored blue. Destruction of the former might be embarrassing because plant construction is still being carried on, and blue prints as well as key construction personnel would be located here. Destruction of the latter, which is adjacent to the rubber plant, might also prolong the recovery period. The plant is new and still has many teething problems. Both these offices should be considered tertiary objectives to be attacked in the event bomb hits of the first waves of bombers obscure the primary and secondary objectives for following waves.

IV. ANTICIPATED RESULTS OF ATTACK

On the assumption that an attempt would be made to reconstruct the works after it was attacked, the following table presents the likely time intervals which would elapse before the plant would be back in operation:

PRODUCTION STAGE OR INSTALLATION DESTROYED	REPLACEMENT TIME	
Butadiene	9	months
Butylene glycol	6–9	months
Acetaldehyde and aldol	2–3	"
Polymerisation	6–9	"
Calcium carbide and acetylene	2–3	"
Transformer station	?	

These periods are, of course, not additive in the event that two or more stages of production are destroyed at the same time. It is evident, therefore, that the effect of successful attack would be probably six months or more production loss.

[A two-page key to sketch map follows.]

SOURCE: National Archives, RG 243, Section 4-1.g. (163), reproduced in Wyman, ed., *America and the Holocaust*, XII:194–97.

1.2 Vrba-Wetzler and Rosin-Mordowicz Reports, April and June 1944 (Excerpts; text from the War Refugee Board translation released 26 Nov. 1944)

[*Vrba–Wetzler Report*]

On the 13th April, 1942 our group, consisting of 1,000 men, was loaded into railroad cars at the assembly camp of SERED. The doors were shut so that nothing would reveal the direction of the journey, and when they were opened after a long while we realized that we had crossed the Slovak frontier and were in ZWARDON. The train had until then been guarded by Hlinka men, but was now taken over by SS guards. After a few of the cars had been uncoupled from our convoy, we continued on our way arriving at night at AUSCHWITZ, where we stopped on a sidetrack. The reason the other cars were left behind was apparently the lack of room at AUSCHWITZ. They joined us, however, a few days later. Upon arrival we were placed in rows of five and counted. There were 643 of us. After a walk of about 20 minutes with our heavy packs (we had left Slovakia well equipped), we reached the concentration camp of AUSCHWITZ.

We were at once led into a huge barrack where on the one side we had to deposit all our luggage and on the other side completely undress, leaving our clothes and valuables behind. Naked, we then proceeded to an adjoining barrack where our heads and bodies were shaved and disinfected with lysol. At the exit every man was given a number which began with 28,600 in consecutive order. With this number in hand we were then herded to a third barrack where so-called registration took place. This consisted of tattooing the numbers we had received in the second barrack on the left side of our chests. The extreme brutality with which this was effected made many of us faint. The particulars of our identity were also recorded. Then we were led in groups of a hundred into a cellar, and later to a barrack where we were issued striped prisoners' clothes and wooden clogs. This lasted until 10 A.M. In the afternoon our prisoners' outfits were taken away from us again and replaced by the ragged and dirty remains of Russian uniforms. Thus equipped we were marched off to BIRKENAU.

AUSCHWITZ is a concentration camp for political prisoners under so-called "protective custody." At the time of my arrival, that is in April of 1942, there were about 15,000 prisoners in the camp, the majority of whom were Poles, Germans, and civilian Russians under protective custody. A small number of prisoners came under the categories of criminals and "work-shirkers."

AUSCHWITZ camp headquarters controls at the same time the work-camp of BIRKENAU as well as the farm labor camp of HARMENSE. All the prisoners arrive first at AUSCHWITZ where they are provided with prisoners' immatriculation numbers and then are either kept there, sent to BIRKENAU or, in very small numbers, to HARMENSE. The prisoners receive consecutive numbers upon arrival. Every number is only used once so that the last number always corresponds to the number of prisoners actually in camp. At the time of our escape, that is to say at the beginning of April, 1944, the number had risen up to 180,000. At the outset the numbers were tattooed on the left breast, but later, due to their becoming blurred, on the left forearm . . .

At the end of February, 1943 a new modern crematorium and gassing plant was inaugurated at BIRKENAU. The gassing and burning of the bodies in the Birch Forest was discontinued, the whole job being taken over by the four specially built crematoria. The large ditch was filled in, the ground levelled, and the ashes used as before for fertilizer at the farm labour camp of HERMENSE, so that today it is almost impossible to find traces of the dreadful mass murder which took place here.

At present there are four crematoria in operation at BIRKENAU, two large ones, I and II, and two smaller ones, III and IV. [The SS numbered them II, III, IV and V, as the gas chamber in Auschwitz I was counted as no. I. *Eds.*] Those of types I and II consist of 3 parts, i.e.: (A) the furnace room; (B) the large hall; and (C) the gas chamber. A huge chimney rises from the furnace room around which are grouped nine furnaces, each having four openings. Each opening can take three normal corpses at once and after an hour and a half the bodies are completely burned. This corresponds to a daily capacity of about 2,000 bodies. Next to this is a large "reception hall" which is arranged so as to give the impression of the antechamber of a bathing establishment. It holds 2,000 people and apparently there is a similar waiting room on the floor below. From there a door and a few steps lead down into the very long and narrow gas chamber. The walls of this chamber are also camouflaged with simulated entries to shower rooms in order to mislead the victims. The roof is fitted with three traps which can be hermetically closed from the outside. A track leads from the gas chamber towards the furnace room. The gassing takes place as follows: the unfortunate victims are brought into hall (B) where they are told to undress. To complete the fiction that they are going to bathe, each person receives a towel and a small piece of soap issued by two men clad in white coats. Then they are crowded into the gas chamber (C) in such numbers that there is, of course, only standing room. To compress this crowd into the narrow space, shots are often fired to induce those already at the far end to huddle still closer together. When everybody is inside, the heavy doors are closed. Then there is a short pause, presumably to allow the room temperature to rise to a certain level, after which SS men with gas masks climb on the roof, open the traps, and shake down a preparation in powder form out of tin cans labelled "CYKLON" "For use against vermin," which is manufactured by a Hamburg concern. It is presumed that this is a "CYANIDE" mixture of some sort which turns into gas at a certain temperature. After three minutes everyone in the chamber is dead. No one is known to have survived this ordeal, although it was not common to discover signs of life after the primitive measures employed in the Birch Wood. The chamber is then opened, aired, and the "special squad" carts the bodies on flat trucks to the furnace rooms where the burning takes place. Crematoria III and IV work on nearly the same principle, but their capacity is only half as large. Thus the total capacity of the four cremating and gassing plants at BIRKENAU amounts about 6,000 daily.

On principle only Jews are gassed; Aryans very seldom, as they are usually given "special treatment" by shooting. Before the crematoria were put into service, the shooting took place in the Birch Wood and the bodies were burned in the long trench; later, however, executions took place in the large hall of one of the crematoria which has been provided with a special installation for this purpose.

Prominent guests from BERLIN were present at the inauguration of the first crematorium in March, 1943. The "program" consisted of the gassing and burning of 8,000 Cracow Jews. The guests, both officers and civilians, were extremely satisfied with the results and the special peephole fitted into the door of the gas chamber was in constant use. They were lavish in their praise of this newly erected installation. . . .

In the meantime, ceaseless convoys of Polish and a few French and Belgian Jews arrived and, without exception, were dispatched to the gas chambers. Among them was a transport of 1,000 Polish Jews from MAJDANEK which included three Slovaks, one of whom was a certain Spira from Stropkow or Vranov.

The flow of convoys abruptly ceased at the end of July, 1943 and there was a short breathing space. The crematoria were thoroughly cleaned, the installations repaired and prepared for further use. On August 3 the killing machine again went into operation. The first convoys consisted of Jews from HENZ-BURG and SOSNOWITZ and others followed during the whole month of August. . . .

On June 27, 1942 I discarded my prisoner's outfit and travelled to AUSCH-WITZ in civilian clothes.

After a journey of 48 hours during which we were coupled up in freight cars without food or water, we arrived at AUSCHWITZ half dead. At the entrance gate the huge poster, "Work brings freedom," greeted us. As the courtyard was clean and well kept, and the brick buildings made a good impression after the dirty and primitive barracks of LUBLIN, we thought that the change was for the best. We were taken to a cellar and received tea and bread. Next day, however, our civilian clothes we taken away, our heads were shaved, and our numbers were tattooed on our forearms in the usual way. Finally, we were issued a set of prisoner's clothes similar to those we had worn in LUBLIN and were enrolled as "political prisoners" in the concentration camp of AUSCH-WITZ.

We were billeted in "Block 17" and slept on the floor. In an adjoining row of buildings separated from ours by a high wall, the Jewish girls from Slovakia, who had been brought there in March and April of 1942, were quartered. We worked in the huge "BUNA" plant to which we were herded every morning about 3 A.M. At midday our food consisted of potato or turnip soup and in the evening we received some bread. During work we were terribly mistreated. As our working place was situated outside the large chain of sentry posts, it was divided into small sectors of 10 × 10 meters, each guarded by an SS man. Whoever stepped outside these squares during working hours was immediately shot without warning for having "attempted to escape." Often it happened that out of pure spite an SS man would order a prisoner to fetch some given object outside his square. If he followed the order, he was shot for having left his assigned place. The work was extremely hard and there were no rest periods. The way to and from work had to be covered at a brisk military trot; anyone falling out of line was shot. On my arrival about 3,000 people, of whom 2,000 were Slovak Jews, were working on this emplacement. Very few could bear the strain and although escape seemed hopeless, attempts were made every day. The result was several hangings a week.

After a number of weeks of painful work at the "BUNA" plant a terrible typhus epidemic broke out. The weaker prisoners died in hundreds. An immediate quarantine was ordered and work at the "BUNA" stopped. Those still alive were sent, at the end of July, 1942, to the gravel pit but there work was even still more strenuous. We were in such a state of weakness that, even in trying to do our best, we could not satisfy the overseers. Most of us got swollen feet. Due to our inability to perform the heavy work demanded of us our squad was accused of being lazy and disorderly. Soon after a medical commission inspected all of us; they carried out their job very thoroughly. Anyone with swollen feet or particularly weak was separated from the rest. Although I was in great pain, I controlled myself and stood erect in front of the commission who passed me as physically fit. Out of 300 persons examined, 200 were found to be unfit and immediately sent to BIRKENAU and gassed. I was then detailed for work at the DAW (Deutsche Aufrüstungswerke) where we had to paint skis. The prescribed minimum to be painted each day was 120. Anyone unable to paint this many was thoroughly flogged in the evening. Another group was employed at making cases for hand grenades. At one time 15,000 had been completed but it was found that they were a few centimeters too small. As punishment several Jews were shot for sabotage.

Somewhere around the middle of August, 1942 all the Jewish girls from Slovakia who lived next to our quarters, on the other side of the wall, were transferred to BIRKENAU. I had the opportunity to talk to them and was able to see how weak and half-starved all of them were. They were dressed in old Russian uniform rags and wore wooden clogs. Their heads were shaven clean. The same day we again had to undergo a strict examination and those suspected of having typhus were removed to the Birch Wood. The remainder were shaven afresh, bathed, issued a new set of clothes and finally billeted in the barracks the girls had just left. By chance I learned that there was an opening in the "clearance squad" and I handed in my application. I was detailed to this task.

This squad consisted of about a hundred Jewish prisoners. We were sent to a far corner of the camp, away from all our comrades. Here we found huge sheds full of knapsacks, suitcases, and other luggage. We had to open each piece of baggage and sort the contents into large cases specially prepared for each category of goods, i.e., combs, mirrors, sugar, canned food, chocolate, medicines, etc. The cases were then stored away. Underwear, shirts, and clothes of all kinds went to a special barrack, where they were sorted out and packed by Jewish girls. Old and worn clothes were addressed to the "TEXTILE FACTORY" at MEMEL, whereas the usable garments were dispatched to a collecting center in BERLIN. Gold, money, bank notes, and precious stones had to be handed over to the political section. Many of these objects were, however, stolen by the

SS guards or by prisoners. A brutal and vile individual who often struck the women is commander of this squad. He is SS "Scharfuhrer" WYKLEFF.

Every day the girls who came to their work from BIRKENAU described to us the terrible conditions prevailing there. They were beaten and brutalized and their mortality was much higher than among the men. Twice a week "selections" took place, and every day new girls replaced those who had disappeared.

During a night shift I was able to witness for the first time how incoming convoys were handled. The transport I saw contained Polish Jews. They had received no water for days and when the doors of the freight cars were open we were ordered to chase them out with loud shouts. They were utterly exhausted and about a hundred of them had died during the journey. The living were lined up in rows of five. Our job was to remove the dead, dying, and the luggage from the cars. The dead, and this included anyone unable to stand on his feet, were piled in a heap. Luggage and parcels were collected and stacked up. Then the railroad cars had to be thoroughly cleaned so that no trace of their frightful load was left behind. A commission from the political department proceeded with the "selection" of approximately 10 percent of the men and 5 percent of the women and had them transferred to the camps. The remainder were loaded on trucks, sent to BIRKENAU, and gassed while the dead and dying were taken directly to the furnaces. It often happened that small children were thrown alive into the trucks along with the dead. Parcels and luggage were taken to the warehouses and sorted out in the previously described manner.

Between July and September, 1942 a typhus epidemic had raged in AUSCHWITZ, especially in the women's camp of BIRKENAU. None of the sick received medical attention and in the first stages of the epidemic a great many were killed by phenol injections, and later on others were gassed wholesale. Some 15,000 to 20,000, mostly Jews, died during these two months. The girls' camp suffered the most, as it was not fitted with sanitary installations, and the poor wretches were covered with lice. Every week large "selections" took place and the girls had to present themselves naked to the "selection committee," regardless of weather conditions. They waited in deadly fear whether they would be chosen or given another week's grace. Suicides were frequent and were mostly committed by throwing one's self against the high tension wires of the inner fence. This went on until they had dwindled to 5 percent of their original number. Now there are only 400 of these girls left and most of them have been able to secure some sort of clerical post in the women's camp. About 100 girls hold jobs at the staff building in AUSCHWITZ where they do all the clerical work connected with the administration of the two camps. Thanks to their knowledge of languages they are also used as interpreters. Others are employed in the main kitchen and laundry. Of late these girls have been able to dress themselves quite well as they have had opportunities to complete their wardrobes which, in some cases, even include silk stockings. Generally speaking they are reasonably well off and are even allowed to let their hair grow. Of course this cannot be said of the other Jewish inmates of the women's camp. It just so happens that these Slovak Jewish girls have been in the camp the longest of all. But if today they enjoy certain privileges, they have previously undergone frightful sufferings.

I was not to hold this comparatively good job with the "clearance squad" for long. Shortly afterwards I was transferred to BIRKENAU on disciplinary grounds and remained there over a year and a half. On April 7, 1944 I managed to escape with my companion.

Careful estimate of the number of Jews gassed in BIRKENAU between April, 1942 and April, 1944 (according to countries of origin).

Poland (transported by trucks)	approximately	300,000
" " " train	"	600,000
Holland	"	100,000
Greece	"	45,000
France	"	150,000
Belgium	"	50,000
Germany	"	60,000
Yugoslavia, Italy and Norway	"	50,000
Lithuania	"	50,000
Bohemia, Moravia and Austria	"	30,000
Slovakia	"	30,000
Various camps for foreign Jews in Poland	"	300,000

approximately 1,765,000[1]

[Rosin-Mordowicz Report]
... The [May 10] transport was received in AUSCHWITZ and BIRKENAU according to the well-known procedure (heads shaven, numbers tattooed, etc.). The men were given numbers beginning with 186,000 and the women were placed in the women's camp. About 600 men, of whom some 150 were between the ages of 45 and 60, were brought to BIRKENAU where they were divided up among various work detachments. The remainder stayed in AUSCHWITZ where they worked in the BUNA plant.

The members of the transport were all left alive and none of them, as had been customary, were sent directly to the crematoria. In the postcards which they were allowed to write, they had to give "Waldsee" as return address.

On May 15 mass transports from Hungary began to arrive in BIRKENAU.

Some 14,000 to 15,000 Jews arrived daily. The spur railroad track which ran into the camp to the crematoria was completed in great haste, the crews working night and day, so that the transports could be brought directly to the crematoria. Only about 10 percent of these transports were admitted to the camp; the balance were immediately gassed and burned. Never had so many Jews been gassed since the establishment of BIRKENAU. The "Special Commando" had to be increased to 600 men and, after two or three days, to 800 (people being recruited from among the Hungarian Jews who had arrived first). The size of the "Clearing Commando" was stepped up from 150 to 700 men. Three crematoria worked day and night (the 4th was being repaired at the time) and, since the capacity of the crematoria was not enough, great pits 30 meters long and 15 meters wide were once more dug in the "Birkenwald" (as in the time before the crematoria) where corpses were burned day and night. Thus the "exterminating capacity" became almost unlimited.

The Hungarian Jews who were left alive (about 10 percent) were not included in the normal camp "enrollment." Although they were shaved and shorn and received convict's clothing, they were not tattooed. They were housed in a separate section of the camp, section "C", and were later transferred to various concentration camps in the German Reich: Buchenwald, Mauthausen, Grossrosen, Gusen, Flossenburg, Sachsenhausen, etc. The women were temporarily quartered in the "gypsy camp" in separate blocks and then also transferred elsewhere. Jewish girls from Slovakia were "block eldests" there.

SOURCE: FDR Library, FDR Papers, WRB Report "German Extermination Camps—Auschwitz and Birkenau," 26 Nov. 1944, reprinted in Wyman, ed., *America and the Holocaust*, XII:1–65.

2

THE FIRST APPEALS TO THE AMERICANS

2.1 Memorandum, Roswell McClelland, War Refugee Board in Switzerland, to Col. Alfred de Jonge, 25 May 1944

The enclosed message was referred to us by a certain Mr. Isaac Sternbuch, representative of the Union of Orthodox Rabbis of the United States of America in Switzerland.

We have had considerable contact with Mr. Sternbuch in the past regarding purely relief matters. Since the question in point, however, is more of a military nature, I felt it advisable to submit to you for whatever action you deem advisable the wire which Mr. Sternbuch wished us to send to his organization in America, particularly since Mr. Getsinger tells me that Mr. Sternbuch has already been in touch with you in this matter.

R.McC.

. . .

To the Union of the Orthodox Rabbis of the United States of America, New York

Gentlemen,

We received news from Slovakia according to which they ask prompt airraids should be made over the two towns Kaschau as transit place for military transports and also Presov as town junction for deportations coming through Kaschau and also the whole railroad line between them where there is a short bridge of about 30 yards. It is the single near route from Hungary to Poland, whereas all the other small and short lines, going eastwards, can be used only in Hungary, but not for the traffic to Poland being already battlefields. Do the necessary that bombing should be repeated at short intervals to prevent rebuilding. Without named two towns just one too long route via Austria remains which is almost impracticable.

Your other messages will be answered separately. The Spanish and Swiss Embassies at Budapest and Bratislava refuse to acknowledge passports and papers of Paraguay and San Salvador which we have sent to Hungary and Slovakia. Kindly have urgent instructions given to the Protective Powers.

Sternbuch.

SOURCE: FDR Library, WRB files, Box 62, Union of Orthodox Rabbis, January–June 1944, reproduced in Wyman, ed., *America and the Holocaust*, XII: 89–91.

2.2 "Report on a Discussion between Y. Gruenbaum and Mr. Pinkerton, General American Consul in the Land of Israel [Palestine], Thursday, June 2, 1944, at the American Consulate," Protocol of 7 June 1944

Mr. Gruenbaum opened the discussion by stating that Mr. A. Dubkin informed him of Mr. P. Lakavmal's [?] desire from a while ago to obtain authoritative information on the development of matters relating to the question of rescue. Thus he [Gruenbaum] is now passing on the latest pieces of news received, and requesting that the [American] consul, Mr. Pinkerton, pass these on to his government. He [Gruenbaum] passed on a detailed description of how things are going in Romania, and on the rescue activities of Jews from there. He expressed his opinion that the widespread publicity given to Mr. Hirschmann's activities have hurt him in a significant way, in terms of his own work. And especially his talking about *"gesher aniyot"* (bridge of ships) that took Jews out of countries of oppression to countries of freedom. It is they who angered the

Germans, and it is now as if they are eager to show that the Americans are not able to give real aid to the Jews under the yoke of the Nazis. He requested that the consul pass this information on to his government.

The consul commented that this matter was already known to him. He requested that what was said on individuals involved in rescue should not turn into an attack on the War Refugee Board of the US. Attacks such as these could only serve to hurt the efforts. It is permissible for me—he said—to attack Mr. Y. Gruenbaum, but it is not permissible for me to talk against the Jewish Agency.

Mr. Gruenbaum switched to the matter of the Turkish ship intended to transport Jewish refugees from Romania. The agreement on this ship was reached on the basis of American responsibility [America as guarantor] that if the ship sinks another one will be supplied to Turkey in its place. Mr. Gruenbaum claimed that after all the publicity given to the ship, he is doubtful as to whether there is really anything to this offer. Instead of this arrangement, he would suggest that pressure be put on the Turks to provide another Turkish ship, under the same conditions, for the very same goal, in order that it should sail without a guarantee from an enemy party, so that they shouldn't [intentionally] sink it. The American consul wrote down these remarks and promised to present them to his government.

Mr. Gruenbaum switched to the matter of Hungary. He described the situation according to the latest news received. He focused primarily on the expulsion [deportation] of jews from Hungary to Poland and emphasized the peril foreseen for these Jews, which the Germans began by deportation and persecution the same way they did in Poland [to the Jews in Poland]. He suggests:

A.) that a stringent warning be given to Hungary (the American consul writes this down to pass on to Washington)

B.) that the American airforce receive instructions to bomb the death camps in Poland.

On this matter, Pinkerton brought up the following point: won't bombing the camps also cause the death of many Jews? And isn't there the concern that German propaganda will spread news that here also Americans are taking part in the destruction of the Jews?

Mr. Gruenbaum answered, that in spite of all this, he sees this operation [the bombing of the death camps] as desirable, because in any event the Jews concentrated in the death camps are destined to die, and maybe with the havoc that would be caused by bombing the camp, some Jews will be able to escape. This and more: The establishment of the camps cost the Germans greatly in financial expense and labor forces, and thus the camps' destruction might disrupt the mass killing process and deter the Germans from building similar death camps in the future, and what more, bombing the camps will cost the Germans the loss of their manpower who guard the camps.

After a brief argument over this suggestion, Mr. Pinkerton stated that he will *not* pass on this suggestion to Washington. Pinkerton advises Gruenbaum to present his suggestion [to bomb the death camps] in writing.

Gruenbaum then suggested bombing the railroad lines between Budapest and Poland. This suggestion, Mr. Pinkerton promised to pass on to his government.

Mr. Gruenbaum suggested to make all efforts to influence Marshal Tito to permit Jews from Hungary and neighboring countries to cross over the borders into his country. The consul mentioned the lack of coordination of labor among the various divisions of the Jewish Agency. A separate division should deal with the issue at hand and he hopes to receive a detailed memo on this issue. Mr. Gruenbaum stated that he was aware of the situation. In any event he wanted to emphasize the point [of bombing the tracks].

Gruenbaum suggested, in relation to the situation in Hungary, that the Allied powers request from the International Red Cross that its employees in Budapest come up with authorized, documented and detailed pieces of news on what is taking place there with the Jews, for this will serve as a pipeline for the passing on of material aid (e.g. food, etc.) for Jews in Hungary. The consul promised to do this.

Within this discussion, Mr. Y. Gruenbaum spoke of the situation in Bulgaria, which also may take on a serious character in the near future. Gruenbaum suggested that a warning be given to Bulgaria, and that it be made possible to send boats over there—since this is being done with Romania. The consul also wrote down this request.

At the conclusion of the discussion, Mr. T[?] Shimsor[?] stated that all these suggestions for the War Refugee Board in Washington were not in his name, but rather in that of Mr. Gruenbaum.

SOURCE: Central Zionist Archives, Jerusalem, translation supplied by USHMM and Richard H. Levy.

2.3 Meeting of the Executive of the Jewish Agency, Jerusalem, 11 June 1944 (excerpt)

Present at meeting: Mr. Ben-Gurion, chairman, Mr. Gruenbaum, Dr. Senator, Rabbi Fishman, Mr. Kaplan, Dr. Schmorak, Dr. Yosef, Mr. Shapiro, Mr. Ben-Zvi, Dr. Hentke, Dr. Granovsky, Mr. Eisenberg
Agenda: 1. rescue matters
       2. discussion of Mr. Gruenbaum and Mr. Pinkerton on rescue matters
       3. Section on Immigrant Absorption. . . .

2. *Conversation between Mr. Gruenbaum and Mr. Pinkerton [American Consul] on Rescue Matters*
MR. GRUENBAUM: I sent to [Jewish Agency] Executive members notes of my

meeting on rescue matters with the General American Consul [Pinkerton]. Among other things I proposed that the Allies bomb the railroad tracks between Hungary and Poland. The Germans are expelling [deporting] 12,000 Jews a day from Hungary to Poland. If they [the Allies] would destroy the railroad tracks, the Germans would be unable for a protracted period of time to carry out their plan.

Mr. Pinkerton promised to relay the proposal to the War Refugee Board.

Also proposed to Mr. Pinkerton was that the Allied airforces bomb the death-camps in Poland, such as: Oswiecim, Treblinka, etc. Mr. Pinkerton claimed that if this would be carried out the Allies will be blamed in the murder of Jews and thus requested that the proposal be presented to him in writing. I [Gruenbaum] promised to consult my colleagues on this matter.

According to our information thousands of Jews are murdered daily in the death-camps in Poland. Only the forced laborers are left alive for a certain amount of time. The victims bodies are not left to be [they're cremated]. Even if we also take into account the fact that if the tracks are bombed while there are Jews on them a portion of them will be killed, the other portion will be able to disperse [run away] and be saved. By the destroyed buildings, they [the Germans] will be unable for a number of months to implement their systematic murder plans.

We received today a piece of information that during ten days 120,000 Jews were expelled [deported] from Hungary.

MR. BEN-GURION: We do not know the truth concerning the entire situation in Poland, and it seems that we will be unable to propose anything concerning this matter.

RABBI FISHMAN: Concurs with Ben-Gurion on this point.

DR. SCHMORAK: It is currently relayed that in Oswiecim exists a large labor camp. It is forbidden for us to take responsibility for a bombing that could very well cause the death of even one Jew.

DR. YOSEF: Also opposes the proposal to request that the Americans bomb the camps, and thus cause the murder of Jews.

Mr. Gruenbaum is not speaking as a private individual, but rather as an institution spokesman. It seems that also the institution to which we are connected should be prohibited from making such a proposal.

DR. SENATOR: Concurs with Dr. Yosef on this point. It is regrettable that Mr. Gruenbaum spoke at all on this matter with the American consul.

CHAIRMAN BEN-GURION: SUMMATION

The opinion of the Jewish Agency's Executive Committee is not to propose to the Allies the bombing of sites in which Jews are located.

SOURCE: Central Zionist Archives, Jerusalem, translation supplied by USHMM and Richard H. Levy.

2.4 Jacob Rosenheim, President, Agudas Israel World Organization (The Union of Universally Organized Orthodox Jewry) to Henry Morgenthau, Secretary of the Treasury and Chairman of the War Refugee Board, 18 June 1944

Dear Mr. Morgenthau:

I beg to approach you in the name of my organization in the following urgent matter of life and death for thousands of innocent Nazi-victims.

Since April, the deportation of Jews from Hungary to the gas-chambers of Poland is relentlessly going on. About ten thousand to fifteen thousand persons *a day* are deported, and up to now, about 300,000 Jews are said to have been doomed to destruction in this way.

Our Rescue-Committee in Switzerland, which is in permanent close contact with Hungary by courier, has recently submitted to the American and British Embassies in Berne the idea of taking measures, to *slow down, at least,* the process of annihilation and thus to preserve a greater number of Jewish lives for the day of liberation.

This slackening of the process of annihilation could be achieved by paralyzing the railroad traffic from Hungary to Poland, especially by an aireal [*sic*] bombardment of the most important railway junctions of KASCHAU and PRESOV, through which the deportation-trains pass. By such a procedure, precious time would be won and thousands of human lives preserved.

On the other hand, every day of delay means a very heavy responsibility for the human lives at stake.

For this reason, we take the liberty of applying to you directly, imploring you for *immediate* decisive assistance in this work of life-rescue.

SOURCE: FDR Library, WRB Records, Box 35, Hungary No. 5, reproduced in Wyman, ed., *America and the Holocaust*, XII:103.

2.5 Maj. Gen. Thomas R. Handy, Assistant Chief of Staff, Operational Plans Division, War Department General Staff, Memorandum for the Record, 23 June 1944

Subject: Proposed Air Action to Impede Deportation of Hungarian and Slovak Jews.

In a letter to the Assistant Secretary of War from the Secretary of the Treasury dated 28 January 1944, Secretary Morgenthau makes reference to the creation, by Executive Order, of a War Refugee Board consisting of the Secretaries of State, Treasury and War. This Board is charged with direct responsibility to the President in carrying out the policy of this Government to take all measures within its power to rescue victims of enemy oppression. This letter was referred to the Deputy Chief of Staff, and in reply the Deputy Chief of Staff in a memo for the Assistant Secretary of War stated: "We must constantly bear in mind however that the most effective relief which can be given victims of enemy persecution is to insure the speedy defeat of the Axis. For this reason, I share your concern over further involvement of the War Department, while the war is on, in matters such as the one brought by Secretary Morgenthau." (See OPD 334.8 War Refugee Board, 28 Jan 44).

By memorandum dated 7 February 44 Lt. Col. Pasco, Assistant Secretary General Staff, informed Colonel Gailey that the British have informed Mr. Morgenthau that they are reluctant to cooperate with the War Refugee Board because the membership of the Secretary of War implies that units or individuals of the armed forces will be used in rescuing refugees. Mr. Bundy, who represents the S/W [Secretary of War] on this Board, requested OPD concurrence to transmission of the following message to the British Government:

"It is not contemplated that such military missions as parachute troop movements will be employed to rescue victims of enemy oppression."

This matter was submitted to General Hull for decision and General Hull agreed to the following message:

"It is not contemplated that units of the armed forces will be employed for the purpose of rescuing victims of enemy oppression unless such rescues are the direct result of military operations conducted with the objective of defeating the armed forces of the enemy." (See OPD 334.8 War Refugee Board 7 Feb 44).

CAD [Civil Affairs Division] D/F [Disposition Form] dated 23 June 44 forwards to OPD for necessary action paraphrase of cable concerning air bombardment of railroad centers to impede deportation of Jews to Poland, which message had been forwarded to the CAD by Mr. McCloy. As this message referred to the Civil Affairs Division by Mr. McCloy for appropriate action, the Operations Division does not consider that it is appropriate for OPD to make reply. Therefore, action taken by OPD was to furnish CAD with a suggested reply to be made by CAD.

T. R. H.

SOURCE: National Archives, RG 165, OPD 383.7, reproduced in Wyman, ed., *America and the Holocaust*, XII:109.

2.6 John W. Pehle, Executive Director, War Refugee Board, Memorandum of 24 June 1944

MEMORANDUM FOR THE FILES:

I saw Assistant Secretary McCloy today on the proposal of the Agudas Israel that arrangements be made to bomb the railroad line between Kassa and Presov being used for the deportation of Jews from Hungary to Poland. I told McCloy that I wanted to mention the matter to him for whatever exploration might be appropriate by the War Department but that I had several doubts about the matter, namely (1) whether it would be appropriate to use military planes and personnel for this purpose; (2) whether it would be difficult to put the railroad line out of commission for a long enough period to do any good; and (3) even assuming that this railroad line were put out of commission for some period of time, whether it would help the Jews in Hungary.

I made it very clear to Mr. McCloy that I was not, at this point at least, requesting the War Department to take any action on this proposal other than to appropriately explore it. McCloy understood my position and said that he would check into the matter.

SOURCE: FDR Library, WRB files, Box 35, Hungary No. 5, reproduced in Wyman, ed., *America and the Holocaust*, XII:104.

2.7 Leland Harrison, U.S. Minister to Switzerland, Bern, to Cordell Hull, Secretary of State, 24 June 1944 ("Paraphrase of Telegram Received")

McClelland sends the following for the War Refugee Board.

Reference is made herewith to Legation's message dated June 17, No. 3867, paragraph three.

Now there is no doubt that the majority of the Jewish population east of the Danube especially in eastern[,] northern, and north eastern Hungary has been deported to Poland. Further reliable information confirming this fact has come in the course of the past two weeks from the following independent sources: (a) Swiss official employee just returned from Budapest, (b) Railway workers in Czech resistance movement, (c) other reliable secret source regard information as to sources as absolutely confidential since any publicity regarding them would endanger lives.

Prior to the deportations, there were two weeks to a month of brutal concentration during which thousands of Jews were crowded together in primitive quarters with insufficient food, clothing and water, regardless of state of health, sex or age. The Hungarian gendarmerie on Laszlo Endre's orders largely carried out this action.

Apparently the actual large scale deportations began about May 15 and lasted until the middle of June. The movement involved 12,000 persons per day: about

7,000 through sub-Carpatho-Russia and 5,000 through Slovakia. Characteristic of such actions, people were deported 60 to 70 per sealed freight wagon for a trip of two to three days without adequate water or food probably resulting in many deaths en route.

Particularly used were the following stretches of railroad:

(1) Caep-Kaschau-[P]resov-Lubotin-Nowyszez in direction of Oszwiscim [sic]; (2) Satoraljaujhaly-Leginamich Klany-Michalovee-Medallaborce.* Also many thousand troops to and from the Polish front were transported daily over this line; (3) Munkacs-Lavoczne; (4) Galanta-Sered-Leopoldstadt-Novemeato-Trencin; (5) Vrutky-Zllina.

It is urged by all sources of this information in Slovakia and Hungary that vital sections of these lines especially bridges along ONE be bombed as the only possible means of slowing down or stopping future deportations. (This is submitted by me as a proposal of these agencies and I can venture no opinion on its utility). . . .

There is little doubt that many of these Hungarian Jews are being sent to the extermination camps of Ausehitz [sic] (Oswiecim) and Birke Nau (Rajska) in western upper Silesia where according to recent reports, since early summer 1942 at least 1,500,000 Jews have been killed. There is evidence that already in January 1944 preparations were being made to receive and exterminate Hungarian Jews in these camps. Soon a detailed report on these camps will be cabled.

SOURCE: National Archives, RG 107, Asst. Sec. of War Files, 400.38 Jews, reproduced in Wyman, ed., *America and the Holocaust*, XII:147–49.

2.8 Memorandum, J. W. Pehle, War Refugee Board, to John J. McCloy, Assistant Secretary of War, 29 June 1944

In connection with my recent conversation with you, I am attaching a copy of a cable just received from our representative in Bern, Switzerland. I wish to direct your attention particularly to the paragraphs concerning the railway lines being used for the deportation of Jews from Hungary to Poland and the proposal of various agencies that vital sections of these lines be bombed.

SOURCE: National Archives, RG 107, Asst. Sec. of War Files, 400.38 Jews, reproduced in Wyman, ed., *America and the Holocaust*, XII:150.

* Various letters in this group illegible.

2.9 War Refugee Board Memorandum, Benjamin Akzin to L. S. Lesser, 29 June 1944

By Cable No. 4041 of June 21, from Bern, McClelland, reporting on the deportation and extermination of Hungarian Jews, states that "there is little doubt that many of these Hungarian Jews are being sent to the extermination camps of AUSCHWITZ (OSWIECIM) and BIRKENAU (RAJSKA) in Western Upper Silesia where according to recent reports, since early summer 1942 at least 1,500,000 Jews have been killed. There is evidence that already in January 1944 preparations were being made to receive and exterminate Hungarian Jews in these camps".

In view of the preeminent part evidently played by these two extermination camps in the massacre of Jews equipped to kill 125,000 people per month, it would seem that the destruction of their physical installations might appreciably slow down the systematic slaughter at least temporarily. The methodical German mind might require some time to rebuild the installations or to evolve elsewhere equally efficient procedures of mass slaughter and of disposing of the bodies. Some saving of lives would therefore be a most likely result of the destruction of the two extermination camps.

Though no exaggerated hopes should be entertained, this saving of lives might even be quite appreciable, since, in the present stage of the war, with German manpower and material resources gravely depleted, German authorities might not be in a position to devote themselves to the task of equipping new large-scale extermination centers.

Aside from the preventive significance of the destruction of the two camps, it would also seem correct to mark them for destruction as a matter of principle, as the most tangible—and perhaps only tangible—evidence of the indignation aroused by the existence of these charnel-houses. It will also be noted that the destruction of the extermination camps would presumably cause many depths among their personnel—certainly among the most ruthless and despicable of the Nazis.

It is suggested that the foregoing be brought to the attention of the appropriate political and military authorities, with a view to considering the feasibility of a thorough destruction of the two camps by aerial bombardment. It may be of interest, in this connection, that the two camps are situated in the industrial region of Upper Silesia, near the important mining and manufacturing centers of Katowice and Chorzow (Oswiecim lies about 14 miles southeast of Katowice), which play an important part in the industrial armament of Germany. Therefore, the destruction of these camps could be achieved without deflecting aerial strength from an important zone of military objectives.

Presumably, a large number of Jews in these camps may be killed in the course of such bombings (though some of them may escape in the confusion). But such Jews are doomed to death anyhow. The destruction of the camps would not change their fate, but it would serve as visible retribution on their murderers and it might save the lives of future victims.

It will be noted that the inevitable fate of Jews herded in ghettoes near the industrial and railroad installations in Hungary has not caused the United Nations to stop bombing these installations. It is submitted, therefore, that refraining from bombing the extermination centers would be sheer misplaced sentimentality, far more cruel than a decision to destroy these centers.

SOURCE: FDR Library, WRB files, Box 35, Hungary No. 5, reproduced in Wyman, ed., *America and the Holocaust*, XII:153.

2.10 A. Leon Kubowitzki, Head, Rescue Department, World Jewish Congress, New York, to J. W. Pehle, War Refugee Board, 1 July 1944

Dear Mr. Pehle:

May I come back to the suggestion I made to Mr. Lesser in the course of the conference I had with him on June 28.

Discussing the apparent determination of the German Government to speed up the extermination of the Jews, I wondered whether the pace of the extermination could not be considerably slowed down if the instruments of annihilation—the gas chambers, the gas vans, the death baths—were destroyed. You will remember that in August and October, 1943, respectively, revolting Jews set fire to installations in Treblinka and Sobibor. The revolt culminated in the escape of a large number of Jews from these camps.

Three governments are directly interested in stopping the massacres: the Soviet Government, whose captured soldiers are being exterminated in the Oswiecim gas chambers, according to a cable received by the Polish Information Center on June 22, a copy of which is attached; the Czechoslovak Government, whose citizens are being murdered in Birkenau; and the Polish Government, for obvious reasons.

The destruction of the death installations can not be done by bombing from the air, as the first victims would be the Jews who are gathered in these camps, and such a bombing would be a welcome pretext for the Germans to assert that their Jewish victims have been massacred not by their killers, but by the Allied bombings.

I submitted to Mr. Lesser that the Soviet Government be approached with the request that it should dispatch groups of paratroopers to seize the buildings, to annihilate the squads of murderers, and to free the unfortunate inmates. Also that the Polish Government be requested to instruct the Polish underground to attack these and similar camps to destroy the instruments of death.

May I add that I think it would be useful to approach also the Czechoslovak Government, so that it may use its influence with the Soviet and Polish Governments to support our request.

May I express the hope that you will consider the suggestion made in this letter as deserving to be acted upon without delay. . . .

P.S. I attach a report, "Three Years in Oswiecim Hell," published by the Polish Jewish Observer on June 16.

SOURCE: FDR Library, WRB Records, Box 35, copy kindly supplied by FDR Library.

2.11 Memorandum, Col. Harrison A. Gerhardt, to Asst. Secretary of War John J. McCloy, 3 July 1944

MEMORANDUM FOR MR. McCLOY:

I know you told me to "kill" this but since those instructions, we have received the attached letter from Mr. Pehle.

I suggest that the attached reply be sent.

H. A. G.

SOURCE: National Archives, RG 107, Asst. Sec. of War Files, 400.38 Jews, reproduced in Wyman, ed., *America and the Holocaust*, XII:151.

2.12 J. J. McCloy, War Department, to J. W. Pehle, War Refugee Board, 4 July 1944

Dear Mr. Pehle:

I refer to your letter of June 29, enclosing a cable from your representative in Bern, Switzerland, proposing that certain sections of railway lines between Hungary and Poland be bombed to interrupt the transportation of Jews from Hungary.

The War Department is of the opinion that the suggested air operation is impracticable. It could be executed only by the diversion of considerable air support essential to the success of our forces now engaged in decisive operations and would in any case be of such very doubtful efficacy that it would not amount to a practical project.

The War Department fully appreciates the humanitarian motives which prompted the suggested operation but for the reasons stated above the operation suggested does not appear justified.

Sincerely,
John J. McCloy

SOURCE: FDR Library, WRB Records, Box 35, Hungary No. 5, reproduced in Wyman, ed., *America and the Holocaust*, XII:152.

3

THE APPEAL TO THE BRITISH

3.1 British Intercept of Cable from Richard Lichtheim to Jewish Agency, Jerusalem, 26 June 1944

[This telegram is of particular secrecy and should be retained by the authorized recipient and not passed on].

[CODE R]   WAR CABINET DISTRIBUTION
                  FROM BERNE TO FOREIGN OFFICE

Mr. Norton.

No. 2949.   D. 7.56. P.M. 26th June 1944.

26th June 1944.   R. 4.00. A.M. 27th June 1944.
                    ****

     Following for Jewish Agency for Palestine from Lichtheim.
     Urgent.

Received fresh reports from Hungary stating that nearly one half total of 800,000 Jews in Hungary have already been deported at a rate of 10,000 to 12,000 per diem. Most of these transports are sent to the death camp of Birkenau near Oswiecim in Upper Silesia where in the course of last year over 1,500,000 Jews from all over Europe have been killed. We have detailed reports about the numbers and methods employed. The four crematoriums in Birkenau have a capacity . . . for . . . gassing and burning 60,000 per diem. In Budapest and surroundings there are still between 300,000 and 400,000 Jews left including those incorporated in labour service but no Jews are left in eastern and northern provinces and according to a letter from our manager of Palestine office Budapest, the remaining Jews in and around Budapest have no hope to be spared. These facts which are confirmed by various letters and reports from reliable sources should be given widest publicity and present Hungarian Government should again be warned that they will be held responsible because they are aiding the Germans with their own police to arrest and deport and thus murder the Jews. In addition the following suggestions have been made, first, reprisals against Germans in Allied hands; second, bombing of railway in lines leading from Hungary to Birkenau; third, precision bombing of death camp installations; fourth, bombing of all Government buildings in Budapest. Please consider these or other proposals, also inform Jerusalem and New York about situation.

[Following three lines handwritten. *eds.*]

Form sent   L.S.

29.6.44   What can be done?

SM   What can be said?

SOURCE: Public Record Office, Kew, PREM 4/51/10, 1370.

3.2 Yitzak Gruenbaum, Jewish Agency Executive, Jerusalem, to Chaim Barlas, Istanbul, 30 June 1944

We have received cables from you and Bader. We have informed Moshe [Shertok] and Stefan [Stephen Wise]. You have probably met with [Yitzhak] Ben-Zvi already. The idea has arisen here about trying to bring about a papal encyclical on the subject of stopping the killing. The Chief Rabbis have made an approach in this matter, asking at the same time for an audience with the Pope. We have relayed to Moshe a proposal from Krausz as well as ours to bring about the bombing of the rail lines connecting Hungary with Poland and of the death camps in Poland. We cannot understand why, despite the experience in Poland, the German executioners are not again meeting organized resistance. Couldn't you send our friends our opinion that resistance should be undertaken? Let us know by telegram what route you have received Krausz's telegram.

SOURCE: Central Zionist Archives, Jerusalem, A 127/544, supplied by David S. Wyman.

3.3 Foreign Secretary Anthony Eden to Winston Churchill, 3 July 1944

PRIME MINISTER

Your minute of June 29th on Berne telegram No. 2949, about the deportation of Jews from Hungary.

2. His Majesty's Government have at a various times made it clear by public declarations that they intended to mete out appropriate punishment for atrocities against the Jews, the latest declaration on this subject being the one I made on the 30th March in Parliament. I stated that satellite governments who dispelled citizens to destinations named by Berlin must know that such actions are tantamount to assisting in inhuman persecution or slaughter. This would not be forgotten when the inevitable defeat of the arch-enemy of Europe came about. I added:

"His Majesty's Government are confident that they are expressing the sentiments of all the Allied Governments in calling upon the countries allied

[262]

with or subject to Germany to join in preventing further persecution and co-operate in protecting and saving the innocent." This declaration has been broad-cast in the appropriate languages.

3. I feel therefore that our attitude has been made clear enough, and there is no point in "inflating the currency" by continually repeating that we propose to punish the guilty. Indeed one could make out a case in favour of the view that the declarations have had the effect of making the anti-Jewish atrocities worse.

4. As regards to military measures, such as bombing, I am ready to consider with the Air Ministry what can be done. We are in fact bombing Budapest already.

SOURCE: Public Record Office, Kew, PREM 4/51/10, 1368–1369.

3.4 Aide-Memoire by Chaim Weizmann and Moshe Shertok, left with Anthony Eden following their interview, 6 July 1944

1) According to messages from the responsible Jewish group in Budapest which have reached representatives of the Jewish Agency in Istanbul, Geneva and Lisbon, 400,000 Hungarian Jews have already been deported to the death-camps. The Geneva message states that most transports have gone to Birkenau in Upper Silesia, where there are four crematoriums with a capacity for gas-sing and burning 60,000 a day, and where, in the course of the last year, over 1,500,000 Jews from all over Europe are reported to have been killed. In and around Budapest there are still over 300,000 Jews awaiting their doom. Ac-cording to the Istanbul message their deportation was to have started this week.

2) It would thus appear that the stage of temporising, in the hope of pro-longing the victims' lives, is over, and some definite steps must immediately be taken if the admittedly remote chance of saving the remnants of Hungarian Jewry is not to be missed. We realise that our proposals for action are unor-thodox, and perhaps unprecedented. But we consider them warranted by the present tragedy, which is also without its parallel or precedent.

3) We have already proposed that

(a) An intimation should be given to Germany that some appropriate body is ready to meet for discussing the rescue of Jews.

(b) A representative of the American War Refugee Board, if necessary, seconded by a British official, should be ready to meet at Istanbul a member of the Nazi group in Budapest, to explore possibilities of rescue.

(c) Joel Brand, and if only possible, his former escort, should be allowed to return to Hungary; Brand being authorised to inform the other side of the course that will have been decided upon.

4) Since the submission of these proposals, one of our friends in Istanbul, a Palestinian, has received a message from the Jewish centre in Budapest urging him to come to Budapest for a discussion, and informing him that his safe return would be guaranteed. While fully realising the risks involved, we would submit that he should be allowed to proceed, preferably together with Joel Brand.

5) That any Gestapo offer to release Jews must have ulterior motives—avowed or hidden—is fully appreciated. It is not, however, improbable that in the false hope of achieving those ends, they would be prepared to let out a certain number of Jews—large or small. The whole thing may boil down to a question of money, and we believe that the ransom should be paid.

6) Apart from the question of Joel Brand's mission, we would make the following urgent suggestions:

(a) That the Allies should publish a declaration expressing their readiness to admit Jewish fugitives to all their territories, and stating that they have in this the support of neutrals (Switzerland, Sweden, Spain, and possibly Turkey), who are prepared to give temporary shelter to Jewish refugees from massacres.

(b) That the Swiss Government in particular should be asked to instruct its representatives in Hungary to inform the local authorities of such readiness, and to issue such documents to the largest possible number of people as might in the interim afford them some protection.

(c) That a stern warning to Hungarian officials, railwaymen, and the population in general, be published and broadcast, to the effect that anyone convicted of having taken part in the rounding-up, deportation and extermination of Jews will be considered to be a war criminal and treated accordingly.

(d) That Marshal Stalin be approached to issue a similar warning to Hungary on the part of the USSR.

(e) That the railway-line leading from Budapest to Birkenau, and the death-camps at Birkenau and other places, should be bombed.

London

6.7.44

SOURCE: Michael J. Cohen, ed., *The Letters and Papers of Chaim Weizmann*, Vol. XXI, Series A, January 1943–May 1945 (Jerusalem, 1979), 321–22.

3.5 Telegram, Moshe Shertok to David Ben-Gurion, Jerusalem, and Nahum Goldmann, Jewish Agency, New York, 6 July 1944

WEIZMANN MYSELF SAW EDEN URGED SPEEDIEST DECISION ON SERIES OF PROPOSALS OF WHICH LEFT SUMMARY AS FOLLOWS ONE ACCORDING BUDAPEST REPORTS REACHING ISTANBUL GENEVA LISBON 400,000 LAREADY [*sic*] SENT DEATHCAMPS GENEVA STATES MOST

TRANSPORTS GONE TO BIRKENAU WHERE FOUR CREMATORIA OP-
ERATING TOTAL CAPACITY 60,000 DAILY [sic]. OVER 300,000 STILL IN
AND AROUND BUDAPEST ACCORDING ISTANBUL THEIR DEPORTA-
TION DUE BEGIN THIS WEEK TWO STAGE OF TEMPORISING THUS
OVER AND DEFINITIVE STEPS IMPERATIVE IF REMOTE CHANCE OF
SAVING REMNANTS NOT TO BE MISSED. WE REALISE OUR PROPOSALS
ARE UNORTHODOX AND UNPRECEDENTED BUT THEY ARE WAR-
RANTED BY TRAGEDY WHICH IS WITHOUT PARALLEL OR PRECEDENT
THREE RECAPITULATES FIRST SECOND FOURTH PROPOSALS SUBMIT-
TED TO HALL AND REPORTED IN OUR TELEGRAM 30.6. FOUR SINCE
SUBMISSIONS ABOVE ONE OF REPRESENTATIVES IN ISTANBUL RE-
CEIVED MESSAGE FROM JEWISH CENTRE BUDAPEST URGING HIM TO
COME TO BUDAPEST FOR DISCUSSIONS AND INFORMING THAT SAFE
RETURN GUARANTEED. WHILE REALISING RISKS INVOLVED WE SUB-
MIT HE SHOULD BE ALLOWED PROCEED PREFERABLY TOGETHER
WITH BRANDT FIVE WE FULLY APPRECIATE GESTAPO OFFERS RE-
LEASE JEWS MUST HAVE ULTERIOR MOTIVES BUT CONSIDER NOT IM-
PROBABLE THAT IN FALSE HOPE ACHIEVING THOSE ENDS THEY
WOULD BE PREPARED LET OUT CERTAIN NUMBER OF JEWS LARGE OR
SMALL. WHOLE THING MAY BOIL DOWN TO QUESTION OF MONEY.
WE BELIEVE RANSOM SHOULD BE PAID. SIX APART FROM QUESTION
OF BRANDT'S MISSION WE URGE FOLLOWING (A) ALLIES SHOULD
PUBLISH DECLARATION EXPRESSING READINESS ADMIT JEWISH FU-
GITIVES TO ALL THEIR TERRITORIES STATING THEY HAVE IN THIS
SUPPORT OF NEUTRALS WHO PREPARED GIVE TEMPORARY SHELTER
(B) SWISS GOVERNMENT SHOULD BE ASKED TO INSTRUCT REPRESEN-
TATIVES IN HUNGARY TO INFORM LOCAL AUTHORITIES OF SUCH
READINESS AND ISSUE SUCH DOCUMENTS TO LARGEST POSSIBLE
NUMBER AS MIGHT IN INTERIM AFFORD PROTECTION (C) STERN
WARNING SHOULD BE BROADCAST TO HUNGARIAN OFFICIALS RAIL-
WAYMEN GENERAL POPULATION THAT ANYONE TAKING PART IN
ROUNDUP AND DEPORTATION WILL BE TREATED AS WAR CRIMINAL
(D) STALIN SHOULD BE APPROACHED TO ISSUE SIMILAR WARNING
TO HUNGARY (E) DEATHCAMPS AND RAILWAYLINE LEADING TO
BIRKENAU SHOULD BE BOMBED. SUMMARY ENDS SECRETARY OF
STATE GAVE US VERY SYMPATHETIC HEARING. EXPRESSED SER-
IOUS MISGIVINGS REGARDING ANY PROPOSAL OR NEGOTIATIONS.
WAR CABINET'S SUGGESTIONS REGARDING BRANDT MISSION AND
OTHER PROPOSALS FOR ACTION HAVE BEEN COMMUNICATED MOS-
COW WASHINGTON REPLIES OUTSTANDING. PROPOSAL REGARD-
ING BADER'S GOING BUDAPEST WILL HAVE TO BE SUBMITTED TO
CABINET. PROMISED RECOMMEND APPROACH TO STALIN ALREADY
ASKED AIRMINISTRY [sic] EXPLORE POSSIBILITY [sic] BOMBING

CAMPS WILL NOW ADD RAILWAYS. ALL OTHER POINTS WOULD BE
CONSIDERED

SHERTOK

SOURCE: Central Zionist Archives, Jerusalem, Z4/14870, supplied by David S.
Wyman

3.6 Memorandum, Anthony Eden to Winston Churchill, 6 July 1944

PRIME MINISTER

I have had another appeal from Dr. Weizmann that we should do something
to mitigate the appalling slaughter of Jews in Hungary. Sixty thousand a day
according to the Jewish Agency's information are being gassed and burnt at the
death camp of Birkenau. This may well be an exaggeration.

2. Dr. Weizmann recognised that there was little His Majesty's Government
could do, but made the following suggestions:

    (a) Something might be done to stop the operation of this death camp

        (i) by bombing the railway lines leading to it (and to similar camps)
and also

        (ii) by bombing the camps themselves so as to destroy the plant used
for the gassing and cremation.

I told Dr. Weizmann that we had already considered (ii) [sic], but that I
would now re-examine it and the further suggestion of bombing the camps
themselves. I am in favour of acting on both these suggestions.

(b) Dr. Weizmann suggested that a greater impression might be made upon
the obduracy of the Hungarians if a warning couched in the strongest terms
were addressed to the Hungarian Government by Marshal Stalin. I told Dr.
Weizmann that I would consider this suggestion. I am in favour of it. You will
remember that the Soviet Government joined His Majesty's Government and
the United States Government in 1942 in a declaration condemning similar
atrocities and pledging themselves to exact retribution. The most appropriate
form of approach would, I think, be a message from yourself to Marshal Stalin.
Would you be willing to do this? . . .

SOURCE: Public Record Office, Kew, PREM 4/51/10, 1365–1366.

3.7 Winston Churchill to Anthony Eden, 7 July 1944

FOREIGN SECRETARY

Is there any reason to raise these matters at the Cabinet? You and I are in
entire agreement. Get anything out of the Air Force you can and invoke me if
necessary. Certainly appeal to Stalin. On no account have the slightest negoti-

ations, direct or indirect, with the Huns. By all means bring it up if you wish to, but I do not think it is necessary.

SOURCE: Public Record Office, Kew, FO 371/42809, 164.

3.8. Anthony Eden to Sir Archibald Sinclair, Secretary of State for Air, 7 July 1944

My dear Archie, [handwritten]

You will remember that I referred in the House last Wednesday to the appalling persecution of Jews in Hungary. On July 6th Weizmann, of the Jewish Agency for Palestine, came to see me with further information about it which had reached the Agency's representatives in Istanbul, Geneva and Lisbon, the main point of which was that, according to these reports 400,000 Hungarian Jews had already been deported to what he called "death camps" at Birkenau in Upper Silesia, where there are four crematoriums with a gassing and burning capacity of 60,000 a day and where, incidentally, in the course of the last year, over one and a half million Jews from all over Europe are reported to have been killed.

Dr. Weizmann admitted that there seemed to be little enough that we could do to stop these horrors, but he suggested that something might be done to stop the operation of the death camps by

(1)   bombing the railway lines leading to Birkenau (and to any other similar camps if we get to hear of them); and

(2)   bombing the camps themselves with the object of destroying the plant used for gassing and burning.

I should add that I told Weizmann that, as you may know, we had already considered suggestion (1) above but that I would re-examine it and also the further suggestion of bombing the camps themselves.

Could you let me know how the Air Ministry view the feasibility of these proposals? I very much hope that it will be possible to do something. I have the authority of the Prime Minister to say that he agrees.

Sincerely,

Anthony Eden [handwritten]

SOURCE: Public Record Office, Kew, AIR 19/218, 46–47.

3.9 Sir Archibald Sinclair to Anthony Eden, 15 July 1944

[*handwritten in top margin by Eden:* A characteristically unhelpful letter. Dept will have to consider what is to be done about this. I think that we should pass the buck to this ardent Zionist, in due course ie, tell Weizmann that we have approached Sir A. Sinclair and suggest he may like to see him. AE July 16]

Dear Anthony, [handwritten]

You wrote to me on the 7th July to ask if anything could be done by bombing to stop the murder of Jews in Hungary.

I entirely agree that it is our duty to consider every possible plan that might help, and I have, therefore, examined:

(a) interrupting the railways
(b) destroying the plant
(c) other interference with the camps.

I am advised that (a) is out of our power. It is only by an enormous concentration of bomber forces that we have been able to interrupt communications in Normandy; the distance of Silesia from our bases entirely rules out our doing anything of the kind.

Bombing the plant is out of the bounds of possibility for Bomber Command, because the distance is too great for the attack to be carried out at night. It might be carried out by the Americans by daylight but it would be a costly and hazardous operation. It might be ineffective, and, even if the plant was destroyed, I am not clear that it would really help the victims. [*handwritten note in margin*: He wasn't asked his opinion of this, he was asked to act. AE]

There is just one possibility, and that is bombing the camps, and possibly dropping weapons at the same time, in the hope that some of the victims may be able to escape. We did something of the kind in France, when we made a breach in the walls of a prison camp and we think that 150 men who had been condemned to death managed to escape. The difficulties of doing this in Silesia are, of course enormously greater and even if the camp was successfully raided, the chances of escape would be small indeed. Nevertheless, I am proposing to have the proposition put to the Americans, with all the facts, to see if they are prepared to try it. I am very doubtful indeed whether, when they have examined it, the Americans will think it possible, and I do not wish to raise any hopes. For this reason, and because it would not be fair to suggest that we favoured it and the Americans were unable to help, I feel that you would not wish to mention the possibility to Weizmann at this stage. I will let you know the result when the Americans have considered it.

Yours ever, *Archie* [handwritten]

SOURCE: Public Record Office, Kew, FO 371/42809, 178–79.

3.10 Sinclair's Assistant Private Secretary to Vice-Chief of Air Staff, 26 July 1944

P.S. to V.C.A.S. [Private Secretary to Vice Chief of Air Staff]

S. of S. [Secretary of State for Air] feels that in all the circumstances it would be best for V.C.A.S. to raise this matter with General Spaatz—possibly in conversation when he is next in the Air Ministry.

2. The Secretary of State feels that it is hardly appropriate for him to approach the Ambassador on a matter of this kind which though partly political, is largely operational.

26.7.44.   A.P.S. to S. of S.

SOURCE: Public Record Office, Kew, AIR 19/218, 33.

3.11 Deputy Chief of Air Staff Bottomley to Acting Chief of Air Staff, 2 August 1944

A.C.A.S.(I)
Copy to: V.C.A.S.
P.S. to S. of S.
D.B. Ops

Reference Minute 1 et seq. I have discussed this subject with General Spaatz, who is most sympathetic. Before we can consider any action, however, it is necessary to know more about the precise location, extent and nature of the camps and installations at Birkenau. It is particularly necessary to have some photographic cover.

2. Will you please have this produced as early as possible, so that the operational possibilities of taking some effective action from the air can be studied by the operational Commands and the Deputy Supreme Commander. I need not emphasize the need for absolute secrecy in this investigation.

2nd August, 1944.   D.C.A.S. [Deputy Chief of Air Staff]

SOURCE: Public Record Office, Kew, AIR 19/218, 33.

3.12 G. W. P. Grant, Air Ministry, to V. F. W. Cavendish-Bentinck, Foreign Office, 13 August 1944

I am perturbed at having heard nothing more from the Foreign Office about the problem of BIRKENAU since Allen telephoned me on the 5th of this month.

2. You will appreciate that as the Secretary of State for Air has instructed the Air Staff to take action on Mr. Eden's request it is a matter of the greatest urgency for me to obtain photographic cover of the camps and installations in

the BIRKENAU area. The information at present in our possession is insufficient for a reconnaissance aircraft to have a reasonable chance of obtaining the cover required and only the Foreign Office can obtain the information which I need.

3. In view of the urgency of the problem which Mr. Eden himself has raised I shall be grateful if I can have a reply, whether it be positive or negative, to my request with the utmost expedition.

4. In his conversation Allen hinted that the Foreign Office were tending to reconsider the importance they had placed upon the liberation of the captives at BIRKENAU. This however does not help me. If in fact further information about the Germans' intentions in that particular camp has caused the Secretary of State for Foreign Affairs to revise his opinion it will be necessary for him to inform the Secretary of State for Air who will, no doubt, then modify or rescind the instructions which he has issued to the Air Staff. Only if and until such official action is taken can the priority of cover of BIRKENAU, which is now of the very highest, be lowered. I therefore shall be most grateful for all the help you can give me either to let me have the information which I require to get the job done or else to clear the position in the event of the Foreign Office having modified its views as to the importance of the task.

SOURCE: Public Record Office, Kew, AIR 19/218, 30–31.

3.13 Richard Law, Foreign Office, to Sir Archibald Sinclair, Air Ministry, 1 September 1944

Dear Archie, [handwritten]

I am writing to thank you on behalf of Anthony for your letter of the 15th July about the suggestion made by certain Jewish Associations that we might stop the murder of Jews by bombing.

For the last month our reports have tended to show that Jews are no longer being deported from Hungary. In view of this fact and also because we understand from the Air Ministry that there are serious technical difficulties in the way of carrying out the suggestion, we do not propose to pursue it.

Yours ever [handwritten]
Richard Law

SOURCE: Public Record Office, Kew, AIR 19/218, 28.

3.14 Deputy Chief of Air Staff Bottomley to Lt. Gen. Carl Spaatz, HQ U.S. Strategic Air Forces, 6 September 1944

You will remember that we discussed some time ago the possibility of bombing objectives in Upper Silesia as a result of representations made by certain

Jewish associations as to the mass murder of Hungarian Jews which was alleged to be taking place in that area.

The Foreign Office have now stated that Jews are no longer being deported from Hungary and that in view of this fact and because of the serious technical difficulties of carrying out bombing they do not propose to pursue the matter further.

This being so we are taking no further action at the Air Ministry and I suggest that you do not consider the project any further.

SOURCE: Public Record Office, Kew, AIR 19/218, 26.

4

THE LATER APPEALS TO THE AMERICANS

4.1 J. J. Smertenko, Emergency Committee to Save the Jewish People of Europe, Inc., to President Franklin D. Roosevelt, 24 July 1944 [Stamped "War Refugee Board, Aug. 1 1944, Dept. of State"]

My dear Mr. President:

In reply to my telegram sent you on July 3, 1944, I have just received a letter from the State Department signed by Mr. George L. Warren, the last paragraph of which states:

> Thus, active attention has been given to all means available for combating these savage practices. In considering the question of applying measures of retaliation, it has been necessary to examine the relation of such measures to the major business of bringing about the early defeat of the Nazi enemy as the really effective way to end the sufferings of the great mass of innocent victims. Anything designed for purposes of retaliation which would divert military energies even momentarily would be inconsistent with the main purpose of defeating the German armies at the earliest possible moment, which must be accomplished if the Jews in Nazi-held territory are to be saved.

The Emergency Committee is in complete accord with your views, as expressed here by Mr. Warren, that nothing be done which will even momentarily divert military energies from the main purpose of defeating the German armies at the earliest possible moment. Nevertheless, I wish to submit most respectfully the view of the Emergency Committee that a number of measures of retaliation can be taken that will be consistent with this purpose and will in fact appreciably aid this purpose.

1. Railways and bridges leading from Nazi-occupied territory to extermination centers in Poland can be destroyed by bombing, specifying that this action is taken in order to prevent the transportation of the Hebrew people of these Axis countries to Hitler's slaughter houses. These railways also serve military purposes and their destruction will be of great benefit to our ally, Soviet Russia.

2. The extermination camps themselves can be bombed, destroying the gas chambers where thousands of people are assassinated daily. This would enable the Hebrew people gathered in these camps to escape and offer them an opportunity to join the underground resistance forces where they can be of help in sabotage and resistance activities.

3. In accordance with the reiterated statements of the American and British Governments that the use of poison gas by Germans and Japanese would be followed by retaliation in kind, a specific statement can be issued that the extermination of Hebrew men, women, and children by the continued use of poison gas will be considered a provocation for retaliation in kind. We respectfully call your attention to the fact that authenticated reports from Czechoslovakian and Polish underground sources have disclosed that over a million and a half persons have been murdered in the poison gas chambers of Auschwitz and Birkenau camps and that the threat of widespread use of the same medium upon the German population will contribute to the disaffection of the German people and may result in a speedier collapse of Hitler's home front.

All these are measures that will not require any additional exertion of military forces nor call for any deviation from the successful military campaigns now in progress. On the contrary, they can be of substantial aid to the campaign of psychological warfare that is being waged simultaneously against our enemy.

At the same time, permit us to call to your attention to the message the Emergency Committee has just received from the International Red Cross Delegation at Washington which states:

RECEIVED FOLLOWING FROM GENEVA QUOTE FOLLOWING ON THE STEPS TAKEN IN BUDAPEST BY THE ICRC IN GENEVA THE HUNGARIAN AUTHORITIES HAVE GIVEN THE COMMITTEE OFFICIAL ASSURANCES THAT TRANSPORTATION OF JEWS BEYOND THE HUNGARIAN FRONTIERS HAS CEASED AND THAT THE INTERNATIONAL COMMITTEE ARE AUTHORIZED TO FURNISH RELIEF TO JEWS WHO ARE INTERNED OR IN FORCED RESIDENCE IN HUNGARY STOP THE COMMITTEE ARE FURTHERMORE EMPOWERED TO COOPERATE IN THE EVACUATION OF ALL JEWISH CHILDREN UNDER TEN YEARS OF AGE WHO ARE IN POSSESSION

OF VISAS TO RECEPTION COUNTRIES AND ALL JEWS IN HUN-
GARY HOLDING ENTRANCE VISAS TO PALESTINE WILL RECEIVE
PERMISSION FROM THE AUTHORITIES TO LEAVE FOR THAT
COUNTRY UNQUOTE.

In view of the agreement between the International Red Cross and the Hungarian Government, we enter the most earnest plea that the United States Government issue as many visas as possible to the children in question and instruct
the War Refugee Board to utilize every possible means to aid the International
Red Cross in evacuating these children immediately from Hungarian territory.
For it is obvious that even though the security of these children has been temporarily assured, their lives are still in danger due to the insufficient food and
shelter provided for them in Hungary.

We also call to your attention to the agreement between the International
Red Cross and the Hungarian Government permitting all Jews in Hungary holding entrance visas to Palestine to leave for that country. We plead with you to
make the strongest possible representation to the British Government requesting
the issuance of such visas in unlimited quantities so that all of the Jews who
can possibly be transported to Palestine may be saved. This need not be interpreted as a political act affecting the future status of Palestine. Temporary Emergency Refugee Shelters can be established in that country for the Hungarian
Jews. Whether they return to Hungary, remain in Palestine, or are settled in
other lands can be decided when the danger is past.

Respectfully yours,
Johan J. Smertenko
Executive Vice-Chairman

SOURCE: National Archives, State Dept. 840.48 Refugees/7-2444, reproduced
in Wyman, ed., *America and the Holocaust*, XII:159–61.

4.2 A. Leon Kubowitzki, World Jewish Congress, to Assistant Secretary of War John J. McCloy, 9 August 1944

My dear Mr. Secretary:
I beg to submit to your consideration the following excerpt from a message
which we received under date of July 29 from Mr. Ernest Frischer of the Czechoslovak State Council through the War Refugee Board:

"I believe that destruction of gas chambers and crematoria in Oswiecim
by bombing would have a certain effect now. Germans are now exhuming
and burning corpses in an effort to conceal their crimes. This could be
prevented by destruction of crematoria and then Germans might possibly
stop further mass exterminations especially since so little time is left to

them. Bombing of railway communications in this same area would also be of importance and of military interest."

Sincerely yours,

A. Leon Kubowitski,

Head, Rescue Department

SOURCE: National Archives, RG 107, Assistant Secretary of War Files, 400.38 Countries C-D-E-F (Box 151), reproduced in Wyman, ed., *America and the Holocaust,* XII:164, transcript supplied by USHMM.

4.3 John J. McCloy to A. Leon Kubowitzki, 14 August 1944

Dear Mr. Kubowitski:

I refer to your letter of August 9 in which you request considerations of a proposal made by Mr. Ernest Frischer that certain installations and railroad centers be bombed.

This War Department has been approached by the War Refugee Board, which raised the question of the practicability of this suggestion. After a study it became apparent that such an operation could be executed only by the diversion of considerable air support essential to the success of our forces now engaged in decisive operations elsewhere and would in any case be of such doubtful efficacy that it would not warrant the use of our resources. There has been considerable opinion to the effect that such an effort, even if practicable, might provoke even more vindictive action by the Germans.

The War Department fully appreciates the humanitarian motives which prompted the suggested operations, but for the reasons stated above it has not been felt that it can or should be undertaken, at least at this time.

Sincerely,

John J. McCloy

Assistant Secretary of War

SOURCE: National Archives, RG 107, Assistant Secretary of War Files, 400.38 Countries C-D-E-F (Box 151), reproduced in Wyman, ed., *America and the Holocaust,* XII:165, transcript supplied by USHMM.

4.4 I. L. Kenen, American Jewish Conference, "Report of Meeting with John W. Pehle, Executive Director and Messrs. Lesser and Frieman of the War Refugee Board," 16 August 1944 (Excerpt)

The committee consisted of Mr. Eugene Hevesi, of the American Jewish Committee, Rabbi Abraham Kalmanowitz, and Rabbi Solomon Metz, of the Vaad Ha-Hazalah, Dr. A. Leon Kubowitzki, of the World Jewish Congress, Mr.

B. Sherman of the Jewish Labor Committee, and I. L. Kenen, secretary, Rescue Commission, American Jewish Conference.

Mr. Kenen introduced the delegation as a committee representing all Jewish organizations, including those affiliated with the Conference and a number outside the Conference, such as the American Jewish Committee and the Vaad-Ha-Hazalah. In addition, he continued, the World Jewish Congress was represented by Dr. Kubowitzki. The organizations had united to expedite rescue measures in view of the situation in Hungary. He said that it was the intention in the future to have representations to the Board made, if possible, by a committee representing all the organizations and thus eliminate duplication of activity. Mr. Pehle said that when he had first taken office, he had hoped that such a unified representation might be achieved but found it impossible at that time. . . .

Dr. Kubowitzki raised the question of the destruction of Nazi extermination facilities. Mr. Pehle doubted that this could be done. He said that a proposal to bomb the facilities had been objected to by Jewish organizations because it would result in the extermination of large numbers of Jews there, and the alternative, he said, was to send an underground detachment. He asked whether we had taken this up with the Polish Government in Exile and he expressed doubt that the Poles could muster the strength for such engagements.

SOURCE: YIVO, AJC Archives, Waldman Series, Box 18, Folder 1, copy supplied by YIVO; transcript supplied by Richard H. Levy.

4.5 War Refugee Board Memorandum, B. Akzin to J. W. Pehle, 2 September 1944

Subject: Urgent message from Rabbi Kalmanowitz

Last night, Rabbi Kalmanowitz called me at home from New York and asked me to deliver to you the following message:

A cable from Sternbuch, transmitted through the Polish embassy, contains the information that on August 26 deportations of Jews from Budapest have begun. Twelve thousand Jews have already been deported to Oswiecim, in Upper Silesia. Sternbuch, in his own name and on the suggestion of the Rabbi of Neutra suggests that further deportations be interfered with by the immediate bombing of the railroad junctions between Budapest and Silesia, viz: Kaschan [–]Presow–Zilina–Galanta–Leopoldorf–Caca–Rudki, as well as the railroad junction at Graz (Austria).

The Polish charge d'affaires, M. Kwapiszewski, has promised to Rabbi Kalmanowitz to transmit a copy of the cable to WRB, but in view of possible delays, the Rabbi wanted my assurance that this matter will be placed before you immediately.

While supporting Sternbuch's and the Rabbi of Neutra's request for action,

Rabbi Kalmanowitz wishes also to emphasize that the renewal of large-scale deportations from Hungary lends particular urgency to his proposals placed before the Board at yesterday's conference.

The Rabbi intends to telephone you this morning regarding this matter and, is ready, despite the Sabbath, to take a train today to Washington, if this should appear necessary in the interest of insuring immediate action.

To the above, I should like respectfully to add the following:

The thought of bombing the railroad junctions between Hungary and Silesia to interrupt the flow of deportations is indeed elementary. You will recall that the thought has been clearly hinted at by McClelland, in 4041 from Bern, dated June 24.

I am aware of the fact that a somewhat similar idea was rejected some time ago by the Department of War—a rejection which quite likely stems from the habitual reluctance of the military to act upon civilian suggestions.

It is submitted, however, that the WRB was created precisely in order to overcome the inertia and—in some cases—the insufficient interest of the old-established agencies in regard to the saving of Jewish victims of Nazi Germany. Repeatedly we refused to take a "no" for an answer when it came from the Department of State. There is nothing in the officials of the Department of War that would make them more sacrosanct or freer from error than the officials of the Department of State.

In the matter of the "Free Port," which, whatever its merits, was certainly not a matter of life and death, Mr. Pehle went to the President.

To be faithful to our task, it would appear most appropriate if the Board took the identical course in connection with the Hungarian emergency.

In the light of the present air superiority of the United Nations, I am certain that the President, once acquainted with the facts, would realize the values involved and, cutting through the inertia-motivated objections of the War Department, would order the immediate bombing of the objectives suggested.

B. Akzin [signature]

P.S. I have promised the Rabbi to see to it that you get this message without delay. I therefore take this unconventional way of sending it straight to your office, not through channels. A copy of the memo goes to my Chief, Mr. Lesser.

SOURCE: FDR Library, WRB, Box 35, reproduced in Wyman, ed., *America and the Holocaust*, XII:166.

4.6 John W. Pehle, War Refugee Board, to John J. McCloy, War Department, 3 October 1944

Dear Mr. McCloy:

You will recall our conversation some time ago concerning the various proposals placed before the Board that extermination centers in Poland be bombed. I understand that the matter is now in the hands of appropriate theatre commanders.

In this connection, there follows for such consideration as it may be worth, the substance of the pertinent portions of a cable recently received from James Mann, Assistant Executive Director of the Board, who is now in England:

"Members of the Polish Government and groups interested in rescue work report that they have reliable information from the Polish underground that in all Polish concentration camps the Germans are increasing their extermination activities.

"The War Refugee Board is urged by them again to explore with the Army the possibility of bombing the extermination chambers and German barracks at largest Polish concentration camps which, they say, are subject to precision bombing since they are sufficiently detached from the concentration camps. The aforementioned persons have promised to furnish me with recent maps which I will forward to Washington by airmail, although I assume the Army authorities have maps of such camps."

Very truly yours,
J. W. Pehle,
Executive Director

SOURCE: National Archives, RG 107, Assistant Secretary of War files, 400.38 Jews, reproduced in Wyman, ed., *America and the Holocaust*, XII:169.

4.7 Memorandum, Col. Harrison A. Gerhardt, to John J. McCloy, 5 October 1944, on Pehle 3 October letter

Memorandum for Mr. McCloy:

1. To note.

2. I recommend no action be taken on this, since the matter has been fully presented several times previously. It has been our position, which we have expressed to WRB, that bombing of Polish extermination centers should be within the operational responsibility of the Russian forces.

SOURCE: National Archives, RG 107, Assistant Secretary of War files, 400.38 Jews, reproduced in Wyman, ed., *America and the Holocaust*, XII:170.

4.8 John W. Pehle to John J. McCloy, 8 November 1944

Dear Mr. McCloy:

I send you herewith copies of two eye-witness descriptions of the notorious German concentration and extermination camps of Auschwitz and Birkenau in Upper Silesia, which have just been received from the Board's Special Representative in Bern, Switzerland, Roswell McClelland whom we have borrowed from the American Friends Service Committee. No report of Nazi atrocities received by the Board has quite caught the gruesome brutality of what is taking place in these camps of horror as have these sober, factual accounts of conditions in Auschwitz and Birkenau. I earnestly hope that you will read these reports.

The destruction of large numbers of people apparently is not a simple process. The Germans have been forced to devote considerable technological ingenuity and administrative know-how in order to carry out murder on a mass production basis, as the attached reports will testify. If the elaborate murder installations at Birkenau were destroyed, it seems clear that the Germans could not reconstruct there for some time.

Until now, despite pressure from many sources, I have been hesitant to urge the destruction of these camps by direct, military action. But I am convinced that the point has now been reached where such action is justifiable if it is deemed feasible by competent military authorities. I strongly recommend that the War Department give serious consideration to the possibility of destroying the execution chambers and crematories in Birkenau through direct bombing action. It may be observed that there would be other advantages of military nature to such an attack. The Krupp and Siemens factories, where among other things cases for handgrenades are made, and a Buna plant, all within Auschwitz, would be destroyed. The destruction of the German barracks and guardhouses and the killing of German soldiers in the area would also be accomplished. The morale of underground groups might be considerably strengthened by such a dramatic exhibition of Allied air support and a number of the people confined in Auschwitz and Birkenau might be liberated in the confusion resulting from the bombing. That the effecting of a prison break by such methods is not without precedent is indicated by the description in the enclosed copy of a recent New York Times article of the liberation from Amiens prison of 100 French patriots by the RAF.

Obviously, the War Refugee Board is in no position to determine whether the foregoing proposal is feasible from a military standpoint. Nevertheless in view of the urgency of the situation, we feel justified in making the suggestion. I would appreciate having the views of the War Department as soon as possible.

Very truly yours,

J. W. Pehle

SOURCE: National Archives, RG 107, Assistant Secretary of War files, 400.38 Countries—Germany, reproduced in Wyman, ed., *America and the Holocaust*, XII:169.

4.9 Memorandum by H. H. F., Operations Division, War Department General Staff, 14 November 1944

Memorandum for Record

1. Memorandum from Executive Director, War Refugee Board, to Assistant Secretary of War enclosing eye-witness stories of German concentration and extermination camps and recommending that these camps be bombed for humanitarian reasons and secondarily for military reasons was forwarded by Assistant Secretary of War's office to OPD for remark and recommendation.

2. Memorandum to Assistant Secretary of War prepared for General Hull's signature concludes that the proposal for the bombing of the concentration and extermination camps is not feasible from a military standpoint at this time and recommends that the Director of War Refugee Board be so informed.

3. A.A.F. (General Loutzenheiser) concurs in the proposed memorandum.

4. Executive to Assistant Secretary of War (Colonel Gerhardt) indicated that a reply to Executive Director War Refugee Board for Mr. McCloy's signature need not be prepared by OPD.

H. H. F.

SOURCE: National Archives, RG 165, OPD 000.5, Section 3, case 53, reproduced in Wyman, ed., *America and the Holocaust*, XII:181.

4.10 John J. McCloy to John W. Pehle, 18 November 1944

Dear Mr. Pehle:

I refer to your letter of November 8th, in which you forwarded the report of two eye-witnesses on the notorious German concentration and extermination camps of Auschwitz and Birkenau in Upper Silesia.

The Operations Staff of the War Department has given careful consideration to your suggestion that the bombing of these camps be undertaken. In consideration of this proposal the following points were brought out:

a. Positive destruction of these camps would necessitate precision bombing, employing heavy or medium bombardment, or attack by low flying or dive bombing aircraft, preferably the latter.

b. The target is beyond the maximum range of medium bombardment, dive bombers and fighter bombers located in United Kingdom, France, or Italy.

c. Use of heavy bombardment from United Kingdom bases would necessitate a hazardous round trip flight unescorted of approximately 2000 miles over enemy territory.

d. At the present critical stage of the war in Europe our strategic air forces are engaged in the destruction of industrial target systems vital to the dwindling war potential of the enemy, from which they should not be diverted. The positive solution to this problem is the earliest possible victory over Germany, to which end we should exert our entire means.

e. This case does not at all parallel the Amiens mission because of the location of the concentration and extermination camps and the resulting difficulties encountered in attempting to carry out the proposed bombing.

Based on the above, as well as the most uncertain, if not dangerous effect such a bombing would have on the object to be attained, the War Department has felt that it should not, at least for the present, undertake these operations.

I know that you have been reluctant to press this activity on the War Department. We have been pressed strongly from other quarters, however, and have taken the best military opinion on its feasibility, and we believe the above conclusion is a sound one.

Sincerely,
John J. McCloy
Assistant Secretary of War

Inc.
Report of two eye-witnesses

SOURCE: FDR Library, WRB, Box 6, German Extermination Camps, reproduced in Wyman, ed., *America and the Holocaust*, XII:169.

NOTES

Editors' Note: As many of the essays in this volume have been previously published, the notes reflect the original citations and have been only marginally changed for stylistic consistency. Some key articles and many key documents relevant to the controversy have been included in the volume, but this fact could not be noted repeatedly for reasons of space.

INTRODUCTION TO THE CONTROVERSY
Michael J. Neufeld

1. *Commentary* 65 (May 1978), 37–46; for a revised version see "Why Auschwitz Wasn't Bombed," in *Anatomy of the Auschwitz Death Camp,* eds. Yisrael Gutman and Michael Berenbaum (Bloomington and Indianapolis, 1994). In two early histories of the failure of the United States to do much about the Holocaust, the 1944 appeals to bomb Auschwitz are discussed only in passing. See Arthur D. Morse, *While Six Million Died* (London, 1967; New York, 1968), 358–61; Henry L. Feingold, *The Politics of Rescue* (New York, 1970), 256–57. Richard H. Levy, in his essay in chapter 8, in this volume, notes that there was a small flurry of interest at the time of the 1961 Eichmann trial in Israel because of the discovery of a document relating to the Palestinian Jewish appeal to London.

2. Letters to the editor and Wyman's responses in *Commentary* 66 (July 1978), 7, 10–12, (Sept. 1978), 24–25, and (Nov. 1978), 19–20; Roger Williams, "Why Wasn't Auschwitz Bombed: An American Moral Tragedy," *Commonweal* (24 Nov. 1978), 746–51; Merton Mintz, "Why Didn't We Bomb Auschwitz: Can John McCloy's Memories Be Correct?" *Washington Post,* 17 Apr. 1983 (which mentions an earlier George Will column supporting bombing).

3. Dino A. Brugioni and Robert G. Poirier, *The Holocaust Revisited: A Retrospective Analysis of the Auschwitz-Birkenau Extermination Complex* (CIA Report ST-79-10001; Washington, D.C., February 1979).

4. Milt Groban, letter to the editor, *Commentary* 66 (July 1978), 10–11.

5. In an interview with the Israeli historian Shlomo Aronson, Albert Speer asserted some years ago that if the Birkenau gas chambers had been destroyed: "Hitler would have hit the roof. . . . He would have ordered the return to mass shooting. And immediately, as a matter of top priority. . . ." Quoted from Aronson's manuscript *Jews' Wars,* chap. 5, pp. 57–58, courtesy of Shlomo Aronson. For the most comprehensive history of the Holocaust, see Raul Hilberg, *The Destruction of the European Jews,* Revised and Definitive Ed., 3 vols. (New York: Holmes & Meier, 1985). Hilberg gives a conservative total of 5.1 million Jewish dead in vol. III, Appendix B. Others have defended figures much closer to the traditional 6 million.

6. Bernard Wasserstein's *Britain and the Jews of Europe 1939–1945* (London and Oxford, 1979), 307–20; Martin Gilbert, *Auschwitz and the Allies* (New York, 1981).

7. More recently, the debate has also had an impact in Israel, where it has been subsumed in arguments over the alleged failure of the leadership of the Yishuv (the half million Jews in the British mandate of Palestine) to do anything about the Holocaust. See Dina Porat, *The Blue and the Yellow Stars of David* (Cambridge, Mass., 1990); Tom Segev, *The Seventh Million* (New York, 1993); and Shabtai Teveth, *Ben-Gurion and the Holocaust* (New York, 1996). Criticisms of the failure of the Allies to bomb Auschwitz have also been increasingly taken for granted there and have been used by Israeli politicians, particularly on the right, to criticize the West—notably Prime Minister Benjamin Netanyahu at the Auschwitz camp on 23 April 1998. See "Netanyahu Says Allies Knowingly Let Jews Die," *Washington Times*, 24 April 1998, A15; David Horovitz, "Why the Allies Didn't Bomb Auschwitz," *World Press Review* 42 (Mar. 1995), 44–45.

8. McCloy's motives are examined by his biographer at greater length, but from a viewpoint very similar to Wyman's: Kai Bird, *The Chairman* (New York, 1992), chap. 10.

9. Michael Marrus, *The Holocaust in History* (New York, 1989), 3–6; Morse and Feingold cited above in note 1. Omer Bartov in "Defining Enemies, Making Victims: Germans, Jews, and the Holocaust," *American Historical Review* 103 (June 1998), 771–816, 801–03, believes the Eichmann trial had a greater impact in the United States. Peter Novick's *The Holocaust in American Life* (Boston and New York, 1999) appeared while this book was in press.

10. For the contrast between American fascination with "precision bombing" and the realities of World War II, see Ronald Schaffer, *Wings of Judgment* (New York, 1986), and Michael Sherry, *The Rise of American Air Power* (New Haven, 1987).

11. See the books by Morse, Feingold, and Wyman previously cited; Monty Noam Penkower, *The Jews Were Expendable* (Urbana, Ill., 1983); Rafael Medoff, *The Deafening Silence* (New York, 1987); Richard Breitman and Alan M. Kraut, *American Refugee Policy and American Jewry, 1933–1945* (Bloomington, 1987); Frank W. Brecher, "David Wyman and the Historiography of American's Response to the Holocaust: Counter-Considerations," *Holocaust and Genocide Studies* 5 (1990), 423–46; Henry L. Feingold, *Bearing Witness* (Syracuse, 1995); Verne Newton, ed., *FDR and the Holocaust* (New York, 1996); William D. Rubinstein, *The Myth of Rescue* (London and New York, 1997); the article by Lucy Dawidowicz cited in note 12; and Weinberg and Lipstadt chapters 1 and 15 in this volume. For Wyman's most recent response to the literature criticizing his book, see the new afterword to the reissue of *The Abandonment of the Jews* (New York, 1998), 341–53.

12. Lucy Dawidowicz, "Could America Have Rescued Europe's Jews?" in *What Is the Use of Jewish History?* (New York, 1992), originally published as "Could the United States Have Rescued the Jews from Hitler?" *This World*, no. 12 (Fall 1985), 15–30.

13. Richard Foregger, "The Bombing of Auschwitz," *Aerospace Historian* (Summer/June 1987), 98–110; "The First Allied Aerial Reconnaissance over Auschwitz during World War II," *Military History Journal* 8 (June 1989), 31–32; "Technical Analysis of Methods to Bomb the Gas Chambers at Auschwitz," *Holocaust and Genocide Studies* 5 (1990), 403–21; "Two Sketch Maps of the Auschwitz-Birkenau Extermination Camps," *Journal of Military History* 59 (Oct. 1995), 687–96.

14. Robert H. Hodges, " 'The Bombing of Auschwitz': A Clarification," and Michael G. Moskow, " 'The Bombing of Auschwitz': A Reply," *Aerospace Historian* (Summer/June 1988), 123–30.

15. See Hilberg, *Destruction*, III: 1132–1140; Porat, *The Blue and the Yellow Stars*, 188–211; Yehuda Bauer, *Jews for Sale? Nazi-Jewish Negotiations, 1933–1945* (New Haven, 1994).

16. Marrus, *The Holocaust in History* (1989 ed.), 156–57.

17. See, for example, Deborah Lipstadt, *Beyond Belief* (New York, 1986), for an illuminating examination of American press skepticism about the persecution of the Jews.

18. William H. Honan, "Historians Warming to Games of 'What If'," *New York Times*, 7 Jan. 1998, A19.

PART 1: ALLIED KNOWLEDGE AND CAPABILITIES
1. THE ALLIES AND THE HOLOCAUST
Gerhard L. Weinberg

1. A fine review is Richard Breitman and Alan M. Kraut, *American Refugee Policy and European Jewry, 1933–1945* (Bloomington, Ind., 1987).
2. See Bernard Wasserstein, *Britain and the Jews of Europe* (Oxford, 1979).
3. Peter Calvacoressi, *Top Secret Ultra* (New York, 1980), 15.
4. F. H. Hinsley, *British Intelligence and the Second World War* (New York, 1981), vol. II, Appendix 5.
5. Ibid., 673.
6. Ibid., 671.
7. Ibid., x–xi.
8. Walter Laqueur, *The Terrible Secret: The Suppression of the Truth about Hitler's "Final Solution"* (New York, 1981).
9. Walter Laqueur and Richard Breitman, *Breaking the Silence* (New York, 1986).
10. *Akten zur deutschen auswärtigen Politik, 1918–1945*, Series D, Vol. 13, No. 515.
11. Ibid.
12. The text has been published repeatedly; it may be found in Walther Hubatsch, ed., *Hitlers Weisungen für die Kriegführung 1939–1945* (Frankfurt/Main, 1962), 129–39, and in *Akten zur deutschen auswärtigen Politik, 1918–1945*, Series D, Vol. 12, No. 617.
13. Norman J. Goda, "Germany and Northwest Africa in the Second World War: Politics and Strategy of Global Hegemony," Ph.D. diss., University of North Carolina, 1991, and "The Riddle of the Rock: A Reassessment of German Motives for the Capture of Gibraltar in the Second World War," *Journal of Contemporary History*, 28 (1993), 297–314.
14. Byron Farwell, *Armies of the Raj: From the Mutiny to Independence, 1858–1947* (New York: Norton, 1989), 310.
15. Jonathan Steinberg, *All or Nothing: The Axis and the Holocaust 1941–1943* (London and New York, 1990).
16. Richard Breitman and Shlomo Aronson, "The End of the 'Final Solution'?: Nazi Plans to Ransom Jews in 1944," *Central European History* 25 (1992), 177–203.
17. Note Jürgen Rohwer, *Die Versenkung der jüdischen Flüchtlingstransporter Struma und Mefkure im Schwarzen Meer (Februar 1942, August 1944)* (Frankfurt/Main, 1965), 31–45.
18. There is an excellent introduction to this issue in Leonard Dinnerstein, *America and the Survivors of the Holocaust* (New York, 1982).
19. Monty Noam Penkower, *The Jews Were Expendable: Free World Diplomacy and the Holocaust* (Urbana, Ill., 1983).
20. See Neil Orpen, *Airlift to Warsaw: The Rising of 1944* (Norman, Okla., 1984).
21. The full text was first published in *Trial of the Major War Criminals before the International Military Tribunal*, 42 vols. (Nuremberg, 1947–49), XXVIII: 628–94.
22. On these matters, see the author's introduction, "The 'Final Solution' and the War in 1943," in *Fifty Years Ago: Revolt amid the Darkness*, U.S. Holocaust Memorial Museum (Washington, DC, 1993), 1–15.

2. AUSCHWITZ PARTIALLY DECODED
Richard Breitman

1. Walter Laqueur, *The Terrible Secret: Suppression of the Truth about the "Final Solution"* (Boston, 1980), esp. 85–86.

2. Martin Gilbert, *Auschwitz and the Allies* (New York, 1981), esp. 130, 339–40.

3. On the basis of more limited sources, I addressed this subject previously in "Allied Knowledge of Auschwitz-Birkenau in 1943–44," in *FDR and the Holocaust*, ed. Verne Newton (New York, 1996), 175–82.

4. Bernard Wasserstein, *Britain and the Jews of Europe 1939–1945* (Oxford, 1979), 307–08.

5. David Engel, *In the Shadow of Auschwitz: The Polish Government-in-Exile and the Jews, 1939–1942* (Chapel Hill, 1987), 202. Darius Stola, "Early News of the Holocaust from Poland," *Holocaust and Genocide Studies* 11 (1997): 1–27, calls some of Engel's arguments into question, but does not discuss specific information about Auschwitz-Birkenau.

6. See F. H. Hinsley et al., *British Intelligence in the Second World War: Its Influence on Strategy and Operations* (Cambridge, 1981), II:669.

7. The addressee(s) is/are missing in the decode. The sender was Liebehenschel of the WVHA.

8. German Police Decodes, no. 3 traffic, 11 June 1942, item 8, Public Record Office (hereafter PRO) HW 16/19.

9. German Police Decodes, 24 Aug. 1942, items 55–56 and 64–65, PRO HW 16/19.

10. For a brief description, Franciszek Piper, "Auschwitz Concentration Camp: How It Was Used in the Nazi System of Terror and Genocide and in the Economy of the Third Reich," in *The Holocaust and History: The Known, the Unknown, the Disputed, and the Reexamined*, ed. Michael Berenbaum and Abraham Peck (Bloomington, Ind., 1998), 371–86.

11. German Police Decodes, 5 June 1942, PRO HW 16/19.

12. German Police Decodes, 17 June 1942, item 16, PRO 16/19.

13. Yehoshoa R. Büchler, "First in the Vale of Affliction: Slovakian Jewish Women in Auschwitz, 1942," *Holocaust and Genocide Studies* 10 (1996): 307.

14. German Police Decodes, 18 Nov. 1942, item 2, PRO HW 16/22.

15. German Police Decodes, 4 June 1942, item 10, PRO 16/19. On Kammler's role in SS construction projects, see Michael Thad Allen, "The Banality of Evil Reconsidered: SS Mid-Level Managers of Extermination through Work," *Central European History* 30 (1997): 287–92.

16. Jean-Claude Pressac, *Die Krematorien von Auschwitz* (Munich and Zurich, 1995) has the most detailed treatment of construction at the extermination camp, but is unreliable on policy decisions. See also Pressac and Robert-Jan van Pelt, "The Machinery of Mass Murder at Auschwitz," in *Anatomy of the Auschwitz Death Camp*, ed. Yisrael Gutman and Michael Berenbaum (Bloomington, Ind., 1994), 183–245.

17. Höss was summoned to a private meeting with Kammler and to a general meeting with all camp commanders led by Oswald Pohl on 25 June 1942, German Police Decodes, 18 June 1942, items 17–18, and 24 June 1942, item 32, PRO HW 16/19.

18. Christopher R. Browning, "A Final Hitler Decision for the 'Final Solution'? The Riegner Telegram Reconsidered," *Holocaust and Genocide Studies* 10 (1996): 5–6.

19. Richard Breitman, *The Architect of Genocide: Himmler and the Final Solution* (Hanover, NH, 1992), 236–38.

20. German Police Decodes, 20 Nov. 1942, items 38–39, PRO HW 16/22.

21. German Police Decodes, 14 Jan. 1943, items 13–16, PRO HW 16/22.

22. The data from the first months were decoded only in May 1942. By June the decodes were almost contemporaneous with the radio reports. See the markings at the top of the data sheets in PRO HW 16/10. Auschwitz was designated as F. British intelligence analysts noted the death totals in hand on some of the data sheets and also highlighted some of the death totals in a summary of 26 Sept. 1942, PRO HW 16/6, part 2.

23. The tables of numbers are in PRO HW 16/10.

24. See ref. Nr. 2325, 17 Aug. 1940, PRO HW 14/6, which mentions that Colonel Tiltman

recently broke the railway ciphers. On the MEW, see Laqueur, *Terrible Secret*, 85–86; Hinsley, *British Intelligence*, I:357–58.

25. German Police Decodes, 16 July 1942, items 40–41, PRO HW 16/20; German Police Decodes, 7 Oct. 1942, items 1–4, PRO HW 16/21.

26. Laqueur, *Terrible Secret*, 86, suggests that some intelligence files were destroyed.

27. Ibid., 238; Chciuk-Celt to Laqueur, 8 Oct. 1979; Chciuk-Celt to Breitman, 24 Feb. 1995.

28. Engel, *In the Shadow of Auschwitz*, 201.

29. Cable from N. [Korbonski], 23 Mar. 1943, for the Polish radio station SWIT, cited by David Engel, *Facing a Holocaust: The Polish Government-in-Exile and the Jews, 1943–1945* (Chapel Hill, NC, 1993), 231, n. 122.

30. Nazi Black Record, from *Poland Fights*, no. 30, 5 Apr. 1943, United States National Archives, Record Group (hereafter NA RG) 165, Box 3138, Poland 6950.

31. The courier is tentatively identified as Jerzy Salski by Engel, *Facing a Holocaust*, 209n.109. But neither the Polish Underground Movement Study Trust nor Tadeusz Chciuk-Celt was able to provide an identification. I am grateful to both for their assistance.

32. The courier said at the outset that he stayed from November 1941 until early December 1942, but his detailed comments about his itinerary contradict his dating. Censorship Report, 5 May 1943, NA RG 226, Entry 191, Box 3, untitled folder. A portion of the document is also quoted by Martin Gilbert, *Auschwitz and the Allies*, 130.

33. Censorship Report, 5 May 1943, NA RG 226, Entry 191, Box 3, untitled folder.

34. Schwarzbart to Representation of Polish Jews, World Jewish Congress, 27 Apr. 1943, Schwarzbart Papers, M2 535, Yad Vashem. I am grateful to Shlomo Aronson for sending me a copy of this cover letter. For the full document, see Censorship Report, 5 May 1943, NA RG 226, Entry 191, Box 3, untitled folder.

35. Gilbert, *Auschwitz and the Allies*, 130.

36. 18 May 1943, NA RG 218, Joint Chiefs of Staff CCS 334, Polish Liaison (Washington), Folder 3.0.

37. Cover note from Josef Zaranski, counselor of the Polish embassy, to Randall, British Foreign Office, 18 May 1943, with memo, Extermination of the Jews of Poland, PRO FO 371/34550 (5628/34/55).

38. Military Attaché (London) Report 907, 17 Mar. 1944, NA RG 165, Box 3138, Poland 6950. Also F. W. Belin to William L. Langer, 10 Apr. 1944, NA RG 226, Entry 16, 66059. Engel, *Facing a Holocaust*, 287, n. 121, mentions a 15 Sept. 1943 cable from Wanda about Birkenau.

39. Gilbert discusses Vrba and Wetzler and the repercussions of their report in *Auschwitz and the Allies*, 192–206, 231–61; quotation from 340. For Vrba's account, see Rudolf Vrba and Alan Bestic, *I Cannot Forgive* (New York, 1964). See also the recent, though tendentious updating by Vrba, "Die missachtete Warnung: Betrachtungen über den Auschwitz-Bericht, 1944," *Vierteljahrshefte für Zeitgeschichte* 44 (1996), 1–24.

3. ALLIED AIR POWER: OBJECTIVES AND CAPABILITIES
Tami Davis Biddle

1. Copy of the report on the Oswiecim camp (dated 30 December 1940), attached to a letter to Air Marshal Sir Richard E. C. Peirse from Count Stephan Zamoyski (4 January 1941), in Folder 9B (Correspondence with CinC, Bomber Command, 1941), Papers of Lord Portal, Christ Church, Oxford.

2. Letter, Peirse to Portal, 8 January 1941, in Portal Papers, Folder 9B. Peirse added: "I feel pretty sure that when our Polish Wellington squadrons are fully trained we shall have a good deal of pressure exerted upon us to let them undertake . . . attacks on targets in Poland."

3. Letter, Portal to Peirse, 12 January 1941, Portal Papers, folder 9B.

4. Letter, Peirse to Sikorski, 15 January 1941, Portal Papers, folder 9B.

5. The most forthright and comprehensive examination of Bomber Command's capabilities in this period can be found in Sir Charles Webster and Noble Frankland, *The Strategic Air Offensive against Germany 1939–1945*, vol. I (London, 1961). For loss rate information, see vol. IV (Annexes and Appendices), 445–446.

6. The one-in-five figure related to total sorties flown. Not all planes sent out, however, would reach the target. If one counts only the planes recorded as attacking the target, then about one in three got within five miles. For the results of the photo-reconnaissance report (the Butt Report), see Webster and Frankland, *Strategic Air Offensive*, IV:205–213.

7. On Peirse's response, see ibid., I:179. For Churchill's comment, see Personal Minute, Churchill to CAS (Portal), 3 September 1941, in the Portal Papers, Folder 2B, Prime Minister's Minutes, July–September 1941.

8. For the 1942 directive, see Webster and Frankland, *Strategic Air Offensive*, I:322–24, and IV:142–48.

9. On the Declaration of December 1942, see Martin Gilbert, *Auschwitz and the Allies* (New York, 1981), 93–105. Despite the fact that information on the mass exterminations was available, many people had great difficulty believing it. Deborah Lipstadt has shown that in a Gallup poll taken in January 1943, nearly 30 percent of those questioned believed that the news of two million Jewish deaths at the hands of the Nazis was "just a rumor." Another 24 percent had no opinion on the question. See Deborah Lipstadt, *Beyond Belief* (New York, 1986), 240–41.

10. Portal quoted in Gilbert, *Auschwitz and the Allies*, 106–07.

11. It should be noted here that a critical means of helping the Jews of Europe had already been forfeited when free governments, including the United States and Britain, had refused to allow increased numbers of Jews to immigrate to their nations in the late 1930s. See David Wyman, *The Abandonment of the Jews* (New York, 1984), esp. 6–9.

12. On this period, see Wesley Frank Craven and James Lea Cate, *The Army Air Forces in World War II* (Chicago, 1948), I:105–35.

13. See Churchill's letters to Roosevelt (16 September 1942) and Harry Hopkins (16 October 1942), along with other relevant correspondence in AIR 8/711, Public Record Office (PRO), London. See also Webster and Frankland, *Strategic Air Offensive*, I:353–63.

14. Craven and Cate, *Army Air Forces*, II:304–07 and 353–57.

15. Ibid., II:371–72.

16. See, for instance, Harris, untitled paper with covering note to Portal, 3 September 1942, in AIR 8/424; Harris to Portal, 21 October 1942, Portal Papers, Folder 9C; Harris to Lord Trenchard, 14 August 1942; and Harris to Trenchard, 25 January 1943, Folder 50, Papers of Sir Arthur Harris, RAF Museum Archive, Hendon, UK.

17. On the general issue of civilian intervention in strategic targeting, see Richard G. Davis, "Royal Air Force/United States Air Force Cooperation," in *Proceedings of the Royal Air Force Historical Society* 9 (1991). My argument regarding Churchill's tendencies is derived from his rate of correspondence with Portal over the years of Portal's service as chief of air staff.

18. Craven and Cate, *Army Air Forces*, II:704.

19. On the American effort to win air superiority over Europe, see Stephen McFarland and Wesley Phillips Newton, *To Command the Sky* (Washington, DC, 1991).

20. On American air strategy and Anglo-American relations, see Tami Davis Biddle, "British and American Approaches to Strategic Bombing: Their Origins and Implementation in the World War II Combined Bomber Offensive," *Journal of Strategic Studies* 18 (March 1995), 91–144.

21. Craven and Cate, *Army Air Forces*, II:564–66.

22. Tami Davis Biddle, "Air War," in Michael Howard, George Andreopoulos, and Mark Shulman, eds., *The Laws of War* (New Haven, 1994); Richard G. Davis, "German Rail Yards and Cities: U.S. Bombing Policy, 1944–1945" *Air Power History* 42 (Summer 1995), 47–63, esp. 52–53.

23. For discussions of accuracy and comparisons between the American and British strategic bombing forces, see W. Hays Parks, " 'Precision' and 'Area' Bombing": Who Did Which, and When?" *Journal of Strategic Studies* 18 (March 1995), 145–74.

24. See Craven and Cate, *Army Air Forces*, II:564–74.

25. See Davis, "German Rail Yards and Cities," 48–49.

26. See Parks, " 'Precision' and 'Area' Bombing," 155–56.

27. Richard G. Davis, *Carl A. Spaatz and the Air War in Europe* (Washington, DC, 1993), 271.

28. Parks, " 'Precision' and 'Area' Bombing," 156.

29. United States Strategic Bombing Survey, Oil Division, Final Report, 2nd ed. (January 1947), 121.

30. See Webster and Frankland, *Strategic Air Offensive*, II: 179–89.

31. See "The Royal Air Force and Clandestine Operations in North-West Europe," in *Proceedings of the Royal Air Force Historical Society* 5 (February 1989), 12 and 22.

32. See "Final Minutes of a Meeting Held on Saturday March 25th to Discuss the Bombing Policy in the Period before 'Overlord,' " in AIR 37/1125, PRO, Kew. On the preinvasion period generally, see Craven and Cate, *Army Air Forces*, III:138–81; and W. W. Rostow, *Pre-Invasion Bombing Strategy* (Austin, 1981). On the organization of the air command arrangements, see generally Davis, "Royal Air Force/United States Air Force Cooperation."

33. Davis, "German Rail Yards and Cities," 54.

34. See, in particular, Alfred C. Mierzejewski, *The Collapse of the German War Economy, 1944–1945* (Chapel Hill, NC, 1988).

35. On heavy bombers for close support, see Davis, *Spaatz*, 453–82; Craven and Cate, *Army Air Forces*, III:228–38.

36. Davis, *Spaatz*, 502–03.

37. Ibid., 426–432.

38. Craven and Cate, *Army Air Forces*, III:173.

39. Ibid., III:172–76.

40. Eisenhower memorandum to Tedder quoted in Davis, *Spaatz*, 430.

41. Goering quoted in ibid., 442.

42. See F. H. Hinsley et al., *British Intelligence in the Second World War*, vol. III, Part 2 (New York, 1988), 497–532.

43. According to the United States Strategic Bombing Survey (USSBS), "Any cloud cover tended to decrease bombing accuracy. Cloud cover became extremely critical as a cause of error once 5/10 coverage was reached. With this cloud cover, the number of visual sightings decreased enormously, and the accuracy on those obtained was poor." USSBS, "Bombing Accuracy, USAAF Heavy and Medium Bombers in the ETO," Military Analysis Division Report No. 3, 1 and 5.

44. Davis, *Spaatz*, 440, 443.

45. They added: "Any relaxation of the tempo of our attacks against his oil installations will provide opportunity for rehabilitation and dispersal. On the other hand a successful campaign against enemy oil at this time may well have repercussions upon the enemy's ability to fight on the French, Italian, and Russian fronts which may prove decisive." CCS 520/3 (Octagon) 12 September 1944, "Control of Strategic Bomber Forces in Europe following the Establishment of Allied Forces on the Continent," Spaatz Papers, Diary, Box 18, Library of Congress Manuscripts Division, Washington, D.C.

46. Davis, *Spaatz*, 440.

47. The idea was straightforward: American bombers would take off from their home bases, fly to deep targets, bomb them, and then land at a designated base in the Soviet Union. The bombers would then stay the night (or perhaps several nights) at the Soviet base before returning home to Western bases. As the American official historians explained, it would offer an opportunity to demonstrate to the Russians "how eager the Americans were to wage war on the German enemy in every possible way and to gain from the Russians a fuller appreciation of the contribution of the strategic air forces to the war effort." See Craven and Cate, *Army Air Forces,* III:309.

48. On the shuttle mission flown on 21 June, a German He 111 aircraft tailed the B-17s and P-51s of the Eighth Air Force. Five hours later, a large group of German bombers attacked the Soviet airfield where the Americans had landed, destroyed or damaged 69 of the 114 B-17s in the force, and ignited virtually all of the aviation gasoline that had been brought into Russia. The surviving aircraft, many patched up, flew back to bases in Italy on 26 June, bombing an oil plant at Drohobycz, in Poland, on the way. There were no shuttle missions flown for a month afterward, in part because the strategic bombers were fully occupied with supporting the ground invasion, and in part because of continuing Soviet objections to targeting plans. In late July and early August, task forces comprised strictly of fighter aircraft made use of Russian bases in order to strafe airfields and railroads in Rumania. On August 6–8, another heavy bomber shuttle mission was flown. On the way to Russia, it attacked a Focke-Wulf factory in Poland, and on the way back it struck the oil refineries at Trzebinia, near Auschwitz. Only one more regular shuttle mission was flown (11–13 September): it targeted an armaments plant at Chemnitz and steelworks in Hungary. See Craven and Cate, vol. III, 311–16.

49. Gerhard Weinberg, *A World at Arms* (New York, 1994), 734.

50. Craven and Cate, *Army Air Forces,* III:316–17.

51. For Slessor's account of the Warsaw Uprising and the dilemma in which he was placed, see *The Central Blue* (New York, 1957), 611–21 (the quote is from 611–12).

52. "Costly and hopeless" are the terms used by the U.S. official historians to describe the feelings toward the mission held by the War Department and the air staff. Their assessment is based in part on a letter from Gen. L. Kuter to Gen. F. Anderson, 3 October 1944. See Craven and Cate, *Army Air Forces,* III:317.

53. Portal-Harris Correspondence, Nov. 1944–January 1945, in Portal Papers, folders 10 B and 10 C; Davis, *Spaatz,* 496; Webster and Frankland, *Strategic Air Offensive,* III:241–43; and F. H. Hinsley et al., *British Intelligence,* III/2:514, 516 and 531.

54. Davis, *Spaatz,* 504.

55. For further detail, see Wyman, *The Abandonment of the Jews,* Chapter XV.

56. McCloy's biographer has written that McCloy "became the country's first national-security manager, a sort of 'political commissar' who quietly brokered any issue where civilian political interests threatened to interfere with the military's effort to win the war." Kai Bird, *The Chairman* (New York, 1992), 175.

57. See memo by Thomas T. Handy, Asst. Chief of Staff, "The Proposed Air Action to Impede Deportation of Hungarian and Slovak Jews," 23 June 1944. Reprinted in David Wyman, ed., *American and the Holocaust* (New York, 1990), XII:107.

58. See Wyman, *The Abandonment of the Jews,* 291; and *America and the Holocaust,* XII:120 and 128.

59. Letter, Sinclair to Eden, 15 July 1944, FO 371/42809, Public Record Office, Kew. It is reprinted in Gilbert, *Auschwitz and the Allies,* 285. Regarding the Americans, Sinclair's exact wording was: "I am proposing to have the proposition put to the Americans, with all the facts, to see if they are prepared to try it. I am very doubtful indeed, whether, when they have examined it, the Americans will think it possible, and I do not wish to raise any hopes."

60. Letter, Richard Law to Chaim Weizmann, 1 September 1944, quoted in Gilbert, *Auschwitz and the Allies*, 306.

61. The text of the Anderson message is reprinted in Wyman, ed., *America and the Holocaust*, XII:174.

62. Pehle's letter to McCloy is reprinted in ibid., XII:175–76.

63. Memorandum for the record, 14 November 1944, OPD 000.5 (8 November 1944), reprinted in ibid, XII:181.

64. For a detailed account of McCloy's thinking and behavior on this issue, see Bird, *The Chairman*, 201–27.

65. During the second raid on Monowitz on 13 September, some bombs fell outside the industrial targets and accidentally landed on Birkenau instead. Gilbert examines the raids taking place near Auschwitz. See *Auschwitz and the Allies*, 282, and 315–17.

4. THE AERIAL PHOTOS OF THE AUSCHWITZ-BIRKENAU EXTERMINATION COMPLEX
Dino A. Brugioni

1. Dino A. Brugioni and Robert G. Poirier, *The Holocaust Revisited: A Retrospective Analysis of the Auschwitz-Birkenau Extermination Complex*, CIA report no. ST-79-10001 (Washington, D.C., February 1979).

PART II: BOMBING AUSCHWITZ: FOR AND AGAINST
INTRODUCTORY REMARKS
Michael J. Neufeld

1. David S. Wyman, "Why Auschwitz Wasn't Bombed," in *Anatomy of the Auschwitz Death Camp*, eds. Yisrael Gutman and Michael Berenbaum (Bloomington and Indianapolis, Ind., 1994), 569–87; "Why Auschwitz Was Never Bombed," *Commentary* 65 (May 1978), 37–46; *The Abandonment of the Jews* (New York, 1984), 288–307, 406–10 (Chapter 15).

2. Wyman, "Why Auschwitz Wasn't Bombed," 569.

3. Wyman also responded to Kitchens and Levy in letters to *The Journal of Military History* 61 (April 1997), 433–37 (with Kitchens's rejoinder), and *Holocaust and Genocide Studies* 11 (Fall 1997), 277–80 (reply to Levy).

5. THE CONTEMPORARY CASE FOR THE FEASIBILITY OF BOMBING AUSCHWITZ
Martin Gilbert

1. With the exception of the interview with Sir Leonard (later Lord) Cheshire, which is from the transcript of the BBC Television documentary "Auschwitz and the Allies," producer Rex Bloomstein, first transmitted on 16 July 1981, all the quotations in this chapter are taken from documents cited in Martin Gilbert, *Auschwitz and the Allies* (New York: Henry Holt/Owl Books, 1982/London: Madarin Books, 1991).

7. THE BOMBING OF AUSCHWITZ RE-EXAMINED
James H. Kitchens III

1. It is, of course, true that information about the annihilation of European Jews began to seep out of Europe by various channels during 1941–42. This information, however, was quite fragmented, was transmitted orally, and usually could not be substantiated by documents, photographs, signals intercepts, or other means of conventional military intelligence. As Walter Laqueur perceptively points out, the credibility of German mass murder at this time was also seriously impaired by public recollection of how German atrocity reports from World War I had been debunked during the 1920s and 30s. Laqueur, *The Terrible Secret* (New York, 1980).

2. The Košice-Prešov line was a key north-south segment of track leading northward out of Hungary over which Jews deported from Budapest to Auschwitz most likely would have traveled. Košice lay in northern Hungary, while Prešov lay almost due north in Slovakia. For a map of the Hungarian and Slovakian rail nets pertinent to the Weissmandel message, one should see Martin Gilbert, *Auschwitz and the Allies* (New York, 1981), 247.

3. See Gilbert, *Auschwitz and the Allies*, 209, 216–17, 219–20, 236–37, 245. Because Gilbert treated the bombing idea as but one element in the unveiling of Auschwitz's horrors, his narration of its initial development is somewhat discontinuous. Despite the complexities of narration, however, *Auschwitz and the Allies* remains the most thorough account of the origins of the bombing idea and its reception during the World War II period.

4. Ibid., 246.

5. David S. Wyman, *The Abandonment of the Jews* (New York, 1984), 292; Bernard Wasserstein, *Britain and the Jews of Europe, 1939–1945* (Oxford, 1979), 308–20; Gilbert, *Auschwitz and the Allies*, 299–311.

6. On 1 July 1944, Leon Kubowitzki, head of the Rescue Department of the World Jewish Congress, wrote to the U.S. War Refugee Board to oppose proposals to bomb Auschwitz. Any bombing would, Kubowitzki thought, itself kill Jews held in the camp and would offer an opportunity for the Germans to make a propaganda advantage of such deaths. Gilbert, *Auschwitz and the Allies*, 256, citing letter of 1 July 1944, War Refugee Board, Box 33, Measures Directed towards Halting Persecutions, F: Hungary No.5.

7. Arthur D. Morse, *While Six Million Died: A Chronicle of American Apathy* (New York, 1968). See especially Morse's remarks on 383. Morse did not introduce the bombing issue, nor did he inculpate Allied military authorities in responsibility for the German genocide.

8. John Morton Blum, *V Was for Victory: Politics and American Culture during World War II* (New York, 1976), 172–181.

9. David S. Wyman, "Why Auschwitz Was Never Bombed," *Commentary* 65 (May 1978), 37–49. The article was unannotated, but at the end the author provided a list of principal archival sources consulted. In a follow-on letter published in July 1978 issue, Wyman offered to furnish a full set of footnotes in exchange for photocopy costs and a self-addressed, stamped envelope.

10. Roger M. Williams, "Why Wasn't Auschwitz Bombed? An American Moral Tragedy," *Commonweal* 105 (24 November 1978), 746–51.

11. Ibid., 750.

12. See, for example, Gilbert's surprising conclusion on 341 that in the summer of 1944, "the American government possessed a great deal of information about Auschwitz, including both its location and its function, *together with the technical ability to bomb both the railway lines leading to the camp and the gas chambers in the camp itself*" [Kitchens's italics].

13. Morton Mintz, "Why Didn't We Bomb Auschwitz?" *Washington Post*, 17 Apr. 1983, D-1, D-2. Alan Brinkley, "Minister without Portfolio," *Harper's* (Feb. 1983), 31–46, is a miniature biography of John Jay McCloy, influential special assistant to Secretary of War Henry Stimson, which includes a lengthy passage on McCloy and the Holocaust.

14. New York, 1984.

15. The author summarized twelve potential rescue measures under the heading "What Might Have Been Done," 331–34.

16. The Vrba-Wetzler report has been published in full in David S. Wyman, ed., *America and the Holocaust* (New York, 1990), "The Extermination Camps of Auschwitz (Oswie-

cim) and Birkenau in Upper Silesia," XII:3–44. (See document 1.2 in Part IV of this volume.)

17. The I. G. Farben works at Monowitz were approximately two and one-half miles east of Auschwitz town and about three to four miles east of the Auschwitz II or Birkenau concentration camp. The Monowitz factory complex produced synthetic oil and rubber and became the object of repeated Allied bombing during the summer of 1944. Monowitz had a separate slave labor camp attached which was not part of the Auschwitz-Birkenau facility.

18. Frantic was the cover name given to long-range USAAF strategic bomber operations which used Russian bases at Poltava, Mirgorod, and Piryatin, all east of Kiev, as staging points. Under the Frantic plan, bombers which normally would have bombed their objectives and returned to bases in England or Italy would instead land in Russia, where they would receive ordnance, fuel, and maintenance. It was not envisioned that these Frantic bases would become permanent homes for heavy bomber groups or their fighter escorts. The first Fifteenth Air Force Frantic mission was carried out on 2 June 1944; D-Day in France delayed the first such Eighth Air Force operation until 21 June. Frantic missions continued throughout the summer of 1944 but were eventually discontinued for various reasons.

19. Wyman, *Abandonment*, 292, quoting O.P.D. D/F (Hull to C.A.D.), 26 June 1944, NA RG 165(1).

20. See *New York Times*, 4 Nov. 1984, C13, and 24 Dec. 1984, 11; *New York Times Book Review*, 16 Dec. 1984, 1, 16; 17 Mar. 1985, 38; 31 Mar. 1985, 34; 7 Apr. 1985, 22; 28 Apr. 1985, 36.

21. In addition to the *New York Times Book Review*, 16 Dec. 1984, 1, 16, see reviews in *Library Journal*, 1 Oct. 1984, 1848; *Nation*, 15 Dec. 1984, 656-57; *Commentary* 72 (Apr. 1985), 70–75; *American Historical Review* 90 (Dec. 1985): 1294–95; *Choice* 22 (Apr. 1985), 1220; *Journal of American History* 72 (June 1985), 186–87.

22. *The Encyclopedia of the Holocaust* (New York, 1990), s.v. "Auschwitz, Bombing of" by David S. Wyman. One should also see Wyman's defense of his previous assertions in a letter to the *Washington Post*, 21 Apr. 1990, A23.

23. For example, Leni Yahil writes in *The Holocaust: The Fate of European Jewry, 1932–1945* (New York, 1990), 639, that "Research has shown that the refusal of the American and British air forces to bomb these installations [Auschwitz and Birkenau] stemmed from their disinclination to be involved with rescue actions per se." For her two-page passage "No Bombing of Auschwitz-Birkenau," Yahil's footnotes 20, 21, 22, and 23, 638–39, cite only Wyman's Ch. XV from *Abandonment of the Jews* and Gilbert, *Auschwitz and the Allies*. See also Michael R. Marrus, *The Holocaust in History* (Hanover, NH, 1987), 193–94, and Michael Berenbaum, *After Tragedy and Triumph: Essays in Modern Jewish Thought and the American Experience* (Cambridge, 1990), 9, 82.

24. See Executive Director Sara J. Bloomfield's letter to the *Washington Post*, 24 Mar. 1990, A19, where she states that "the United States and its allies, fully aware of the murder factories in Poland, failed to act and *even declined to bomb the death camps, though the knowledge and the opportunity existed*" [Kitchens's italics]. *The Directory of American Scholars* (New York: R. R. Bowker Co., 1982), History, "Wyman, David S.," I:847, lists the author as a special advisor to the Council.

25. *New York Tribune*, 23 Apr. 1990, 1.

26. Equipped with a mix of B-17 Flying Fortresses, B-24 Liberators, and escort fighters, the Fifteenth Air Force made up the USAAF's strategic bombing force in the Mediterranean Theater of Operations after the spring of 1944. By May it was operating several hundred heavy bombers and fighters from a complex of bases around Foggia on the eastern coast of southern Italy. Though slightly younger as an organization, the Fifteenth Air Force

grew to become comparable in size, striking power, and effectiveness with the USAAF's Eighth Air Force which operated out of England after August 1942.

27. The letter is in *Commentary* 65 (July 1978), 10–11.

28. Richard S. Levy, reviewer for *Commentary*, was an associate professor of history at the University of Chicago and a specialist in anti-Semitism, Jewish history, immigration history, and Holocaust studies; Leonard Dinnerstein, reviewer for the *Journal of American History*, was professor of history at the University of Arizona and a specialist in American Jewish history; Jonathan D. Sarna, reviewer for *Library Journal*, was an assistant professor of history at Hebrew Union College and a specialist in American Jewish history; B. Kraut, reviewer for *Choice*, was an associate professor of Judaica at the University of Cincinnati and a specialist in modern Jewish history and modern Judaism. See *Directory of American Scholars*, vol. 1, *History, passim*.

29. Richard Foregger, "The Bombing of Auschwitz," *Aerospace Historian* 34 (Summer 1987), 98–110.

30. Two commentaries on Foregger's article did subsequently appear in *Aerospace Historian*, but neither came from the Holocaust studies community or from academic historians. Both included a number of digressions from the basic questions, and neither added anything substantive to the basic Wyman-Foregger dialogue. See Robert H. Hodges, "The Bombing of Auschwitz': A Clarification," and Michael G. Moskow, "The Bombing of Auschwitz': A Reply," in *Aerospace Historian* 35 (Summer 1988), 123–29.

31. Amherst, MA, 1968.

32. Wyman defined "nativistic nationalism" as an attitude held by patriotic and veterans' groups which reflected pride in "100 percent Americanism," a sentiment which he thought manifested a certain anti-alienism. Many nativistic nationalists sought to limit immigration, if not to deport aliens, as deleterious to the American body politic.

33. Wesley Frank Craven and James Lea Cate, eds., *The Army Air Forces in World War II*, vol. III, *Europe: ARGUMENT to V-E Day, January 1944 to May 1945* (Chicago, 1951); Charles Webster and Noble Frankland, *The Strategic Air Offensive against Germany, 1939–1945*, vol. III (London, 1961).

34. Phillip Birtles, *Mosquito: A Pictorial History of the DH98* (London, 1980).

35. Glenn Infield, *The Poltava Affair* (New York, 1973).

36. James F. Sunderman, ed., *World War II in the Air: Europe* (New York, 1963).

37. Sunderman's *World War II in the Air: Europe* contains elementary tables of USAAF aircraft characteristics in an appendix. These tables, however, are far from adequate for assessing the aircraft in question. No information, for example, is presented about the B-25J models which equipped the USAAF's Twelfth Air Force squadrons in the Mediterranean Theater in 1944.

38. C. Martin Sharp and Michael J. F. Bowyer, *Mosquito* (London, 1967). Although older than Birtles's book, *Mosquito* is a much more detailed and informative work containing twenty-three appendices and a detailed text with important data not found in Birtles. Michael J. F. Bowyer's 2 *Group R.A.F.: A Complete History, 1936–1945* (London, 1974), also could have enlightened Wyman about special Mosquito operations analogous to camp attacks, and Philip J. R. Moyes's *Bomber Squadrons of the R.A.F.*, new edition (London, 1976), could have furnished order of battle data about Mosquito units, but neither is cited.

39. There are also indications that the writer selectively used the sources he does cite: the RAF Bomber Command's 17 April 1942 operation against the M.A.N. diesel engine works at Augsburg, for example, had many similarities to one model of assault on Auschwitz and is described at length in Webster and Frankland's official history, yet it is not noted in *Abandonment*.

40. Most, but not all, of the USAF Historical Research Center's files are duplicated on 16mm

microfilm at the Office of Air Force History, Bolling AFB, Washington, D.C., and it is conceivable that Wyman or a proxy performed research there. If that were the case, however, there is no bibliographic statement in *Abandonment* to suggest it.

41. The USAF Historical Research Center is a direct reporting unit of headquarters USAF in Washington, D.C. Its collections originated with the institution of a USAAF historical program in 1942; files collected at the Pentagon during the war, together with unit histories up to that point, were moved to Maxwell in the late 1940s to support research and education at the Air University. Today the Center holds approximately sixty million pages of documents on approximately three linear miles of shelving, of which approximately one-third to one-half treat the World War II period.

42. The Mediterranean Allied Air Forces was a joint USAAF-RAF command in the Mediterranean Theater which controlled all of the Allied air power assets there. MAAF's major elements included the Fifteenth and Twelfth AFs and several large constituent elements from the RAF such as 205 Group and the Balkans Air Force. The Historical Research Center's MAAF microfilm collection reproduces the MAAF headquarters files from formation of the force in 1943 to approximately late 1944.

43. An examination of the Spaatz documents cited in Chapter XV, footnotes 34, 40, 41, 49, 57, 62, and 75 reveals that these are uniformly correspondence, cables, and minutes of staff meetings and not the war plans, studies, reports, and operational records upon which Spaatz and Eaker based their opinions and decisions. Thus, this selection of sources from personal papers also reflects Wyman's focus on bombing policy rather than the operational constraints surrounding policy.

44. See Wyman, *Abandonment*, 301–02.

45. An excellent plan drawing of Crematory and Gas Chamber III at Birkenau has been published in Anna Pawelczynska, *Values and Violence in Auschwitz*, trans. by Catherine S. Leach (Berkeley, 1979), 31. Another less detailed plan is in Rudolf Höss, *Death Dealer: The Memoirs of the SS Kommandant at Auschwitz*, ed. Stephen Paskuly (Buffalo, NY, 1992). The Paskuly edition also contains several external and internal photographs of Birkenau's gas chambers and crematoria which are helpful in analyzing them as bombing targets.

46. The maps and diagrams of Auschwitz provided in Gilbert, *Auschwitz and the Allies*, 193 and 195, are indispensable references to the problem of the area's camps as aerial targets. These maps and diagrams were published three years before *Abandonment* appeared. Diagrams of Auschwitz I ("Main") and of Birkenau are also available in Pawelczynska, *Values and Violence in Auschwitz*, 26–27.

47. The large slave labor camp at I. G. Farben's Monowitz works also killed hundreds of thousands through overwork, disease, starvation, and other causes, but presumably because it possessed no easily targetable gas chambers or crematoria and existed as a labor adjunct to the chemical works it was not included as a potential target in Wyman's thesis.

48. Dino Brugioni, "Auschwitz-Birkenau: Why the World War II Photo Interpreters Failed to Identify the Extermination Complex," *Military Intelligence* 9 (Jan.–Mar. 1983): 50–55, and Dino Brugioni and Robert G. Poirier, *The Holocaust Revisited: A Retrospective Analysis of the Auschwitz-Birkenau Extermination Complex* (Washington, DC, 1979), NTIS ST-7910001, are indispensable for understanding the problem of interpretation and intelligence appreciation of the Auschwitz aerial photographs made in 1944.

49. Two important pieces of evidence indicate just how little was known about the Holocaust in Allied intelligence circles. USAFHRC 512.6162-1, 10 Oct. 1944, "Axis Concentration Camps and Detention Camps Reported as Such in Europe," British War Office (M1 14), 10 Oct. 1944 (originally Secret, declassified 22 Sep. 1972) was a 105-page report which attempted to summarize the concentration camp intelligence then in hand. An examination of this document, prepared at the highest levels of the wartime intelligence ap-

paratus, clearly shows that the Allies had no exact knowledge of the number of camps the Germans were operating, where the camps were located, how many internees there were, or to what overall purpose the detainees were being held. This document is not included in Wyman's bibliography or notes. A footnote in F. H. Hinsley et al., *British Intelligence in the Second World War* (London, 1988), III/2:736, states that Ultra—the most sensitive intelligence available to the Allies from intercepted radio traffic—made scarcely any references to concentration camps. "There were," the authors note, "no Sigint [signal intelligence] references to the extermination camps" before April 1945 apart from "a few Police decrypts in the second half of 1944 and early 1945 about the movement into concentration camps of Jews from France, Hungary, and the Baltic States and about the use of camp inmates as forced labor." The reason, of course, was that for clarity and security the Germans used land lines not subject to eavesdropping wherever possible.

50. Gilbert, *Auschwitz and the Allies*, 190–239; Wyman, *Abandonment*, 288–96.

51. Several maps associated with the Vrba-Wetzler report have been published. Document 1, "The Extermination Camps of Auschwitz (Oswiecim) and Birkenau in Upper Silesia," November 1944, in Wyman, *America and the Holocaust*, vol. XII, reproduces three sketches from a copy in the FDR Library, OF 5477, War Refugee Board, German Extermination Camps-Auschwitz and Birkenau. Another sketch, taken from an original in the Public Record Office, is available in Foregger, "The Bombing of Auschwitz," 98–99.

52. Foregger, "The Bombing of Auschwitz," 108. The sketch map, titled "Topographical Sketch of the Concentration Camp at Oswiecim/Auschwitz" is reproduced in Foregger's article. It bears the notation "Drawn according to the description of a former prisoner of the camp."

53. Sharp and Bowyer, *Mosquito*, 241.

54. Vis airfield was lengthened to 3,600 feet in the autumn of 1944.

55. USAFHRC 638.01-1, 1943-1944, AAF Engineer Command, Mediterranean Theater of Operations (Prov.), "Airfields in the Mediterranean Theater of Operations"; USAFHRC 638.245, Jul.–Aug. 1944 and Jul. 1945, HG AAF Engineer Command, Mediterranean Theater of Opertions (Prov.), "Airfields Status Report," 1 July 1944. The July 1945 edition of "Airfield Status Report" has a small map of the airfield. For the absence of permanent combat units on the island, see USAFHRC 622.6318, Jan–Dec. 1944, HQ MAAF, "Order of Battle—Mediterranean Allied Air Forces, Royal Air Force," monthly reports stating the duty stations of each Allied combat unit in the MTO. Vis' primitive, precarious, and clandestine existence is made clear from USAFHRC 622.01–1, MAAF Microfilm Project, Roll 272, Section 376, "Defense of Vis," and Section 377, "Use of Vis for Operation of Advanced Air Forces." On 18 June 1944, RAF 242 Group specifically warned HQ MAAF about the dangers of aircraft making forced landings there. "Your A245 [message dated] 2 May," it advised, "is being continually ignored and situation on Vis is becoming increasingly intolerable. On 16 June 5 Liberators and 1 Lightning landed there. This frequent landing and crash landing of heavy aircraft seriously jeopardizes operations and could easily lead to disastrous consequences." USAFHRC 622.01-1, MAAF Microfilm Project, Roll 272, Section 377, "Use of Vis for Operation of Advanced Air Forces."

56. Wyman made no effort to identify the Luftwaffe order of battle defending Auschwitz-Birkenau, and it is surprising that subsequent commentators such as Hodges and Moskow have largely ignored the question in favor of generalities about the effectiveness of the German fighter force in mid-1944.

57. For the figure of seventy-nine guns around Monowitz, see the 5th Bombardment Wing's intelligence briefing for the wing's 20 Aug. 1944 attack on the Farben works in "Annex to Operations Order No. 671 for 20 August 1944." USAFHRC WG-5-HI, Aug. 1944, Unit History, 5th Bombardment Wing, Aug. 1944. German heavy flak pieces ranged from 88 to 128mm. The most numerous German antiaircraft weapon, the 88mm Flak 36, had a

maximum horizontal range of 16,200 yds. (9.2 mi.) and a maximum vertical range of 13,000 yds. (7.3 mi.); thus many pieces emplaced around Monowitz would have coincidentally covered most, if not all, of the Birkenau camp area.

58. A MAAF map of "Approximate Freya Location and Coverage—Western Mediterranean" dated 29 Mar. 1944 shows three Freya sites at Bar, Durazzo, and Fier as positively located and a further four sites at Zara, Split, Dubrovnik, and Lesh as known or believed to exist. These Freya radars operated on several frequencies in the A, B, C, D, and other bands; intruders could be detected at ranges from twelve miles for very low flying planes to sixty miles for those flying at 8,000–10,000 feet. By 31 May, MAAF had also detected several other types of radars in the Dubrovnik area. This meant that German radars could track any aircraft flying at medium altitudes out of USAAF bases in southern Italy from a few minutes after take-off all the way across the Adriatic. *Freyas* could also scan 360°, permitting a degree of tracking inland. Sites in the vicinity of Precko, Sinj, Banja Luka, Vukovar, and other locations permitted German fighter control to follow raids from Yugoslavia to southern Poland. As a rule of thumb, the lower an intruder's altitude, the more difficult tracking became, until, at altitudes of 200–250 ft. or less, radar detection became nearly impossible. Sustained flight to avoid radar detection, however, would have imposed a variety of handicaps and hazards, and interception of voice radio communications always remained a possibility. USAFHRC 622.011, MAAF Microfilm Project, Roll 132, Section 194, "Radar Intelligence—Pt. 1."

59. Documentation of the location of German fighter units in the Balkans and western Hungary at a given moment is quite difficult. In order to maximize its fighter assets, the Luftwaffe became adept at frequently and quickly moving its units from one airfield to another in a way unknown to the Allies; within a day's time, intercepting units might use one airfield as a home base but could be ordered to leapfrog across considerable distances to concentrate against a perceived threat. Assessment of this kind of shifting defense is further complicated by loss of at least 95 percent of the Luftwaffe's operational records at war's end. I am greatly indebted to Henry L. de Zeng IV, a lifelong student of the Luftwaffe in the Balkans, for his invaluable assistance in documenting the German order of battle from diverse published and archival sources.

60. USAFHRC 137.306-3, Jan. 1943–May 1945, USSBS, Military Analysis Division Report No. 3, *A Study on the Bombing Accuracy of the USAAF Heavy and Medium Bombers in the ETO*, 3 November 1945. This USSBS study found that the actual average circular error on ten target complexes in the study ranged between 825 and 1,175 feet. The average circular error of USAAF strategic bombers in Europe diminished from 3,400 feet in January 1943 to a rough average of 1100 feet during 1944–45. In the Fifteenth AF, approximately 30 percent of bombs fell within 1,000 feet of the aiming point during 1944–45.

61. Williams, "Why Wasn't Auschwitz Bombed?" 751.

62. *Auschwitz and the Allies*, 195.

63. Höss, *Death Dealer*, 359, 363.

64. In an independent calculation made in 1983, Pierre M. Sprey, a weapons analyst in the Office of the Assistant Secretary of Defense, estimated that 135 bombers would have been necessary to destroy 50 percent of the gas chambers, crematoria, rail sidings, and loot structure and that one-third of the 1,350 bombs dropped would have hit the prisoner barrack area. Mintz, "Why Wasn't Auschwitz Bombed?" *Washington Post*, 17 Apr. 1983, D2.

65. For details of the mission, see USAFHRC 520.332, 24 Aug. 1944, "Eighth AF Mission Report [for Operation 568], 24 August 1944." Casualty figures are from "Die Toten des Bombenangriffs vom 24. August 1944," a written report of SS-Hauptsturmführer d. R. Gerhard Schiedlausky, medical officer at Weimar, to Chef des Amt D III of the WVHA

Berlin-Oranienburg dated 27 August 1944, attached to a 1 October 1991 letter from Sqdn. Leader Stanley A. Booker (Ret.) to the USAFHRC Inquiries Branch. Sqdn. Leader Booker was incarcerated in Buchenwald at the time of the raid and witnessed it and the aftermath from an internee's perspective. A copy of Sqdn. Leader Booker's letter, together with the SS report, is on file at USAFHRC, Inquiries Branch, internal reference file "Buchenwald." A copy is also in the author's possession.

66. Craven and Cate, eds., *The AAF in World War II*, make one brief reference to AZON in vol. III, *Europe: ARGUMENT to V-E Day*, 728. This scarcely acknowledges the existence of AZON bombs and says nothing about their technology or M.T.O. testing. The reason for this is almost certainly the cloak of security surrounding guided weapons at the time Craven and Cate were writing (1951 in the case of vol. III): largely because of such security considerations, the Fifteenth Air Forces's report on the accuracy and effectiveness of AZON bombs was not declassified until 1972. See USAFHRC 670.310-1, Fifteenth AF, Operations Analysis Section, "AZON Bombing-Fifteenth AF," 2 October 1944, declassified by Executive Order 11652 on 10 Mar. 1972. Such security considerations also help explain why Sunderman, *World War II in the Air*, makes no mention of the weapon. There was no reason for Infield to mention AZON in connection with Poltava, and the USSBS says little, if anything, about the bomb, probably because as a weapon in development it played no significant part in the strategic air war.

67. USAFHRC 670.310-1, Fifteenth AF, Operations Analysis Section, "Azon Bombing—Fifteenth Air Force," 2 Oct. 1944. I am also indebted to Dr. Kenneth A. Werrell and Ernest Helton for access to their findings on AZON bombing presented in a forthcoming unit history of the 301st Bomb Group and to David Friday, M.A. candidate in history at Auburn University, whose thesis deals with the wartime development and testing of AZON.

68. A hi-lo-hi mission would have entailed a high altitude approach to the target, a low altitude run-in and bomb release, and a high altitude return to base.

69. James Dugan and Carroll Stewart, *Ploesti: The Great Ground-Air Battle of 1 August 1943* (New York, 1962), 222.

70. Webster and Frankland, *Strategic Air Offensive*, I:441–43.

71. The range of the B-25Js operated by Twelfth Air Force's 57th Bomb Wing in the summer of 1944 was 1350 miles with 3,000 lbs. of bombs. Adverse winds, a zig-zag route, navigational errors, or other factors might well have caused critical fuel shortages, even allowing for the possibility of emergency landings on Vis.

72. During the summer of 1944, Twelfth Air Force B-25s totaled 192 aircraft in 310th, 321th, and 340th Bomb Groups under the 57th Bomb Wing. USAFHRC 622.6318, Jul. 1944, HQ MAAF, Order of Battle—Mediterranean Allied Air Forces, Royal Air Force, as at 31st July 1944, 9–10.

73. Kenn Rust, *The Twelfth AF Story* (Temple City, CA, 1975), 35.

74. Wyman, *Abandonment*, 303.

75. USAFHRC 622.424-6, Aug. 1943–Aug. 1944, HQ MAAF, Ploesti Records Obtained in Roumania.

76. USAFHRC GP-82-HI(FI), Jun. 1944, 82nd Fighter Group Unit History, June 1944, 2; USAFHRC GP-1-HI(FI), Jun. 1944; 1st Fighter Group Unit History, June 1944, 2.

77. Wyman, *Abandonment*, 303.

78. " 'The Bombing of Auschwitz': A Clarification," *Aerospace Historian* 35 (Summer 1988), 124. The *Aerospace Historian* simply described Hodges as "a former USAAF pilot." There is no indication that he had any flying time in Mosquitoes or had any personal familiarity with the aircraft.

79. Wyman, *Abandonment*, 303–63.

80. USAFHRC 622.6318, Jan.–June 1944, HQ MAAF, Order of Battle—Mediterranean Allied

Air Forces, Royal Air Force, as at 30th June, 1944, 15–16, 18, 22. Although one cannot be certain, it is doubtful that Munday, a long-serving and highly experienced archivist at the Air Historical Branch, misinformed Wyman. The author believes it more probable that Wyman, not especially familiar with the complexities of the Mosquito family, simply asked Munday how many D.H.98s were present in the Mediterranean Theater in June 1944, and the archivist correctly replied with a gross total of forty-four.

81. In an unusual break with normal mission assignments, No. 627 Squadron, a target-marking unit from 3 Group, Bomber Command, executed the 31 December 1944 strike against the Gestapo headquarters in Oslo, Norway. So far as the author can determine, this was the only such operation ever mounted by this squadron. Sharp and Bowyer, *Mosquito,* 369.

82. Between 3 October 1943 and 26 May 1944, 2 Group Mosquitoes carried out 155 day-bombing operations and about 1,600 sorties; 464 Squadron executed 78 sorties between 21 and 30 June and 421 sorties between 1 October and 31 December 1944. Operational losses for D.H.98 Mosquito F.B. Mk. VIs (the type used by 140 Wing) averaged 8 percent per month for the sixteen months between January 1944 and April 1945; losses reached 20 percent during February 1945. Sharp and Bowyer, *Mosquito,* 235–59; Michael J. F. Bowyer, 2 *Group R.A.F.: A Complete History, 1936–1945* (London, 1974), 355–415, 473–77.

83. See, for example, Williams's statement that "A strong case can be made for the feasibility and effectiveness of bombing several targets connected with the Hungarian episode of the Final Solution: Auschwitz . . . and the rail lines leading to it; [and] the Budapest railroad yards." Williams, "Why Wasn't Auschwitz Bombed?" 746.

84. For example, in the spring of 1944, the Operational Research Section of IX Bomber Command reported that a 250-lb. general purpose bomb crater on a single-track railroad would take about six hours to repair, and that of a 100-lb. bomb 3.5 hours. Out of a box formation of eighteen aircraft, 5.2 hits with 100-lb. bombs and 3.1 hits with 250-lb. bombs might be expected. "The total hours delay thus produced by a single attack of 18 Marauders loaded with 30 100 lb bombs will be 5.2 × 3.5=18.2 hours, and loaded with 14 250-lb. bombs it will be 3.1 × 6=18.6 hours. These are the hours of daylight delay [in rail traffic]. British experience is that repair cannot be made at night. The delay per mission of 18 planes may be, therefore, taken as 24 hours regardless of whether 100-lb. or 250-lb. bombs are carried." The report concluded, "It is seen that, if the present bombing accuracy is to be expected in these operations, about 1.1 attacking boxes are required per line cut if 100-lb bombs are used, or about 1.4 attacking boxes per line cut if 250-lb. bombs are used." HQ IX Bomber Command, Operational Research Section, "Railway Networks as Joint Objectives for the IX Bomber Command and IX Air Support Command," 18 Mar. 1944, in USAFHRC 534.02, Mar. 1944, History of IX Bomber Command. Bridges were tougher but more rewarding targets. In July 1944, the 1st Operations Analysis Section of Fifteenth Air Force stated that "The probability of obtaining a successful hit on a bridge depends to a marked degree upon its size and construction." It calculated that thirty-six aircraft (one bomb group) each carrying ten 500-lb. bombs had a 19 percent probability of one hit on a bridge 20 × 300 ft.; a 46 percent probability on a bridge 30 × 600 ft.; and a 76 percent probability on a bridge 30 × 1400 ft. In effect, to be reasonably sure of damaging a 30 × 1000 ft. bridge (100 percent probability of one hit), about two bomb groups (50 to 65 aircraft) would have to be dispatched. Absolute certainty of destroying the structure would have required many more aircraft. See HQ IX Bomber Command, 1st Operations Research Section, "Effect of Size and Construction of a Bridge on Probability of Obtaining a Successful Hit," in USAFHRC 670.310-1, Fifteenth AF, Operational Analysis Reports, 1944–1945.

85. See Michael A. Baker's letter to the *Washington Post,* 14 Apr. 1990, A17, in which he writes that "Most critics of the 'no-bomb' policy toward the camps agree that the camps

were difficult targets. Their criticism is that the infrastructure of rail lines, rolling stock, etc., were never attacked. . . . Destroying the transport used by the SS could have saved many who were shipped to the camps in the final year of the war while denying the German army much of its needed transport."

86. Roger A. Freeman, *Mighty Eighth War Diary* (New York, 1981), *passim.*

87. The best single source on the air war against German transportation remains USAFHRC 137.312, 20 Nov. 1945, USSBS, Transportation Division, "The Effects of Strategic Bombing on German Transportation." The ninety-page report contains ninety-nine exhibits, including maps, tables, photographs, and graphs.

88. Department of State, "Laws and Customs of War on Land" (Hague, IV), 18 Oct. 1907, *Treaties and Other International Agreements of the United States* of America, 1776–1949, I:648.

89. War Department, *Rules of Land Warfare*, FM 27-10 (Washington, 1 October 1940), 12. The three examples of "undefended places" given in the manual are: (1) a fort or fortified place, (2) a town surrounded by detached forts, the whole considered as fortified, and (3) "A place that is occupied by a combatant military force or through which a force is passing."

90. See Ronald Schaffer, *Wings of Judgment* (Oxford, 1985). Air war commanders Arnold, Spaatz, Eaker, Doolittle, Anderson, Quesada, LeMay, and Brereton and their staffs were well aware of the moral implications of strategic bombing, and although some of them drifted towards acceptance of Douhetian ideas as the air war in Europe progressed, few if any, lost a repugnance for the killing of wholly innocent civilians.

91. USAFHRC K239.0512-1754, Oral History Interview with Lewis F. Powell dated 26 Feb. 1985. The interview includes subsequent clarifications requested by Chief of Air Force History Dr. Richard Kohn, and Powell's statement is included in these supplementary comments. Maj. Gen. Carl Spaatz commanded the U.S. Strategic Air Forces in Europe (USSTAF) between 6 Jan. 1944 and 3 June 1945. Lewis F. Powell served as a staff intelligence officer with the Army Air Forces. He was trained in Ultra at Bletchley Park, England, during February and March 1944, and in April and May 1944 toured operational commands in the Mediterranean Theater. In May 1944 he became Special Security Representative to Headquarters, U.S. Strategic Air Forces in Europe and in August became Chief of Operational Intelligence of the USSTAF. These wartime experiences gave Powell an insider's view of high-ranking Allied air commanders and the intelligence that was available to them.

8. THE BOMBING OF AUSCHWITZ REVISITED: A CRITICAL ANALYSIS
Richard H. Levy

1. Gideon Hausner, *Justice in Jerusalem* (New York, 1966), 243–44, 344–45; Prosecution Document T/1177 from the Eichmann Trial; Central Zionist Archives Z4/14870. The 11 July document shows Weizmann's pessimistic opinion of the practical value of bombing Auschwitz. Its relationship to the prosecution of Eichmann is unclear.

2. *The Guardian*, 31 May, 3 and 7 June 1961; *Sunday Telegraph* (London), 4 June 1961; and *Jewish Chronicle* (London), 16 Nov. 1962, 25, 43, 14 Dec. 1962, 23, and 11 Jan. 1963, 7.

3. Parliamentary Debates, Commons, Fifth Series, vol. 642 (1961), 202–03. Many documents were later opened to the public.

4. David S. Wyman, "Why Auschwitz Was Never Bombed," *Commentary* 65 (May 1978), 37–46. See also "Letters from Readers" 66 (July 1978), 7 and 10–12; 66 (Sep. 1978), 24–25; and 66 (Nov. 1978), 19–20; David S. Wyman, *The Abandonment of the Jews* (New York, 1984), 288ff.

5. Frank W. Brecher, "David Wyman and the Historiography of America's Response to the Holocaust: Counter-Considerations," *Holocaust and Genocide Studies* 5 (1990), 423–46.

See also Wyman's response in the same issue, 485–86; Lucy S. Dawidowicz, "Could the United States Have Rescued the European Jews from Hitler?" *This World,* no. 12 (Fall 1985), 15, reprinted as "Could America Have Rescued Europe's Jews?" in *What Is the Use of Jewish History?* (New York, 1992); Richard Foregger, "The Bombing of Auschwitz," *Aerospace Historian* 34 (1987), 98–110. See also Robert H. Hodges, "The Bombing of Auschwitz: A Clarification" and Michael G. Moskow, "The Bombing of Auschwitz: A Reply," *Aerospace Historian* 35 (1988), 123–29; James H. Kitchens III, "The Bombing of Auschwitz Re-examined," *Journal of Military History* 58 (Apr. 1994), 233–66; Richard Foregger, "Technical Analysis of Methods to Bomb the Gas Chambers at Auschwitz," *Holocaust and Genocide Studies* 5 (1990), 403–21. See also *Holocaust and Genocide Studies* 6 (1991), 442–43.

6. Martin Gilbert, *Auschwitz and the Allies* (New York, 1982), 236–37. Both dates are given for the second telegram. Gilbert treats these early appeals for railway bombing as quite distinct from the later appeals for bombing Auschwitz itself.

7. Raul Hilberg, *The Destruction of the European Jews* (Chicago, 1961), 543.

8. Wyman, "Auschwitz," 38, and Wyman, *Abandonment,* 290; and Gilbert, *Auschwitz,* 219–20.

9. Gilbert, *Auschwitz,* 223.

10. Wyman, "Auschwitz," 38, and *Abandonment,* 290. The reference to American censorship does not appear in the 1978 article. Gilbert, *Auschwitz,* 236.

11. Wyman, "Auschwitz," 39, and *Abandonment,* 292; and Gilbert, *Auschwitz,* 237. Richard Breitman, "Allied Knowledge of Auschwitz-Birkenau in 1943–1944," in Verne W. Newton, ed., *FDR and the Holocaust* (New York, 1996), 175, has identified several intelligence items relating to Auschwitz which reached the West between March 1943 and January 1944. Some of these were public, others known only to Jewish organizations. He asserts on this basis that planning a bombing raid on Auschwitz might have begun in early 1944. For reasons which may have included failure to separate the intelligence wheat from the chaff, or sheer disbelief, these early reports do not seem to have prompted anyone to propose military action of any kind. The Gruenbaum/Pinkerton and Rosenheim communications and many other documents cited in this study reflect what their authors knew or believed when they were written. The issue of disbelief is thoroughly considered by Deborah E. Lipstadt, *Beyond Belief* (New York, 1986).

12. Gilbert, *Auschwitz,* 246. The WRB in Berne had received information about Auschwitz a week earlier. That communication did not include a bombing appeal. It is not clear whether they passed the 24 June request to bomb the gas chambers and crematoria on to Washington at that time. Wyman, "Auschwitz," 39, and *Abandonment,* 294.

13. Gilbert, *Auschwitz,* 251–52.

14. Ibid., 255.

15. Ibid., 269.

16. Wyman, "Auschwitz," 40, and *Abandonment,* 295; Gilbert, *Auschwitz,* 246 and 262–65.

17. Wyman, "Auschwitz," 40, and *Abandonment,* 295.

18. Wyman, *Abandonment,* 291.

19. Gilbert, *Auschwitz,* 238.

20. Wyman, *Abandonment,* 292–93.

21. B. Akzin, Memo of 29 June, cited in Wyman, "Auschwitz," 40, and *Abandonment,* 295; Gilbert, *Auschwitz,* 246–47.

22. Gilbert, *Auschwitz,* 256.

23. Jacob Fishman, *Morgen Journal* (New York), June 27, 1944. I am indebted to Dr. R. Medoff for a translation of the three relevant sentences from the original Yiddish. Medoff interprets the words "I am still thinking about the idea" as meaning that Fishman

believed that, on balance, an air raid would be justified. In my opinion, if this was in fact Fishman's belief, he would have said so.

24. Gruenbaum's Memorandum of 7 June, Central Zionist Archives S 26/1232; Minutes of the Meeting of the Jewish Agency Executive, 11 June, Central Zionist Archives. Gruenbaum's letter of 21 June to Barlas, Central Zionist Archives S 26/1284. Gruenbaum's correspondence, but not the minutes of the meeting of the Executive, were noted by Yehuda Bauer, *American Jewry and the Holocaust* (Detroit, 1981), 496n31.

25. Gilbert, *Auschwitz*, 314–15. Gilbert says that "news of yet more deportations from Hungary had begun to reach the Jewish Agency in Jerusalem, following the overthrow of Admiral Horthy, and the return of the Gestapo to Budapest." But the telegram from Gruenbaum which he cites says only that the newly installed Hungarian Government had ordered the deportations to begin again. The overthrow of Admiral Horthy, and the return of the Gestapo to Budapest did not take place until the middle of October, a month later.

26. *Sunday Telegraph* (London), 4 June 1961, 15.

27. Wyman, "Auschwitz," 44–45, and *Abandonment*, 302. In a letter published in *Holocaust and Genocide Studies* 11 (Fall 1997), 277–80, Wyman claims that I have made an "astounding error that collapses . . . [the] entire argument" of this chapter since, he says, "Ben Gurion and the rest of the JAE changed their position before the end of June to support the bombing of Auschwitz." However, he cites no primary sources in support of his claim, and only offers two secondary sources neither of which gives any primary source on the specific question at issue. When and if primary documents emerge supporting the hypothesis that "Ben Gurion and the rest of the JAE changed their position," Wyman's claim will deserve to be taken seriously. Weizmann's attitude, as shown by the appeal to the British government in early July, was quite distinct and is presented in the text. Shertok's part in the affair may have been that of a messenger, as his own opinion on the subject of bombing is unknown.

28. Milt Groban, Letter to the Editor, *Commentary*, July 1978, 11. Charles M. Bachman, Letter to the Editor, *Commentary* 66 (Nov. 1978), 20.

29. Gilbert, *Auschwitz*, 267–69.

30. Ibid., 271–72.

31. Ibid., 284–85.

32. Wyman, "Auschwitz," 39, and *Abandonment*, 292; Gilbert, *Auschwitz*, 238.

33. *Jewish Chronicle* (London), 16 Nov. 1962, 25, 43.

34. Wyman, "Auschwitz," 42, and *Abandonment*, 300.

35. For example Solly Zuckerman, *From Apes to Warlords* (New York, 1978), 217ff; David R. Mets, *Master of Airpower: General Carl A. Spaatz* (Novato, CA, 1988), 199ff; Lord Tedder, G.C.B., *With Prejudice* (Boston, 1967), 502ff; Wesley F. Craven and James L. Cate, eds., *The Army Air Forces in World War II* (Washington, 1983), III:72ff.

36. Foregger, "Technical Analysis," 412–14.

37. Hilberg, *Destruction*, 547.

38. Gilbert, *Auschwitz*, 286–87.

39. Wyman, "Auschwitz," 43, and *Abandonment*, 300.

40. Wyman, *Abandonment*, 300.

41. Gilbert, *Auschwitz*, 266.

42. Ibid., 255, 265, 279–80.

43. Martin Gilbert, *Churchill: A Life* (New York, 1991), 783.

44. Hilberg, *Destruction*, 549.

45. Gilbert, *Auschwitz*, 266.

46. Martin Gilbert, private communication, 22 Mar. 1994.

47. Bernard Wasserstein, *Britain and the Jews of Europe 1939–1945* (Oxford, 1979), 319–20.

48. Hilberg, 537; Mario D. Fenyo, *Hitler, Horthy, and Hungary* (New Haven, 1972), 212.

49. Gilbert, *Auschwitz*, 266; "The Strategic Bomber Strikes Ahead" in Craven and Cate, eds., *The Army Air Forces in World War II*, III:290.

50. Wasserstein, *Britain*, 312.

51. Gilbert, *Auschwitz*, 272.

52. Ibid., 278ff.

53. Gideon Hausner, *Justice in Jerusalem* (New York, 1966), 243; Abba Eban, *My People* (New York, 1968), 427; Wasserstein, 310; Chaim Barlas, *Hatzalah Bimei Shoah*, 293-95; Norman Rose, *Chaim Weizmann: A Biography* (New York, 1986), 394.

54. Gilbert, *Auschwitz*, 262ff.

55. Ibid., 285.

56. Wyman, "Auschwitz." 40, and *Abandonment*, 295–296; and Gilbert, *Auschwitz*, 303.

57. Rafael Medoff, *The Deafening Silence* (New York, 1988), 160.

58. The full text of McCloy's letter to Kubowitzki of 14 August 1944 appears in Wyman, *Abandonment*, 296. The original is on permanent display in the Holocaust Museum in Washington.

59. Wyman, "Auschwitz," 43, 45; and *Abandonment*, 301.

60. Olga Lengyel, *Five Chimneys* (Chicago, 1947).

61. Uwe Dietrich Adam, "The Gas Chambers" in Francois Furet, ed., *Unanswered Questions* (New York, 1989), 151.

62. Leni Yahil, *The Holocaust: The Fate of European Jewry, 1932–1945* (New York, 1990), 527.

63. Jean-Claude Pressac, *Auschwitz: Technique and Operation of the Gas Chambers* (New York, 1989), 253.

64. Foregger, "Technical Analysis," 403.

65. Foregger, "Bombing," 106.

66. Hausner, *Justice in Jerusalem*, 345.

67. Foregger, "Technical Analysis," 403.

68. Wyman, "Auschwitz," 44, and *Abandonment*, 304.

69. Pressac, *Auschwitz*, 132, 165, 171.

70. Foregger, "Bombing," 106–08.

71. Hodges, "Bombing," 125.

72. Dino A. Brugioni and Robert G. Poirier, *The Holocaust Revisited: A Retrospective Analysis of the Auschwitz-Birkenau Extermination Complex* (Washington, DC, 1979); Dino A. Brugioni, "Auschwitz-Birkenau: Why the World War II Photo Interpreters Failed to Identify the Extermination Complex," *Military Intelligence 9* (January–March 1983), 50–55.

73. Kitchens, "Bombing," 248–49.

74. Milt Groban, "Letter to the Editor," *Commentary* 66 (July 1978), 10.

75. Gilbert, *Auschwitz*, 162; Danuta Dombrowska, "Majdanek," *Encyclopedia Judaica* (Jerusalem, 1974), XI:794–95.

76. Shlomo Aronson, cited by Lucy S. Dawidowicz, "Could the United States," 173.

77. Pressac, 253; Miklos Nyiszli, *Auschwitz: A Doctor's Eyewitness Account* (New York, 1960), 84–89.

78. Hilberg, *Destruction*, 629.

79. Wyman, "Auschwitz," 43, 44; and *Abandonment*, 301, 304. The book reads "There is no doubt that destruction of the gas chambers and crematoria would have saved many lives"; Milt Groban, "Letter to the Editor," and Wyman, "Reply to Letter to the Editor," *Commentary* 66 (July 1978), 10, 12.

80. Lucy S. Dawidowicz, *The War against the Jews 1933–1945* (New York, 1986), 140–42.

81. Wyman, "Auschwitz," 44, and *Abandonment*, 304. The 1978 article says 450,000, not 437,000; the lower figure agrees with Hilberg.

82. Gilbert, *Auschwitz*, 285.

83. *Jewish Chronicle,* 16 Nov. 1962, 25, 43. This interview followed the revelations at the Eichmann trial.

84. *Sunday Telegraph,* 4 June 1961, 15. This interview followed the revelations at the Eichmann trial.

85. From taped interview with Martin Gilbert, 1982; private communication, 14 Oct. 1993.

86. Herbert Loebel, "Letter to the Editor" *Commentary* 66 (July 1978), 7, 10; and "Letter to the Editor" *Holocaust and Genocide Studies* 6 (1990), 442.

87. Wasserstein, *Britain and the Jews of Europe,* 19–320.

88. Brugioni and Poirier, *Holocaust Revisited,* 11.

89. Pressac, *Auschwitz,* 253.

90. Gilbert, *Auschwitz,* 285.

91. C. Martin Sharp and Michael J. F. Bowyer, *Mosquito* (London, 1967), 241–44, photographs on 96–97. On the Amiens raid see *Jewish Chronicle,* 16 Nov. 1962, 25 and 43.

92. Hilberg, *Destruction,* 584.

93. Lawrence H. Blum, "Letter to the Editor" *Commentary* 66 (July 1978), 7.

94. Wyman's response to Blum, *Commentary* 66 (July 1978), 11.

95. Wyman, *Abandonment,* 409–63.

96. Ibid., 303.

97. *Sunday Telegraph,* 4 June 1961, 15.

98. Dawidowicz, "Could the United States," 171; Foregger, "Bombing," 108–09. In "Technical Analysis," Foregger includes the Mosquito among aircraft that could fly from Foggia to Auschwitz and return, but does not assert that it could carry a useful bomb load; Hodges, "Bombing," 124; Kitchens, "Bombing," 258–61.

99. Sharp and Bowyer, *Mosquito,* Appendix 4, "Summary of Mosquito Variants," 393–400; Appendix 5, "Mosquito Operational Performance and Loads," 401–03.

100. Compare discussions of other episodes in Sharp and Bowyer, *Mosquito,* 254. Richard H. Levy, "The Bombing of Auschwitz Revisited: A Critical Analysis," in *FDR and the Holocaust,* 242–43; Hodges, 124; Sharp and Bowyer, *Mosquito,* 351.

101. Wyman, *Abandonment,* 303.

102. Ibid.

103. Craven and Cate, *Army Air Forces,* III:283. Foregger ("Technical Analysis," 409) also considered the raid on Ploesti. In his view, the average error in this type of attack made it uncertain that one of the facilities at Auschwitz could have been hit; but there would have been inmate casualties.

104. Groban, Letter to the Editor, 10–11; Kitchens, "Bombing," 251–52; Sharp and Bowyer, *Mosquito,* 230.

105. Wyman, *Abandonment,* 302.

106. Groban, Letter to the Editor, 10.

107. Craven and Cate, *Army Air Forces,* III:305–06.

108. Gilbert, *Auschwitz,* 195.

109. Ibid., caption to Figure 28.

110. Ibid., 310; Wyman, *Abandonment,* 299; Craven and Cate, *Army Air Forces,* III:642; see also Kitchens.

111. Gilbert, *Auschwitz,* 321. Gilbert quotes 1980 recollections of Nahum Goldmann. Goldmann frowned on the objection of "General" (actually Field-Marshal) Dill to killing thousands of prisoners, but was apparently unaware that Kubowitzki and others shared Dill's view. Goldmann's "few dozen bombs" also appear in Medoff, *The Deafening Silence,* 159.

112. Gilbert, *Auschwitz,* 195.

113. Kitchens, "Bombing," 255.

114. Gilbert, *Auschwitz,* 321.

115. Foregger, "Technical Analysis," 408.
116. Roger M. Williams, "Why Wasn't Auschwitz Bombed: An American Moral Tragedy," *Commonweal* 105 (24. Nov. 1978), 751.
117. Wyman, *Abandonment*, 303.
118. Loebel, *Commentary*, 7, 10, and *Holocaust and Genocide Studies* 6 (1991), 442.
119. John J. McCloy, in interview with Morton Mintz, *The Washington Post*, 17 Apr. 1983.
120. Aaron Lerner, "Letter to the Editor" *Commentary* 66 (July 1987), 7.
121. Mets, *Master of Airpower*, 237.
122. Wyman, *Abandonment*, 410, note 78.
123. Wyman, "Auschwitz," 40, and *Abandonment*, 295.
124. Wyman, "Auschwitz," 40, and *Abandonment*, 296; Gilbert, *Auschwitz*, 312.
125. Gilbert, *Auschwitz*, 277–78.
126. Ibid., 285.
127. Ibid., 300–01.
128. Hausner, *Justice in Jerusalem*, 243.
129. Wasserstein, *Britain*, 313.
130. Ibid., 313–16. A review and subsequent exchange (John Fox, *European Studies Review* 10 (Jan. 1980), 138–46; and 10 (October 1980), 487–92) air sharp differences on these documents. As the authors of the documents thought they were involved in preparing to bomb Auschwitz, it may be possible to draw conclusions about motives. But these civil servants and officers did not know that a British operation had been ruled out since 15 July, and only an American operation was under consideration. If Sinclair had found a practical way for the RAF to bomb Auschwitz, the whole affair would have started in mid-July. The last half of July was spent, so far as this issue is concerned, waiting for Spaatz to visit the Air Ministry. Gilbert, *Auschwitz*, 301–19.
131. Foregger, "Bombing of Auschwitz," 104–08.
132. Wyman, "Auschwitz," 45, and *Abandonment*, 305.
133. Sir John Slessor, *The Central Blue* (New York, 1957), 615 ff. Yahil, *The Holocaust*, 638–39, says British planes bombed Warsaw in support of the Polish uprising. This is wrong.
134. Winston S. Churchill, *Triumph and Tragedy* (London, 1954), 113–28.
135. Mets, *Master of Airpower*, 231.

9. COULD THE ALLIES HAVE BOMBED AUSCHWITZ-BIRKENAU?
Stuart G. Erdheim

1. David S. Wyman, "Why Auschwitz Was Never Bombed," *Commentary* 65 (May 1978), 37–49; David S. Wyman, *The Abandonment of the Jews* (New York, 1984); James H. Kitchens III, "The Bombing of Auschwitz Re-examined," *The Journal of Military History* 58 (April 1994), 233–66. Kitchens's article has since been republished in *FDR and the Holocaust*, Verne W. Newton, ed. (New York, 1996), 183–217, and is Chapter 7 in this volume. Levy's article, "The Bombing of Auschwitz Revisited: A Critical Analysis," first appeared in *FDR and the Holocaust*. A revised version was published in *Holocaust and Genocide Studies* 10:3 (Winter 1996), 267–98 and is reprinted here as Chapter 8. References to Levy are to the *HGS* version, while those to Kitchens come from his April 1994 article. This chapter will deal only with those parts of Kitchens and Levy that are applicable to operational questions.
2. Kitchens, "Auschwitz Re-examined," 264–65.
3. U.S. Library of Congress, Manuscript Division, Carl A. Spaatz Papers, Subject File– 1929–45, 2 Aug. 1944. Note that Bottomley correctly refers to Birkenau, not Auschwitz, as the target.
4. The political will to follow through on the feasibility study was not sustained. Ibid., Minute from D.C.A.S. Bottomley, 6 Sep. 1944. Bottomley quotes the Foreign Office

stating that Jews are no longer being deported from Hungary, and that "because of the serious technical difficulties," they do "not propose to pursue the matter further." This determination, obviously, was made without photographic cover or a feasibility study having ever been done by the Air Ministry in the prior month.

5. This was not really an error at all. The map referred to did not have a north arrow indicator. The 'error' occurs only if one assumes that north is toward the top of the page. With the relative positions of Birkenau, Auschwitz I, and the Oswiecim railroad station accurately depicted, however, correlation with aerial photography would have clarified any possible confusion.

6. Richard Foregger, "Two Sketch Maps of the Auschwitz-Birkenau Extermination Camps," *Journal of Military History* 59 (October 1995), 687–96. Foregger also writes that the "expert photo-analysts,"—Brugioni, Poirier, and Stanley—all "state that the extermination facilities could not have been identified with the photographic equipment and techniques available in 1944," 691–6. Their actual argument, however, is that the extermination facilities would not have been identified without at least some knowledge that they existed. The errors in the sketch maps are overshadowed by the information that they and the rest of the report provide on the existence of the killing facilities, along with the layout of the camp. Brugioni clearly states that with the Vrba-Wetzler report, photo-interpreters would have located the gas chambers and crematoria (see n. 12 and accompanying text). Foregger, like Kitchens, simply ignores Brugioni on this most critical point. If applied elsewhere, Foregger's argument could lead us to question if photo-interpreters would have discovered V-1 weapons and enemy radar if they were unaware of their existence and not specifically tasked to look for them.

7. Francis H. Hinsley, *British Intelligence in the Second World War* (London, 1979), I:279. The CIU "became the headquarters of a central photographic library, and the supplier to all three services of charts, plans and models as well as of the operational intelligence derived from photo reconnaissance." Hinsley, *British Intelligence*, III/1:318–19; II: 654; Sir Basil Embry, *Mission Completed* (London, 1957). Embry was Commander of No. 2 Group, which executed the Amiens Prison raid, and many of the Gestapo headquarters raids including that of 11 Apr. 1944 in the Hague. For this mission, Embry states that only "after having the building and approaches to it photographed and modeled, I reported that the mission was perfectly feasible," 265. (No. 2 Group was the only unit to have its own modeling section, against the express orders of the Air Ministry.) See also n. 9.

8. Intercepts received by ULTRA revealed German Air Force (GAF) anxiety about Allied photo reconnaissance. On 5 August 1944, Luftlotte 2 reported "for the benefit of other commands their regular experience of low-level attacks on single buildings, generally headquarters, by small formations of fast aircraft. These followed a previous aerial reconnaissance in detail." See "History of US Strategic AF Europe vs. GAF," June 1945, SRH-013, RG 457 (National Security Agency), Box 8, Entry 9002, p. 230.

9. Embry, *Mission Completed*, 261. "The first step I took was to have the prison photographed and modeled by our modeling section."

10. RG 243, Aiming Point Report, 1.g. (163) Oswiecim, 21 Jan. 1944. The sketch map included in this report is dated May 1943 with the notation, "Not to scale—from memory." It does include some errors. Allied Intelligence was aware that in "May 1943—At least 2 trains of 20 carloads each arrived daily." USAFHRC 512.6162-1, 10 Oct. 1944, 27. It is not clear whether the latter information came from the same source that drew up the sketch map, despite the coincidence of the May 1943 date. Roy Stanley, *WWII Photo Intelligence* (New York, 1981), 346–48. Reports from ground sources in the summer of 1943 indicated a large concentration camp in the area with approximately 65,000 inmates. He incorrectly adds that there was no mention of gassing. See n. 50 and text.

11. Brugioni, now retired, founded and worked as an analyst at the CIA's National Photo-graphic Interpretation Center (NPIC). He discovered the aerial imagery of Auschwitz in 1978 along with Robert Poirier, also with the CIA.

12. Dino Brugioni, "Auschwitz-Birkenau: Why the World War II Interpreters Failed to Iden-tify the Extermination Complex," *Military Intelligence* 9 (Jan.–March 1983), 55, reprinted in a revised form as chapter 4 in this volume. Italics are mine.

13. Kitchens, "Auschwitz Re-examined," 246.

14. Hinsley, *British Intelligence*, III/1:552. The three sources for flak intelligence were: (1) photo reconnaissance, (2) operational reports from the Allied bombers themselves, (3) GAF Enigma.

15. RG 18, Box 1083, 55th BW, Intelligence Annex No. 175, 12 September 1944. 1.a. (1) "Oswiecim—Intense flak, possibly accurate, will be encountered. Pinpoint positions of guns shown on E Section Map No. 1574; 2 June 1944, and amendments . . . 17 Aug 1944 . . . 19 Aug 1944 . . . 25 Aug 1944 . . . When last attacked, on 20 Aug 1944, MIH was en-countered, but Heavy Guns have been added since that date. Course, axis, and rally prescribed avoid maximum exposure to flak." Stanley, *WWII Photo Intelligence*, 254, 262. "Once photoscale was known, the size of any object on the ground covered by a frame could be determined by measuring image size on the photo and then multiplying by the scale." (The altitude at which photos were taken and the focal length of the lens was the basis for determining the scale of a photograph. This information along with the PR unit, sortie no., date and time of day was noted on each photo to aid the P.I.s.) Photo 8-18 of a wireless station at Bourges. Caption reads, "Knowledge of latitude, day and time would permit use of sun angle, shadow, and trigonometry to compute antenna height," p. 262.

16. Target Information Sheet dated 18 July 1944, RG 243, 3 a. (2154) Oswiecim, Box 124. Place: 'Oswiecim or Auschwitz.' [Information is for target I. G. Farben plant only.] Sec-tion (iii): "The obstructions to low flying within the target area consist of chimneys and cooling towers, the highest being the chimney on the boiler house which is approx. 400 ft. high. A power line runs N. from the Transformer Station . . . with pylons 90 ft. high except over the river where they are 120 ft." Obtaining this information was apparently routine. The Target Sheet for the Tzerbinia Oil Plant states that information regarding obstructions to low flying attacks is not included, but adds that, "If this information is required . . . it will be obtained and supplied at short notice on application to A.I. 3(c)1." RG 243, 3.a.(2856) Tzerbinia, Box 157, Target Sheet. Hinsley notes the ability of A.I. 3(c)1 to provide information quickly, including sending it by air to the 15th AF in Italy. Hinsley, *British Intelligence*, III/1:318–19.

17. Bertram Schwartz, Letter to the Editor, *Journal of Military History* 60 (Jan. 1996), 209. The forested area west of crematoria IV and V is correctly indicated on the sketch map. Rudolf Vrba and Alfred Wetzler, "The Vrba-Wetzler Report," *44070: The Conspiracy of the Twentieth Century* (Bellingham, WA, 1989), 317.

18. Birkenau was a huge camp, almost half the size of the I. G. Farben synthetic oil and rubber plants nearby, and had a unique footprint, easily distinguishable from the air. It was surrounded for miles around by mostly farmland on three sides, north, west, and south. On the east it was separated by a marshaling yard from the much smaller Ausch-witz I, Main camp.

19. It is not likely, for example, that anything other than photo-reconnaissance was used for attacks on German headquarters buildings behind enemy lines mentioned in n. 8. De-tailed PR was adequate in those cases where other information was not available.

20. Hinsley, *British Intelligence*, III/1:318–19. "Aiming Point Reports on a broad range of [manufacturing] plants" were prepared with the assistance of British and American ex-perts. William J. Casey, *The Secret War against Hitler* (Washington, D.C., 1988), 79.

21. Vrba, *44070: The Conspiracy*, 284, 290–91. "The prisoners work in all the aforementioned factories" [Krupp, Siemens, DAW]. "I was ordered together with 200 other Slovak Jews to work in the German armament factories at AUSCHWITZ, but we continued to be housed in BIRKENAU. . . . The gaps in our ranks caused by deaths were replaced daily by prisoners from BIRKENAU." Postwar memoirs confirm this, with accounts of the now infamous men's and women's orchestras that accompanied the prisoners as they left for work and returned to the camp. See Fania Fenelon, *Playing for Time* (New York, 1979), 38. The number of prisoners of Birkenau "employed" as slave laborers rose from 40 percent in April to 50 percent in August 1944. Franciszek Piper, "The System of Prisoner Exploitation," *Anatomy of the Auschwitz Death Camp*, edited by Y. Gutman and M. Berenbaum (Bloomington, Ind., 1994), 49–35.

22. See n. 50 and text re: Breitman article.

23. Kitchens, "Auschwitz Re-examined," 297.

24. It was considerably smaller than the four at Birkenau anyway. Franciszek Piper, "Gas Chambers and Crematoria," Gutman and Berenbaum, eds., *Anatomy*, 159, 165.

25. Vrba, *44070: The Conspiracy*, 285. "We had some 150 dead daily and their bodies were sent for cremation to AUSCHWITZ," 292. It is not noted in the sketch map of Auschwitz I.

26. Embry, *Mission Completed*, 279. Regarding the third attack by the RAF on the Gestapo in Denmark, Embry writes "we had difficulty in finding the target, a house in a thickly populated area and well camouflaged with netting."

27. Constance Babington-Smith, *Air Spy* (New York, 1957), 198–99.

28. RG 243, 3.a. (454), Brüx, Target Sheet.

29. R. V. Jones, *The Wizard War* (New York, 1978), 430; Babington-Smith, *Air Spy*, 234.

30. USAFHRC 512.6162-2, June 1944, 5.

31. RG 18, Box 3900, 90th P.R. Wing, Interrogation Report 26th Feb. 1944, and Daily Information Summary, 27 Feb. 1944; Wyman, *Abandonment*, 299.

32. Bernard Wasserstein, *Britain and the Jews of Europe*, 1939–1945 (Oxford, 1979), 313.

33. Martin Gilbert, *Auschwitz and the Allies* (New York, 1982), 262. Roswell McClelland claims the Foreign Office had a copy by 27 June, *Washington Post*, 27 Apr. 1983, Letter to the Editor.

34. Wasserstein, *Britain and the Jews of Europe*, 315. This intermediary role of the Jewish Agency was unnecessary since as of 1941 the JIC had empowered ISTD "to approach the Allied Governments-in-Exile . . . as a source of topographical intelligence." Hinsley, *British Intelligence*, II:9.

35. RG 373, Can: C1172 Fr: 5022; June 26, 1944; Mission: 60/PR522 60SQ; Focal length: 6 inches; altitude: 30,000 feet; Scale: 1:60,000. With a scale of 1:60,000, every inch equals .946 miles. A 36-inch lens at an altitude of 27,000 feet produced a scale of 1:9,000, which would have provided excellent detail of the crematoria.

36. Letter from Charles Barry (PR pilot with S.A.A.F. 60 SQ) to Anthony Rider, 1 Mar. 1979, RG 373, "Aerial Photographs of Auschwitz and Birkenau."

37. Stanley, *WWII Photo Intelligence*, 348.

38. Most PR sorties covered several targets. The crew on the 4 April mission to Auschwitz also obtained imagery of Cieazyn [sic] A/C plant, Bogumin O/R, and the Gleiwitz O/R. Two other areas to be photographed were obscured by clouds. The total time of the sortie was 5 hours using a Mosquito Mk. IX. Public Record Office (PRO), AIR27/568, Interrogation Report dated 4 Apr. 1944, Sortie No. 60 PR 288. (The EOU had mistakenly thought there was an oil refinery at Gleiwitz, which the imagery confirmed was not the case. RG 243 3.a [1072] Gleiwitz, Germany.)

39. Richard Breitman, "Allied Knowledge of Auschwitz-Birkenau in 1943–1944," in *FDR and the Holocaust*, ed. Verne W. Newton (New York, 1996), 180.

40. In an attempt to verify a report received about ammo dumps being placed next to a

British POW camp at Auschwitz to deter bombing of the Farben plant, the 60 PR Squadron was tasked to photograph the POW camp. The PR sortie to Auschwitz on 4 April (piloted by Charles Barry), occurred only 11 days after Roosevelt's 24 March statement concerning the imminent annihilation of Hungarian Jewry.

41. RG 243, 1.g. (141)—Blechhammer South, E.O.U. Aiming Point Report No. III.B. 19, dated 15 Mar. 1944, "C.I.U. Plan No. D/154a based on photographs of 6/10/42 and 20/8/43." RG 243, Damage Assessment Report, 3.a. (314) Blechhammer South. The imagery indicates that the 20 Aug. 1943 mission was flown by the 540 PR Squadron based in England. Two days after the Ploesti raid of 1 Aug. 1943, a PR Mosquito of the S.A.A.F. 60 Squadron photographed the bomb damage. The round-trip from its Benghazi base was almost 2,400 miles. Dugan, *Ploesti*, 235. The distance from English bases to Auschwitz was less than 1,700 miles round-trip, well within PR Mosquito range. From the Blechhammer PR missions it is evident that Stanley in *World War II Photo Intelligence*, 340, is incorrect in stating that "initially Mosquitos [only] from lower Italy could reach Southern Poland."

42. Babington-Smith, *Air Spy*, 214-215. The author, a WWII P.I., writes that in the search for what they thought might be "rail-served rocket-launching sites," any signs of new railway spurs were closely observed.

43. Brugioni, "Auschwitz-Birkenau," 50; Stanley, *WWII Photo Intelligence*, 349.

44. The vague and noncommittal phrase, "before the end of 1944" ignores the considerable amount of information known early enough to plan an attack on Birkenau designed to help save Hungarian Jewry.

45. Kitchens, "Auschwitz Re-examined," 246–49.

46. USAFHRC 512.6162-2, June 1944, 5. For 1944, the report indicates, "another report states that 150,000 names were listed as having passed through this camp." Not mentioned is the Vrba-Wetzler report's detailed description of the gas chambers and crematoria at Birkenau (not Auschwitz I), and the estimate of 1,765,000 Jews having been gassed in Birkenau between April 1942 and April 1944. Vrba, Wetzler, "The Vrba-Wetzler Report," *44070: The Conspiracy*, 316. In August, Air Marshal Bottomley correctly stated that Birkenau, not Auschwitz, was the killing camp; see n.3. The October 10 report, while mentioning Majdanek as a killing camp, is unable to identify it as the camp the Russians overran in July 1944 with its gas chambers and crematoria intact, a fact widely published in the American and British press at the time. Wyman, *Abandonment*, 324.

47. Hinsley, *British Intelligence*, II:671, appendix 5. "Between 18 July and 30 August 1941, police decrypts on at least seven occasions gave details of mass shootings, in the central sector, of victims described variously as 'Jews,' 'Jewish plunderers,' 'Jewish bolshevists' or 'Russian soldiers' in numbers ranging from less than a hundred to several thousand. On 7 August the SS Cavalry Brigade reported that it had carried out 7,819 'executions' to date in the Minsk area, and on the same day von dem Bach, commander of police in the central sector, reported that 30,000 executions had been carried out since the police arrived in Russia. In the southern sector between 23 and 31 August 1941, the shootings of Jews, in groups numbering from 61 to 4,200, was reported on 17 occasions. . . ."

48. Martin Gilbert, *The Second World War: A Complete History* (New York, 1989), 226. Whether informed of these decrypts or not, Roosevelt was also aware of the Final Solution. See Breitman, "Allied Knowledge of Auschwitz-Birkenau in 1943–1944," in *FDR and the Holocaust*, 116. See also Wyman, *Abandonment*, 72–73.

49. Wyman, *Abandonment*, 75.

50. Casey, *The Secret War against Hitler*, 218.

51. Richard Breitman, "Allied Knowledge of Auschwitz-Birkenau," 179.

52. *The Public Papers and Addresses of FDR: 1944–45, Victory and the Threshold of Peace*, comp. Samuel I. Rosenman (New York, 1969), XIII: 104.

53. RG 373, "Aerial Photographs of Auschwitz and Birkenau," Mission: 60 PR 288 60 SQ, 4 April 1944, Can: F5631 Frame: 4028.

54. "INTELLIGENCE ANNEX TO OPERATIONS ORDER FOR TWENTY AUGUST: OS- WIECIM . . . SHOWED DEFINITE INDICATIONS OF ACTIVITY ON RECENT COVER AND MOVE IN OF FIFTY [50] FLAK GUNS . . . FLAK OSWIECIM NOW SHOWS SEVEN NINE [79] HEAVY GUNS," USAFHRC 670.332, 20 Aug. 1944. The addition of battery no. (5), with four flak guns in the July 8th imagery, bringing the total to 33 guns, is the only increase seen in the photographs of April through July. The significant addition of flak guns can be seen starting with the August 9th imagery, increasing steadily in the August 12th and August 20th photos. RG 373, "Aerial Photographs of Auschwitz and Birkenau." Charles Coward, a British officer interned at the British POW camp at Auschwitz, reported that 2 US bombers dropped leaflets warning non-combatants to leave the area in advance of Allied bombing. Taking the threat seriously, the German staff, headquartered near the Farben plant, exchanged places with the British whose camp was located in the town of Auschwitz three miles away. Because of the move, 39 POWs were killed in the 20 Aug. raid. The American warning also gave the Germans enough time to increase the flak and smoke screen defenses in August. See John Castle, *The Password Is Courage* (London, 1954), 179, 174.

55. This assumes the heavy guns are 88mm model 36, the most widely produced flak gun, which had a horizontal range of 9.2 miles. Werner Müller, *The Heavy Flak Guns, 1933– 1945* (Westchester, PA, 1990), 139. Batteries (8) and (10) are out of range. While batteries (1), (2), (5), and (12) are within range of "bombs away," battery no. (5) added in July, and half of the guns (12) did not have the range for the bomb run.

56. Kitchens, "Auschwitz Re-examined," 251–57. ". . . many pieces emplaced around Monowitz [I. G. Farben plant] would have coincidentally covered most, if not all, of the Birkenau camp area." Of the 79 guns, only battery no. (12), consisting of 6 groups of 3 guns each, is at Farben. More flak was situated at the eastern approach to the plant than at the plant itself, placing them even further from Birkenau, and beyond the extreme range of many of these guns. This is probably the reason why the approach for the 13 September raid was from the west, unlike the 20 August raid which came from the east. After that raid, the Germans increased the flak on the eastern approaches to the plant, which was successfully picked up by the P.I.s.

57. RG 373, "Aerial Photographs of Auschwitz and Birkenau," Mission: 464 BG: 4M97, 13 Sep. 1944, Can: B8413 Frame: 3V1. This is one of the photos annotated by the CIA.

58. In August or later, an approach from the north to avoid the greater concentration of newly added flak guns emplaced south of the Farben plant [(2), (13), (3), (4), (5)] might have been considered, rallying right (west) after bombs away. By 9 August, a large battery (13) had been added approximately three and one-half miles south of Auschwitz I which would have been the closest to bombers attacking from the south. RG 373, "Aerial Photographs of Auschwitz and Birkenau," Mission: USEC/R-79, 9 August 1944, Can: B6912 Frame: 1019. By 20 August, batteries (3) and (4), 3 miles south of Farben had been added, and (1) and (2) had been strengthened. Ibid., Mission: USEC/R-86, 20 Aug. 1944, Can: B10658 Frame 5020.

59. Flak batteries (7) and (9) were added to two existing ones, (8) and (5), at the eastern approaches of Farben. RG 373, "Aerial Photographs of Auschwitz and Birkenau," Mission: 60 PR/694, 25 Aug. 1944, Can: F5366 Frame: 5024. While possibly part of the flak alignment in August, battery (6), southeast of Farben, is seen only on captured German imagery taken sometime after the September raid, but is too distant to appear in Allied imagery, RG 373, TU GX 894, 1269K, Exp. 51.

60. This is assuming that radar picked up the attackers and sounded the alarm. If it did not, the surprise would be its own defense. At Monowitz, German soldiers and civilians

ran to the shelters during air raids. During the bombing at Blechhammer, whose slave labor camp was a satellite of Auschwitz, the "SS abandoned the watch towers." For the Buchenwald raid, see n. 83 and text, Gilbert, *The Second World War*, 591, 631.

61. Kitchens, "Auschwitz Re-examined," 251–52. Wesley Frank Craven and James Lea Cate, eds., *The Army Air Forces in World War II*, vol. III, *Europe: Argument to V-E Day, January 1944 to May 1945* (Chicago, 1951). Due to attrition and the inability of the GAF to adequately train new fighter pilots, the limited number of experienced pilots and fuel available negated the significance of the number of radar sites. Craven and Cate, *The AAF in World War II*, III:179. Hinsley, *British Intelligence*, III/1:317.

62. Intelligence Annex No. 156 1.(7), RG 18 Box 1084, 55th BW, 20 Aug. 1944. This contrasts with the heavier defenses for Austria in the west.

63. "Frantic" missions went through Russia for refueling.

64. RG 18 Box 1398, 390 BG Mission File 8/7/44–8/12/44.

65. Ibid., "Intelligence Annex Nr. 1;4. Section Three."

66. RG 18 Box 509, 99th BG, Operations Order No. 672, 21 Aug. 1944.

67. RG 18, Box 13, 2nd BG Narrative Report, 20 Aug. 1944. "1. *Enemy Resistance, A. Fighters.*"

68. RG 18, Box 1018, 5th BW, "Special Narrative Report—Mission 20 August 1944—Oswiecim—483rd Bombardment Group."

69. RG 18, Box 509, 99th BG—Mission Reports. 5th Daily Intelligence Report.

70. RG 18 Box 26, 2nd BG—Mission Summaries. "Operations Order Number 671," dated 19 Aug. 1944.

71. RG 18 Box 1083, 55th BW. "Intelligence Annex No. 175," 12 Sep. 1944.

72. Craven and Cate, *The AAF in World War II*. Of the 500 B-17 and B-24 bombers dispatched to bomb oil refineries in Poland and Czechoslovakia by Fifteenth AF on 20 August, only 4 aircraft did not return, III:299. On 7 July, the GAF did turn up in force, attacking 1,000 bombers sent against synthetic oil plants. Of the 300 enemy aircraft encountered, "70 were destroyed and damaged." RG 243, Box 50, USSBS, 15th AF "Historical Summary First Year of Operations, 1 November 1944," (Env. 58).

73. Craven and Cate, *The AAF in World War II*, II:565. The actual statistics bear this out only for the spring and summer months. See note below.

74. RG 243, M1013, Roll 5, "Weather Factors," Table IX, Eighth Air Force Weather Abortives, and Table X, Fifteenth Air Force Bombers Abortive Due to Weather. The percentages of abortive sorties in 1944 for the two Air Forces are as follows: 8th AF: Apr—23.1%, May—17.9%, June—11.4%, July—12.4%, Aug—10.8%, Sept—8.0%; 15th AF: Apr—13.1%, May—10.9%, June—7.8%, July—4.6%, Aug—2.8%, Sept—11.1%.

75. David A. Hackett, ed. *The Buchenwald Report* (Boulder, CO, 1995), 95. The original report was produced by the Intelligence Team of the Psychological Warfare Division of the Supreme Headquarters of the Allied Forces.

76. Hackett, *Buchenwald Report*, 95.

77. Ibid., 305. Testimony of Robert Leibrand, a former prisoner at Buchenwald.

78. Hackett, *Buchenwald Report*, 115, 95. Besides 384 dead, 600 were seriously wounded. The total population of Buchenwald at the end of August 1944 was 82,391 inmates.

79. Hackett, *Buchenwald Report*, 304.

80. RG 243 3.a. (3037) Weimar. Photo title reads: (SAV-457-480-6-) (24-8-44) (826—12"—24,500 × WEIMAR). RG 18 Box 1450, 401st BG, Mission Reports, 8-24-44, Photo title reads: (SAV-401C/567-9) (24-8-44) (42-1026747-233 00) (WEIMAR). Stanley, *World War II Photo Intelligence*; photograph of a P.I. marking the damaged areas on a bomb assessment photo of Buchenwald with caption that reads: "The concentration camp (upper right) was not hit," 251.

81. Kitchens, "Auschwitz Re-examined," 254. There were 144 B-17 bomber sorties with five bombers lost, four to enemy aircraft, one unknown. Bombing altitude was between

24,000 and 26,000 feet. While the 79 AA guns at Auschwitz in August, even with 30–40 percent out of range were more than at Buchenwald, the B-25s at Toulon proved that high accuracy in the face of 82 AA guns was possible from 13,000 feet, where the flak was even more deadly. The April–July period, with only 29–33 AA guns, 9–12 of which were out of range of attacking bombers, compares more favorably with the reported 12 guns at Buchenwald, where bombers also experienced persistent and effective attacks from enemy fighters prior to reaching the target. RG 18 Box 1450, 401st BG, Mission Summary Report, 24 Aug. 1944.

82. In *World War II Photo Intelligence*, 347, Stanley writes: "Slave labor camps were common throughout Nazi Europe—indeed were expected near defense industries."

83. Franciszek Piper, "The System of Prisoner Exploitation," 49–35. The percentages given are postwar figures, available for the male population only. For February and November 1943 figures, which included women, the percentages of those "employed" were slightly higher. As mentioned in n. 21, the Vrba-Wetzler report revealed that inmates at Birkenau worked outside the camp, without estimating precise numbers.

84. Hackett, *Buchenwald Report*, 95.

85. Ibid. The sentiment was expressed by Shalom Lindenbaum, a survivor of Auschwitz, of the raids at Monowitz: "Those bombardments elevated our morale and, paradoxically, awakened probably some hopes of surviving, of escaping from this hell." Gilbert, *Second World War*, 591.

86. RG 18 Box 1450, 401 BG Mission Reports, 8-24-44. While many inmates died at the camp, it was not an extermination camp like Birkenau.

87. Though it could be argued that before D-Day V-weapons were viewed as a serious threat to the invasion forces, air commanders almost unanimously viewed CROSSBOW as a diversion to be avoided. In the spring of 1944, "Spaatz, Vandenberg, Vandenberg, and Brereton frequently conveyed to General Arnold their rising concern about the CROSS-BOW diversion." Craven and Cate, *The AAF in World War II*, III:100.

88. The total number of British civilians killed by V-2 attacks was 2,754. V-1 attacks killed 6,184, while conventional German bombing of England killed 51,500. Brian Johnson, *The Secret War* (New York, 1978), 180. The total British death toll for both V-1 and V-2 weapons for the entire war was *less* than *one* day of killing at Birkenau in the spring and summer 1944.

89. See Buchenwald discussion above regarding inmates at Birkenau working outside the camp.

90. John S. Conway, "The Significance of the Vrba-Wetzler Report on Auschwitz-Birkenau," in *44070: The Conspiracy*, p. 358.

91. RG 18 Box 1865, 15th AF Operational Analysis, "Bombing Accuracy—Aiming Errors and Pattern Dimensions," dated 31 Oct. 1944, 3. This percentage difference was for August–September 1944. The data for the Jan.–July period was not available.

92. Twelfth AF medium bombers placed 67 percent of bombs within 600' of the A.P. in April–May and 78 percent from June–August. RG 243 (2) K Medium Bomber Operations, Jan. 1–Aug. 28, 1944. B-25J's had a still air range of 1,350 miles with a 3,000 lb. bomb load. They would have required bomb bay fuel tanks, which were regularly used and available in the MAAF. N. L. Avery, *B-25 Mitchell: The Magnificent Medium* (St. Paul, MN, 1992), 41, 63–65. Besides U.S. forces, the RAF's 205 Group in Italy had 6 squadrons of Wellington Mk.X medium-bombers. Hilary St. George Saunders, *Royal Air Force, 1939–1945* (London, 1974), 3:406–08. USAFHRC 622.6318, June 1944, The MAAF/RAF Order of Battle, 8.

93. Jean Labayle Couhat, *French Warships of World War II* (London, 1971), 24, 47.

94. Dino Brugioni, "Precision Pays Off," *Air Force Magazine* (June 1982), 90–91. Brugioni was a member of the 321 BG and flew in this mission. Escort, often provided in the MAAF by P-38s, was imperative for the longer route to Birkenau. The flak defenses,

however, would have been less, about 65 AA (within range) in August, and a third prior to that. Average accuracy for the 321 BG was over 90 percent within a 600-ft. radius. With that kind of accuracy, the crematoria could have been destroyed without hitting any barracks.

95. Lewis H. Brereton, *The Brereton Diaries* (New York, 1946), 194. The raid by 521 bombers was conducted from Allied bases in North Africa (heavy bombers, flying 2000 miles round trip), and Pantelleria (medium bombers, somewhat closer).

96. Babington-Smith, *Air Spy*, 165.

97. Conrad Crane, *Bombs, Cities and Civilians* (Lawrence, KS, 1993), 46.

98. Gilbert's map is flawed in at least two other details: (1) It shows only two railroad sidings inside the camp instead of three; (2) The date of the construction progress at the 'Mexico' camp is not noted, making it impossible to determine how many of the new barracks are within 1000 feet, if any. This map is not reprinted in Kitchens's republished article in *FDR and the Holocaust*.

99. RG 18, Box 1865, 15th AF Operational Analysis, "Bombing Accuracy—Aiming Errors and Pattern Dimensions," 31 Oct. 1944, 6. Between January and July, the 15th Air Force used 3-aircraft fronts 15 percent of the time vs. 7 percent for 6-aircraft and 78 percent for 9- and 12-aircraft. In August-September the figures were: 3-aircraft front = 47 percent; 6-aircraft = 37 percent; 9- and 12-aircraft = 16 percent. Those averages that include the 8th AF would be weighted with an even greater percentage of large fronts. USAFHRC 137.306–3, 3, 6. On the average, an 18-aircraft box had a lower level of accuracy than a 9-aircraft box. The combination of a weakened GAF and increasingly strong fighter escort allowed the use of smaller boxes, when desired. For raids with hundreds of bombers, however, the use of smaller boxes was too cumbersome.

100. RG 18, Box 1865, 15th AF Operational Analysis, "Bombing Accuracy—Aiming Errors and Pattern Dimensions," 31 Oct. 1944, 6. "The first two or three boxes over the target achieve an order of accuracy substantially superior to that obtained by the remaining boxes," due primarily to smoke obstruction by bombs of the earlier groups. The need to use less accurate PFF and/or offset techniques, instead of visual bombing for later groups, is evident from the briefing notes for the 20 August Auschwitz raid which involved 5 groups: ". . . since we are the last group over it will certainly be covered with smoke from otheres [sic] bombing. To hit the MPI on our portion of the target, outside check points will most certainly have to be used." RG 18 Box 509, 99th BG, Mission Reports. Another common problem of large formations was congestion which could prevent a good run up. On the 13 Sep. 1944 six-group raid on Blechhammer North, interfering groups prevented the lead squadron of the 2nd BG from bombing the primary target and forced the remaining three squadrons into a short bomb run. The 463rd BG could not bomb at all: ". . . the Group was crowded off the run by other Groups, so could not bomb the primary target . . . the group leader decided to get rid of the bombs on the first target of any kind. Bombs were dropped on the town of Oswiecim, Poland." RG 18, Box 1012, 5th BW "Bombing-Navigation Analysis for 13 Sept. 44." (Another report stated that these bombs were dropped on a "small unidentified village . . . midway between Oswiecim and Cracow," RG 18, Box 13, 5th BW Final Strike Assessment Report, 9/13/44, p. 1). While Kitchens notes (p. 253) that bombs commonly fell a mile or more away from their targets, he makes no distinction as to the size of the formation of which such large errors were probably the result. For example, 'creepback,' common in large formations, is hardly a factor with smaller ones. On the massive Hamburg raid of July 25, 1943, 'creepback' resulted in "a carpet of incendiary bombs stretched back for seven miles." Charles Webster and Noble Frankland, *The Strategic Air Offensive against Germany, 1939–1945* (London, 1961), II:152.

101. USAFHRC 137.306-3, p. 9. For a 400'-wide target, a three-aircraft front had a 46 percent

advantage over a 9-aircraft front. Heavy bombers using more than a three-aircraft front generally had patterns resembling squares, which were less compact and more inaccurate.

102. On the Buchenwald raid, an error in range caused 40 percent of the bombs of a later group to fall short into a wooded area, resulting in no collateral damage. RG 18, Box 982, 351st BG, Operations and Missions, 24 Aug. 1944.

103. RG 18, Box 1865, 15th AF Operational Analysis, "Bombing Accuracy—Aiming Errors and Pattern Dimensions," 31 Oct. 1944, 3, 8. Large errors in range are "probably due to the frequency of malfunctions of the release mechanism," or premature or accidental release. Since these large errors represent 'scatter' beyond 1000 feet, Kitchens's estimate of 25 to 30 percent falling in the barracks area is overstated, not to mention that only deflection errors on one side would have landed in the barracks area. Also, there are four deflection sightings per group with a three-plane front as opposed to two sightings for the larger fronts, ensuring better deflection accuracy.

104. Ploesti was attacked at low level by 38 P-38 fighter bombers (46 were dispatched), of the 82nd Fighter Group, escorted by 39 fighters from the 1st Fighter Group.

105. The P-38s were dive bombing through a total of 471 flak guns, releasing their bombs from an altitude above the opaque smoke screen. Through either a breakdown in discipline or unclear orders, two of the escorting squadrons veered off to attack Do 217s, and were in turn attacked by Fw 190s, thus unable to protect the dive-bombers at the target. Simply stated, it was a "poorly conceived raid," Leon Wolff, *Low Level Mission* (London, 1958), 216.

106. Kitchens, "Auschwitz Re-examined," 259.

107. Craven and Cate, *The AAf in World War II*, III:283. The authors were writing about the June 1944 mission. Barrage balloons, while numerous at Ploesti, are not mentioned in any report relating to Auschwitz, or seen on any of the photo imagery.

108. RG 243, Box 200, Ploesti—Summary of Operations, Env. 754.

109. RG 18 Box 509, 99th BG, Mission Reports. Briefing notes for the August 20 raid on Auschwitz discuss flak defenses: "Over the target heavy, intense flak may be expected. It isn't anywhere near a [sic] bad as Ploesti . . ." The 79 guns protecting Auschwitz in August were about one-third of the total for heavy guns at Ploesti in June, while the 29 guns at Auschwitz in June represent only 13 percent of Ploesti's heavy guns. With the 237 light AA at Ploesti versus none at Auschwitz, we see the unquestionable defensive difference in the two targets. USAFHRC-(GP-82-HI TO GP-82-SU-OP-S), INTELLIGENCE ANNEX TO OPERATIONS ORDER FOR TEN JUNE, "TOTAL FOR THIS AREA TWO THREE FOUR [234] HEAVY AND TWO THREE SEVEN [237] LIGHT GUNS." Despite this virtual fortress, the skilled pilots of the 82nd FG were able to inflict moderate damage on the primary objectives. P.I.R. No. G189, 10 June 1944.

110. USAFHRC-(GP-82-HI to GP-82-SU-S), Narrative Report, 10 June 1944. The P-38s flew 650 miles (still air) to Ploesti with one 1000-lb. bomb and one 300-gallon belly tank. After climbing over the Yugoslavian mountains they proceeded to the target on the deck, where mileage is lower than at higher altitudes. Twenty miles from Ploesti they commenced a second steep climb to bombing altitude in a severe barrage of antiaircraft guns. (This would have been similar to the climb over the 5000-foot Tatra range south of Auschwitz, minus the flak barrage.) Besides their bomb load, they also carried enough ammunition to fight off aggressive enemy aircraft, and even strafe targets of opportunity (including rolling stock, motor transport, an A/D, and gun positions) on the way home. Out of 38 planes, 8 were lost, while 11 others received damage. Only two planes ran out of gas and could not make it home.

111. RG 18, Box 333, 332nd FG, Foler Aug–Sept '44. "Narrative Mission Report No. 57" dated 20 August 1944: The mission was "to provide penetration escort for 5th Bomb Wing to Oswiecim Oil Refinery." 7. Enemy Air-Resistance and Activity: "16 plus ME

109's and FW 190's came in from the East on the last flight of our fighters. We turned into them and they turned back East and climbed out of range. No attack on the bombers."

112. "Heavy flak is not effective against high speed aircraft at very low altitudes but becomes [sic] to become effective at or slightly above the altitude at which light flak loses its effectiveness," which is approximately 4,500 feet: The Fifth Wing Combat Manual, RG 18, Box 1015, 5th BW. The following anecdotal observation of an airman who flew in the August 1943 low-level raid at Ploesti is useful: "The most telling fire from the ground was coming from agile 37mm and 20mm guns. . . . Many of the big 88's were silent for long stretches of the battle. They were not maneuverable enough to hit low-flying bombers. . . ." James Dugan and Carroll Stewart, *Ploesti* (New York, 1962), 121. Stymied by slow bombers, the German 88mm guns would be even less effective against fast fighters. In discussing attacks by low-level Mosquitos against V-1 targets, Basil Embry noted that "Heavy gun defenses did not seriously bother the Mosquito operations," Embry, *Mission Completed*, 259.

113. Wasserstein, *Britain and the Jews of Europe*, 312.

114. Gilbert, *Auschwitz*, 285.

115. USFHRC 622.6318, June 1944, The MAAF/RAF Order of Battle, 8.

116. Denis Richards and Hilary St. George Saunders, *Royal Air Force 1939–1945, The Flight Avails*, Appendix V, Principal Operational aircraft of the RAF, 2:373. The mileage given is a straight line distance, with a 25 percent reduction providing the operating radius. The Wellington could probably carry four to six 500-lb. bombs to Birkenau.

117. A transcript from the 1982 interview is in the author's possession. Cheshire's interview appeared in the 1983 BBC documentary "Auschwitz and the Allies," produced by Rex Bloomstein.

118. Levy's error stems in part from a misreading of the appendices of *Mosquito*. In Appendix 8 the authors write: "The weights, armament, bomb load quoted . . . are . . . for peace-time. . . ." "Under wartime conditions these aircraft flew at a very much higher all-up weight and hence were able to carry a much larger quantity of fuel and greater bomb load." C. Martin Sharp and Michael F. Bowyer, *Mosquito* (London, 1971), 409.

119. Hilary St. George Saunders, *Royal Air Force*, III:406–08.

120. Richards and St. George Saunders, *Royal Air Force*, II:373.

121. Craven and Cate, eds., *The AAF in World War II*, III:382.

122. John Terraine, *A Time for Courage* (New York, 1985), 495–96.

123. Wyman, *Abandonment*, 303.

124. Jack Fishman, *When the Walls Came Tumbling Down* (New York, 1983), 107, 134.

125. Out of a total of 700 inmates, 100 were slated to be executed, though it appears only 24 were to be shot on the 19th. Twelve of those to be killed on the 19th managed to escape. Sharp and Bowyer, *Mosquito*, 243–44.

126. Fishman, *When the Walls Came Tumbling Down*, 183. Bad weather had delayed the mission by ten days, not one as Kitchens indicates. Embry, *Mission Completed*, 263.

127. Wyman, *Abandonment*, 291.

128. Ibid., 296.

129. The Army Air Force Statistical Digest (WWII), Prepared by the Office of Statistical Control, December 1945, Tables 120 and 128, 222, 229. Effective sorties of heavy and medium bombers in July (which are mid-range for this period), are: Heavy—10,825, Medium—4,447. Ibid., Table 120,222. A mission of 100 heavy bombers or 50 medium bombers would represent about one-third of one day's sorties in the MTO, while a 100-fighter escort would be between one-fifth and one-seventh of one day's fighter sorties.

130. John Slessor, *Central Blue* (New York, 1957), ". . . it is sometimes necessary to face up

to the fact that 500 casualties today may well save 5,000 in the next month," 615. This kind of decision anguished Embry at Amiens and elsewhere—"a hateful responsibility I had to carry alone both then and on several further occasions," Embry, *Mission Completed*, 262—but one made nonetheless. Ball-bearing factories, for example, were a top priority in 1943, until the cost of bombers lost and airmen killed outweighed the benefit of destroying this target system; and so the attacks were put on hold. On the other hand, the collateral deaths of many French civilians in the "Transportation" and CROSSBOW raids did not deter these attacks. Eisenhower, backed by Roosevelt, rebuffed Churchill's attempt to limit attacks against French rail targets, claiming the collateral civilian deaths were outweighed by military necessity. Casey, *The Secret War against Hitler*, 87.

131. Wyman, *Abandonment*, 305–307.

132. Chaz Bowyer, *The Wellington Bomber* (London, 1986), 182–84.

133. Slessor, *Central Blue*, 615.

134. Breitman, "Allied Knowledge of Auschwitz-Birkenau," 180.

135. Höss, the commandant of Auschwitz, describes several priority projects that were prevented from being built in 1944 owing to a shortage of materials. *KL Auschwitz Seen by the SS* / Höss, Broad, Kramer (New York, 1984), 125.

136. By late 1943, three of the six death camps, Belzec, Sobibor, and Treblinka, had been destroyed by the Germans themselves. Kulmhof (Chelmno), which had been closed since 1943, reopened briefly in June and July, but was a small camp without the possibility of being enlarged on short notice. Raul Hilberg, *The Destruction of the European Jews* (New York, 1985), III:979–80. Majdanek, a small camp in comparison to Auschwitz, had stopped using its gas chambers in November 1943, well before being overrun by the Russians in July 1944. Uwe Dietrich Adam, "The Gas Chambers," *Unanswered Questions* (New York, 1989), 152–53.

137. Verne Newton, ed., *FDR and the Holocaust*, 16.

10. BOMBING AUSCHWITZ: U.S. FIFTEENTH AIR FORCE AND THE
MILITARY ASPECTS OF A POSSIBLE ATTACK
Rondall R. Rice

1. This essay was initially published in *War in History* 6 (1999): 205–29, and the current version contains only minor editorial changes and improvements. For their assistance and advice, I would like to thank Professors Alan E. Steinweis, Peter Maslowski, and Edward Homze of the University of Nebraska–Lincoln, and Professor Dennis Showalter of Colorado College.

2. See Davis S. Wyman, "Why Auschwitz Was Never Bombed," *Commentary* 65 (May 1978), 37–46; Bernard Wasserstein, *Britain and the Jews of Europe, 1939–1945* (New York: Oxford University Press, 1979); and Martin Gilbert, *Auschwitz and the Allies* (New York: Henry Holt, 1981).

3. See James H. Kitchens III, "The Bombing of Auschwitz Reexamined," *The Journal of Military History* 58 (Apr. 1994), 233–66; Richard Foregger, "The Bombing of Auschwitz," *Aerospace Historian* 34 (June 1987), 98–110; Richard Foregger, "Technical Analysis of Methods to Bomb the Gas Chambers at Auschwitz," *Holocaust and Genocide Studies* 5 (1990), 403–21; and Richard Foregger, "Two Sketch Maps of the Auschwitz-Birkenau Extermination Camps," *The Journal of Military History* 5 (Oct. 1995), 687–96.

4. See David S. Wyman, *The Abandonment of the Jews: America and the Holocaust, 1941–1945* (New York: Pantheon, 1984).

5. U.S., President, Executive Order 9417, "Establishing a War Refugee Board," 22 Jan. 1944, Record Group (RG) 165, Records of the War Department General and Special Staffs, CAD 383.7, National Archives, College Park, MD.

6. See the collections of Ira Eaker, Henry Arnold, and Carl Spaatz for dates around 13 Aug. 1944; these are in the Library of Congress (LC) Manuscripts Division.

7. See Wesley F. Craven and James L. Cate, eds., *The Army Air Forces in World War II*, 7 vols. (Chicago: The University of Chicago Press, 1949), vol. III: *Europe: Argument to V-E Day, January 1944 to May 1945*, 316–17, for information on the Warsaw airlifts. Messages to and from Spaatz contain the best information on the air leaders' views on the missions and are in the Carl Spaatz Collection, Box 18, Official Diary, and Box 139, Occupied Countries, both in LC Manuscripts Division.

8. Gilbert, *Auschwitz and the Allies*, 339–40.

9. Richard Breitman, *Official Secrets: What the Nazis Planned, What the British and Americans Knew* (New York: Hill and Wang, 1998), 110–21.

10. For more information on how ULTRA was used in the Mediterranean Theater, see Ralph Bennett, *ULTRA and Mediterranean Strategy* (New York: William Morrow, 1989).

11. Office of Strategic Services, no title, numbered 04968, copy in United States Holocaust Research Institute (USHRI) Subject File: Camps—Auschwitz.

12. OSS Report, 15 Oct. 1943, copy in USHRI Subject File: Camps–Auschwitz.

13. "Oswiecim Synthetic Oil and Rubber Works, Poland," Target Information, United States Air Force Historical Research Agency (USAFHRA), Maxwell Air Force Base, Alabama, File Number 670.424.

14. Ibid.

15. Message to WRB from McClelland, Number 4291, 6 July 1944, copy in USHRI Subject File: Camps—Auschwitz Bombing to Camps—Auschwitz WRB Report.

16. Message to WRB from McClelland, Number 4295, 6 July 1944, copy in USHRI Subject File: Camps—Auschwitz Bombing to Camps—Auschwitz WRB Report.

17. U.S., Executive Office of the President, War Refugee Board, *German Extermination Camps—Auschwitz and Birkenau*, Nov. 1944, copy in USHRI Subject File: Camps—Auschwitz Bombing to Camps—Auschwitz WRB Report. Arrival date confirmed by Gilbert, *Auschwitz and the Allies*, 327.

18. Interviews with Sedge Hill, Dick Anderson, Gale Christianson, and John Parks, 451st Bombardment Group Reunion, Fairmont Army Airfield, Fairmont, Nebraska, 15 June 1996.

19. Milton Groban, personal letter to author, 12 May 1996.

20. Ibid.

21. Interview with Milton Groban, Glencoe, Illinois, 22 June 1996.

22. Kitchens, "The Bombing of Auschwitz Reexamined," 248–49, and Foregger, "Two Sketch Maps of the Auschwitz-Birkenau Extermination Camps," 696.

23. Kitchens, "The Bombing of Auschwitz Reexamined," 249.

24. Spaatz to Arnold, 19 Mar. 1944, Carl Spaatz Collection, Box 14, Personal Diaries, LC Manuscripts Division.

25. Yehuda Bauer, *A History of the Holocaust* (New York: Franklin Watts, 1982), 314.

26. Franciszek Piper, "Gas Chambers and Crematoria," in *Anatomy of the Auschwitz Death Camp*, eds. Yisrael Gutman and Michael Berenbaum (Bloomington: Indiana University Press, 1994), 165–66.

27. Bauer, *A History*, 314.

28. Leni Yahil, *The Holocaust: The Fate of European Jewry* (New York/Oxford: Oxford University Press, 1990), 529.

29. Again, Breitman (*Official Secrets*) shows that the Allies may have known sooner, but the required aircraft and support assets would not have been in place to bomb earlier than June 1944. Also, one still must account for the information flow from the highest and most secret levels of government down to the air units for planning; intelligence available at high levels does not always mean immediate availability for aircrews and planning.

30. Marvin Downey, ed., *Fifteenth Air Force, History* (Wright Field, Dayton, Ohio: Headquarters Air Material Command, 1946), 23–31 (and supporting charts on unnumbered pages between these). Document available at USAFHRA, File Number 670.01–1 Vol. 1, c.1.

31. Statistical Control Office, USSTAF, *Daily Operations Report, Eighth and Fifteenth Air Forces*, 7 June 1944, USAFHRA File Number 519.308–2.

32. Numbers derived by taking the last *Daily Operations Report* from each week from 7 June to 30 October and averaging the numbers. Reports used were: 7, 14, 21, and 28 June; 7, 14, 21, and 28 July; 7, 14, and 28 Aug.; 7, 14, 21, and 30 Sep. 1944.

33. Downey, 75–76, USAFHRA File Number 670.01–1 Vol. 1, c.1.

34. Craven and Cate, *The Army Air Forces in World War II*, III:27–28.

35. Ibid., 280–81.

36. Office of the Director of Operations, Headquarters Mediterranean Allied Air Forces, *Bombing Directive*, 15 June 1944, USAFHRA File Number 670.01–3C, Annex 19.

37. Office of the Director of Operations, Headquarters Mediterranean Allied Air Forces, *Bombing Directive*, 3 Aug. 1944, USAFHRA File Number 670.01–3C, Annex 19.

38. Spaatz to Commanders of Eighth, Fifteenth, and Mediterranean Allied Air Forces, *Target Priorities*, 1 Sep. 1944, USAFHRA File Number 670.01–3C, Annex 19.

39. Office of the Director of Operations, Headquarters Mediterranean Allied Air Forces, *Bombing Directive*, 13 Sep. 1944, USAFHRA File Number 670.01–3C, Annex 19.

40. Spaatz to Arnold, message K4035, 4 Mar. 1944, USAFHRA File Number 519.308–1.

41. Spaatz to Arnold, message U61850, 8 May 1944, USAFHRA File Number 519.308–1.

42. Craven and Cate, *The Army Air Forces in World War II*, III:291.

43. Headquarters Fifteenth Air Force, Office of the Assistant Chief of Staff A-2, *Special Intelligence Report No. 63*, 10 July 1944, USAFHRA File Number 670.6012–63.

44. Headquarters Fifth Wing, *Operations Order No. 671*, 19 Aug. 1944, and A-2 Section, Headquarters Fifth Wing, *Annex to Operations Order No. 671 for 20 August 1944*, 19 Aug. 1944, USAFHRA File Number 670.332.

45. Headquarters 55th Bomb Wing, *Operations Order Number 156*, 19 Aug. 1944, USAFHRA File Number 670.332.

46. Headquarters 55th Bomb Wing, *Intelligence Annex No. 156 to Operations Order No. 156*, 19 Aug. 1944, USAFHRA File Number 670.332.

47. Milton Groban, Personal Combat Diary, Mission 25/26, 20 Aug. 1944.

48. Headquarters Fifteenth Air Force, Office of the Assistant Chief of Staff A-2, *Special Intelligence Report No. 67*, 24 Aug. 1944, USAFHRA File Number 670.6012–67.

49. Headquarters 97th Bombardment Group (H), Group Intelligence Office, *Special Narrative Report: Mission: 20 August 1944—Oswiecim Synthetic O/R, Poland*, 20 Aug. 1944, USAFHRA File Number 670.332.

50. Headquarters Fifteenth Air Force, Office of the Assistant Chief of Staff A-2, *Special Intelligence Report No. 68*, 26 Aug. 1944, USAFHRA File Number 670.6012–68.

51. Headquarters 55th Bomb Wing (H), *Operations Memorandum Number 175*, 12 Sep. 1944, USAFHRA File Number 670.332.

52. See separate reports by Headquarters 460th, 464th, 465th, and 485th Bombardment Groups (H), *Narrative Mission Report*, 12 and 13 Sep. 1944, USAFHRA File Number 670.332.

53. Interviews with Sedge Hill, Dick Anderson, Gale Christianson, and John Parks, 451st Bombardment Group Reunion, Fairmont, Nebraska, 15 June 1996; Groban interview.

54. Headquarters, Fifteenth Air Force, *Intelligence Plan*, 24 Aug. 1944, USAFHRA File Number 670.01–3C. Annex 19.

55. Headquarters 5th Wing, *Annex to Operations Order No. 671 for 20 August 1944*, 19 Aug. 1944, USAFHRA File Number 670.332.

56. See separate reports by Headquarters 99th, 301st, 97th, 2nd, and 483rd Bombardment Groups, *Special Narrative Mission Report: Mission: 20 August 1944—Oswiecim Synthetic Oil Works, Poland,* 20 Aug. 1944, USAFHRA File Number 670.332.

57. Headquarters 55th Bomb Wing (H), *Intelligence Annex No. 175 to Operations Order No. 175,* 12 Sep. 1944, USAFHRA File Number 670.332.

58. See separate reports by Headquarters 460th, 464th, 465th, and 485th Bombardment Groups, *Narrative Mission Report,* 13 Sep. 1944, USAFHRA File Number 670.332.

59. Rudolf Höss, *Commandant of Auschwitz: The Autobiography of Rudolf Hoess,* trans. Constantine Fitz-Gibbon (London: Weidenfeld and Nicolson, 1959), 191, and Rudolf Vrba and Alan Bestic, *I Cannot Forgive* (New York: Grove, 1964), 233.

60. Rudolf Lusar, *Die deutschen Waffen and Geheimwaffen des 2. Weltkrieges und ihre Weiterentwicklung* (Munich: J. F. Lehmanns, 1971), 232.

61. Piper, "Gas Chambers and Crematoria," 158–62.

62. *The Extermination Camps of Auschwitz (Oswiecim) and Birkenau in Upper Silesia,* 14, copy in USHRI Subject File: Camps—Auschwitz.

63. See Dino A. Brugioni and Robert G. Poirier, *The Holocaust Revisited, a Retrospective Analysis of the Auschwitz-Birkenau Extermination Complex* (Washington, D.C.: Central Intelligence Agency, 1979); and Dino A. Brugioni, "Auschwitz-Birkenau: Why the World War II Photo Interpreters Failed to Identify the Extermination Complex," *Military Intelligence* 9, no 1 (Jan.–Mar. 1983), 50–55 (see Chap. 4 in this volume).

64. Piper, "Gas Chambers and Crematoria," 166.

65. Plates of the original plans, as well as the development and plans for Auschwitz, are in Debórah Dwork and Robert-Jan van Pelt, *Auschwitz: 1270 to the Present* (New York: W. W. Norton, 1996).

66. Foregger, "Technical Analysis of Methods to Bomb the Gas Chambers at Auschwitz," 404 and 417n6.

67. Groban interview.

68. Foregger, "Technical Analysis of Methods to Bomb the Gas Chambers at Auschwitz," 407.

69. See separate reports by Headquarters 460th, 464th, 465th, and 485th Bombardment Groups (H), *Narrative Mission Report,* 12 and 13 Sep. 1944, USAFHRA File Number 670.332.

70. U.S. War Department, *Handbook for Bombardiers,* TM1–251, 31 Mar. 1941, 48.

71. Using Tables I and II from ibid., 57–58.

72. Formula in ibid., 47.

73. Table IV, ibid., 60.

74. Chart 9, ibid., 80–81.

75. First Operations Analysis Section, Fifteenth Air Force, *Bombing Accuracy—Aiming Errors and Pattern Dimensions,* 31 Oct. 1944, USAFHRA File Number 670.310–1, 1.

76. R. J. Overy, *The Air War 1939–1945* (New York: Stein and Day, 1981), 139–42.

77. David MacIssac, ed., "Summary Report (European War)," 30 Sep. 1945, *The United States Strategic Bombing Survey,* 10 vols. (New York: Garland, 1976), I:5.

78. First Operations Analysis Section, Fifteenth Air Force, *Development of Radar Bombing—Fifteenth Air Force,* 18 Jan. 1945, USAFHRA File Number 670.310–6.

79. First Operations Analysis Section, Fifteenth Air Force, *Bombing Accuracy,* 20 Aug. 1944, Daily Bombing Accuracy Reports, USAFHRA File Number 670.56–3.

80. Craven and Cate, *The Army Air Forces in World War II,* III:14–16.

81. Groban interview.

82. Ibid.

83. Headquarters Eighth Air Force, H2X Intelligence Program, 12 Apr. 1944, 1–4, USAFHRA File Number 670.317–3, vol. I; Assistant Chief of Staff A-3, Fifteenth Air Force, *Bombs*

through the Undercast, A Pathfinder Manual of Operation and Technique, copy acquired from Milton Groban.

84. First Operations Analysis Section, Fifteenth Air Force, *Report on PFF-Synchronous Bombing—Fifteenth Air Force,* 20 Sep. 1944, USAFHRA File Number 670.310–1.

85. Groban interview. Groban displayed original film copies of Pathfinder radar images for several of his targets, including Auschwitz.

86. First Operations Analysis Section, Fifteenth Air Force, *Optimum Tactics for Current Level of Bombing Accuracy,* 23 Oct. 1944, USAFHRA File Number 670.310–1, 5.

87. First Operations Analysis Section, Fifteenth Air Force, *Bombing Accuracy—Aiming Errors and Pattern Dimensions,* 31 Oct. 1944, USAFHRA File Number 670.310–1, 1–2.

88. Twenty-Eighth Statistical Control Unit, Fifteenth Air Force, *The Statistical Story of the Fifteenth Air Force,* USAFHRA File Number 670.308–2, 11.

89. First Operations Analysis Section, Fifteenth Air Force, *Bombing Accuracy,* 30 Apr. 1945, USAFHRA File Number 670.56–2.

90. Ibid.

91. *The Statistical Story of the Fifteenth Air Force,* USAFHRA File Number 670.308–2, 12.

92. Downey, *Fifteenth Air Force History,* 63–68. See also the charts on aircrew manning and aircraft availability, Tables 3 and 5. The tables, on unnumbered pages, appear facing pages 63 and 68, respectively.

93. See Vrba, *I Cannot Forgive,* 124–40.

PART III: NEW PERSPECTIVES ON THE CONTROVERSY
INTRODUCTORY REMARKS
Michael J. Neufeld

1. Henry L. Feingold, *The Politics of Rescue* (New York, 1970), 257.

2. See also Peter Novick, *The Holocaust in American Life* (Boston/New York, 1999).

11. AUSCHWITZ
Walter Laqueur

1. Walter Laqueur, *The Terrible Secret: Suppression of the Truth about the "Final Solution"* (London, 1980; reissued with a new Introduction, New York, 1998).

12. BOMBING AUSCHWITZ AND THE POLITICS OF THE JEWISH QUESTION DURING WORLD WAR II
Henry L. Feingold

1. There are those who are convinced that *precision bombing* and *pickle-barrel bombing* were propagandistic terms used by the USAAF, which had paradoxically chosen daylight bombing to avoid the moral onus of killing civilians in the manner the RAF did with night area bombing. The strategy was gradually abandoned when the losses proved unacceptable. The fire raid on Tokyo and finally the use of the atomic bomb on Hiroshima on 6 August 1945 marked a total reversal of the initial strategy. See Ronald Schaffer, *Wings of Judgment: American Bombing in World War II* (New York, 1986).

2. William Rubinstein argues that neither Gen. Eisenhower, who alone had command authority to order such a raid, nor President Roosevelt ever received a formal request to bomb Auschwitz. See *The Myth of Rescue: Why the Democracies Could Not Have Saved More Jews from the Nazis* (London, 1997), 245–44.

3. An unsuccessful effort to create such a historical context can be found in Arno J. Mayer, *Why Did the Heavens Not Darken?: The "Final Solution" in History* (New York, 1988). The only article in this collection that uses the contextual approach is Gerhard L. Wein-

berg's "The Allies and the Holocaust." Unfortunately, Weinberg does not concern himself with a key contextualization question: Why did a powerful modern nation like Germany allow a figment of its demonic imagination, the "Jewish question," to become the centerpiece of its reasons for going to war, destroying itself and a good part of Europe in the process?

4. The contention is challenged by William Rubinstein who argues that the receiving nations, especially the United States, were in fact generous to the refugees. After October 1941, all emigration of Jews from German-occupied areas was prohibited.

5. When Washington and London finally declared such a warning on 17 December 1942, it listed depredations against Jews among a long list of victims, including Cretan peasants.

6. The raid on Monowitz on 20 Aug. 1944, which so many *kazetniks* witnessed and cite today as evidence that bombing was a possibility, came as a result of a change in strategy aimed at destroying the Reich's synthetic-fuel–producing capacity. What was unresolved and what the inmates could not have known was the kind of bombing that would have had to be done to destroy the gas chambers and crematoria. Buna was subject to saturation bombing which—if used to destroy Crematoria II and III of Birkenau, which handled 75 percentage of the capacity of Auschwitz—would have taken the lives of a large number of the inmates at the same time.

7. The rescue resolutions, first publicized at the massive "Stop Hitler Now" rally held at Madison Square Garden on 21 Mar. 1943, contained twelve suggestions including the need to negotiate with Germany through neutral agencies and nations, the preparation of sanctuaries for those who might be rescued, the establishment of a War Crimes Commission, and the usual request to open the doors of Palestine.

8. Bernard Wasserstein, *Britain and the Jews of Europe* (Oxford, 1979), 308. Two additional requests for retaliatory bombing were made in January and February 1943, but were rejected by the RAF's Bomber Command ostensibly for fear that Berlin would then escalate the terror beyond the Allied will to respond. Releasing prisoners by precision bombing was later implemented when the RAF successfully attacked the Amiens prison in France on 18 Feb. 1944.

9. Ibid., 306.

10. As the blanket bombing of German cities intensified, incidents of lynching of *Terrorflieger* by German civilians did occur. A May 1944 law permitted their immediate execution without court-martial. See Mitchell G. Bard, *Forgotten Victims: The Abandonment of Americans in Hitler's Camps* (Boulder, CO, 1994), 44.

11. See *The Goebbels Diaries, 1942–1943*, ed. Louis P. Lochner (New York, 1948), 13 Dec. 1942, 241.

12. Ibid., 17 May 1943, 239–40, 382.

13. Ibid., 13 Dec. 1942, 241.

14. Tami Davis Biddle, "Allied Air Power: Objectives and Capabilities" (chapter 3 in this volume), p. 46.

15. *Goebbels Diaries*, 10 May 1943, 366.

16. An official of the Russian Jewish Congress, part of a delegation visiting American Holocaust museums, expressed doubt that the Russian public would welcome the memorialization of the Jewish victims of the Holocaust. "The soil for a museum," he observed, "is different than in America." Clyde Haberman, "Painful Epoch Bracketed by Optimism," *New York Times*, 26 June 1998, B1.

17. Only at the Teheran Conference was shuttle bombing discussed with the Russians. It concerned the ongoing air war and reaching targets in the East, not bombing Auschwitz.

18. The "stupendous power of a solitary person over the historical process" is examined by Joachim C. Fest, *Hitler* (New York, 1975), 7–8.

13. Monday-Morning Quarterbacking and the Bombing of Auschwitz
Williamson Murray

1. At present, there is no complete edition of the diaries, but rather a bad collection of many of the more controversial diary entries, edited by Arthur Bryant. The diaries themselves are available in the B. H. Liddell Hart archives at King's College University of London. For the Bryant editions, see: Arthur Bryant, *The Turn of the Tide: A History of the War Years Based on the Diaries of Field-Marshal Lord Alanbrooke, Chief of the Imperial General Staff* (Garden City, NY, 1957).

2. This was patently not the case with the Soviet leadership, which after all had killed millions of its own citizens through mass starvation, purges, and sheer bungling incompetence over the years before the German invasion. And in the conduct of military operations during the war, that leadership displayed not the slightest compunction in sacrificing its soldiers and citizens on the altar of the needs of the state.

3. The grim joke that was going around the Reich in late 1944 had a real base in the Germans' fear of the coming punishment: "Enjoy the war while it lasts, because the peace will be hell."

4. For all the massive efforts to ask why the Western Allies failed to respond to the Jews in their hour of desperate need, one finds virtually nothing on why the Soviets did absolutely nothing—either in the air or on the ground—to stop the slaughter at Auschwitz. And they were much closer.

5. This brings up the important point that decrypts of what was occurring with regard to the Holocaust did exist, but given the extraordinary demands of the preparations for the invasion of France, there is no reason why senior Allied military leaders would have had time to read such information—nor was Bletchley Park interested in such information; it too was overburdened with the task of keeping track of German military intentions and the movement of German military forces.

6. See Williamson Murray, *Luftwaffe* (Baltimore, MD, 1985), 273.

7. Public Record Office, DEFE 3/166, KV 6673, 6 June 1994 1944, 2356Z.

8. Speer Memorandum to Hitler, 29 July 1944, Speer Collection, Imperial War Museum, FD 2690/45 GS, vol. 3.

9. Speer Papers, Imperial War Museum, FD 2690/44.

10. It was during the three weeks before the invasion and the three weeks following it that much of the killing of the Hungarian Jews took place. Even had the Allies been fully informed of what was occurring, they could not have taken the focus off the invasion and the military targets on which air and ground commanders were concentrating their efforts.

11. With the significant difference that in World War I the combatants regularly rotated divisions in and out of the fighting, while in the fighting in Normandy combat divisions in the American, British, and Canadian forces remained constantly in combat from their initial commitment through to the end of the war. For what this meant to the individual soldier, see Stephen Ambrose, *Citizen Soldiers* (New York, 1998).

12. In fact, the damage inflicted on Caen and the resulting rubble probably did as much to slow the advance of British troops as did the initial resistance of German defenders.

13. Lt. Gen. Fritz Bayerlein, divisional commander of *Panzer Lehr*, records that the bombardment "was hell. . . . The planes kept coming overhead like a conveyor belt, and the bomb carpets kept coming down. . . . My front line looked like a landscape on the moon and at least seventy percent of my personal were out of action—dead, wounded, crazed, or numb." Quoted in Richard G. Davis, *Carl A. Spaatz and the Air War in Europe* (Washington, D.C., 1992), 472.

14. If there were a set of decisions, the changing of which might have saved the lives of hundreds of thousands of Jews and Gentiles, it was not the bombing of Auschwitz, but

rather Montgomery's failure to open up Antwerp in early September and encompass the destruction of the Fifteenth Army. The accomplishment of that specific task when ordered might well have ended the war in April or even March 1945, thereby saving hundreds of thousands of lives.

15. Quoted in Martin Gilbert, *The Holocaust: A History of the Jews of Europe during the Second World War* (New York, 1985), 695.

16. Those who believe that such bombing might have done significant damage are urged to consult the map on the level of accuracy that 170 B-17s enjoyed in their attack on the Schweinfurt ball-bearing factories in August 1943 in Martin Middlebrook, *The Schweinfurt-Regensburg Mission* (New York, 1983), 205.

14. THE BOMBING OF AUSCHWITZ: COMMENTS ON A HISTORICAL SPECULATION
Richard G. Davis

1. Michael Viatteau, "Netanyahu Says Allies Knowingly Let Jews Die," Agence France-Presse, *Washington Times*, 24 Apr. 1998, A15. The opinions expressed in this chapter by Richard G. Davis are his own and do not reflect the official position of the U.S. Air Force or the Department of Defense.

2. The number of lives spared at Birkenau death camp would depend on the precise date on which the camp ceased operations and whether or not the Germans resorted to alternate methods of execution and corpse disposal other than gas chambers and crematoria. It would appear that the average daily death rate at the camp from 7 July 1944 (when the Hungarian mass deportations ceased) and early November 1944 (when the Germans discontinued mass killings) was between 1,100 and 1,400. German policy forbade the camp administration to retain records of the precise number of killings. Some surviving inmates kept an oral record of the arriving trains, but could only estimate the numbers selected for death. See David S. Wyman, *The Abandonment of the Jews* (New York, 1984), 304, who puts the figures at 50,000 deaths between 7 July and 20 August, and 100,000 further deaths between 21 August and November. Also see Martin Gilbert, *Auschwitz and the Allies* (New York, 1981), 326, who states that 34,000 died in October 1944. Wyman cites several sources, none dated later than 1970, for his estimates. I accept at face value Wyman's numbers of those exterminated, although I would argue that not all of them would have been saved unless, by some unlikely miracle, the camp had entirely ceased operations on 7 July 1944.

   Immediately after the war, the Soviet government announced that four million people may have died at the camp; Norman Davies, "Auschwitz," in I. C. B. Dear, *The Oxford Companion to World War II* (New York, 1995), 77. In 1981, Gilbert, *Auschwitz and the Allies*, 343, put the total of Jewish deaths at the camp, from June 1942 through June 1944, at 1.5 million. Finally, in 1991, the Auschwitz Museum issued a revised total death count of 1.2 to 1.5 million victims, 800,000 of whom were Jews; Dear, *Oxford Companion*, 77. Clearly, there can never be an authoritative death total.

3. For a detailed description of the air operations in support of Warsaw, see Neil Orpen, *Airlift to Warsaw: The Rising of 1944* (Norman, OK, 1984).

4. During "Big Week" (20–25 Feb. 1944), when the Americans lacked sufficient long-range escort fighters in Italy, 657 of the Fifteenth's heavy bombers attacked aircraft-manufacturing targets in southern Germany and Austria. Eighty-eight bombers fell victim to the German defenses, a loss rate of 13.4 percent, far in excess of the 5 percent that the AAF considered unsustainable. On 25 February, the Fifteenth lost 25 percent of its attacking aircraft, a loss rate above that suffered by the Eighth in its famous attacks on Schweinfurt.

5. Gilbert, *Auschwitz and the Allies*, 191.

6. Richard G. Davis, draft manuscript, "The Combined Bomber Offensive: A Statistical

History," forthcoming, Frank Cass & Co., Ilford, Essex. This manuscript lists every bombing and mining sortie flown by aircraft of RAF Bomber Command, RAF No. 205 Group, and all the heavy bomber sorties of the U.S. Eighth, Ninth, Twelfth, and Fifteenth Air Forces, from 1 January 1942 through 8 May 1945, by effective sorties, combat losses, tonnage and type of bomb dropped, target, and method of sighting.

7. On the night of 25–26 June, 109 bombers of RAF No. 205 Group dropped 182.6 tons of high explosives on the Budapest Shell oil refinery. The Fifteenth followed on 27 June with a 113-plane raid and 289.8 tons on Budapest's Rakos marshaling yard, and on 30 June when 20 bombers, using the highly inaccurate H2X radar bombing device, attacked the city with 60 tons of high explosives. Two weeks earlier, 14 June 1944, 189 American heavy bombers attacked Budapest's Shell and Fantos oil refineries.

8. See Gilbert, *Auschwitz and the Allies*, 266, and Richard H. Levy, "The Bombing of Auschwitz Revisited: A Critical Analysis," in this volume. The Allies, of course, never made such plans. What the Hungarians had apparently picked up, perhaps through an intentional leak, was the retransmittal through diplomatic channels, by the American or British legation in Berne, Switzerland, to their governments, of pleas received from Jewish relief committees in Budapest. Whenever the origin of the Hungarian intercepts and the credence accorded them, they gave the government a pretext to bow to the international pressure exerted upon it.

9. See C. Martin Sharp and Michael J. F. Bowyer, *Mosquito* (London, 1995), 143–45, and 235–59. The detailed discussion of attack tactics and missions flown by Mosquitoes in daylight bombing raids in these two chapters convincingly demonstrates that Mosquitoes did not use the steep-angle dive-bombing (which would allow bombs to penetrate below ground level) and invariably struck only targets such as aboveground buildings, rail facilities, and industrial plants.

10. Notes of meeting at General Wilson's HQ, 30 Apr. 1944, Library of Congress, Manuscripts Division, The Papers of Carl A. Spaatz, Diary File.

11. Clouds over the target forced half the American sorties sent against the nearby Blechhammer synthetic-oil complexes to use H2X radar. According to wartime operations analysis reports of the Eighth Air Force's bombing, visual bombing was seventy times more accurate than radar bombing through one hundred percent clouds. See Operational Analysis Section, Eighth Air Force, "Report on Bombing Accuracy Eighty Air Force 1 September 1944 through 31 December 1944," 20 April 1945, USAF History Support Office, Bolling AFB, Washington DC, microfilm reel A5883, starting frame 566.

12. Davis, CBO Statistical History.

13. Weinberg, "The Allies and the Holocaust," chapter 1 in this volume.

14. Minute, AM Norman Bottomley, Deputy Chief of the RAF Staff, to the Vice Chief of the RAF Staff (Intelligence), 2 Aug. 1944, reproduced in part IV, Documents, in this volume.

15. Spaatz may even have turned the matter over to his target planning officers. Forty-six years later, former U.S. Supreme Court Justice Lewis F. Powell, Jr., one of Spaatz's intelligence officers, while admitting that after such a long time "memories grow dim," hinted as much when he wrote: "I do not recall any real interest at General Spaatz's headquarters in bombing Auschwitz or any other German death camp. To the extent that there was discussion, we were concerned that more internees would be killed than Germans. Our objective was to bring the war to an early end. This was far more important than bombing any particular German death camp." (Letter, Powell to Richard G. Davis, 5 July 1990). Given Spaatz's request for photography, what information did his headquarters examine in determining that a raid would cause too much collateral damage? Is it possible that they already had some photos of the camp available to them in London?

The official "Target Information Sheet" on the Monowitz facility, dated 18 July 1944 and prepared by RAF Intelligence, based on the 4 Apr. 1944 overflight, covers only the plant, and not Birkenau. It would have been of little value to Spaatz's people. (For a copy of this "Target Information Sheet," see AFHSO microfilm, Reel A5286, frames 156–63.) Minute, Bottomley to Spaatz, 6 Sep. 1944, in part IV, Documents, in this volume.   16.

17. See Forrest Pogue, *The United States Army in World War II*, subseries: *The European Theater of Operations*, volume: *The Supreme Command* (Washington, DC, 1954), 307.

18. Minute, Churchill to Eden, 7 July 1944, reprinted in part IV, Documents, in this volume.

15. THE FAILURE TO RESCUE AND CONTEMPORARY AMERICAN JEWISH HISTORIOGRAPHY OF THE HOLOCAUST: JUDGING FROM A DISTANCE
Deborah E. Lipstadt

1. Whenever I give public lectures on the Holocaust, the topic of the bombing provokes the most discussion and argument. In Jewish circles, the audience is often reluctant to hear anything that might sound like a "justification" or "rationalization" of Allied inaction. Other scholars have reported similar reactions.

2. Bernard Wasserstein, *Britain and the Jews of Europe 1939–1945* (Oxford, 1979), 143–57.

3. During a stop in Germany to lecture at a number of universities, I saw a sign over a large book display in a prominent Frankfurt bookstore: "Books Commemorating the Fiftieth Anniversary of the Liberation of Germany." I was tempted to ask the manager, liberation from whom? the Nazis? The sign reflected the German delusion—now effectively punctured—that the Nazis had invaded and occupied their country for twelve long years.

4. My thanks to Laurie Patton for her help in developing this idea. An expanded discussion of synechdocical thought can be found in Laurie Patton, "From Magic to Commentary: Imagining the Vedic Enemy," forthcoming in Ithamar Gruenwald and Moshe Idel, eds., *Proceedings of the Conference on Magic and Magic in Judaism*.

5. Richard Breitman, "The Failure to Provide a Safe Haven for European Jewry," in Newton, ed., *FDR and the Holocaust*, 137, 143.

6. The Allies could have assisted people in neutral territories. This in turn might have made it easier for additional numbers of Jews to escape into those territories. I do not mean to discount the importance of saving even a few lives. However, many of the people I encounter cannot be dissuaded from the notion that "bombing Auschwitz would have changed everything," as I was recently told. Had the United States and other nations adhered to a more benevolent immigration policy in the 1930s, thousands of people who were sent to their death would have been saved.

7. Breitman, "The Failure," 138n1.

8. Frank W. Brecher, "David Wyman and the Historiography of America's Response to the Holocaust: Counter-Considerations," *Holocaust and Genocide Studies* 5 (Fall 1990), 423–46; Henry Feingold, "Review of David Wyman's *The Abandonment of the Jews: America and the Holocaust, 1941–45,*" in Verne Newton, ed., *FDR and the Holocaust* (New York, 1996), 146.

9. Herbert Druks, *The Failure to Rescue* (New York, 1977), 98.

10. William Perl, *The Holocaust Conspiracy: An International Policy of Genocide* (New York, 1989) as quoted in William D. Rubinstein, *The Myth of Rescue* (New York, 1997), 7.

11. Druks, *Failure*, viii.

12. Rafael Medoff, *The Deafening Silence* (New York, 1987), 35, 184, 186.

13. Yitshaq Ben-Ami, *Years of Wrath, Days of Glory: Memoirs from the Irgun* (New York, 1982), 326.

14. Perl also accuses Jewish leaders of doing Britain's "dirty work," in preventing Jews from escaping from Europe to Palestine. William Perl, *Operation Action: Rescue from the Holocaust* (New York, 1983), 85, 246–47.

15. Lucy Dawidowicz, *What Is the Use of Jewish History?* (New York, 1992), 189–96.

16. For a searing critique of the report and the commission behind it, see ibid., 179–89.

17. Saul S. Friedman, "The Power and/or Powerlessness of American Jews, 1939–1945," in Seymour M. Finger, *American Jewry during the Holocaust: A Report by the American Jewish Commission on the Holocaust* (New York, 1984), Appendix 8, pp. 18, 19, 42. This volume is commonly known as *The Goldberg Report*.

18. Davidowicz, "Indicting American Jews," 186.

19. David Kranzler, *Thy Brother's Blood: The Orthodox Jewish Response during the Holocaust* (New York, 1987), 65.

20. Ibid., 68–69.

21. Finger, Appendix 3, p. 15.

22. Yehuda Bauer, *Jews for Sale?* (New Haven, 1994), 258.

23. J. J. Goldberg, *Jewish Power* (New York, 1996), 134. For an expanded discussion of this point, see Deborah Lipstadt, "The Holocaust: Symbol and 'Myth' in American Jewish Life," *Forum*, 40 (Winter 1981), 73–88, and "America and the Memory of the Holocaust, 1950–1965," *Modern Judaism* 16 (1996), 195–214.

24. Many Jews, particularly religious leaders, who had been deeply engaged in ecumenical dialogue were deeply resentful of the churches' silence during this period. One rabbi expressed his disappointment: "I had hoped and prayed that mankind, and especially Christianity, had learned a lesson from the Holocaust. I had hoped that they had learned that the ultimate sin was silent acquiescence in the Nazi genocide. To my dismay, in 1967, it became apparent that nothing had been learned and nothing had actually changed." Joseph D. Herzog, "I Walked with Martin Luther King, Jr.," *Jewish Spectator* (Summer 1979), 19.

25. Milton Himmelfarb, "The 1967 War," *Commentary* (October 1967), reprinted in *The Jews of Modernity* (New York, 1973), 344.

26. Ibid.

27. Goldberg, *Jewish Power*, 134.

28. Psalms 146:3.

29. Feingold, "Review," 56.

30. An official of a civil rights organization told the predominantly Jewish audience at a New York City Board of Education hearing on school integration: "Hitler made a mistake when he didn't kill enough of you." When the organization, Congress of Racial Equality (CORE), to which many Jews belonged, refused to discipline him, deep pain was added to deep outrage. Robert Weisbord and Arthur Stein, *Bittersweet Encounter* (New York, 1972), 175; *New York Times*, February 9, 1966. A radio station in New York City broadcast a poem by a fifteen-year-old African American. Dedicated to Albert Shanker, then president of the teachers' union, it included the verse: "Hey, Jewboy, with that yarmulka on your head/You pale-faced Jewboy, I wish you were dead." The student complained that she was "sick of hearing about [Jewish] suffering in Germany." On the same station, another African-American guest opined that "Hitler didn't make enough lamp shades out of Jews." *New York Times*, January 24, 1969; *Village Voice*, February 6, 1969; Weisbord and Stein, 175–77. Ironically, these incidents occurred on the Julius Lester show. A number of years later, Lester converted to Judaism and currently teaches at the University of Massachusetts's Jewish Studies program.

31. Nathan Glazer, *American Judaism* (Chicago, 1972), 181.

32. Ibid., 173.

33. Ibid.

34. M. J. Nurenberger, *The Scared and the Doomed: The Jewish Establishment vs. the Six Million* (New York, 1985), 31.

35. Perl, *Operation Rescue*, 128.

36. Karen Greenberg, "The Burden of Being Human: An Essay on Selected Scholarship of the Holocaust," in Newton, *FDR and the Holocaust*, 36–37; Goldberg, *Jewish Power*, 135–36.

37. From a speech given by the author in Boston's Faneuil Hall in the fall of 1972 at a women's rally for Soviet Jewry.

38. Goldsberg, *Jewish Power*, 114.

39. Lipstadt, "Symbol and Myth," 73–88.

40. Yehuda Bauer, "The Goldberg Report," *Midstream* 2 (1985), reprinted in Michael Marrus, ed., *The Nazi Holocaust: Historical Articles on the Destruction of European Jews* (Westport, CT, 1989), VIII:942.

41. Nurenberger, *The Scared and the Doomed*, 31.

42. Monty Penkower, *The Jews Were Expendable* (Chicago, 1983), 145, 339n70.

43. Arthur J. Goldberg and Arthur Hertzberg, "Commentary from Commission Members on American Jewry and the Holocaust," in Finger, Appendix 3, p. 8.

44. Medoff, *Deafening Silence*, 176–77, 180; Saul S. Friedman, "The Power and/or Powerlessness," 38.

45. Douglas Wilson, "Thomas Jefferson and the Character Issue," *Atlantic* (November 1992), as quoted in Goldberg, *Jewish Power*, 113.

46. William J. Vanden Heuvel, "The Holocaust Was No Secret," *New York Times Magazine*, December 22, 1996, 30–31; Arthur Schlesinger, Jr. "Did FDR Betray the Jews? Or Did He Do More than Anyone Else to Save Them?" in Newton, *FDR and the Holocaust*, 159–61.

47. William J. Vanden Heuvel, "An Amplification," in Newton, *FDR and the Holocaust*, 164.

48. Rubinstein, *Myth of Rescue*, 3–4.

49. Walter Laqueur, "Fait Accompli," *New Republic*, March 24, 1997, 42.

50. Bauer, *Jews for Sale?* 258.

PART IV: DOCUMENTS
INTRODUCTION

1. For more detail, see Miroslav Karny, "The Vrba and Wetzler Report," in Yisrael Gutman and Michael Berenbaum, eds., *The Anatomy of the Auschwitz Death Camp* (Bloomington, Ind., 1994), 553–68.

VRBA-WETZLER AND ROSIN-MORDOWICZ REPORTS

1. The best current estimates are that about 1.1 million people were murdered in the Auschwitz gas chambers and camp system up to liberation at the end of January 1945; about one million of these were Jewish.

SELECT BIBLIOGRAPHY

Bauer, Yehuda. *Jews for Sale? Nazi-Jewish Negotiations, 1933–1945*. New Haven: Yale University Press, 1994.

Berenbaum, Michael, and Abraham Peck, eds. *The Holocaust and History: The Known, the Unknown, the Disputed, and the Reexamined*. Bloomington and Indianapolis: Indiana University Press, published in association with the United States Holocaust Memorial Museum, 1998.

Biddle, Tami Davis. "British and American Approaches to Strategic Bombing: Their Origins and Implementation in the World War II Combined Bomber Offensive," *Journal of Strategic Studies*, 18 (March 1995), 91–144.

Bird, Kai. *The Chairman: John J. McCloy and the Making of the American Establishment*. New York: Simon & Schuster, 1992.

Braham, Randolph L. *The Politics of Genocide: The Holocaust in Hungary*. Revised and Enlarged Edition. 2 vols. New York: The Rosenthal Institute for Holocaust Studies, Graduate Center/CUNY and Social Science Monographs, Boulder, distributed by Columbia University Press, 1994.

Breitman, Richard. *The Architect of Genocide: Himmler and the Final Solution*. New York: Knopf, 1991.

———. *Official Secrets: What the Nazis Planned, What the British and Americans Knew*. New York: Hill and Wang, 1998.

———, and Shlomo Aronson. "The End of the 'Final Solution'?: Nazi Plans to Ransom Jews in 1944," *Central European History* 25 (1992), 177–203.

———, and Alan M. Kraut. *American Refugee Policy and American Jewry, 1933–1945*. Bloomington: Indiana University Press, 1987.

Brugioni, Dino A. "Auschwitz-Birkenau: Why the World War II Photo Interpreters Failed to Identify the Extermination Complex." *Military Intelligence* (Jan.–Mar. 1983), 50–55.

———, and Robert G. Poirier. *The Holocaust Revisited: A Retrospective Analysis of the Auschwitz-Birkenau Extermination Complex*. ST-79-10001. Washington, D.C.: Central Intelligence Agency, February 1979.

Cesarani, David, ed. *Genocide and Rescue: The Holocaust in Hungary 1944*. Oxford and Washington, D.C.: Berg Publishers, 1997.

Craven, Wesley Frank, and James Lea Cate. *The Army Air Forces in World War II*, 7 vols. Chicago: University of Chicago Press, 1948–1958.

Davis, Richard G. *Carl A. Spaatz and the Air War in Europe*. Washington, D.C.: Smithsonian Institution Press for the Center for Air Force History, 1993.

Engel, David. *Facing a Holocaust: The Polish Government-in-Exile and the Jews, 1943–1945*. Chapel Hill: University of North Carolina Press, 1993.

———. *In the Shadow of Auschwitz: the Polish Government-in-Exile and the Jews, 1939–1942*. Chapel Hill: University of North Carolina Press, 1987.

Erdheim, Stuart G. "Could the Allies Have Bombed Auschwitz-Birkenau?" *Holocaust and Genocide Studies* 11 (Fall 1997), 129–70.

Feingold, Henry L. *Bearing Witness: How America and Its Jews Responded to the Holocaust.* Syracuse: Syracuse University Press, 1995.

———. *The Politics of Rescue: The Roosevelt Administration and the Holocaust, 1938–1945.* New York: Holocaust Library, 1970.

Foregger, Richard. "The Bombing of Auschwitz." *Aerospace Historian* (Summer/June 1987), 98–110.

———. "The First Allied Aerial Reconnaissance over Auschwitz during World War II." *Military History Journal* 8 (June 1989), 31–32.

———. "Technical Analysis of Methods to Bomb the Gas Chambers at Auschwitz." *Holocaust and Genocide Studies* 5 (1990), 403–21.

———. "Two Sketch Maps of the Auschwitz-Birkenau Extermination Camps." *Journal of Military History* 59 (Oct. 1995), 687–96.

Gilbert, Martin. *Auschwitz and the Allies.* New York: Holt, Rinehart and Winston, 1981.

Gutman, Yisrael, and Michael Berenbaum, eds. *Anatomy of the Auschwitz Death Camp.* Bloomington and Indianapolis: Indiana University Press, published in association with the United States Holocaust Memorial Museum, 1994.

Hilberg, Raul. *The Destruction of the European Jews.* Revised and Definitive Edition. 3 vols. New York: Holmes & Meier, 1985.

Hinsley, F. H., et al. *British Intelligence in the Second World War: Its Influence on Strategy and Operations.* 3 vols. in 4. London: Her Majesty's Stationery Office, 1979–88.

Hodges, Robert H. "Auschwitz Revisited: Could the Soviets Have Bombed the Camp?" *Air Power History* (Winter 1997), 74–75.

———. " 'The Bombing of Auschwitz': A Clarification." *Aerospace Historian* (Summer, June 1988), 123–26.

Horovitz, David. "Why the Allies Didn't Bomb Auschwitz." *World Press Review* 42 (Mar. 1995), 44–45.

Kitchens, James H., III. "The Bombing of Auschwitz Re-examined." *Journal of Military History* 58 (April 1994), 233–66.

Laqueur, Walter. *The Terrible Secret: The Suppression of the Truth about Hitler's "Final Solution."* New York: Penguin, 1981.

———, and Richard Breitman. *Breaking the Silence.* New York: Simon & Schuster, 1986.

Levy, Richard H. "The Bombing of Auschwitz Revisited: A Critical Analysis." *Holocaust and Genocide Studies* 10 (Winter 1996), 267–98.

Lipstadt, Deborah. *Beyond Belief: The American Press and the Coming of the Holocaust 1933–1945.* New York: Free Press, 1986.

Marrus, Michael R. *The Holocaust in History.* Hanover, N.H.: University Press of New England, 1987/New York: Meridien, 1989.

Medoff, Rafael. *The Deafening Silence.* New York: Shapolsky Publishers, 1987.

———. "New Perspectives on How America, and American Jewry, Responded to the Holocaust." *American Jewish History* 84 (Sept. 1996), 253–66.

Morse, Arthur D. *While Six Million Died: A Chronicle of American Apathy.* New York: Random House, 1968.

Moskow, Michael G. " 'The Bombing of Auschwitz': A Reply." *Aerospace Historian* (Summer, June 1988), 127–30.

Newton, Verne, ed. *FDR and the Holocaust.* New York: St. Martin's Press, 1996.

Novick, Peter. *The Holocaust in American Life.* Boston and New York: Houghton Mifflin, 1999.

Orpen, Neil. *Airlift to Warsaw: The Rising of 1944.* Norman: University of Oklahoma Press, 1984.

Penkower, Monty Noam. *The Jews Were Expendable: Free World Diplomacy and the Holocaust*. Urbana: University of Illinois Press, 1983.

Porat, Dina. *The Blue and the Yellow Stars of David*. Cambridge, Mass.: Harvard University Press, 1990.

Rice, Rondall R. "Bombing Auschwitz: US 15th Air Force and the Military Aspects of a Possible Attack," *War in History* 6 (1999), 205–29.

Rubinstein, William D. *The Myth of Rescue: Why the Democracies Could Not Have Saved More Jews from the Nazis*. London and New York: Routledge, 1997.

Schaffer, Ronald. *Wings of Judgment: American Bombing in World War II*. New York: Oxford University Press, 1986.

Schwartz, Bertram, and James H. Kitchens III. "Could the Allies Have Bombed Auschwitz?" (Letters to the Editor). *Journal of Military History* 59 (1995), 205–15.

Sherry, Michael. *The Rise of American Air Power: The Creation of Armageddon*. New Haven: Yale University Press, 1987.

Teveth, Shabtai. *Ben-Gurion and the Holocaust*. New York: Harcourt Brace, 1996.

Vrba, Rudolph. "Die missachtete Warnung: Betrachtungen über den Auschwitz-Bericht, 1944." *Vierteljahrshefte für Zeitgeschichte* 44 (1996), 1–24.

———, and Alan Bestic. *I Cannot Forgive*. New York: Grove Press, 1964.

Wasserstein, Bernard. *Britain and the Jews of Europe 1939–1945*. London: Institute of Jewish Affairs, and Oxford: Clarendon Press, 1979.

Webster, Sir Charles, and Noble Frankland. *The Strategic Air Offensive against Germany 1939–1945*. 4 vols. London: Her Majesty's Stationery Office, 1961.

Weinberg, Gerhard L. *A World at Arms: A Global History of World War II*. New York: Cambridge University Press, 1994.

Williams, Roger M. "Why Wasn't Auschwitz Bombed? An American Moral Tragedy." *Commonweal* 105 (24 Nov. 1978), 746–751.

Wyman, David, ed. *America and the Holocaust*, vol. 12. New York: Garland, 1990.

———. *The Abandonment of the Jews: America and the Holocaust 1941–1945*. New York: Pantheon Books, 1984.

———. "Why Auschwitz Was Never Bombed." *Commentary* 65 (May 1978), 37–46. (See also letters to the editor and Wyman's responses on the same in *Commentary* 66 [July 1978], 7, 10–12; [Sept. 1978], 24–25; and [Nov. 1978], 19–20.)

Yahil, Leni. *The Holocaust: The Fate of European Jewry, 1932–1945*. New York: Oxford University Press, 1990.

ABOUT THE EDITORS

MICHAEL J. NEUFELD is a curator and historian at the National Air and Space Museum, Smithsonian Institution, Washington, D.C. A native of Alberta, Canada, he received his Ph.D. from Johns Hopkins in 1984. He is the author of *The Skilled Metalworkers of Nuremberg* (1989) and *The Rocket and the Reich* (1995), and he edited and introduced Yves Béon's *Planet Dora: A Memoir of the Holocaust and the Origins of the Space Age* (1997). Currently he is researching and writing a scholarly biography of Dr. Wernher von Braun.

MICHAEL BERENBAUM is director of the Sigi Ziering Institute: Exploring the Ethical and Religious Implications of the Holocaust and adjunct professor of theology at the University of Judaism. He is former president of the Survivors of the Shoah Visual History Foundation and former director of the Research Institute and former project director of the United States Holocaust Memorial Museum. He has authored or edited twelve books, including *The World Must Know* (1993), *Anatomy of the Auschwitz Death Camp* (1994), and *The Holocaust and History: The Known, the Unknown, the Disputed and the Reexamined* (1998).

ABOUT THE CONTRIBUTORS

TAMI DAVIS BIDDLE is associate professor of national security at the U.S. Army War College. She has taught at Duke University and has held fellowships from the Social Science Research Council, the Smithsonian Institution, the Harvard Center for International Affairs, and the Brookings Institution. While maintaining an active interest in the history of the Cold War, she has completed a book on interwar Anglo-American strategic bombing doctrine: *Rhetoric and Reality in Air Warfare: The Evolution of British and American Ideas About Strategic Bombing, 1914–1945* (Princeton, 2002). Biddle has also contributed "British and American Approaches to Strategic Bombing: Their Origins and Implementation in the World War II Combined Bomber Offensive," to John Gooch, ed., *Air Power: Theory and Practice* (London, 1995), and "Air Power," to Michael Howard, George Andreopoulos, and Mark Shulman, eds., *The Laws of War* (1994).

RICHARD BREITMAN is professor of history at American University and editor-in-chief of *Holocaust and Genocide Studies.* He is the author, among other works, of *The Architect of Genocide: Himmler and the Final Solution* (1991) and of *Official Secrets: What the Nazis Planned, What the British and Americans Knew* (1998), from which chapter 2 of this volume is drawn.

DINO A. BRUGIONI is a native of Missouri. During World War II, he flew sixty-six bombardment and a number of reconnaissance missions over Europe. After the war, he received B.A. and M.A. degrees in foreign affairs from George Washington University. He joined the Central Intelligence Agency in 1948 and became an expert on Soviet industrial installations. He was selected as a member of the cadre of founding officers of the National Photographic Interpretation Center, where he was involved in the exploitation of U-2, SR-71, and satellite imagery in strategic and crisis situations. Brugioni has received a number of awards for his work, including a citation from President Kennedy for his performance in the Cuban missile crisis, and more recently the "Pioneer in Space" medal from the U.S. government. He has written extensively on the application of aerial and spatial imagery to intelligence, historical, and environmental problems. He is also a Civil War buff and has written articles and a book on the war in the west.

RICHARD G. DAVIS received his Ph.D. from George Washington University in 1986. Since 1980, he has been employed by the U.S. Air Force as a civilian historian. (The opinions expressed in his chapter are his own and do not reflect the official position of the U.S. Air Force or the Department of Defense.) His *Carl A. Spaatz and the Air War in Europe* was jointly published by the Office of Air Force History and the Smithsonian Institution Press in 1993. He has completed two book-length manuscripts: a statistical history of the Combined Bomber Offensive and a security-classified study of the bombing of Iraq in the Persian Gulf War. Davis is currently working on two projects: a short history of B-29 operations in the Korean War and a biography of Gen. Henry A. (Hap) Arnold.

STUART G. ERDHEIM received a master's degree in philosophy and a doctor of divinity degree from Yeshiva University in 1982. Since 1990, he has been working in the film industry and has recently produced a documentary on the bombing of Auschwitz-Birkenau entitled, "They Looked Away," narrated by Mike Wallace of the CBS show 60 *Minutes.*

HENRY L. FEINGOLD is emeritus professor at the Graduate Center and Baruch College of CUNY, where he taught Holocaust and American Jewish history. He currently serves as the director of the Jewish Resource Center of Baruch College. He is the author of *The Politics of Rescue: The Roosevelt Administration and the Holocaust, 1938–1945* (1970) and *Bearing Witness: How America and Its Jews Responded to the Holocaust* (1995). He is the editor of the five-volume *The Jewish People in America,* and he wrote its fourth volume, *A Time for Searching: Entering the Mainstream, 1920–1945* (1992). He is currently writing a history of the Jewish question in American foreign relations.

MARTIN GILBERT is the official biographer of Winston S. Churchill and is the author of more than fifty books, including *The Holocaust* (1979), *Auschwitz and the Allies* (1981), *Israel* (1998), and *The Routledge Atlas of the Holocaust* (3rd ed., 2002). He has been a fellow of Merton College Oxford since 1962 and an honorary fellow since 1994. He was knighted in 1995.

JAMES H. KITCHENS III is an independent scholar. He received his Ph.D. in history from Louisiana State University in 1974 and is the author of a history of the Huntsville Division of the U.S. Army Corps of Engineers (1978). For eleven years, he was a reference archivist at the Air Force Historical Research Agency at Maxwell Air Force Base, Alabama. In addition to his article on the bombing of Auschwitz, originally published in the *Journal of Military History* in 1994, he has written on early modern European history and on the history of the Luftwaffe.

WALTER LAQUEUR is cochair of the International Research Council at the Center for Strategic and International Studies, Washington, D.C., and holder of the Kissinger Chair. He has taught at Brandeis, Harvard, the University of Chicago, Johns Hopkins, and Tel Aviv University. His last academic position was that of university professor at Georgetown University. He was also director of the Institute of Contemporary History and Wiener Library, London, and is founder and coeditor of the *Journal of Contemporary History*. Among his books are *The Terrible Secret: The Suppression of the Truth about Hitler's "Final Solution"* (1980, 1998) and *Breaking the Silence* (with Richard Breitman, 1986, 1996). He has also edited *The Holocaust Encyclopedia* (2001).

RICHARD H. LEVY is a retired nuclear engineer. He received a B.A. in mathematics from Cambridge and a Ph.D. in engineering from Princeton. Since his retirement, he has written on the bombing of Auschwitz (in the journal *Holocaust and Genocide Studies*) and has lectured on the same subject in Washington, D.C., London, and Tel Aviv.

DEBORAH E. LIPSTADT is Dorot Professor of Modern Jewish and Holocaust Studies at Emory University. She is the author of *Beyond Belief: The American Press and the Coming of the Holocaust, 1933–1945* (1986) and *Denying the Holocaust: The Growing Assault on Truth and Memory* (1993).

WILLIAMSON MURRAY is professor emeritus at Ohio State University. He has taught at Yale and the U.S. Military Academy and has been a visiting professor at the London School of Economics, the Naval War College, and the Air War College. He has also been a Secretary of the Navy Fellow at the Naval War College, Matthew C. Horner Professor in Military Theory at Marine Corps University, and the Charles A. Lindbergh Professor in Aerospace History at the National Air and Space Museum. In 1998–1999, he was Harold K. Johnson Professor of Military History at the Army War College. He is the author of *The Change in the European Balance of Power, 1938–1939* (1984), *The Luftwaffe* (1985), *German Military Effectiveness* (1992), and *The Air War in the Persian Gulf* (1994). His edited works include *Military Effectiveness* (with Allan Millett, 1988); *Calculations, Net Assessment and the Coming of World War II* (with Allan Millett, 1992); *The Making of Strategy, Rulers, States, and War* (with MacGregor Knox, 1994); and *Military Innovation in the Interwar Period* (with Allan Millett, 1996).

RONDALL R. RICE, a captain in the United States Air Force, is a 1989 U.S. Air Force Academy graduate. Rice, who holds a bachelor's degree in military history, earned his M.A. in modern European history from the University of Nebraska at Lincoln in 1996. His military assignments as an intelligence specialist have included the Persian Gulf war and a NATO unit in Germany, and he was director of tactical reconnaissance for NATO air operations over Bosnia-Herzegovina. From 1996 to 1999, he returned to the Air Force Academy as an assistant professor, where he directed the Holocaust course and taught courses on world, German, and modern European history. Rice is currently being sponsored by the Air Force in his pursuit of a Ph.D. in military history at the University of North Carolina, Chapel Hill.

GERHART M. RIEGNER died in Geneva on 3 December 2001. He was born in Berlin in 1911 and studied law and political sciences at the Universities of Freiburg im Breisgau, Heidelberg, and Berlin. After his suspension on 1 April 1933 as an official of the Tribunal of First Instance in Berlin, he left Germany. At the creation of the World Jewish Congress in 1936, he joined the staff of the organization and directed its international legal work. During World War II, his office in Geneva became the main source of information on the fate of the European Jews. He served the WJC in many capacities, notably as secretary general from 1965 to 1983. He was awarded many high honors and in 1999 published his memoirs, entitled *Ne jamais désespérer*.

GERHARD L. WEINBERG is William Rand Kennan, Jr., Professor of History Emeritus at the University of North Carolina at Chapel Hill. He has also taught at the Universities of Chicago, Kentucky, and Michigan, and he has directed the American Historical Association's project for microfilming captured German documents. He is the author of numerous articles in both American and German journals, as well as of many books. Among his best known are *Germany and the Soviet Union, 1939–1941* (1954); *Hitlers Zweites Buch* (1961); *The Foreign Policy of Hitler's Germany* (2 vols., 1970, 1980); *World in the Balance: Behind the Scenes of World War II* (1981); and *A World at Arms: A Global History of World War II* (1994). His most recent work is *Germany, Hitler, and World War II: Essays in Modern German and World History* (1995).

COPYRIGHT ACKNOWLEDGMENTS

The editors wish to thank the following publishers and institutions for granting the right to republish copyright material in this book:

- Indiana University Press for Gerhard L. Weinberg's "The Allies and the Holocaust" from *The Holocaust and History* (1998), edited by Michael Berenbaum and Abraham J. Peck.
- Farrar, Straus and Giroux, Inc., and Penguin UK, for "Auschwitz Partially Decoded" by Richard Breitman, a revised version of Chapter 7 of *Official Secrets: What the Nazis Planned, What the British and Americans Knew* (1998), published by Hill and Wang, an imprint of Farrar, Straus and Giroux, and Penguin Books Ltd.
- The Society for Military History for James H. Kitchens III's "The Bombing of Auschwitz Re-examined," from *The Journal of Military History* 58 (April 1994), 233–66.
- Oxford University Press and *Holocaust and Genocide Studies* for "The Bombing of Auschwitz Revisited: A Critical Analysis" by Richard H. Levy, from *HGS* 10 (Winter 1996), 267–98, and "Could the Allies Have Bombed Auschwitz-Birkenau?" by Stuart G. Erdheim, from *HGS* 11 (Fall 1997), 129–70.
- Martin Gilbert for rights to two maps from *Auschwitz and the Allies* (1981) used by James H. Kitchens III in "The Bombing of Auschwitz Re-examined" as base maps for his illustrations.
- St. Martin's Press and the Franklin and Eleanor Roosevelt Institute for "Allied Knowledge of Auschwitz-Birkenau in 1943–1944" by Richard Breitman, parts of which have appeared in his contribution "Auschwitz Partially Decoded," and for an earlier version of "The Bombing of Auschwitz Revisited: A Critical Analysis" by Richard H. Levy, both published in Verne Newton, ed., *FDR and the Holocaust* (New York: St. Martin's, 1996).
- Edward Arnold Publishers, Limited, for "Bombing Auschwitz: U.S. Fifteenth Air Force and the Military Aspects of a Possible Attack," by Rondall R. Rice, an earlier version of which appeared in *War in History*, 1999; 6:205–29; copy-

In addition, Dino A. Brugioni's contribution, "The Aerial Photos of the Auschwitz-Birkenau Extermination Complex," is a lightly revised version of his article "Auschwitz-Birkenau: Why the World War II Photo Interpreters Failed to Identify the Extermination Complex," from *Military Intelligence* (Jan.–Mar. 1983), 50–55, a U.S. Government (Department of Defense) publication.

INDEX

Adam, Uwe Dietrich, 113
Aegean islands, 22
aerial photography
  modern interpretation of World War II
    photos, 52–57
  World War II practice of acquiring and
    interpreting, 52–57, 87–88, 130–33, 135–36
Aerospace Historian, 4, 84
Agudas Israel World Organization, 48, 65–66, 103, 254
aircraft production
  American, 39
  German, Allied air attacks on, 164–65, 207
Air Ministry (British)
  examines feasibility of bombing Auschwitz, 70–
    75, 224
  opposed linkage of bombing and retaliation, 196
  rejects Auschwitz bombing appeal, 81
air power
  Allied, objectives and capabilities of, 35–51
  American belief in, 3
  historical studies of, 85–86
air raids, planning process of, 89–90
air war over Germany
  Allied losses, 206–7
  lynching of downed pilots, 319n.10
  success of, by 1944, 102, 165
Akzin, Benjamin
  memos in favor of Auschwitz bombing, 67–
    68, 104
    memo to J. W. Pehle, quoted, 275–76
    memo to L. S. Lesser, quoted, 258–59
  urged action on Auschwitz, 9, 106
  urged Pehle to go directly to Roosevelt, 122
Alanbrooke, Lord (Sir Alan Francis Brooke), 204
Albright, Madeleine, 228
Allen, Roger, 73
Allies
  anti-Semitism among, 9, 22, 198, 225–26
  conduct of War, Soviet objection to, 198
  and the Holocaust
    condemnation of, 38, 138–39
    extent of knowledge of, 27–34, 191
    inaction during, 39, 234–35
    indifferent to fate of Jews, supposedly, 127
    lack of concern with, supposed, 201–3
    policies as affecting, 15–26
    refusal to engage the "Jewish Question," 194,
      200–203

war aim
  and public opinion, 22, 198
  total and quick victory, 9, 22–23, 26, 49, 77–
    78, 85, 190, 195, 198, 206, 225
  was not explicitly to save Jews, 194–203
American Gathering of Jewish Holocaust
  Survivors, 82
American Jews
  leaders, criticized for inaction during
    Holocaust, 230–36
  Orthodox criticisms of Reform and secular
    Jews, 231–32
Americans
  accused of complicity in Holocaust, 81
  and British, coordination of war efforts, 39–
    41
  intelligence reports passed to, 32–33
  response to the Holocaust, as it was
    occurring, 227–33
Amiens, German prison camp at, bombing of
  (1944), 67, 90
  attack method, 96, 149, 218
  difficulty of, as target, 145, 152
Anderson, Gen. Frederick, 49
antiaircraft guns, German, 91, 139–41, 165–68,
  294n.57
anti-Semitism
  among Allied populations, 9, 22, 198, 225–26
  "Jewish," 234
  postwar, 200–201, 233
Antwerp, 211
Arabian peninsula, 20
Arab-Israeli War of 1967 (Six-Day War), 3, 232–33
Arabs, in Palestine, British policy toward, 16–17
Ardennes offensive, 209
Armenians, genocide against, 226
Arnold, Gen. Henry "Hap," 158
Aronson, Shlomo, 23
Atlantic Charter (1941), 203
Augsburg, Allied air attack against M.A.N. diesel
  engine works at (1942), 93–95
Auschwitz (town) (also called Oswiecim), 127
Auschwitz bombing controversy (among
  historians), x, 1–10, 201–3
  current interest in, reason for, 201–3, 229
  a "dialogue of the deaf," 4, 201
  origins of, 101–26
  overview of, 80–100

Auschwitz bombing controversy (*continued*)
  as part of wider study of rescue efforts in
    World War II, 186–87, 193
Auschwitz bombing proposal (of 1944)
  actions that might have been taken, 139–41,
    143–52, 174–79
    bombing the rail lines leading to
      Auschwitz, 48, 102–11
    commando raid to blow up crematoria, 78
    heavy bombing in daylight, 120
    low level attack, 147–49, *148* (map)
  arguments against, 36–39, 49–51, 67–73, 81
    a diversion from main war effort, 153, 162,
      190, 195, 212, 221–22
    it would kill camp prisoners, 99, 105, 143–
      47, 172–79, 213
    technical difficulties, 188
    unlikely to limit loss of life, 193–94
  arguments for, 70
    moral effect, 111–12, 213
    as precedent for intervening in future
      atrocities, 215
    prisoners were doomed anyway, 145, 178
    to save lives, 214–15, 314n.136
    to send a message, 214–15
    to show indignation, 68
    to slow the killing, 67–68
    symbolic effect, 25–26
  casualties expected from, 92–93, *94* (map), 98–
    99, 121
  commanders consulted on, 49, 72, 121–24
  contemporary appeals to bomb, 6, 27, 35–39,
    48–51, 57, 65–78, 80–81, 102–4, 112–13, 122–
    25, 134, 193, 200, 214
    denied, 36–38, 66–69, 71–72, 81, 107, 113, 153,
      195
  feasibility question, 5–8, 24–26, 65–75, 107, 116–
    21, 127–28, 152–79, 218–26
    never tested, because not even tried, 192
    should vs. could question, 127–28, 153–56
  German probable response, 179, 223, 281n.5
  how many lives could have been saved, 7, 25,
    113–16
  ideal months to attack (July and August,
    1944), 163, 223–25
  intelligence and planning necessary to carry
    out, causing delay, 159–63, 223–24
  international law aspects of, 99
  opponents of, 105–6, 112–13, 121, 122
  placed in the context of the War, 201–3
  political considerations, 122–24, 154–63
Auschwitz complex (as a whole)
  antiaircraft defenses at, 91, 139–41, *140* (map),
    167–68, 294n.57
  fighter aircraft at or near, 91, 141–42, 165–68
  industrial activities at, 28–29, 133
  maps of, 77, *88* (map), 89
  photo-reconnaissance of, 1, 49, 51
    existed already, before Auschwitz bombing
      proposal, 57, 133–36
    present-day interpretation of, 52–57
  raids on (summer 1944), 127, 133, 142
Auschwitz I ("Main Camp"), 28, 54, 113

aerial photography of, 52
Crematorium I at, out of service, 131, 169
truth about, as extermination camp, when
  evident, 137
Auschwitz II (Auschwitz-Birkenau)
  bombing proposals. *See* Auschwitz bombing
    controversy; Auschwitz bombing
    proposal
  crematoria at (Crematoria II–V), 31, 33, 87,
    132, 169–70
    assessing as targets, 169–79
    capacity and extent of use, 114, 162
    confusion over number of, 113
    as difficult targets, 87, 115–16, 117, 218, 221
    as easy and worthwhile targets, 131–32, 155
    feasibility of destroying them, 75
  executions at, 28, 32
  gassing facilities, in two buildings, 169
  Himmler's visit to, 29
  intelligence reports on, 66–67, 72–73, 81, 89,
    103, 134, 160–63
  liberation of, by Soviets, 50, 200
  map and photo-reconnaissance requested, 72–
    73, 123–24, 129–36, 224
  present-day interpretation of, 52–57, 87
  maps of, in escapees' reports, 129–30
  population and mortality statistics, 27, 31, 32–
    33, 92, 162–63, 321n.2, 325n.1(2)
  targeting of
    difficulty, due to distance and
      inaccessibility, 89–91, 187–88, 215
    not considered a priority, by some, 128
  truth about, as extermination camp
    first thought to be a concentration camp, 133
    little awareness of, by average American at
      the time, 195
    not known to lower level American
      commanders, 161
    obscure nature of activities at, 27–34, 159
    revealed from escapees' reports, 27, 65–66,
      76–77, 129
    revealed from underground reports, 31–34,
      65–66, 82, 135
    surmised from German police intercepts,
      18, 27–30, 137–38
    when evident, 103, 137–39, 159–63, 188–89,
      222–23
Auschwitz III (Auschwitz-Monowitz)
  aerial photography of, 54
  bombing of, 51, 77, 319n.6
  industrial activities at, 28–29
  intelligence reports on, 160
  prisoner of war camp at, 160, 308n.54
  slave laborer deaths at, 293n.47
  See also Farben, I. G., complex
Austria, emigration from, difficulty of, 15
Avranches, 211

B-17 Flying Fortress bomber, 42, 91, 163, 164, 220
B-24 Liberator bomber, 91, 150, 163, 220
B-25 Mitchell bomber, 90, 95, 119, 219
B-29 Superfortress bomber, 164
Babi Yar, 115, 200

Balkan Air Force (British), 150
Balkans, Germans in, 225
Barlas, Chaim, letter from Yitzak Gruenbaum
    to, quoted, 262
Barry, Charles, 135
Bauer, Yehuda, 232, 234
Bayerlein, Lt. Gen. Fritz, 320n.13
Bedouins, airlift of food to, 154, 202
Belgium, transports from, 33
Belzec, 6, 314n.136
Ben-Ami, Yitshaq, *Years of Wrath, Days of Glory:
    Memoirs from the Irgun*, 231
Ben-Gurion, David, 105–6, 121, 236
    cable from Moshe Shertok to, quoted, 264–66
Ben-Tzvi (JAE board member), 105
Berlin, bombing of (1943–44), 43, 206
Birkenau. *See* Auschwitz II
Blechhammer, refineries at, Allied air attacks on,
    133, 135, 166, 167, 216
Bletchley Park decoding operation, 17–18
Blizna, 133
Blood for Trucks ransom proposal (1944), 193, 195
Blum, John Morton, *V Was for Victory*, 81
Board of Deputies of British Jews, 200
Bohemia-Moravia, transports from, 33
Bohlen, Allied air attacks on, 208
Bohumin, Allied air attacks on, 216
Bomber Command (British)
    area bombing policy of, 41, 195–98
    capabilities of, 37–38, 116–17
    losses, 37, 206–7
    oil supply bombing campaign, 209
    operating methods of, 43
    range of, 215
bombing
    accuracy of, 37, 43, 84, 92, 96, 120, 145–47, 169–
        79, 211
    aerial photography during, 52
    area, 37–43, 47, 120, 172, 195–98
    blind, 173
    British vs. American policies, 39–43
    daylight, 39–41, 120, 143–47
    dive, 119, 147–49, 219
    in formations, 174
    high-altitude, 39–41, 91–93, 120, 143–47
    low-altitude, 93, 147–49
    nighttime, 39–40, 120, 150
    planning process
        assessing the probability of destroying the
            target, 169–72
        determining the radius of accuracy, 120
        determining the tonnage necessary, 120–21
        model-making of target as aid to, 129
    precision, "pinpoint"
        American belief in, 3
        British abandonment of, 74–75
        claimed, 41–43, 102, 211
        meaning of World War II term, 172, 318n.1
    radar aids, 38, 42–43, 173–74, 218
    strategic
        legal and moral objections to, 42, 99, 197–
            98, 298n.90
        reasons why undertaken, 37–38

summer, 150
visual, 174
weather and, 42–43, 143
Bosnian war (1990s), 24
Bottomley, Air Marshal N. H., 72, 128, 134
    letter to Carl Spaatz, quoted, 270–71
    memo to Air Staff, quoted, 269
Bradley, Lt. Gen. Omar, 44
Brand, Joel, 6
Bratislava, Jewish leadership in, 65, 76
Breitman, Richard, 23
    and Alan Kraut, *American Refugee Policy and
        European Jewry*, 230
    and Walter Laqueur, *Breaking the Silence*, 19
Brereton, Gen. Lewis, 145
Britain
    colonialism of, German propaganda about,
        196
    decoding program of, 27–30, 228
    immigration restrictions, during Depression,
        16
    Indian Muslim troops of, in Palestine, 16, 21
    parliamentary debate on Auschwitz
        controversy (1961), 101
    pre-War policy, 16–17
British Expeditionary Force, 16
Brittany, 211
Brugioni, Dino A., 1, 87–88, 130
Brüx, oil plant in, 132–33
    Allied air attacks on, 208
Buchenwald, 18, 199
    Allied air attack on (1944), 92–93, 143–45
Budapest
    air attack on (April 1944), 216
    air attack on (July 1944), and end of
        deportations, 69, 110, 197, 217–18
    Jewish leadership in, 76
Bulgaria
    surrender to Soviets, 225
    warnings to, re extermination program, 192
Butt report (on Bomber Command accuracy), 37
bystanders, claimed innocence and ignorance of
    Holocaust, 228–29

Caen, Allied air attacks at, 210–11
Cairo conferences (1943), 202
Calvacoressi, Peter, *Top Secret Ultra*, 17–18
Cambodia, mass extermination in, 226
Carter, Pres. Jimmy, x
Casablanca conference (1943), 40, 202
Casey, William, 138
Caucasus campaign (1942), 23
Cavendish-Bentinck, William, 134
    letter from G. W. P. Grant, quoted, 269–70
Central Intelligence Agency, 52
Central Interpretation Unit (Medmenham,
    England) (CIU), 54, 129, 133
Chciuk-Celt, Tadeusz, 30–31
Chelmno (Kulmhof), 215, 314n.136
Chemnitz, Allied air attacks on, 208
Chernovtsi (Czernowitz), 187
Cheshire, Leonard, 74–75, 117, 118, 150–51
Chorzow, 68

Christian churches, felt to be indifferent to
Jewish suffering, 324n.24
Churchill, Winston
failure of vision of, re Final Solution,
supposedly, 202, 214, 225
favored bombing German cities, 195
favored reprisals for German atrocities, 38–
39
letter from Anthony Eden, quoted, 262–63
memo from Anthony Eden, quoted, 266
memo to Anthony Eden, quoted, 266–67
personally ordered raids on difficult targets,
159, 215
remarks about air power, 37, 39
speech about "crime without a name"
(August 1942), 138
urged to condemn the Nazi extermination
program, 106, 192
urges action be taken on Auschwitz, 48–50,
57, 69–70, 77, 107, 122, 123, 125, 222–23,
225
war planning by, 40, 46–47, 125, 204, 314n.130
Circular Error Probable, 171
cities, bombing of, 37–38, 40–43, 47, 172
intended to break German morale, 198
as retaliation, pros and cons, 195–98
civilians, bombing of
collateral deaths from, 220, 314n.130
intentional, 44, 146, 197–98
codes, German, Allied deciphering of, 17–19, 27–
30, 138, 222, 228
Cologne, Allied air attacks on, 195
Combined Bomber Offensive (CBO)
(POINTBLANK), 40, 158, 164
Combined Chiefs of Staff, 121, 202
Commentary, 1, 81
Commissar order (to German troops, to execute
Soviet political prisoners) (1941), 199
Committee of Operations Analysts (COA)
(U.S.), 40
Commonweal, 1, 81
communications, German, disruption of, toward
end of War, 19–20
communism, Jewish links with, claimed, 199,
200
concentration camps
aerial photography of, 53, 55–57
air raids on, welcomed by prisoners, 144, 218
Allied forces not briefed on, 161
Allied knowledge of, 55, 133, 136–39, 159
Allied proposed response to, 38–39
escapes from, 118
German reports about, decoded by British, 17–
19
German system of, 155
mortality statistics, kept by Germans, 29–30
Soviet system of, 200
See also death camps
Copenhagen, 219
cremation ditches, 115–16, 155
crematoria, aerial photographs of, 56
Crimean Tatars, 200
Croatia, 20

Czechoslovakia
Government in Exile, 67, 103, 112, 134
transports from, 30
Czechowice oil refinery, Allied air attack on, 166

Dachau, 18
Dawidowicz, Lucy, 4
death camps, Nazi system of, 155, 215–16
deciphering operations in World War II, 17–20,
27–30
de Jonge, Col. Alfred, memo from Roswell
McClelland, quoted, 249–50
Depression, The, and immigration restrictions in
all countries, 15–16
D.H.98 Mosquito light bombers, 86, 90, 91, 95–
98, 118–19, 218–19
fighter bomber version of, 151–52
photo-reconnaissance version of, 119
Dill, Sir John, 121
Dinnerstein, Leonard, 292n.28
Dominican Republic, 194
Doolittle, Gen. James (Jimmy), 143, 195, 207
Dresden, fire raid on (1945), 196, 209
Drohobycz, 288n.48
Druks, Herbert, *The Failure to Rescue*, 230
Dubova oil refinery, Allied air attack on, 166
Dutch records facility, Allied attack on, 218–19

Eaker, Gen. Ira C., 121, 133, 135, 220
Eastern Europe, air targets in, 187–88
Eastern Front
and liberation of Jews, 212
Soviet advance in, 46, 187–88
Soviet halt at Warsaw, 159, 224
Vernichtungskrieg (war of annihilation) policy,
194, 199
Eban, Abba, 232
Eden, Anthony
letter from Archibald Sinclair, 116, 123
quoted, 267–68
letter to Archibald Sinclair, 149
quoted, 267
letter to Winston Churchill, quoted, 262–63
meeting with Chaim Weizmann, 102, 106–7,
111
memo from Chaim Weizmann and Moshe
Shertok, quoted, 263–64
memo from Winston Churchill, quoted, 266–
67
memo to Winston Churchill, quoted, 266
requested by Chaim Weizmann to bomb
Auschwitz, 69–71, 103
requested by Churchill to take action on
Auschwitz, 48–49, 77, 122, 225
requests Archibald Sinclair to take action on
Auschwitz, 48–49, 70–71, 77, 107, 122
Egypt, 20–21
Eichmann, Adolf
monitoring of activities of, 28
trial of, 3, 101
Eighth Air Force (U.S.)
bombing campaigns, 41, 46, 92
capabilities of, 164

losses, 206–8
not briefed on concentration camps, 161
oil supply bombing campaign, 166
Operation Overlord support, 211, 224
rail bombing campaigns, 98, 220
range of, 215
8th Army (British), 21
82nd Fighter Group (U.S.), 96, 219
Einsatzgruppen (German mobile killing units), 17–19, 229
Eisenberg (JAE board member), 105
Eisenhower, Gen. Dwight, 225, 314n.130, 318n.2
and air operations, 45, 46, 104, 121–22
Commander for the European Theater, 220
and Operation Overlord, 43–44, 210
Embry, Sir Basil, 304n.7, 314n.130
Encyclopedia of the Holocaust (Macmillan), 82
Engel, David, 27
Enigma machine, 17–18, 28
Ent, Brig. Gen. Uzal, 93
Erdheim, Stuart G., 4, 7
Essen, Allied air attacks on, 195
"euthanasia" program, German, 196
Évian-les-Bains conference (1938), 194
extermination program, Nazi
Allies' condemnation of (December 1942), 38
beginnings of, by shooting, 17–20, 115, 138
Himmler's order to discontinue at Auschwitz, 221
improvisation in methods of, 115–16
rail transportation essential to, 101
special death camps for, 155
See also death camps; *Einsatzgruppen*; Final Solution; Holocaust

Farben, I. G., complex
aerial photographs of, taken during World War II, 52, 54, 129–30, 216
Aiming Point Report of 21 Jan. 1944, quoted, 240–42
Allied air attacks on, 77, 120, 133, 166–68, 170, 173, 216, 220, 223
intelligence reports on, 160
oil refinery, 170
synthetic rubber (Buna) plant, 28–29
Feingold, Henry L., 4
The Politics of Rescue, 3, 230
Fifteenth Air Force (U.S.)
A-2 staff of, 166
aerial photographs taken by, 57
Auschwitz bombing by, feasibility of, 90–100
bombing campaigns, 42, 46, 120
Budapest attack, 217
capability and mission of, 157–79, 216, 220
chain of command for, 121
formation of, 41, 143, 291n.26
losses, 96, 208, 321n.4
Ploesti attack, 45, 96, 207–8
target priorities of, from MAAF, 164–65
Fifteenth Army (German), 211
fighter planes
American, escort, 41
German, 141–42, 165–67

Final Solution
Allied intelligence about, 76
high priority given by Nazis to, 116
silence about, in Germany, 196–97
See also Holocaust
Finger, Seymour M., *American Jewry during the Holocaust: A Report by the American Jewish Commission on the Holocaust* (*"Goldberg Report"*), 324n.17
Finland, surrender to Soviets, 225
Fishman, Jacob, 105, 106
"Floradora" material, 19
Focke-Wulf factory in Poland, 288n.48
Fogg, John E., 110
Foggia air base, 90, 102, 119, 143, 187, 200
Foregger, Richard, 4, 87, 129, 157
"The Bombing of Auschwitz" in *Aerospace Historian*, 84, 96
Foreign Office (British)
asked for information re Auschwitz, 72–73
opposed linkage of bombing and retaliation, 196
reports on Auschwitz received by, 89, 103, 134
France
Allied invasion of. *See* Operation Overlord
Jews in, German intention to kill, 22
transports from, 33, 72, 190
Vichy, 197
Frankfurter, Felix, 234
Free French, 211
French North Africa, 20
Friedman, Saul, *No Haven for the Oppressed*, 230, 231
Frischer, Ernest, 112–13
Fry, Varian, "The Massacre of the Jews" article in *New Republic*, 191–92

gas chambers. *See* Auschwitz II.
genocide
inaction in face of, 225–26
by Soviets, 200
unprecedented and therefore unnoticed, 56, 88
See also Holocaust
Gerhardt, Col. Harrison A., 68
memos to John McCloy, quoted, 260, 277
Germans
anti-Semitism of, 196
belief by many that the war was lost, 191
bystanders among, self-claimed, 228–29
possibly unaware of the Final Solution, 197
prisoners in concentration camps, 29
Germany
anti-Semitic measures by Nazis, prior to World War II, 15
archives lost, now evidenced only in intercepts, 19–20
codes, intercepted and decoded by Allies
diplomatic, 19
police, 17–19, 138, 222
desperation of, toward end of war, fearing retaliation, 320n.3
emigration from, difficulty of, 15
intention of, to kill all Jews, 20–26

Germany (*continued*)
negotiations with, to rescue Jews, 23–24, 198
propaganda
anti-Semitic slant of, 22, 39, 200
counter-atrocity campaign, about Allied
terrorism and colonialism, 196
war aim, the "Jewish Question," 202–3, 319n.3
warnings and reprisals to, proposed, re
extermination program, 67, 69, 195–97
Gestapo
camps and headquarters, Allied air attacks
against, 96–97, 118, 145, 149, 219
negotiating with, to rescue Jews, 6–7, 191, 193,
195
Gilbert, Martin, 27, 32, 33, 84, 103, 157
Auschwitz and the Allies, 2, 82, 86
Gleiwitz, 168
Globocnik, Odilo, 29
Goda, Norman, 20
Goebbels, Joseph, 196, 197
Goering, Hermann, intercepted message from, 45
Goldberg, Arthur J., 235
"*Goldberg Report*," 231
Goldhagen, Daniel, *Hitler's Willing Executioners*,
228–29
Goldmann, Nahum, 120, 231
cable from Moshe Shertok to, quoted, 264–66
Goodwin, Doris Kearns, 156
Granovsky (JAE board member), 105
Grant, G. W. P., letter to V. Cavendish-
Bentinck, quoted, 269–70
Great Britain. *See* Britain
Greece
aid to famine sufferers in, 202
Jews of, German intention to kill, 22
transports from, 33
Groban, Milton, 1–2, 84, 161, 167, 173
Gruenbaum, Yitzak, 81, 102–3, 105–6
letter to Chaim Barlas, quoted, 262
memo by Pinkerton of a discussion with,
quoted, 250–52
Gryn, Hugo, 75
Gustloff Works at Buchenwald, bombing of, 143–
44
Gydnia, 215
Gyor, 166
Gypsies, 25, 30, 33

Hague Convention, 99
Hamburg, Allied air attacks on, 195
Handy, Maj. Gen. Thomas R., memo for the
files, re War Refugee Board, 254–55
Hantke (J.A.E. board member), 105
Harris, Sir Arthur ("Bomber")
Berlin campaign, 43
city bombing policy, 37, 40, 47
interviews with, 107, 117, 150
Transportation Plan, 108
Harrison, Leland, telegram to Cordell Hull,
quoted, 256–57
Hertzberg, Arthur, 235
Hilberg, Raul, *The Destruction of the European
Jews*, 3

Himmelfarb, Milton, 232
Himmler, Heinrich, 118, 221
inspection of Auschwitz by, 29
Hinsley, F. H., *British Intelligence in the Second
World War*, 18, 136
Hiroshima bombing, 318n.1
history (discipline)
judging the past by contemporary standards
(presentism), 35, 201, 235
need for counterfactual analysis ("why it
happened"), 186–87
pitfall of, as guidance for wartime leaders,
204
"what if" speculations and "Monday-morning
quarterbacking," 4–5, 8–10, 35, 204
Hitler, Adolf
own words on intention to destroy Jews, 20–
21, 203
probable reaction to bombing Auschwitz,
281n.5
and treatment of prisoners of war, 197
Hodges, Robert H., 96
Holocaust (Shoah, Final Solution)
Allied policies contributing to, 15–26, 81
Allies' condemnation of (1942), 138–39
Allies' knowledge of, as it was occurring, 17–
20, 27–34, 76, 80–81, 88, 136–39, 188–89,
191, 194–95, 227–33, 307n.48
Allies' lack of ability to interfere with, 39
Allies' lack of concern with, seemingly, 201–3
appeals to Allied leaders to stop, 106, 192, 198
archives pertaining to, 19
bystanders' claimed innocence of, 228–29
continuing interest in, 227–36. *See also*
Auschwitz bombing controversy
disbelief in, in the West, 286n.9, 288n.48,
289n.1
German policy of, 76, 116, 196–97
historical studies of, 3–5, 81–87
how it could be stopped
a contemporary proposal, 192
only by Allied troops on the ground, 212–
13
by warning of reprisals, 67, 69, 195–97
See also Auschwitz bombing proposal
and Israel, 282n.7
Jews having learned the lesson of, 232, 234
a museum of, not wanted in Russia, 319n.16
number of Jews killed, 113, 115, 229
popular awareness of, after the War, 3, 9, 35
Soviet response to, 199–200
Holocaust (1978 TV miniseries), 3, 52
Holocaust and Genocide Studies, 4
Hoover, Pres. Herbert, 15
Hopkins, Harry, 39, 205
Horthy, Miklós, 69, 218
Höss, Rudolf, 29, 168
Hull, Cordell, telegram from Leland Harrison
to, quoted, 256–57
Hull, Maj. Gen. J. E., 49
human intelligence, Allied, 30–34
humanitarian missions in World War II, 154,
202

Hungary
  Jews of
    concentration of, prior to deportation,
      102
    Hitler's displeasure with survival of, 20
    negotiations to save, 191
    numbers deported and numbers saved, 108,
      217
    protected for a while from Nazi attack, 218
    transports from, 48, 65–66, 69, 80, 102–8, 162,
      189, 212, 223, 225
      Allied warning to stop, 69, 110, 192, 197, 217
      demand to end, from puppet regime, 69,
        217–18
      ended, 106, 108–11, 217

immigration, restrictions on, by all countries,
    during Great Depression, 15–16
industries, German, Allied air attacks on, 39–43,
    164, 172
intelligence agencies, Allied, records of
  declassification of, 28
  historians urged to research, 79
  kept secret indefinitely, 18
Iran, 20
Iraq, 20
Irgun/Bergson/Revisionist camp, 231
Israel
  impact of the Holocaust in, 282n.7
  leftist critics of, 233–34
  military power of, 234
Italian front, 44, 164
Italy
  Allied air bases in, 90, 102, 119, 143, 150, 152,
    187, 200
  Jews in
    fascist regime's protection of, 21–22
    German intention to kill, 22

Jarvik, Laurence, Who Shall Live and Who Shall
    Die?, 231
Jerusalem, Grand Mufti of, Hitler's promise to,
    20
Jewish Agency (JA)
  appeals of, re Auschwitz, 69–71, 81, 102, 122,
    125, 134, 200
  cable from Richard Lichtheim to, quoted, 261–
    62
  draft note re bombing (July 1944), never sent,
    101, 111–12, 123
  and intelligence on Hungary, 197
  locates map of Auschwitz, 72–73
  Rescue Committee of, 81
Jewish Agency Executive (JAE), 102
  minutes of a meeting of, excerpts, quoted, 252–
    53
  refusal to ask for Auschwitz bombing, 105–6
"Jewish Question" (Germany's)
  Allies' attempt to ignore, 200–203
  importance of, to German war aims, 202–3,
    319n.3
  as Nazi propaganda strength, 194–203
  See also Final Solution

Jews
  abandonment of
    by Allies, claimed, 82, 194, 229
    by fellow Jews, claimed, 236
  Allies' refusal to consider as special case, 194
  extermination of (1940s). See Holocaust
  Germany's intentions to destroy worldwide,
    20–26
  interests of, marginal to Allied thinking, 17–
    26, 50, 190
  prisoners in concentration camps, 29, 31, 113
  refugees
    feared by British of flooding Palestine, 73
    numbers admitted to United States, 16
    resettlement proposals, 193
  survival of, 26, 189–92, 198–99, 201–3
  traditional persecution and exclusion, 15, 202
  underground, 65, 76, 80, 89
  See also American Jews
Joint Intelligence Sub-Committee (JIC), 134
Joint Photographic Reconnaissance Committee
    (JPRC), 134
Joseph, Dr., 105
Journal of Military History, 4
Judeo-Bolshevism (Nazi term), 199, 200

Kalmanowitz, Abraham, 275
Kammler, Hans, 29
Kaplan (JAE board member), 105
Katowice, 68, 133, 168
Katyn Forest massacre, 200
Kenen, I. L., report of meeting with John Pehle,
    quoted, 274–75
Kiev, 187
  air bases near, 200
Kitchens, James H., III, 4, 127, 157
Klemperer, Victor, 188
Kopecky, Jaromir, 67, 76
Korbonski, Stefan, 31
Kos, deportation of Jews from, failure of Allies
    to prevent, 189–90
Košice, railway at, 66, 80, 81
Krakow, 167
Kranzler, David, 231
Krzesinski, 215
Kubowitzki, Leon, 78
  letter from John McCloy, quoted, 274
  letter to John McCloy, quoted, 273–74
  letter to J. W. Pehle, quoted, 259–60
  opposed to Auschwitz bombing, 105–6, 112–13,
    121, 122
kulaks, Soviet murder of, 200

labor, forced, 28–29
Lancaster bomber, 93–95, 117
Laqueur, Walter, 10, 27
  The Terrible Secret, 19, 188
Law, Richard, letter to Archibald Sinclair,
    quoted, 270
Leclerc, Gen. Jacques, 211
Lengyel, Olga, Five Chimneys, 113
Lesser, L. S., memo from Benjamin Akzin to,
    quoted, 258–59

Levy, Richard H., 4, 127, 292n.28
liberals
  Jewish American, condemned by
    neoconservatives, 233
  non-Jewish, anti-Israel politics of, 233–34
Lichtheim, Richard, 69, 197
  cable to Jewish Agency, quoted, 261–62
Lindenbaum, Shalom, 310n.85
Lipstadt, Deborah E., 3
Lookstein, Haskel, xiii
Lublin, 29
Luftwaffe (German air force)
  in air war over Germany, 206–7
  Allied air attacks on production and support
    facilities, 164
  Allied aim to engage and destroy aircraft, 41
  fighter defenses, usual tactics, 141–42, 165–67
  fuel shortage, limiting flights, 209
Lutzkendorf, Allied air attacks on, 208

Madison Square Garden rescue resolutions
    (1943), 198, 319n.7
Majdanek, 115, 216, 307n.46, 314n.136
Marrus, Michael, 8–9
Marshall, George C., 225
Mayer, Arno J., Why Did the Heavens Not
    Darken?, 318n.3
McClelland, Roswell, 67, 68, 160
  memo to Col. Alfred de Jonge, quoted, 249–
    50
McCloy, John J., 288n.56, 290n.13
  approached by Pehle re Auschwitz bombing
    appeal, 48–50
  Auschwitz bombing appeals to, 66–69, 103–4,
    112–13
  blamed for inaction, 121
  contacts with War Refugee Board, 48–50, 103
  letters from John Pehle, quoted, 277, 278
  letter from Leon Kubowitzki, quoted, 273–74
  letters to John Pehle, quoted, 260, 279–80
  letter to Leon Kubowitzki, quoted, 274
  memos from Harrison Gerhardt, quoted, 260,
    277
  memo from John Pehle to, quoted, 257
  rejection of bombing appeals, 68–69, 72, 107,
    113, 153, 195
McNair, Lt. Gen. Leslie, 211
Me 109 fighter (German), 167
Mediterranean Allied Air Force (MAAF), 86, 88,
    133, 164, 220
Mediterranean Allied Photographic
    Reconnaissance Wing (MAPRW), 54, 133
Mediterranean campaign (1942–43), 21–22
Medoff, Rafael, 230, 235
Merlin, Samuel, 231
Merseburg-Leuna, Allied air attacks on, 45, 208
Middle East campaign (1942), 20–21
military history, 186–87
Ministry of Economic Warfare (British), Railway
    Research Service, 30
Mintz, Morton, "Why Didn't We Bomb
    Auschwitz" Washington Post article, 82
Mischlinge, 25

Montgomery, Field Marshall Bernard Law, 211
Moravska Ostrava, Allied air attacks on, 216
Mordowicz, Czeslaw, 66
Morgen Journal, 299n.23
Morgenthau, Henry, Jr., 234
  letter from Jacob Rosenheim to, quoted, 254
Morocco, 20
Morse, Arthur D., While Six Million Died, 3, 81,
    230
Moscow conference (1943), 202
Munday, Eric, 97
museums, looted artworks in, 228
Muslim troops in British army, 16, 21
Mussolini, fall of, 191

National Air and Space Museum (Smithsonian),
    x, 5
National Archives, Air Force records in, 86
National Photographic Interpretation Center
    (U.S.), 52
National Security Agency, records of, 18
Nazis
  ideology, re Judeo-Bolshevism, 199–200
  propaganda, re "Jewish Question," 194–203
neoconservatives, American Jewish, 233
Netanyahu, Benjamin, 214, 226, 236, 282n.7
Netherlands, transports from, 30, 33
Neufeld, Michael, xi
New Left (American), 233
New Republic, 191
New York Times, 83
Norden bombsight, 42, 219
Normandy
  ground war in, 210, 224
  invasion of. See Operation Overlord
North African campaign, 20–21
Nurenberger, M. J., 233
  The Scared and the Doomed: The Jewish
    Establishment vs. the Six Million, 234

Odertal, refinery at, Allied raid on, 142, 216
Office of Strategic Services (OSS) (U.S.), 33,
    160
Office of War Information, 192
oil industry, German, Allied air attacks on, 45–
    48, 133, 164–65, 207–9, 221
  success of, in shortening the War, 208–9,
    224
Omaha Beach, 210
Operation Barbarossa. See Eastern Front
Operation Cobra (breakout from Cherbourg
    peninsula, 1944), 44, 211
Operation Crossbow (attack on V-1 and V-2
    sites, 1944), 44–45, 144, 207
Operation Frantic (shuttle bombing, 1944), 82,
    215–16
Operation Market Garden (to seize bridge at
    Arnhem, 1944), 44, 211
Operation Overlord (Normandy invasion, 1944),
    43–44, 164, 210, 224
  aerial photography in preparation for, 54
  air support of, 43–44, 107, 108, 211, 224
  command authority during, 121–22

crucial to winning the War, 209–12
preparation for, 41, 54, 207
Oslo, 219
Oswiecim. *See* Auschwitz

P-38 Lighting fighter-bomber
  dive bombing by, 119, 147–49, 219
  precision bombing by, 95–96, 121
  range of, 90
  vulnerability of, 91
P-51 Mustang, 97
Palestine
  British mandate, 16
  British policy to limit Jewish immigration
    into, 16–17, 21, 73, 193
  Jews in, 20–21
Paris, liberation of, 211, 224
Pathfinder radar, 173
Patton, Gen. George, 211
Peenemünde, attacks on, 46
Pehle, John W.
  approaches John McCloy with doubts re
    Auschwitz bombing appeal, 48–50, 66,
    103–4, 106
  letter from Leon Kubowitzki, quoted, 259–60
  letters from John McCloy, quoted, 260, 279–
    80
  letters to John McCloy, 68, 107
    quoted, 277, 278
  memo for the files, re bombing appeal,
    quoted, 256
  memo from Benjamin Akzin, quoted, 275–76
  memo to John McCloy, quoted, 257
  urged by Akzin to go directly to Roosevelt,
    122
  urges action be taken on Auschwitz, 48–50
Peirse, Sir Richards, appeal to, to bomb
  Auschwitz, 35–38
Penkower, Monty, *The Jews Were Expendable*,
  24, 234–35
Perl, William, 233
  *The Holocaust Conspiracy: An International
    Policy of Genocide*, 230
  Operation Action: Rescue from the Holocaust, 231
Pinkerton, L. C., 102, 105, 122
  memo by, of a discussion with Y.
    Gruenbaum, quoted, 250–52
Piper, Franciszek, 284n.10
Pius XII, Pope, 67, 192, 217
Ploesti, Rumania, refineries at
  air attacks on (1944), 45, 96, 207–8, 209
    aircraft used, 150
    bomber losses, 93, 96, 119, 147–49
    bombing accuracy, 96
  antiaircraft defenses of, 147–49, 208, 219
Pohl, Oswald, 29
POINTBLANK. *See* Combined Bomber
  Offensive
Poirier, Robert, 1, 52
Poland
  Government-in-Exile, 72, 195
    reports of, re ongoing atrocities, 27, 30–33,
      36, 135

Polish prisoners in concentration camps, 29,
  31
  transports from, 30
  underground in, 24, 31
  uprising (1944), 74, 124–25, 154, 202
Poland Fights, 31
Polish Home Army, 124, 154
Politz, attacks on, 45
Porat, Dina, *Blue and the Yellow Stars of David*,
  236
Portal, Sir Charles, 43
  denies request to bomb Auschwitz, 36–38
  opposition to proposed reprisals, 39
Posen, 215
Powell, Lewis F., 99, 322n.15
Prešov, railway at, 66, 80, 81
Pressac, Jean-Claude, 113–14, 284n.16
Pripet Marshes, 212
prison camps, Allied air attacks against, 96–97,
  152
  welcomed by prisoners, despite danger, 144,
    218
prisoners of war, German-held
  camps for, aerial identification of, 56
  captured Soviet troops, 199
  downed American Jewish pilots, 161
  mistreatment of, 196–97
propaganda, German, 22, 39, 196, 200
Protestants, German, 192

radar, American, bombing aids, 38, 42–43, 173–
  74, 218
radar, German (Freya), 91, 141, 142
radio, use of, by Germans, 28–29
rail transportation
  generally, bombing often ineffective, 107–8,
    189
  German
    Allied air attacks on, 44, 98–99, 207, 220
    intelligence about, 30
Ranke, Leopold von, 186
Red Cross, complicity in Holocaust, 228
refugees, Jewish
  numbers admitted to United States, 16, 194
  and Palestine, 73
  worldwide refusal to receive, 194
Reich Security Main Office (RSHA), 28
rescue
  attempts, 186–87, 193
    few saved by, 26
    little money available for, at the time, 190–
      91
    low priority given to, 190
    negotiation with Axis powers, 23–24, 191,
      198
  failure to try, 227–36
  organizations and countries active in, 24, 81,
    105, 158, 189, 190
  proposals, 23–24
    Auschwitz bombing proposal as special
      case, 193
    history of Allies' rejection of, 194–95
    numerous but not practical, 193

rescue (*continued*)
a race against time, to save the remainder, 189–92
winning the War claimed as best means of, 190, 195, 198, 206
Rescue Resolutions (Madison Square Garden, New York, 1943), 198, 319n.7
retaliation or reprisals for Holocaust, 67, 69, 195–97
aimed at Germany's allies and satellites, 197
bombing policy of, suggested, 195–98
proponents and opponents of, 38–39, 96
Rhodes and Kos, deportation of Jews from, failure of Allies to prevent, 189–90
Rice, Rondall R., 4
Riegner, Gerhart, 67
activities in Geneva during the War, 76–79
Riga, destruction of Jews of (1941), 78
Roma (Gypsies), 25, 30, 33
Rome
Allied air attack on, 145–46
taking of (June 1944), 224
Rommel, Gen. Erwin, 21
Roosevelt, Col. Elliott, 57
Roosevelt, Pres. Franklin D.
and Auschwitz bombing proposal, 57, 122–24, 214
aware of Nazi extermination activity, 307n.48
and Churchill, 125
command authority of, to order military action, 115, 121–24, 215
critics and defenders of policy re Holocaust, 233, 235
establishes War Refugee Board, 104
failure of vision of, supposedly, re stopping the Holocaust, 156, 202, 225, 233
immigration policy, 16
letter from J. J. Smertenko, quoted, 271–73
ordered Warsaw air drops, 159
pre-War preparations, 21, 39
speech condemning Final Solution (March 1944), 138–39
urged to stop Nazi extermination campaign, 106, 192, 198
war planning by, 46–47, 50, 205
war policies, 42
was never formally requested to bomb Auschwitz, 318n.2
Rosenheim, Jacob, 48, 66, 68, 103, 107
letter to Henry Morgenthau, quoted, 254
Rosin, Arnost, 66
Rosin-Mordowicz report, 66
excerpts from, quoted, 248–49
Royal Air Force (British) (RAF)
Air Historical Branch, 86
area bombing policy, 195–98
asked to bomb Auschwitz, 66
bases in Italy, 150, 152
capabilities and mission of, 35–43, 172
205 Group, 150, 216
See also Bomber Command
Rubinstein, William D., *Myth of Rescue*, 235–36
Rublee-Schacht ransom offer, 193, 195

Rumania
Allied air attacks on, 216, 288n.48. *See also* Ploesti, Rumania
Jews of, negotiations to save, 191
switches sides, trapping German army, 225
warnings to, re extermination program, 192, 197
Russia
post-Soviet, anti-Semitism in, 200–201
Soviet. *See* Soviet Union
Russians
nationalism of, encouraged in World War II, 200
prisoners in concentration camps, 29
Rwanda, genocide in, 226

St. Louis refugee ship, 3
Salski, Jerzy, 285n.31
Sarna, Jonathan D., 292n.28
Saving Private Ryan (movie), 210
Schapira (JAE board member), 105
Schindler, Oskar, 229
Schindler's List (movie), 227
Schlesinger, Arthur, 235
Schmorek, Dr., 105
Schwarzbart, Dr. Ignacy, 32
Schweinfurt, Germany, bombing raid on, 41
Segev, Tom, *The Seventh Million*, 236
selections of prisoners, 28–29, 30, 33
Senator, Dr., 105
Sherer, Rabbi Morris, 231–32
Sherman, A. J., 83
Shertok, Moshe, 69, 103, 106–7, 111–12
cable to David Ben-Gurion and Nahum Goldmann, quoted, 264–66
memo to Anthony Eden, quoted, 263–64
Shoah. *See* Holocaust
shuttle bombing (via Soviet bases), 46–47, 188, 200, 215–16, 288n.47, 288n.48
See also Operation Frantic
Sikorski, Gen. W., 36, 195
Silesia
maps of, 77
Soviet taking of, 209
Sinclair, Sir Archibald
asked by Eden to take action on Auschwitz, 48–49, 70–71, 77, 107, 122
letter from Anthony Eden, quoted, 267
letter from Richard Law, quoted, 270
letter to Anthony Eden, 112, 116–18, 149–50
quoted, 267–68
memo to Vice Chief of Air Staff, quoted, 269
negative about feasibility of bombing, 123, 153
Sinti (Gypsies), 25
slave labor, 28–29, 293n.47
Slavs, German war against, 199
Slessor, Sir John, 47, 154
Slovakia (puppet state), 28, 197
Jewish underground in, 76, 80, 89
transports from, 33
Smertenko, J. J., letter to Franklin D. Roosevelt, quoted, 271–73
smoke screens, 147, 173
Sobibor, 6, 29, 314n.136

Sonderkommandos, 115
Soviet Union
    advances on the Eastern Front, 46–47, 159, 187–88, 224
    air bases in, 46–47, 125, 188, 200
    anti-Semitic policy of, 22–23
    concentration camp system, 200
    conflict with Allies, over conduct of War, 198
    desire to avoid linkage with the "Jewish Question," 199–200
    Jews in, position of, 199–200, 234
    prisoners of war, 31, 199
    war aim of, 199–200
    war conduct of, 22–23
Spaatz, Gen. Carl A.
    argued against the Warsaw air drop, 125
    command authority of, 41, 121–22, 217, 220
    consulted about Auschwitz bombing, 49, 72, 123–24, 128, 133, 224
    letter from N. H. Bottomley, quoted, 270–71
    mentioned, 146, 158, 162
    policy of attacking German oil supply, 45–48, 164–66, 207
Special Operations Executive (SOE) (British), 43
Speer, Albert, 115, 281n.5
Sprey, P. M., 121
SS (Schutzstaffel)
    Economic-Administrative Main Office (WVHA), 28, 29–30
    guards, character of, when in danger, 141, 144
    negotiating with, to rescue Jews, 191
Stalin
    appeal to, to stop Nazi extermination, 106
    opposed shuttle bombing, 216
    resistance to Allied demands, 188
Stanley, Col. Roy, 135
Sternbuch, Isaac, 102, 103
Stimson, Henry L., 290n.13
Stroop report, 25
Students for a Democratic Society, 233
submarine pens, German, Allied bombing of, 40, 164
Sweden, 109
Switzerland, 109, 191
    complicity in Holocaust, 228
    Jews saved by, 190, 192
Syria, 20
Szolnok oil refinery, Allied air attack on, 166
Sztójay, Döme, 110, 217

tasking (in aerial photography), 53–54
Tedder, Sir Arthur, 44, 45, 74
Teheran conference (1943), 202
Ternopol, 187
Teveth, Shabtai, Ben-Gurion and the Holocaust, 236
Thaelmann, Ernst, 199
Theresienstadt, 78
Tokyo
    fire raids on, 318n.1
    first raid on (1942), 195
Toulon harbor, Allied air attack on, 145, 220
Transportation Plan (of railway bombing), 108

transports, German, Allied intelligence about, 28–30
    See also under individual countries
Treblinka, 6, 32, 314n.136
Trujillo, Rafael, 194
Trzebinia, oil plant, Allied air attacks on, 141, 215, 288n.48
Turkey, rescue of Jews by, 189, 190
Twelfth Air Force (U.S.), 95, 220
Twining, Lt. Gen. Nathan F., 217

ULTRA
    intelligence reports from, 45, 159–60, 207, 208
    operation at Bletchley Park, 222
Union of Orthodox Rabbis, 102
United States
    Hitler's anticipation of war with, 20
    immigration restrictions, during Great Depression, 15–16
    pre-War neutrality of, 85
    pre-War preparations, 21, 39
United States Air Force Historical Research Center, 86
United States Army Air Forces (USAAF)
    bombing campaigns over German-held territories, 102, 124–25
    capabilities and mission of, 39–43, 117, 172
    industry as target of, 39–43
    number of planes, 39
    records of, Auschwitz issues sparse in, 158
United States Holocaust Memorial Council, 83
United States Holocaust Memorial Museum (Washington D.C.), ix, 19
    symposium on the Auschwitz bombing controversy (April 1993), 5
United States Strategic Air Forces (USSTAF), 41
United States Strategic Bombing Survey (USSBS), 43
Upper Silesia
    antiaircraft defenses of, 141
    map of, 77
    targets in, 133

V-1 and V-2 rockets
    Allied air attacks
        on factories making, 144
        on launch sites of, 44–45, 207, 219
    locating sites of, 133
    reprisals for use of, 195
Vanden Heuvel, William, 235
Vatican, 67, 109
VB-1 AZON bomb, 93
Veesenmayer, Edmund, 110, 217
Vernichtungskrieg (war of annihilation) policy, 194, 199
Vichy France, 197
Vienna, Allied air attacks on, 167
Vis air base, 90, 91
Vitkovice, 167
Vrba, Rudolf (aka Walter Rosenberg), 34, 88–89, 129, 169
Vrba-Wetzler report
    excerpts from, quoted, 242–48

Vrba-Wetzler report (*continued*)
how it reached the West, 65
intelligence deficiencies of, supposed, 88–89, 129–35
intelligence value of, 77, 82, 129–36, 160, 169
moral effect of, 61, 222–23
not made widely available, 56, 112
not the first to report Nazi atrocities, 34

Wallenberg, Raoul, 24, 111, 229
"Wanda" (codename of a Polish informant), 33
war, decision-making in, pressures of, 204
War Crimes Commission, suggested, 319n.7
War Department (U.S.), 48–50
"H.H.F." memo for record, quoted, 279
Operations Division (OPD), 158
rejection of Auschwitz bombing appeal, 66–69, 71–72, 81
War Refugee Board contacts with, 48–50, 103–5, 158
War Refugee Board (WRB)
Auschwitz bombing appeals relayed to, 48, 66, 72, 102–5
contacts with War Department, 48–50, 103–5, 158
founding and role of, 104, 122, 158
reports on Auschwitz received by, 66–67, 81, 89
rescue work, 24
Warsaw
air dropping of supplies to (1944), 159
aircraft used, 150
example of a humanitarian mission, 202
example of a long dangerous mission with little hope of success, 24, 74, 124–25
example of a political not military requirement, 153, 154–55, 158–59, 215–16
Soviet hindrance to, 46–47
ghetto, destruction of, 25
Washington Post, 82, 83
Wasserstein, Bernard, 157
Britain and the Jews of Europe, 2, 149
weaponeering (in bombing planning), 169–72
weather, effect on bombing, 42–43, 143
Weinberg, Gerhard L., 7–8
Weissmandel, Rabbi Michael Dov, 80–81
Weizmann, Chaim
meeting with Eden, 102, 106–7, 111
memo to Eden, 106–7, 111–12
and Moshe Shertok, memo to Anthony Eden, quoted, 263–64
relations with Churchill, 125

requests bombing of Auschwitz, 69–70, 73, 103, 123
Wellington Mk.X medium bomber, 38, 150
Western Front
early success predicted, 225
operations (1944), 205–12
Wetzler, Alfred, 34, 88–89, 129, 169
White Paper (British, 1939), 16
plea to rescind, 193
Wiesel, Elie, x
Williams, Roger, "Why Wasn't Auschwitz Bombed?" *Commonweal* article, 81–82
Wilson, Gen. Maitland, 220
Wise, Stephen S.
criticisms of, 230–31
efforts on behalf of European Jews, 235
Wolfe, Gen. James, quoted on war, 204
World Jewish Congress, 122
desires Auschwitz to be bombed, 72, 81, 112–13
Representation of Polish Jews within, 32
Rescue Department, 105
World War I, atrocity reports in, 288n.48
World War II
aim of Allies
total and quick victory, 190, 195, 198, 206
was not to save Jews, 194–203
military vs. political goals in, 154–55, 188
quick victory seen by end of 1944, 225
Second Front sought by Soviets, 198
Wyman, David, 4–5, 7, 81, 157
The Abandonment of the Jews: America and the Holocaust 1941–1945, 2, 4, 61, 82–100, 127, 201, 230
Paper Walls: America and the Refugee Crisis, 1938–1941, 84–85, 230
"Why Auschwitz Was Never Bombed" *Commentary* article, 1–3, 61, 81–82, 84, 101, 103, 127, 201, 230

Yalta conference (1945), 202
Yiddish press in New York, 105
Yishuv, 236, 282n.7
Yugoslavia, 91
genocide in (1990), 226
Jews in, German intention to kill, 22

Zamoyski, Count Stephan, 36
Zeitz, Allied air attacks on, 208
Zionism, 231–32, 236
Zuckerman, Prof. Solly, 74, 108
Zwickau, Allied air attacks on, 45, 208
Zyklon-B, 3, 115